FLOWERS
in the **WALL**

Global Indigenous Issues Series

SERIES EDITOR: Roberta Rice, Assistant Professor, Department of Political Science, University of Calgary

ISSN 2561-3057 (Print) ISSN 2561-3065 (Online)

The Global Indigenous Issues series explores Indigenous peoples' cultural, political, social, economic and environmental struggles in para-colonial and post-colonial societies. The series includes original research on local, regional, national, and transnational experiences.

No. 1 · **Flowers in the Wall: Truth and Reconciliation in Timor-Leste, Indonesia, and Melanesia**
by David Webster

UNIVERSITY OF CALGARY
Press

FLOWERS *in the* WALL

Truth and Reconciliation in Timor-Leste, Indonesia, and Melanesia

Edited by
David Webster

Global Indigenous Issues Series
ISSN 2561-3057 (Print) ISSN 2561-3065 (Online)

© 2017 David Webster

University of Calgary Press
2500 University Drive NW
Calgary, Alberta
Canada T2N 1N4
press.ucalgary.ca

This book is available as an ebook which is licensed under a Creative Commons license. The publisher should be contacted for any commercial use which falls outside the terms of that license.

LIBRARY AND ARCHIVES CANADA CATALOGUING IN PUBLICATION

    Flowers in the wall : Truth and Reconciliation in Timor-Leste, Indonesia, and Melanesia / edited by David Webster.

(Global indigenous issues series ; 1)
Includes bibliographical references and index.

Issued in print and electronic formats.
ISBN 978-1-55238-954-6 (softcover).—ISBN 978-1-55238-955-3 (open access PDF).—
ISBN 978-1-55238-956-0 (PDF).—ISBN 978-1-55238-957-7 (EPUB).—
ISBN 978-1-55238-958-4 (Kindle)

    1. Truth commissions—Timor-Leste. 2. Truth commissions—Indonesia.
3. Truth commissions—Solomon Islands. 4. Human rights. 5. Collective memory.
6. Reconciliation. I. Webster, David, 1966-, editor

JC580.F56 2017   323.4'9   C2017-906773-7
                                                                           C2017-906774-5

The University of Calgary Press acknowledges the support of the Government of Alberta through the Alberta Media Fund for our publications. We acknowledge the financial support of the Government of Canada. We acknowledge the financial support of the Canada Council for the Arts for our publishing program.

This book has been published with the support of Bishop's University Senate Research Committee.

Cover image: Colourbox #3052510
Copyediting by Ryan Perks
Cover design, page design, and typesetting by Melina Cusano

Table of Contents

Illustrations	ix
Abbreviations	xi
Acknowledgements	xv

1. Introduction: Memory, Truth, and Reconciliation in Timor-Leste, Indonesia, and Melanesia — 1
   DAVID WEBSTER

2. Incomplete Truth, Incomplete Reconciliation: Towards a Scholarly Verdict on Truth and Reconciliation Commissions — 23
   SARAH ZWIERZCHOWSKI

SECTION I
Memory, Truth, and Reconciliation in Timor-Leste — 39

3. East Timor: Legacies of Violence — 45
   GEOFFREY ROBINSON

4. Shining *Chega!*'s Light into the Cracks — 63
   PAT WALSH

5. *Politika Taka Malu*, Censorship, and Silencing: Virtuosos of Clandestinity and One's Relationship to Truth and Memory — 79
   JACQUELINE AQUINO SIAPNO

6	Development and Foreign Aid in Timor-Leste after Independence LAURENTINA "MICA" BARRETO SOARES	93
7	Reconciliation, Church, and Peacebuilding JESS AGUSTIN	109
8	Human Rights and Truth FERNANDA BORGES	117
9	*Chega!* for Us: Socializing a Living Document MARIA MANUELA LEONG PEREIRA	121

SECTION II
Memory, Truth-seeking, and the 1965 Mass Killings in Indonesia — 125

10	Cracks in the Wall: Indonesia and Narratives of the 1965 Mass Violence BASKARA T. WARDAYA	131
11	The Touchy Historiography of Indonesia's 1965 Mass Killings: Intractable Blockades? BERND SCHAEFER	145
12	Writings of an Indonesian Political Prisoner GATOT LESTARIO	155

SECTION III
Local Truth and Reconciliation in Indonesia — 161

13	Gambling with Truth: Hopes and Challenges for Aceh's Commission for Truth and Reconciliation LIA KENT AND RIZKI AFFIAT	167
14	All about the Poor: An Alternative Explanation of the Violence in Poso ARIANTO SANGADJI	185

SECTION IV
Where Indonesia meets Melanesia: Memory, Truth, and Reconciliation in Tanah Papua — 199

15 Facts, Feasts, and Forests: Considering Approaches to Truth and Reconciliation in Tanah Papua — 205
    TODD BIDERMAN AND JENNY MUNRO

16 The Living Symbol of Song in West Papua: A Soul Force to be Reckoned With — 233
    JULIAN SMYTHE

17 Time for a New US Approach toward Indonesia and West Papua — 261
    EDMUND MCWILLIAMS

SECTION V
Memory, Truth, and Reconciliation in Solomon Islands — 273

18 The Solomon Islands "Ethnic Tension" Conflict and the Solomon Islands Truth and Reconciliation Commission — 279
    TERRY M. BROWN

19 Women and Reconciliation in Solomon Islands — 293
    BETTY LINA GIGISI

SECTION VI
Bringing it Home — 297

20 Reflecting on Reconciliation — 299
    MAGGIE HELWIG

21 Conclusion: Seeking Truth about Truth-seeking — 309
    DAVID WEBSTER

Bibliography — 325
Index — 345
Contributors — 359

Illustrations

Fig. 1.1	Popular monument to victims of mass killings outside the local Catholic church, Liquiça, Timor-Leste. Photo: David Webster.
Fig. 1.2	Sign welcoming visitors to the *Chega!* exhibit at the former Comarca prison facility, Balide, Dili, Timor-Leste. Photo: David Webster.
Fig. 3.1	Burned-out building, Dili, Timor-Leste, 1999. Photo: Jess Agustin.
Fig. 4.1	Entry to *Chega!* exhibit, Dili, Timor-Leste. Photo: David Webster.
Box 4.1	Centro Nacional *Chega!* is born.
Fig. 5.1	Display from Archives and Museum of the Timorese Resistance, Dili, Timor-Leste. Photo: David Webster.
Fig. 7.1	Jess Agustin (right) with Bishop Carlos Belo, Dili, Timor-Leste. Photo courtesy of Jess Agustin.

Abbreviations

ACbit	Asosiasaun *Chega!* Ba Ita (Tetun); *Chega!* for Us Association
AJAR	Asia Justice and Rights
ASEAN	Association of Southeast Asian Nations
BRA	Badan Reintegrasi Damai Aceh (Indonesian); Aceh Peace Reintegration Agency
BRICS	Brazil, Russia, India, China, and South Africa
Brimob	Brigade Mobil (Indonesian); Mobile Brigade (of the National Police)
CAVR	Comissão de Acolhimento, Verdade e Reconciliação (Port.); Commission for Reception, Truth and Reconciliation (Timor-Leste)
CCSEAS	Canadian Council for Southeast Asian Studies
CNRT	Congresso Nacional de Reconstrução de Timor (Port.); National Congress for Timorese Reconstruction
CONEFO	Conference of the New Emerging Forces
CSIS	Centre for Strategic and International Studies (Indonesia)
CTF	Commission for Truth and Friendship (Indonesia and Timor-Leste)
DAC	Development Assistance Committee (of the OECD)
Densus 88	Detasemen Khusus 88 (Indonesian); Special Detachment 88 (of the Indonesian police)
DOM	daerah operasi militer (Indonesian); military operations zone
ETAN/Canada	East Timor Alert Network (Canada)
ETAN/US	East Timor and Indonesia Action Network (United States)

xi

Fretilin	Frente Revolucionária de Timor-Leste Independente (Port.); Independent East Timor Revolutionary Front
GAM	Gerakan Aceh Merdeka (Indonesian/Acehnese); Free Aceh Movement
GANEFO	Games of the New Emerging Forces
GIDI	Gereja Injili di Indonesia (Indonesian); Indonesian Evangelical Church
GLF	Guadalcanal Liberation Front
GRA	Guadalcanal Revolutionary Army
HIVOS	Humanistisch Instituut voor Ontwikkelingssamenwerking (Dutch); Humanist Institute for Co-operation
HRW	Human Rights Watch
ICTJ	International Center for Transitional Justice
IFM	Isatabu Freedom Movement (Solomon Islands)
Interfet	International Force for East Timor
IPMG	International Peace Monitoring Group (Solomon Islands)
JI	Jemaah Islamiyah (Indonesia)
KKR	Komisi Kebenaran dan Rekonsiliasi (Indonesian/Acehnese); Truth and Reconciliation Commission (Aceh)
KNPB	Komite Nasional Papua Barat (Indonesian); West Papua National Committee
Komnas-HAM	Komisi Nasional Hak Asasi Manusia (Indonesian); National Human Rights Commission (Indonesia)
Kopassus	Komando Pasukan Khusus (Indonesian); Special Forces Command (of the Indonesian army)
KWI	Konferensi Waligereja Indonesia (Indonesian); Indonesian Council of (Catholic) Bishops
LoGA	Law for Governing of Aceh
MEF	Malaitan Eagle Force
MIT	Mujahedeen Indonesia Timur; Eastern Indonesia Mujahedeen
MoU	Memorandum of Understanding
MSG	Melanesian Spearhead Group

OECD	Organisation for Economic Co-operation and Development
OPM	Organisasi Papua Merdeka (Indonesian); Free Papua Movement
Otsus	Otonomi khusus (Indonesian); special autonomy
PKI	Partai Komunis Indonesia (Indonesian); Indonesian Communist Party
PNG	Papua New Guinea
PNI	Polisi Nasional Indonesia; Indonesian National Police
PNTL	Polícia Nacional de Timor-Leste (Port.); Timor-Leste National Police
RAMSI	Regional Assistance Mission to Solomon Islands
RPKAD	Resimen Pasukan Komando Angkatan Darat (Indonesian); Army Forces Commando Regiment (now Kopassus)
RSIPF	Royal Solomon Islands Police Force
SICA	Solomon Islands Christian Association
SITRC	Solomon Islands Truth and Reconciliation Commission
SDA	Seventh-day Adventist
SSEC	South Seas Evangelical Church
TNI	Tentara Nasional Indonesia (Indonesian); Indonesian National Army
TPA	Townsville Peace Agreement
TRC	Truth and Reconciliation Commission
ULMWP	United Liberation Movement of West Papua
UNMIT	United Nations Mission in Timor-Leste
UNTAET	United Nations Transitional Administration in East Timor
UNTEA	United Nations Temporary Executive Authority (Tanah Papua)
UNTF	United Nations Trust Fund
WPAT	West Papua Advocacy Team
ZEEMS	Zona Espesial Ekonomia Merkadu Sosial (Tetun); Social Market Economy Special Zone

Acknowledgements

Flowers in the Wall is the end product of a larger project which aimed at contributing to policy discussions in Canada, and serves as the capstone to that larger project on Memory, Truth and Reconciliation. The project has been realized collaboratively between authors, a team at Bishop's University, and with the support of members of two Canadian non-governmental organizations which work to connect Canada and the Asia Pacific region: the Pacific Peoples' Partnership, based in Victoria BC and active in Indigenous rights campaigning across the Pacific; and the Canadian Catholic Organization for Development and Peace, based in Montreal. Material related to this project is online at http://reconciliationtim.ca/ http://reconciliationtim.ca/

This research was supported by the Social Sciences and Humanities Research Council of Canada, particularly through a Connections Grant that supported a workshop at the University of Ottawa held in 2015. Additional support was provided by Bishop's University through the Senate Research Committee and the Crossing Borders Research Cluster—Indigeneity and Race Research Axis.

First thanks belong to the chapter authors, both those who offered their insights at the original Ottawa workshop and those who provided valuable contributions later. It has been a privilege to work with each of them. In addition, thanks are due to Bella Galhos, April Ingham, Micheline (Mika) Lévesque, and Melissa Marschke and her organizing team at the 2015 Canadian Council for Southeast Asian Studies CCSEAS conference. I am indebted for information, wisdom and connections shared by the post-CAVR technical secretariat, by friends in Dili, and by the wider global community active around human rights in Timor-Leste and Indonesia – and as always, to my family and especially to Sean, more than I can say.

The project would not have been possible without research assistance at Bishop's University from Sarah Zwierzchowski, Cynthia Dawn Roy, and Nicholas Chlumecky. The University of Calgary Press team, especially Brian Scrivener, Helen Hajnockzy, Alison Cobra, Melina Cusano, and Ryan Perks, were tireless and supportive in seeing the project through to publication.

Chapter 3 previously appeared in the *Journal of Asian Studies*. Chapter 16 was first published in *Indonesia*. Some material draws on a working paper originally written for *Active History* (activehistory.ca).

1

Introduction: Memory, Truth, and Reconciliation in Timor-Leste, Indonesia, and Melanesia

DAVID WEBSTER

> *Everything will be crushed / Everything will be broken / Everything will become dusty / New buds will appear, flourishing the flat land / We will pray / We will sing the songs of ancestors / We will* tebe *form / We will* bidu *Circling the stones of the sacred house / A big mat will be spread out / We all will sit down / Our hearts will be soft / Our heads will be cool / Telling the truth / Recounting the wrong doings / The happiness of love will appear / The beauty of peace will be green / Flourish and flourish / Flourish everlastingly*
>
> —Abé Barreto Soares, "Flourish Everlastingly"[1]

Circles, Stones, Songs

In Suai, a town in the southwestern corner of Timor-Leste (East Timor[2]), there is a circle of stones. Built by local people, it stands near the church where, in 1999, members of the pro-Indonesia Laksaur militia massacred as many as two hundred people with grenades, guns, and machetes.[3]

The killings at Our Lady of the Rosary Church are one of the many threads that tie Canada to Timor-Leste. Among the dead was the parish priest, Father Hilario Madeira. He had spent time in Canada, twinning his parish with one in Windsor, Ontario. "The blood of martyrs is the seedbed of the church," his Canadian counterpart, Father Jim Roche, told me after Father Hilario's death. "But it's not supposed to happen to people you know. It's supposed to happen to those nameless people over there."[4]

There are two monuments to the Suai church massacre, just as there are memorials—both official and popular—scattered over the country. Cenotaph-like, one of the Suai monuments inscribes the names of the dead in marble. The other stands nearer the church, on the site where the bodies of the dead were brought to be burned by men wanting to erase not only their victims' lives, but the truth of their killing. This circle of stones is unpolished, but on each one, local people have carved the name of a loved one lost in 1999.[5] The stones sing out their lives and the truth of what happened there.

On this site, too, local people remember the truth of the Suai church massacre. One such example, a re-enactment scripted by Timorese human rights advocate Filomena dos Reis, is recounted in the documentary film "Circle of Stones." The documentary, made in English for international viewers, was possible only because local women invited Australian filmmaker Jen Hughes into their circle.[6] It connects local communities and international audiences. That is the aim of this book, also.

Like a community reconciliation ceremony, *Flowers in the Wall* tries to circle the truth. It circles around truth commission reports, around truth and reconciliation processes fighting to be born, around the struggles of people trying to turn truth commission reports into "living documents"[7] that can shape national futures. When truth and reconciliation is seen as an event, not as an ongoing process, it roots are shallow.

This is not a traditional academic book grouping discrete chapters on discrete topics. Instead, we aim to present an integrated narrative about

1.1: Popular monument to victims of mass killings outside the local Catholic church, Liquiça, Timor-Leste. Photo: David Webster.

recent truth and reconciliation processes in a part of the world sprawling from Sumatra to Solomon Islands, from the islands of Southeast Asia into the islands of the Melanesian Pacific. The authors include scholars and human rights practitioners, engaged academics, and informed advocates whose conversations and comparisons spawned this collection. We see the hope embodied in truth commissions and in reconciliation processes in post-conflict societies. We see links between the disparate experiences of different places: the way gender concerns came to take a more central place in Timor-Leste and Solomon Islands truth commissions; the efforts to embody Indigenous traditions in truth-seeking processes; the vital role of civil society; the importance of seeing truth-seeking as a process that goes before and comes after truth commissions. We also see the barriers to true reconciliation. When calls to seek truth are denied, conflicts persist. When truth commission reports are not followed up, their impact is weakened.

"You have already consumed me," writes Mama Yosepha Alomang, a famous Papuan advocate of Indigenous rights, in chapter 16. She is referring to the predatory impulses of global mining companies in her homeland, but could just as well be describing global governments, whose role in local conflicts cannot be overlooked. International economics and politics are crucial to understanding local conflicts.

What follows are thoughts in a conversation about truth and reconciliation across different places in which the authors are taking part. They are also notes and stanzas in a song that we are trying to perform together. The chapters in this book do not try to stand alone, but rather contribute to a single story about several places.

One of those sites of memory is the Comarca, a former prison and torture facility in Dili, the Timorese capital. Today visitors can enter the "dark cells" that once held prisoners of conscience and tour an exhibit that fills much of the old prison and which chronicles the human rights history of Timor-Leste and the work of the Timorese truth commission, known by its acronym CAVR. The Comarca housed the truth commission's offices and is still home to a follow-up institution dedicated to carrying on the memory and work of truth and reconciliation. Above its entrance are carved the words: "CAVR has shown that flowers can grow in a prison."

The title of this collection draws from that image, as well as from the pieces of creative writing that open three of its chapters. Indonesian poet Wiji Thukul's metaphor of flowers growing until they crack the wall of tyranny leads off chapter 10. They evoke both Canadian poet Leonard Cohen's image of a crack in everything to let the light shine in (which opens chapter 4), and the words of Timorese poet Abé Barreto Soares, noted above, about new buds flowering in a blasted land. The flowers stand for individuals who strive for peace, for reconciliation, for remembering, for truth. Walls and wastelands look permanent, but humble flowers can make the wall crumble or the wasteland bloom: for flowers, too, are perennial.

Memory, Truth, Reconciliation

Truth and reconciliation commissions are an increasingly common tool for addressing the aftermath of conflicts in the global South. Eight formed in the 1980s; twelve in the 1990s; and at least nineteen in the first decade of the twenty-first century.[8] Truth commissions, in other words, are not going

1.2: Sign welcoming visitors to the *Chega!* exhibit at the former Comarca prison facility, Balide, Dili, Timor-Leste. Photo: David Webster.

away. In fact, they have spread from post-conflict zones in the global South (especially Latin America and Africa) to developed countries, most notably Canada and Germany. Appearing as a "restorative justice" alternative to the "retributive justice" model of criminal prosecutions of human rights violators, they answer a clear need in many societies.[9] And they are said to offer the bonus of building reconciliation between communities previously in conflict—most famously, in post-apartheid South Africa, where the country was to be healed by a truth and reconciliation commission. As chapter 2 explains, scholars have offered a mixed verdict on the South African experience of reconciliation and the model of truth commissions it bequeathed. Nevertheless, the increasing use of truth and reconciliation commissions around the world demonstrates that the tool meets the perceived needs of multiple societies.

This book surveys the truth and reconciliation experience in a part of the world that has drawn less attention in the "transitional justice" literature: the islands of Southeast Asia and the Melanesian region of the Southwest Pacific. It does so with a focus on three countries: Timor-Leste, Indonesia (including both national and local spaces), and Solomon Islands. Indonesia and Timor-Leste are part of Southeast Asia, but this region shades eastwards into Melanesia, which includes the Indonesian-ruled land of Papua.

Timor-Leste was occupied by the Indonesian army for twenty-four years (1975–99) before regaining its independence. Under military rule, more than a hundred thousand civilians died from war-induced famine and slaughter—a death toll approaching the levels of the Cambodian genocide, which also started in 1975. After the Timorese won their freedom, they formed a truth and reconciliation commission with two goals: to reconcile divided communities after a long-running conflict, and to reconcile the new country with its own tumultuous past by crafting a narrative that for the first time would tell the truth through Timorese testimony rather than outside research about what had happened between 1975 and 1999. The Commission on Reception, Truth and Reconciliation (CAVR) is considered to be one of the more substantive truth commissions to date.[10] The findings of its five-volume report, entitled *Chega!* (Portuguese for "no more" or "enough"), were confirmed by a subsequent joint Timorese-Indonesian Commission on Truth and Friendship.[11]

Truth commissions in Timor-Leste are examples of a preference for "restorative" over "retributive" justice. In the aftermath of a brutal military occupation, the Timorese government's desire for cordial relations with a post-dictatorship Indonesia combined with a lack of will in the international community to lead to the choice of a truth commission rather than a criminal tribunal like those established for Rwanda, the former Yugoslavia, and, in a far more limited fashion, Cambodia and Sierra Leone. Compassion was selective, and neither the Timorese government nor other governments heeded calls for a tribunal. Although the truth commission was a necessity, it also sought to be a virtue. Beyond the work of victim support, it aimed to tell the first national history grounded in Timorese testimony. The result was an agreed national narrative of what had happened under near-genocidal conditions and thus a "usable past" for independent Timor-Leste.[12]

Indonesia has itself experienced a succession of mass violence throughout its history, starting under Dutch colonial rule and continuing periodically since the proclamation of an independent Republic of Indonesia in 1945. The most severe violence came as the army, under General Suharto, seized power from the country's first president, Sukarno, in 1965–66.[13] Encouraged and directed by military leaders, mass violence claimed hundreds of thousands of lives. Where Sukarno had promoted a brand of left-wing nationalism, Suharto's "New Order" clamped down on dissent and promoted a form of crony capitalism. The New Order imposed an official version of history that blamed the Indonesian Communist Party (PKI) for the "1965 events," as they were euphemistically dubbed. Only since the fall of Suharto in 1998 has it become possible to discuss and debate the 1965 events, though to date the truth remains contested.

Indonesia has long struggled to define itself as a united nation, and the arrival of democratic government after Suharto's fall has done nothing to change this. It spans hundreds of islands and as many ethnic groups, with the nationalist slogan "from Sabang to Merauke" defining the westernmost and easternmost points of the national territory. It also highlights the tentative nature of the Indonesian state's borders. Merauke is in Papua, home to an independence movement that predates Indonesian annexation. Sabang is located in Aceh, a province considered to be the most strongly Islamic in Indonesia.

In 1976, the Free Aceh Movement (Gerakan Aceh Merdeka, or GAM) declared the province's independence, sparking decades of guerrilla warfare with the Indonesian National Army. The armed conflict ended only in 2005 with a pact between GAM and the Indonesian government that in effect permitted the group's leaders to take power in provincial elections while keeping Aceh within the Indonesian national fold. Former rivals henceforth shared power in a more open Indonesia. But the conflict left scars, as all conflicts do, in the form of lives lost and in a legacy of human rights troubles. Talk of a truth commission to follow the peace process stalled for years, though it never vanished entirely. In 2016, the Aceh provincial government finally created its own truth commission, with a plan to leave the commission's doors open permanently.

Meanwhile, regional conflicts flared in many other parts of Indonesia. Often described as "ethnic conflicts," they also showed the scars of repression under the New Order and the revived aspirations for local control.

Some of the most enduring violence centred on the island of Sulawesi, today one of the front lines in the global "war on terror." Yet coverage of these conflicts has tended to overlook their local and historical roots. Different regional conflicts have been met with different efforts at peace and reconciliation between divided communities.

Indonesia's post-Suharto government consented to a referendum on Timorese independence, but all subsequent governments have otherwise clung to the idea of national unity. In particular, they have stridently resisted calls for a referendum, or even dialogue, in Tanah Papua (the land of Papua).[14] Papua came under Indonesian rule in 1963 and it remains the site of a struggle between an independence movement and Indonesian rule. A major line of division is identity: while Indonesia claims to be a multi-ethnic state, Papuan nationalists have long asserted a Melanesian identity, one they contrast with the Indonesia's "Asian" identity. One of the major Papuan demands to emerge is for *pelurusan sejarah*, a setting straight of the historical record. This can be likened to a call for a truth and reconciliation process, as it does not focus on the political future, but rather on how two sides in a conflict address the past, and to what extent historical injustices can be righted in an effort to reach peaceful future outcomes. In other words, Papuans seek truth. The Indonesian government has tried to resolve this ongoing conflict with a "special autonomy" package that granted considerable local self-government, along with the promise of a truth commission that has so far gone unfulfilled due to objections from the still-influential Indonesian army. History is a battlefield.

Papuan nationalists' embrace of a Melanesian ethnic identity links Papua to the final area covered in this volume: Solomon Islands.

Solomon Islands became independent from Britain in 1978. The country experienced mass internal violence from 1998 to 2004. When the violence ended, a Solomon Islands Truth and Reconciliation Commission was formed with three national and two international members. Inspired directly by South Africa's famous TRC, the commission could point to successes but not to a lasting legacy. Its impressive report was at first not released to the public for fear that it would enflame rather than cool tensions. This has now changed, but unlike Timor-Leste, Solomon Islands lacks a follow-up institution to continue the commission's work and preserve its archival and institutional memory.

In sum, the cases here run the gamut from a relatively strong commission (Timor-Leste's CAVR) through commissions whose actions are dictated by politics (the joint Indonesian-Timorese CTF, Solomon Islands TRC, and now Aceh's TRC) to areas still awaiting truth processes as the prerequisite for reconciliation (Papua and much of Indonesia).

The truth commission model, developed for the global South, has begun to be implemented in the developed world, most prominently in Canada. The Truth and Reconciliation Commission of Canada, which has looked into residential schools for Indigenous peoples, opened with an event that featured senior members of truth commissions from the global South (including Timor-Leste) sharing potential lessons.[15] This book suggests that there are mutually beneficial lessons to be learned from truth and reconciliation experiences in Timor-Leste, Indonesia, Melanesia, and Canada, and that these cases offer lessons for truth and reconciliation processes in other contexts.

History, Narratives, Phases

Truth and reconciliation processes have implications for conflict resolution.[16] This book aims to create, synthesize, and share knowledge about issues of conflict resolution in which the conflicts are partly driven by clashing historical narratives. When each side in a conflict disagrees on what happened in the past, it is not easy to engage in dialogue about ways of moving forward. We also address truth-seeking efforts in the wake of conflict.

Several chapters analyze and interrogate officially-crafted narratives and efforts from non-governmental voices to put forward counter-narratives. For reconciliation to take place, official narratives must make space for alternative tellings. Truth commissions can embody what Priscilla Hayner calls "official truth-seeking,"[17] but they can also offer a platform for alternative stories about the past to emerge, and for unofficial memory to penetrate through cracks in the official story. Onur Bakiner argues that in some cases truth commissions are more valuable for their "indirect" effect on civil society than for their ability to directly convince governments to implement their recommendations.[18] The chapters in this book underline that conclusion by highlighting the vital role of civil society and considering truth and reconciliation as a process rather than simply an institutional exercise in which a commission forms, researches the past, aids victims and survivors, and produces a final list of recommendations. Bottom-up aspects are as important to truth and reconciliation *processes* as the top-down workings of a truth commission.

It is important to underline, as several chapters in this volume do, that this requires seeing women's experiences, women's roles, and women's participation more clearly. Conflict and human rights violations are gendered, and truth and reconciliation processes must acknowledge this if they are to be effective.

The best truth commission reports are not simply history texts but road maps towards greater respect for human rights, and it is groups and advocates outside government who are sometimes best equipped to follow that road map. In the words of Murray Sinclair, chief commissioner of the Canadian TRC: "As commissioners, we have described for you a mountain. We have shown you the path to the top. We call upon you to do the climbing."[19] In response, Canadian ecumenical justice coalition KAIROS produced an educational resource booklet entitled *Strength for Climbing: Steps on the Journey of Reconciliation*.[20] This is the sort of responsive partnership work that has been carried out for some time by others in Canadian and international civil society. The Pacific Peoples' Partnership, based in Victoria, British Columbia, has a long record of helping to build ties between First Nations communities on Vancouver Island and Indigenous Papuan communities. The Canadian Catholic Organization for Development and Peace did extensive work in Indonesian-occupied East Timor on strengthening civil society.

Civil society's role in truth and reconciliation is vital. It falls to non-governmental groups to disseminate truth commission reports, to bring them to wider audiences, and even to do much of the work of implementing their recommendations. Indonesian and Timorese activists call this "socialization" (to translate into somewhat awkward English the Indonesian-language term *sosialisasi* and the Tetun-language derivative *sosialisasaun*). Civil-society groups may be the key agents in bringing about change—both in terms of pushing to implement change after a truth commission delivers its report, and in trying to create truth and reconciliation processes where they do not, yet, exist. Commissions are often preceded by a popular struggle for justice in the face of past wrongs, a theme seen in Papuan campaigns to "set history straight." They are as often followed by a popular struggle to see justice done, not just in the words of a commission report, but in society's deeds in the aftermath of that report.

This conclusion implies also that there are phases in truth and reconciliation processes: a "before" and an "after" that are as important as the truth commission itself. In her research on wars, political scientist Cynthia Enloe has argued that we should see war not simply as an event bounded by start and end dates, but as a process with "pre" and "postwar" phases.[21] This framework can be applied to truth and reconciliation commissions, too. Truth commissions are a valuable tool, but they often lack follow-up mechanisms to implement their recommendations. The existing literature looks in detail at the operational phases of truth commissions. It is now starting to pay more attention to the campaigns to establish truth processes, to efforts to implement truth commission recommendations, and to the role of activists and civil-society organizations in creating the context for truth commissions and pushing for follow-up action.

Origins, Scope, Methodology

This book's origins lie in a workshop held at the University of Ottawa in October 2015 on Memory, Truth and Reconciliation in Southeast Asia.[22] The workshop aimed to share research and experience between academics, Canadian advocates of human rights in Southeast Asia, and people directly involved in the cases described below. The mix of academic and advocacy perspectives lies at the heart of this book's approach. Some authors write in an academic voice; others write from their wealth of experience as advocates; and many authors combine these two approaches. Every effort has been made to maintain the voice of contributors, including the orality of some texts. It is important also to note that chapters inform one another, with themes running like threads through them.

Starting with research questions about truth and reconciliation processes in Indonesia and Timor-Leste, we followed the story to include Melanesian cases as well, both from Indonesian-ruled Papua and from the independent Solomon Islands. As a result, this book includes coverage of all truth commissions to date held in Southeast Asia (Timor-Leste and a joint Indonesia–Timor-Leste commission) and the Southwest Pacific (the Solomon Islands TRC). It also explores, quite deliberately, cases in which the promises of a truth commission did not materialize. This is the case in Indonesia with respect to the mass killings that took place in the aftermath of the 1965 military coup, and in Indonesian-governed Papua. The lack to date of truth commissions does not mean there will never be a truth-seeking process. Indonesian-ruled Aceh is moving, after considerable delay, to create a process. What might future truth commissions look like? Some authors consider this question for locales that have not (yet) had a commission.

Methodologically, our focus on "socialization" is an attempt to implement current methods among researchers rooted in Indonesian civil society. The attention it pays to campaigns to "rectify" the past is inspired by historical approaches that emphasize a "usable past" but attempt to shift the agency in this quest from state to civil-society actors. This project highlights two less-studied aspects of truth commissions. First is the ways in which truth commissions seek to define and disseminate an agreed-upon "truth" about past events and to deploy that truth in ways that will serve the present.[23] Second is the focus in many commission reports on follow-up aspects that relate to memory and memorialization. We aim to incorporate a more historical note into the existing literature on truth commissions while also highlighting the way stories told by truth commissions are framed as authoritative truths and, driven by witness and victim testimony, as an emerging form of historical narrative creation.

Outline of Chapters

Truth commissions have often been studied through the lens of the most famous commission, South Africa's TRC, which was formed after the end of apartheid in 1994. In this and other scholarly accounts, truth commissions are often found at best to be partially successful, and at worst fatally flawed. Sarah Zwierzchowski's chapter provides an overview of the academic literature on truth commissions, noting their basis in Western positivist notions about truth and the way they are often yoked to government aims. This is increasingly seen as a weakness. "What will you do with our stories?" some Solomon Islanders asked. They want to explore outcomes beyond the simple completion of a government report.[24] We argue that one of the goals of civil-society organizations concerned with truth and reconciliation is to see that these stories are used—that is, heard and acted upon, not filed away or treated simply as evidence for a report.

Following the introductory essays, this book is organized into five sections that cover five geographic areas (Timor-Leste; Indonesia's national memory of the 1965 killings; Indonesian regional conflicts; Tanah Papua, a Melanesian space ruled by Indonesia; and, further into the Melanesian Pacific, Solomon Islands). A closing section connects these truth and reconciliation processes to Canada and looks for lessons that might be applicable to the wider study of truth and reconciliation.

Timor-Leste's significant truth commission makes it the logical starting point. Denied any prospect of a tribunal along the lines of those established in Rwanda and the former Yugoslavia, or even a mixed tribunal like the one set up in Cambodia, Timor-Leste hosted an impressive Commission on Truth, Reception, and Reconciliation, and followed it up with a joint Indonesia–Timor-Leste Commission on Truth and Friendship.

Neither commission was divorced from Timorese history. Geoffrey Robinson's historical overview opens the Timor-Leste section by examining "repertoires of violence" from the twentieth century that carry on influencing the independent Timor-Leste of the twenty-first. After Indonesian rule came to an end in 1999, there were high hopes that the "cycle of impunity" would be broken and perpetrators of mass violence held accountable through international legal processes. These hopes were dashed as neither the post-independence Timorese government nor the international community pushed to have justice done. As processes like the UN-mandated Serious Crimes Unit faltered, the CAVR emerged as the closest thing to an avenue for accountability. Robinson is both a leading scholar of these topics and a human rights researcher whose extensive report on the violence he witnessed as part of the UN mission in East Timor in 1999 forms volume 5 of the *Chega!* report.

Pat Walsh, a senior adviser to the CAVR with a history in Timor advocacy going back decades, picks up the story with a close focus on the commission itself. It was, he stresses, a Timorese institution driven by Timorese voices, not an attempt to impose a cookie-cutter version of truth commissions. Walsh debunks suggestions that the commission was imposed by the United Nations or based on outside models by painting it as very much a local creation. It was intended as a forward-looking road map with lessons on human rights and recommendations on accountability, not simply as a new official version of Timorese history. A decade after its completion, the report still has much to offer. As Walsh points out, the recent decision by the Timor-Leste government to establish an institute of memory, the Centro Nacional *Chega!* (*Chega!* National Centre), to implement many of the recommendations made by both the CAVR and the CTF, will give both commissions a new lease of life. The impact of this initiative, however, may depend most of all on current debates over historical memory and historical justice in Indonesia, the former occupying power.

The fate of Timorese truth-seeking processes will also depend on Timorese politics and economics. Most Timorese political leaders are former guerrillas or clandestine youth activists—a legacy that still shapes Timorese politics. This theme is examined by Jacqueline Aquino Siapno, a scholar who has worked in Timor-Leste, Australia, Europe, and North America. She traces the legacy of a violent occupation into "post-conflict" independent Timor-Leste, revealing the ways in which former independence activists continue to use clandestinity as both method and identity. This has shaped the independent Timor-Leste state in multiple ways. Timor-Leste today grapples with its past, with notions of truth, and with the desire for reconciliation in ways that are shaped by the experiences of clandestine activism in the days before freedom, and also by the often colonialist approaches of the international governments and individuals who have exerted an influence over the country since independence. Siapno's analysis draws on her own years as an academic and activist in Timor-Leste and on the experiences of her late husband, the leader of a major political party and the former speaker of the Timor-Leste parliament.

Timor-Leste also joined the international community as one of Asia's poorest countries. This economic legacy informs reconciliation processes. Mica Barreto Soares, a Timorese academic and former officer with the UN Development Programme in Timor-Leste, offers an overview of the successes and challenges of development in a country that combines oil wealth with widespread poverty. Timor-Leste has its own development plan, but it cannot escape global development strategies. Barreto Soares discusses the country's positioning between the liberal state-building approach championed by the United States and other Western donors and the emerging challenge of Chinese aid models that stress "non-interference" but also imply outside influence on Timor-Leste's future direction. Memory and continued calls for reconciliation and justice intertwine with development. It is not simply a case of "goodbye conflict, hello development," as banners in

Dili occasionally proclaim. Rather, development must address the wounds of the past if it is to move forward.

The final three chapters on Timor-Leste are more personal in tone but they, too, draw out thematic threads. Along with the Philippines, Timor-Leste is one of two majority-Catholic countries in Asia. Religion clearly informs reconciliation, all the more so given the historic role of the Timorese Catholic Church. Jess Agustin draws on his own solidarity work in Canada and Timor-Leste as an officer with the Canadian Catholic Organization for Development and Peace to describe the role of the Timorese church during the independence struggle. He points to a tension between its role as bastion of the Portuguese colonial state and its alliance with popular movements during the Indonesian occupation. Both approaches to the church's role shape its attitude towards the independent Timor-Leste state, towards Timorese civil society, and towards reconciliation—itself a Christian concept in many ways. Building a culture of peace, he concludes, remains a key need today, and that requires healing.

In thinking about religion, Agustin's meditation is also a reflection on the key role played by civil society. This theme shines through the testimony of two Timorese women that closes this section. While most political leaders and parliamentarians avoided calls to implement the CAVR report's recommendations, Fernanda Borges, during her time as a member of parliament, sought to place the report's findings at the centre of the policies of the independent Timor-Leste. Her chapter reproduces in edited form a speech she delivered on Human Rights Day in 2010, a powerful statement of the case for a victim-centred approach to reconciliation even after the *Chega!* report's completion.

This section's concluding testimony comes from Maria Manuela Leong Pereira, director of ACbit, (Asosiasaun *Chega!* Ba Ita, or "*Chega!* for Us Association"). If the calls for a victim-centred approach continue today, they originate mostly from outside government—from human rights organizations and other groups located in Timorese civil society. In an interview conducted for this book, she speaks about ACbit's socialization efforts and insists that the report is not over, but rather that *Chega!* remains a "living document" belonging to all of the Timorese people.

In sum, the Timor-Leste section links the inheritance of a violent past and a shared struggle for recognition of Timorese identity and Timorese freedom to a contested present in which truth and reconciliation processes intersect with the contemporary challenges of effective governance, economic development, and popular participation. Timor-Leste was not a blank slate when it regained independence in 2002: memories of the past shape the present and the future of the country.[25] Moreover, the publication of a truth commission report did not end the truth and reconciliation process. Indeed, it continues today.

The next section moves the story to Indonesia. The country has faced truth and reconciliation challenges on both the national and local levels, with increasing demands for an accounting over the "events" of 1965–66 in which hundreds of thousands of people were killed in a violent military takeover of the country that brought General Suharto to power. Unresolved tensions from 1965 led to a promise, by a post-dictatorship elected government, to create a historical truth commission, but that promise was abandoned soon afterwards.

This section opens with history. Advocate, researcher, and Jesuit priest Baskara Wardaya provides an overview of the 1965 events before moving to his main topic, the way the mass violence and repression of 1965 have been remembered by the state and by victims and their families. The Suharto regime developed an all-encompassing narrative that blamed violence on the PKI, which was alleged to have masterminded a coup attempt. The "impenetrable wall" of this official narrative could not be challenged during the three decades of Suharto's New Order. Since the fall of Suharto, victims and human rights groups have tried a number of creative ways to break silences and offer different tellings of 1965, all in an attempt to make cracks in the wall of state-imposed official "truths."

The 1965 events are not just an Indonesian story: they are an international story as well. Bernd Schaefer also touches on narratives of 1965, but from an international perspective. The state narrative rests on an alleged collusion between the PKI and the People's Republic of China, which implies that Chinese records would be valuable as part of a multi-archival truth-seeking effort into what happened in 1965, and what role was played by global actors, including the United States, other Western countries, the Soviet Union, and China. Schaefer's chapter closes with a road map for what an Indonesian truth commission into 1965 might address, and how international records could inform its truth-seeking efforts. There is no immediate prospect of Indonesia's government holding a truth-seeking process into the mass killings of the 1960s. Still, truth and reconciliation processes inform debates about 1965, and Schaefer's thoughts on the shape of a possible commission draw on these global conversations as well as on the Indonesian civil-society voices described in Wardaya's account.

This section closes, again, with personal testimony—this time from the letters and diary of Gatot Lestario, an Indonesian political prisoner arrested after the 1965 coup and executed twenty years later. His letters shed light on the experience of the *tapol* (*tahanan politik*, or political prisoner) in Suharto's New Order. His words are reproduced from letters on file at TAPOL, the Indonesia Human Rights Campaign, in London. They were provided, along with a translation of parts of the prisoner's diary, by TAPOL founder Carmel Budiardjo, herself a political prisoner (1965–71) during the New Order.

Indonesian debates about truth and reconciliation do not take place only at the centre, nor are they concerned only with the past. They are also present throughout the archipelago, especially in conflict-ridden areas. We take a close look at a truth process in formation in Aceh and a failed reconciliation effort in Central Sulawesi.

Aceh was promised a truth commission in the peace settlement that ended three decades of warfare in the province. As with the 1965 events, government promises of truth-seeking in Aceh were not transformed into action. In this section's opening chapter, Australian researcher Lia Kent and Acehnese researcher Rizki Affiat explore a new model being tried in Aceh: a truth and reconciliation commission mandated by the provincial government, with the stated intention of being permanent. The authors explore this way of "gambling with truth," assessing the potential benefits and and pitfalls of the Acehnese approach.

Diverse Indonesia has seen the emergence of twenty-first-century tensions between different groups in several regions, and consequent efforts to build reconciliation processes for more recent conflicts. Are these simply "ethnic" or "religious" conflicts, as most accounts argue? Arianto Sangadji, a former human rights campaigner on Eastern Indonesia's island of Sulawesi and now a Canada-based scholar, argues that the prevailing interpretation has it wrong by way of a close analysis of the class-based roots of conflict in Poso, in Central Sulawesi province. Government-led reconciliation efforts there have failed because they saw the local conflict as one based in religious splits between Christians and Muslims; because they ignored class elements; because they took a top-down approach rather than one based in grassroots civil-society leadership; and because they treated the Indonesian state as a neutral arbiter rather than as one of the parties to a complex, multi-level conflict.

Perhaps the most intractable and troublesome challenge to Indonesian unity is the conflict, ongoing since the 1960s, on the western half of the island of New Guinea—now defined by the Indonesian government as the provinces of Papua and West Papua, but treated by local Papuan nationalists as a single territory that is still seeking its right to self-determination. The conflict in Tanah Papua, subject of the next section, may also be one of the most serious human rights challenges in today's Indonesia. Anthropologically, as Papuan nationalists always point out, Papua, inhabited by people with darker skin and curlier hair than the Malayo-Polynesian people of most of Indonesia, is part of Melanesia. Whether this claim is accepted or disputed, it underpins a sense of Papuan identity that continues to feed a widespread movement for Papuan independence.

The Papua section again moves from history to recent context to testimony, ending with a reflection on the role of the key outside actor, the United States. NGO worker Todd Biderman and researcher Jenny Munro offer a close description of current human rights troubles in Papua and the challenges those troubles put in the path of reconciliation. In an echo of the failure in Sulawesi, they see current "reconciliation" processes conducted by Indonesian state agents as missing important aspects of local agency. Is reconciliation possible when the truth is so disputed, and the Indonesian government's truth is seen as "non-truth" by so many Papuans? Based on a close involvement with Papuan partners over many years, Biderman and Munro consider what a Papuan truth and reconciliation process might look like, and what lessons flow from Papuan centring of the natural environment for global truth and reconciliation processes.

Julian Smyth asks related questions in her examination of the role of music and song in Papuan resistance struggles. In an oral tradition, Papuan identity is expressed through word and song, which become at once both "living symbol" and "participative practice." Indigenous traditions and lived experiences are at the centre of Smyth's account of song and identity, and she illustrates the troubles inherent in any effort to resolve the conflict through the dominant security and development approaches.

Like other conflicts, this one is both local and international. Former US diplomat Edmund McWilliams, who now coordinates the West Papua

Advocacy Team, takes aim at US policy as the key lever in creating a genuine reconciliation process in Papua. He analyzes the current human rights situation and the "compromises with the truth" that run through annual US government human rights reports on Indonesia. While post-Suharto Indonesia is relatively democratic, the New Order mentality seems to live on in Papua, where human rights violations are widespread. Many of these violations can, in part, be laid at the feet of the American business interests exploiting Papuan natural resources. This has led successive US governments to back the continued military occupation of Papua, rather than promote a stable, democratic, and demilitarized Indonesia with full respect for human rights. Reconciliation requires the Indonesian army to leave Papua and allow free dialogue.

The next section moves further into Melanesia, with two accounts of the experience of the only Melanesian country to hold a truth commission: Solomon Islands. This was a mixed national-international commission, struck after an internal conflict within the country. A pair of chapters on the Solomon Islands experience comes from two participants, one offering a historical account and the other describing how gender entered the commission's deliberations.

At the time of the conflict, Canadian Anglican Terry Brown was the bishop of Malaita, a diocese of the Church of Melanesia. His chapter recounts the history of this conflict and the truth and reconciliation process that followed after a ceasefire agreement was finally reached. The commission's report was secret until Brown published it online himself in order to ensure that its results were available to the public. His chapter tells this story and assesses the strengths and weaknesses of the Solomon Islands TRC final report, the silence from government and media that followed its release, and the value that still lies in the commission's powerful final report.

Betty Lina Gigisi worked as one of the gender officers on the Solomon Islands TRC, and her chapter recounts her own experience in attempting to have women's rights and women's status included in politics. She briefly describes the work done and the form of the commission and argues that to be effective, truth commissions must include a gender perspective.

The book's closing section attempts to connect truth and reconciliation processes in Southeast Asia and the Southwest Pacific to similar processes in Canada. Maggie Helwig, an Anglican priest with many years of solidarity work behind her, draws connections to the Truth and Reconciliation Commission of Canada, which completed its work in 2015. Canada's TRC focused on "Indian residential schools" and issued a broader set of calls to action that together amount to a plea for a renewed relationship between Indigenous peoples and Canadians descended from settlers. Canada's TRC did not exist in isolation; rather, it was embedded in global truth and reconciliation processes as well as in the painful legacy of residential schools. Helwig highlights the Canadian TRC's focus on systems of oppression rather than individuals and its efforts to "socialize" a counter-narrative about Canadian history before considering what lessons it might offer for truth commissions and processes in other countries.

The conclusion, finally, aims to draw together the various threads that make up the book, to contribute to the literature on truth and reconciliation commissions and transitional justice, and to inform current policy debates on how governments and societies can, and should, face the violence and conflict in their own past.

Notes

1. Abé Barreto Soares, "Flourish Everlastingly," *Dadolin* (blog), 1 October 2008, http://dadolin.blogspot.ca/2008/10/poetical-expression-1.html (accessed 10 February 2017). Tebe is a Timorese dance, usually performed by men and women holding hands in a circle; Bidu is another traditional Timorese dance, usually performed by men.

2. The official name, the Democratic Republic of Timor-Leste, was determined at independence. Timor-Leste is Portuguese for "East Timor." The two names are used interchangeably in this book.

3. See "The Suai Church Massacre," *Chega! The Final Report of the Timor-Leste Commission for Reception, Truth, and Reconciliation*, http://www.laohamutuk.org/Justice/99/bere/CAVRSuaiChurch.pdf (accessed 10 February 2017).

4. Father Jim Roche cited in David Webster, "East Timorese: Destroy Their Religion, Destroy Their Identity," *Catholic New Times* (Toronto), 3 October 1999.

5. Lia Kent, *The Dynamics of Transitional Justice in East Timor* (New York: Routledge, 2012), 176.

6. *The Circle of Stones*, directed by Jen Hughes and Filomena dos Reis, 2001, https://archive.org/details/TheCircleOfStones (accessed 10 February 2017). See also *Suai Media Space*, 20 November 2008, http://www.suaimediaspace.org/2008/11/20/the-circle-of-stones-uploaded-at-last/ (accessed 10 February 2017).

7. The concept of a "living document" is borrowed from Manuela Leong's contribution to this book.

8   Priscilla B. Hayner, *Unspeakable Truths: Facing the Challenge of Truth Commissions* (New York: Routledge, 2010). See also Greg Grandin, "The Instruction of Great Catastrophe: Truth Commissions, National History, and State Formation in Argentina, Chile, and Guatemala," *The American Historical Review* 110, no. 1 (2005): 46–67; Joanna R. Quinn, *The Politics of Acknowledgement: Truth Commissions in Uganda and Haiti* (Vancouver: UBC Press, 2011).

9   Kent, *Dynamics of Transitional Justice*; John Roosa, "How Does a Truth Commission Find Out What the Truth Is? The Case of East Timor's CAVR," *Pacific Affairs* 80, no. 4 (2008): 569–80; David Cohen, *Indifference and Accountability: The United Nations and the Politics of International Justice in East Timor* (Honolulu: East-West Center Special Reports Number 9, June 2006). See also Elizabeth F. Drexler, "Fatal Knowledges: The Social and Political Legacies of Collaboration and Betrayal in Timor-Leste," *International Journal of Transitional Justice* 7, no. 1 (2013): 74–94; Lia Kent "Local Memory Practices in East Timor: Disrupting Transitional Justice Narratives," *International Journal of Transitional Justice* 5, no. 3 (2011): 434–55; and Johammes Langer, "Including and excluding civil society in the truth commission of Timor Leste," *Perspectivas Internacionales* 11, no. 1 (2015): 89–114.

10 See Hayner, *Unspeakable Truths*.

11 *Chega! The Final Report of the Commission for Reception, Truth, and Reconciliation Timor-Leste*. The occupation of Timor-Leste is chronicled, among other sources, in António Barbedo de Magalhães, *Timor Leste : ocupação Indonésia e genocídio* (Porto : Universidade do Porto, 1992); Carmel Budiardjo and Liem Soei Liong, *The War Against East Timor* (London: Zed Books, 1984); James Dunn, *East Timor: A Rough Passage to Independence* (Australia: Longueville, 2004); Clinton Fernandes, *The Independence of East Timor: Multidimensional Perspectives—Occupation, Resistance and International Political Activism* (Eastbourne, East Sussex: Sussex Academic Press, 2011); Jill Jolliffe, *East Timor: Nationalism and Colonialism* (St Lucia: University of Queensland Press, 1978); Jose Ramos-Horta, *Funu: The Unfinished Saga of East Timor* (Boston: Red Sea Press, 1987); Geoffrey Robinson, *If You Leave Us Here, We Will Die: How Genocide Was Stopped in East Timor* (Princeton and Oxford: Princeton University Press, 2010); and Awet Tewelde Weldemichael, *Third World Colonialism and Strategies of Liberation: Eritrea and East Timor Compared* (Cambridge: Cambridge University Press, 2013).

12 Charles S. Maier, *The Unmasterable Past: History, Holocaust, and German National Identity* (Cambridge, MA: Harvard University Press, 2009); David Webster, "History, Nation and Narrative in East Timor's Truth Commission Report," *Pacific Affairs* 80, no. 4 (2008): 581–91. On the evolution of Timorese nationalism, see Michael Leach, *Nation-Building and National Identity in Timor-Leste* (London: Routledge, 2017).

13 The modern spelling system for Indonesian and Malaysian is being used here, thus Sukarno and Suharto rather than Soekarno and Soeharto. Like many Indonesians, both Sukarno and Suharto use only one name.

14 Tanah Papua (the Land of Papua) in this book refers to the territory that was officially called Netherlands New Guinea before 1962, West New Guinea in 1962–63, the Indonesian province of West Irian (later Irian Jaya) until 2000, and the Indonesian province of Papua after 2000. It also includes the new province of West Papua, split from Papua province in 2003 (originally under the name West Irian Jaya). Contributors

use the terms *Tanah Papua*, *Papua*, or *West Papua* interchangeably except where stated otherwise. On Papuan history under Indonesian rule, see, among other sources, Carmel Budiardjo and Liem Soei Liong, *West Papua: The Obliteration of a People* (London: Tapol, 1988); Danilyn Rutherford, *Laughing at Leviathan: Sovereignty and Audience in West Papua* (Chicago: University of Chicago Press, 2012); and S. Eben Kirksey, *Freedom in Entangled Worlds* (Durham, NC: Duke University Press, 2012).

15 This was recalled, for instance, by TRC Canada Commissioner Murray Sinclair, in his Woodrow Lloyd lecture at the University of Regina, 24 February 2016.

16 See, for instance, International Center for Transitional Justice, "Challenging The Conventional: Can Truth Commissions Strengthen Peace Processes?" Multimedia website, March 2016, https://www.ictj.org/challenging-conventional-truth-commissions-peace/index.html (accessed 10 February 2017).

17 Hayner, *Unspeakable Truths*, 8.

18 Onur Bakiner, *Truth Commissions: Memory, Power and Legitimacy* (Philadelphia: University of Pennsylvania Press, 2016).

19 Cited in Dan Lett, "A Mountain Waiting to be Climbed," *Winnipeg Free Press*, 3 June 2015, http://www.winnipegfreepress.com/local/a-mountain-waiting-to-be-climbed-305943201.html (accessed 10 February 2017).

20 KAIROS Canada, *Strength for Climbing: Steps on the Journey of Reconciliation* (Toronto: KAIROS Canada and Mennonite Church Canada, 2015), http://www.anglican.ca/wp-content/uploads/KAIROS_StrengthForClimbing.pdf (accessed 10 February 2017).

21 Cynthia Enloe, *Nimo's War, Emma's War: Making Feminist Sense of the Iraq War* (Princeton, NJ: Princeton University Press, 2010).

22 Workshop materials are available online on the project web site, https://memorytruthreconciliation.wordpress.com/ (accessed 10 February 2017).

23 Greg Grandin, "Chronicles of a Guatemalan Genocide Foretold: Violence, Trauma, and the Limits of Historical Inquiry," *Nepantla* 1, no. 2 (2000): 391–412.

24 Louise Vella, "'What Will You Do with Our Stories?' Truth and Reconciliation in the Solomon Islands," *International Journal of Conflict and Violence* 8, no. 1 (2014): 91–103.

25 See Douglas Kammen, *Three Centuries of Conflict in East Timor* (New Brunswick, NJ: Rutgers University Press, 2015).

Incomplete Truth, Incomplete Reconciliation: Towards a Scholarly Verdict on Truth and Reconciliation Commissions

SARAH ZWIERZCHOWSKI

Since their emergence as political and legal institutions in South America in the 1980s, truth and reconciliation commissions have become the dominant international paradigm for resolving tensions and preventing further atrocities in the aftermath of intrastate conflicts. These truth commissions generally operate on a purely Western understanding of objective truth and reconciliation as a means of securing political unity, overriding traditional and alternative reconciliation practices. In the same vein, the commissions conclude by producing a report that serves to present a uniform narrative of the past and a commitment to future co-operation that is presumed to be unanimous. While truth commissions are upheld at an international level, major critiques of these processes revolve around the strict forms and narratives inherent in them. Truth commissions have an undeniable value, but these critiques are valid and should be considered. Both truth and reconciliation can be sought and enacted in a variety of ways, taking many different forms, but existing examples have not adequately mined alternative solutions, nor have they addressed the potential and necessity for multiplicities of truths and reconciliations.

This chapter will examine scholarly evaluations of truth and reconciliation commissions. It will begin with a general analysis of the purpose of truth commissions, their functions, and the results expected of them. Attention will then be turned to the scholarship pertaining to the Truth and Reconciliation Commission in South Africa. Academics first began paying attention to the proceedings and results of truth commissions in the 1990s and the popularity of the subject in academia has since increased. The scholarship shows that conceptual understandings of commissions depend on idealistic and politically impractical expectations. The case of the South African TRC demonstrates how scholars have struggled to reconcile their expectations with an often disappointing reality. Overwhelmingly, scholars looking at existing case studies have determined that all truth commissions fall short of completing or respecting their mandates; as a result, reconciliation is only ever partially achieved. The scholarship identifies several main reasons for this failure, including the interference of political factions, the uneven participation of religious institutions, the unclear definitions of the very concepts of truth and reconciliation found in TRC mandates, and the marginalization of particular victims and alternative reconciliation practices.

Setting the Standards for Evaluating Truth Commissions

There have been many attempts to pin down reconciliation and its implications in political and social realms, though most scholars admit that reconciliation can take many forms in different contexts. Erin Daly and Jeremy Sarkin note that while there is unanimity that reconciliation can repair divided societies, there is no consensus on what reconciliation entails or requires.[1] Reconciliation can take on various political, cultural, and socio-economic implications. The combined enthusiasm for reconciliation and the lack of understanding of its mechanics or consequences create serious challenges for governments and communities, who are equally unsure of what results to promise or what to expect from reconciliation processes. Methods of measuring the success of reconciliation or how long such processes should be in effect remain undetermined. Reconciliation is used to describe various kinds of healing, ranging from personal to interpersonal, and including the rebuilding of communities and the attainment of national stability and peace. Daly and Sarkin argue that reconciliation offers the possibility for healing divided societies undergoing political transition, but only if societies articulate reconciliation within their own political and historical contexts. A structural conception of reconciliation would prove useful for such societies and transitional governments should create political and economic structures rooted in the needs of their societies that are inclusive, allowing all involved to participate in public life equitably.

Though it has proven difficult to pin down an exact definition of or expectation for reconciliation, scholars have acknowledged the existence of various reconciliation practices. Johann Galtung identified twelve broad practices of reconciliation: the exculpatory nature-structure-culture approach; the reparation/restitution approach; the apology/forgiveness approach; the theological/penitence approach; the juridical/ punishment approach; the codependent origination/karma approach; the historical/truth commission approach; the theatrical/reliving approach; the joint sorrow/healing approach; the joint reconstruction approach; the joint conflict resolution approach; and the *ho'o ponopono* approach.[2] He argues that there is no one solution for every situation and that, in fact, none of the identified approaches alone can properly address the complexities that emerge following serious conflicts. These approaches are ineffective because they cannot end the cycle of violence nor can they reconcile the involved parties to each other; they are each loaded with various assumptions regarding the nature of truth and community, and so they cannot address multiplicities of experiences and needs. For example, Westerners would recognize *ho'o ponopono* as a practice that is culturally specific to Hawai'i, but Western theological and juridical approaches to reconciliation are considered universal solutions for transitional societies. The above approaches would be most effective when paired or grouped together, though no society has thus far undertaken this alternative.

All forms of reconciliation depend on understandings of the role of forgiveness in the aftermath of conflict. Mark R. Amstutz focuses on the concept of forgiveness itself as played out in the proceedings of truth commissions to determine whether a nation can move past serious injustices and atrocities and what role forgiveness can play in countries experiencing political conflict.[3] Amstutz argues that political forgiveness cannot act as a guarantor that human rights violations and conflicts will be forgotten. Instead, forgiveness must be understood as an ethic that demands that political actors confront their guilt and responsibility through an exploration and acknowledgement of the truth. It also requires that political actors express remorse, preferably sincerely, offering reparations and submitting to punishment. Political forgiveness is not the only option for achieving reconciliation, but truth commissions are nonetheless most promising when they empower victims and restore community ties. Legal retribution is effective in promoting and protecting the rights of individuals, but a communitarian approach emphasizing social and political goods is effective when communities are divided.

In her widely read book *Unspeakable Truths*, Priscilla B. Hayner remarks that while truth-seeking commissions aim to allow countries to move forward by acting as a public stage for forgiveness, state violence and abuse leaves a legacy that is not easily overcome.[4] There is a need in such societies to rebuild victims' trust in their government, the police, and the armed forces. While some have suggested that countries should merely try to move forward by forgetting past atrocities, this cannot provide a solid foundation for a democracy. Though Truth and Reconciliation Commissions (TRCs) are gaining attention on an international level, there remain misconceptions regarding the manner in which they operate and the impact they can have for victims, perpetrators, policies, and society as a whole. In addition, the contingency of truth causes many discrepancies, depending on the mandates and resources governments allocate to fund commissions, as well as the views of the panelists of the commissions. Because of these misconceptions, there remain doubts that truth commissions can serve as mechanisms for individual accountability, especially since they are sometimes offered up as alternatives to criminal tribunals for those responsible. Criminal remedies cannot be discussed without considering the political context of states or the perceived alternative. Trials and TRCs can perform different functions, but their goals can also overlap.

The relationship between truth-seeking mechanisms and criminal justice mechanisms is crucial, as Vasuki Nesiah has demonstrated.[5] Each process has its complexities and positive and negative attributes in dealing with serious community divisions by revealing the truth and punishing those that have done wrong. A perfect mechanism would be able to accomplish both tasks, but truth commissions have often failed to deliver consequences to perpetrators and courts have marginalized the needs of victims to speak out about their experiences. Nesiah argues that the pursuits of justice and truth can and should be complementary, rather than put in opposition, as has been the paradigm in the field of international conflict resolution until recently. Courts focus on questions of guilt and innocence, determining appropriate punishments for perpetrators, and truth commissions allow victims to speak their piece and be reconciled to their oppressors. These two functions are very important and one cannot be adopted without the other if serious reconciliation and societal healing are to be attained. The pitting of truth against justice represents a false dichotomy because each concept and its corresponding institution can be so diverse and offer a variety of solutions.

In all of the scholarship mentioned thus far, authors have understood the potential of commissions to bring the dominant and oppressed groups together to reconcile and smoothly transition from intrastate conflict to reconstruction. Robert I. Rotberg emphasizes that commissions can provide meaningful inquiry and careful research that allows a society to engage in a collective apology.[6] He argues that state apologies drawn from the investigations of commissions achieve more healing and provide a durable foundation for reconciliation. Commissions and other restorative judicial institutions contribute to the process of reconciliation by allowing victims to express their grievances to their perpetrators and learn more about the atrocities that affected them. From a political perspective, the research conducted by commissions lends an informed sincerity to an official apology. The South African Truth and Reconciliation Commission is noted as a successful turning point by many scholars because it operated as though reconciliation were possible despite the many challenges it faced and it solved many problems that previous commissions had confronted. The commission process has its flaws, but if nothing else its commitment to truth-finding and truth-telling allows for more compelling and sincere apologies following intrastate conflict.

The proliferation of literature related to truth and reconciliation commissions continues and scholars have presented a more nuanced understanding of their workings and goals. Onur Bakiner looks back on the now thirty-year history of TRCs, noting that they embody the modern desire to address the wrongs of the past.[7] The success of TRCs has been mixed, stemming from the political nature of these institutions, which involve interest groups from all levels of society who seek to advance their own agendas. The political nature of the commissions is a product of the fact that those involved "constantly make choices when they define such basic objectives as truth, reconciliation, justice, memory, reparation, and recognition, and decide how these objectives should be met and whose needs should be served."[8] As a result, the task of evaluating the achievements and weaknesses must follow from an understanding of the interests, values, and expectations that inform the political dimensions of each TRC. Commissions frequently struggle to strike a balance between the interests of the governments that sponsor them, the religious groups that support and promote them, and the victims relying on them for moral support and reconciliation. The limits imposed on TRCs by these competing groups necessarily affect the progress and outcomes of their work, especially when their goals are described in narrow terms to begin with.

While truth commissions are an increasingly popular phenomenon globally, scholarly assessments have tended to find fault with many of their aspects. Based on the theoretical outlines explored above, the consensus emerges that most truth commissions have fallen short of their potential and left an unresolved or unsatisfactory legacy. Taking texts devoted to the TRC in South Africa as a case study, it becomes clear that, despite their various contributions to reconciliation and political transition, TRCs have been found lacking for a variety of reasons. In South Africa, analysts have located the TRC's shortcomings in intervention from political parties and factions, the uneven participation of religious institutions, ambiguities in its mandate regarding the very concepts of truth and reconciliation, and its marginalization of those victims who preferred alternative routes to achieving reconciliation.

Healing from Apartheid: Truth and Reconciliation in South Africa

Though truth and reconciliation commissions had been in existence under other names for over a decade, the TRC in South Africa drew unprecedented international attention, thereafter popularizing the term *truth commission*. All future truth commissions had to look back to the South African experience for lessons both positive and negative. This response was due to a number of factors, including the high profile of its most ardent proponents, its use of public hearings, and the controversy surrounding its policy of granting amnesty to perpetrators in exchange for testimony. The

South African TRC is noted for its attempt to create a new national truth to replace the national narrative of the apartheid regime, for granting amnesty to some individual perpetrators who admitted their actions, and for giving victims a chance to tell their stories in a public forum in an attempt to create national reconciliation.[9] In the words of Gillian Slovo: "The TRC's great virtue, it was suggested, was to exchange retributive justice (or legal punishment) for restorative justice: a justice that would direct attention to the needs and participation of the victims and, in that way, help repair the damage done." These hearings were "shot through with accounts of what had happened to individuals and with lamentations of pain and suffering. People had come to mourn. To be heard. To put their truths on record. There lies the paradox: the wonder of the TRC, and the thing for which it is best known, resides not in its original purpose—to provide amnesties—but in its by-product, the victims hearings."[10]

In 1995, the Promotion of National Unity and Reconciliation Act was passed by the South African parliament and over the course of the following months seventeen commissioners were selected from nominations made by private citizens, churches, and political parties. The TRC was empowered to grant amnesty to individual perpetrators, to conduct searches and seize evidence, and to subpoena witnesses, but its mandate was limited to "gross" human rights violations. Its period of investigation was set to cover the period from May 1960 to the elections of May 1994.[11] In 1998, the TRC's five-volume report was presented to the South African parliament. It immediately drew criticism due to its downplaying of the liberation struggle on the part of the African National Congress and the strict narrative of reconciliation presented in the report. A great deal of public attention in South Africa has since focused on the lack of community and institutional reparations extended by the government.[12] The failures of the TRC remain contestable, while some continue to argue in its favour.

The failure of South Africa's TRC to achieve reconciliation is apparent from surveys done among the population since the commission's closure in 1998. Truth commissions operate on the assumption that knowledge of the past can lead to acceptance and reconciliation, and that the truth can allow citizens to reconcile and embrace a democratic future. Using statistical analysis, James L. Gibson argues that there has been moderate, though incomplete, reconciliation in South Africa, thanks in part to the work and findings of the TRC. Data from popular surveys undertaken in South

Africa reveals a racial divide between the reconciled and the unreconciled: among South Africans of Asian origin and Coloured South Africans, accepting the truth has heightened their feelings of reconciliation. Among white South Africans, truth leads to reconciliation, but those who already felt reconciled were more prepared to accept the truth about apartheid. Among black South Africans, however, truth has not led to reconciliation and reconciliation has not led to truth. These results give a mixed impression of the impact of the truth and reconciliation process, demonstrating that the outcome depends on one's race and personal experiences with the apartheid system.

The political influences that plagued the Truth and Reconciliation Commission in South Africa are significant in understanding its failure, though many scholars have chosen to focus on larger conceptual issues. The TRC mandate, however, was given a decidedly political slant, which necessarily affected its impact and results. Graeme Simpson argues that the commission's primary mandate to determine responsibility for politically motivated human rights violations and ensure reconciliation on a political level limited the truths that the TRC could access and reveal.[13] The TRC delivered a politically whitewashed version of the truth about apartheid. Truth clashed with reconciliation: the role of the commission in fostering reconciliation and preventing future human rights violations was constrained by the conception that apartheid was based on political differences. Specific categories for victims and perpetrators were therefore established in political terms at the opening of the TRC's work. The focus on individuals blurred the systemic issues of racism that lay at the centre of the apartheid system. This misconception of the past further mystified, rather than revealed, the truth. Right-wing political parties, fearing what the TRC would make public about their participation in apartheid, decried it as a witch hunt and openly rejected its legitimacy as a forum for reconciliation. Due to these attacks, the TRC's mandate was made sufficiently ambiguous to avoid allegations of political bias. The imperative to appear as fair as possible from all political vantage points seriously limited the extent to which the TRC could uncover the truth, promote reconciliation, and deliver justice. Ultimately, the political tensions in the TRC have allowed issues of longstanding and deep-seated social imbalances to remain ignored.

Some scholars have identified the influence of religious institutions on the TRC in South Africa as the source of its inability to properly promote both truth and reconciliation. Russell H. Botman, for example, stressed that the history of apartheid is equally political and religious; the apartheid stance of "separation of races" developed out of the Dutch Reformed Church's mission policy, which itself stemmed from debates over the position of Indigenous converts in the church throughout the nineteenth century.[14] In other words, through apartheid, the original segregation policies of the Dutch church were extended towards all aspects of individual and political life. Botman notes that as apartheid was dismantled and reconciliation became a national focus, the role of religion in the creation and perpetuation of apartheid posed a major problem. Throughout the process, restorative justice was favoured as the most Christian approach, but this drew criticism that the process was taking the airs of a Christian initiative. While Christian leaders like Anglican archbishop Desmond Tutu served as TRC commissioners, the Dutch Reformed Church did not participate meaningfully in the process and merely published its own report, in which it admitted its part in apartheid, though in a calculated way. These issues relating to the participation of the church prevented a deep reconciliation from taking place.

Hugo van der Merwe has written extensively on the outcome of the South African TRC, arguing that many different factors contributed to its incomplete mandate and its ambiguous success. Van der Merwe notes that the end of the apartheid era challenged church leaders in general to struggle against a serious source of social division in South Africa—apartheid itself.[15] He argues that, while this struggle in the name of justice allowed the church to legitimize itself as a political actor with power to promote change and reconciliation, the institution continues to struggle to clearly define its role in the reconciliation process and has negatively impacted the process as a result. The church's broad reach and moral influence over the general population granted them a potentially powerful role in all major societal discussions and activities; this potential, however, can only be realized through principled commitment, for which there is no clear strategy or even enthusiasm. Church leaders believe their institution is especially qualified to undertake the challenge of reconciliation since they see reconciliation as a distinctly Christian and biblical concept. Practical strategies for church participation, however, have not been fully fleshed out, and potential has not become reality. The church's exclusionary claims on reconciliation have contributed to these problems because secular developments in reconciliation have been neglected. The role of the churches in the TRC was ambiguous, presenting both a positive and a negative influence on the reconciliation process.

Some scholars have argued that the TRC failed to reconcile all South Africans because truth and reconciliation had already been defined narrowly in its mandate, the result of negotiations among the African National Congress and the apartheid government. In an earlier publication, van der Merwe discusses the impact of the TRC on reconciliation in two particular communities that experienced violence during apartheid.[16] While it attempted to mold its processes based on a multitude of inputs, the TRC often lacked a coherent approach to the questions of justice and reconciliation. He argues that competing interpretations of these key concepts created tensions both within the TRC and between the TRC and the community, which can be seen in its hearing proceedings. The tension that stands out the most is that between top-down approaches to restorative justice and reconciliation, as adopted by the TRC itself, and bottom-up approaches, which were preferred by local communities. While the TRC's intervention in particular communities resulted in both successes and challenges, significant ideas about reconciliation and justice emerged during the hearings. There was a clear engagement with the ideas of reconciliation, justice, and forgiveness and a broad acceptance of restorative justice as embodied in the TRC's amnesty policy over the punitive justice that would have been possible through the work of an international criminal tribunal. There was some resistance to the top-down conceptions of restorative justice as offered by the TRC and communities pushed for a bottom-up approach to justice as an alternative.

Later, in collaboration with Audrey R. Chapman, van der Merwe compared the TRC mandate with its actual results to determine how much the mandate was respected and when it was limited by various factors.[17] They argue that the TRC did not adequately deliver the truth, reconciliation, and justice described in its mandate, although this failure does not negate the fact that TRC made significant contributions to South Africa's transition from apartheid to an inclusive democratic state. The TRC's role should not be idealized but rather clearly understood, because it set the precedent for other commissions. The TRC uncovered both "macro truths" (related to contexts, causes, and patterns of humans rights abuses) and "micro truths" (related to specific events); both truths join together to determine responsibility, but the types and levels of responsibility vary. Van der Merwe and Chapman conclude that the TRC's truth-finding mandate was poorly realized because it lacked a coherent conception and process for such work. Its public hearings were innovative, but storytelling is an ineffective route to the objective truth.

Perhaps due to the need to balance the interests of South Africa's major political parties, the TRC's narrow mandate prevented a significant exploration of the root causes or origins of apartheid. More recently, Paul Gready has argued that the paradigm for transitional justice and human rights has not properly addressed structural violence, in particular the wealth inequality and social and criminal violence that remain as legacies of unresolved violent conflicts.[18] The TRC in South Africa was conceived post hoc based on a mandate and manner of work that had already been forced upon it; as a result, concepts of truth, justice, and reconciliation were weak, hampering the progress of the commission's work. Gready posits that human rights need to be reimagined in three ways: truth commissions must use a broader understanding of human rights, emphasizing economic, social, and cultural rights, in addition to legal and political rights. Holistic approaches to transitional justice work that blend traditional and non-traditional practices should be adopted because they show great potential for community reconciliation. A balance must be struck between the demands of law and politics and those of interests and values, while making absolute claims and moral judgments. Truth commissions also require a deeper understanding of how the past and present interact, encouraging continuity and change. By allowing for public discussion and constituency-building, the influence and significance of truth commissions on national consciousness could be strong. But in order to do so, truth commissions must also address economic and social inequality—something the South African TRC failed to do.

At the behest of the South African parliament, the TRC presented reconciliation as a foregone conclusion to be embodied in the conclusions of its report. Claire Moon argues that reconciliation in South Africa was presented as the closure of the story of apartheid, narrated by the TRC report and constructed to frame the ways in which the violence of the past was related in the testimony of victims. Further, reconciliation as an institution of transitional discourse is necessarily constructed to fit a prescribed narrative form.[19] She identifies the TRC in South Africa as a definitive case of "the construction of reconciliation as a widespread and hegemonic discourse of political transition," one that addresses the shortcomings of previous commissions and sets a precedent for those that would follow them.[20] She asserts that reconciliation is constructed and in no way inherent; rather it is a political practice that is controlled by societal elites. The TRC narrated South Africa's past as defined by political violence undertaken and perpetuated by the state and its agents, in addition to those who opposed the state. It also narrated a present that constituted a confessional story told in the testimonies of victims and perpetrators alike. The confessional story was constructed as a stage for a future story about reconciliation and reunification on a national and community level.

Most significantly, scholars have argued that the use of the hegemonic Western ideal of truth commissions marginalized victims who preferred to present their testimony in the contexts of traditional, local, or alternative reconciliation practices. Philipa Rothfield examines reconciliation as a normalization process and the forms of resistance to reconciliation found in South Africa, including why people sought to resist it.[21] Reconciliation requires looking into the past to address losses and damages, but also to mend divisive conflicts to ensure that past atrocities are not repeated. It is in some ways apart from justice, allowing parties in conflict to unite to vent their differences and claims against each other, concluding with an agreement to move forward together. Rothfield argues that national reconciliation processes are necessarily ambivalent towards victims of violence due to the tension between the needs of society and the needs of individuals. Resistance to reconciliation is not necessarily pathological, but can "enact a critical stance towards the sociality of reconciliation on behalf of the singularity of corporeal life."[22] In the South African TRC, the state attempted to create a single narrative of South African history during the apartheid years; in order to achieve this, victims and perpetrators had to be clearly identified and allowed to speak their piece. Unreconciled victims, by contrast, were described as morally deranged obstacles to a stable national future. Yet resistance for many survivors was actually an act of defiance and an assertion of agency after experiencing dehumanizing events.

Some scholars have analyzed specific examples of the alternative approaches to truth and reconciliation processes enacted in South Africa since the end of the TRC's mandate.[23] For example, Kay Schaffer argues that the South African TRC initiated a process of reconciliation and nation building by allowing victims of apartheid to engage in truth-telling and forgiveness, though in a lopsided manner. Acts of remembrance staged in South Africa since the closing of the TRC simultaneously celebrate the country's strong sense of diversity and reveal the social divisions that continue to plague it. Some stagings adopt top-down approaches to national reconstruction while others emphasize interpersonal exercises; both can lead to redemption, but the former marginalizes dissonant voices and the latter emphasizes the singularity of each victim's experiences. Further, the contradictions and tensions within the TRC highlight the challenges of reconciliation and nation building and a need to recognize that victims may be drawn to different methods of reconciliation. She points to the alternate testimony of a witness whose son had been murdered during apartheid: her testimony had deviated from the expected narrative of victimization and resilience and seemed to lack chronological or logical sequence; she was subsequently ignored and marginalized in order to further that overarching narrative. TRC testimony continues to be contested and alternative reconciliation methods allow unconventional victims to speak their piece.

In the same vein, Richard Wilson notes that the TRC, as well as the Human Rights Commission and the Commission for Gender Equality in South Africa, created new moral and cultural leadership in the country, constituting a new hegemony to represent the transition undertaken by South African society.[24] Human rights replaced apartheid as the guiding narrative for the new South Africa. This new hegemony was first presented as part of the effort to ensure accountability for past state crimes and to decide whether human rights violators should be pardoned or punished. The TRC set out to perform two main functions, truth-telling about apartheid and reconciling various groups within the nation with each other. The TRC's account of apartheid was constrained by an excessive legalism and positivist methodology that prevented the successful creation of a coherent and inclusive socio-political history. Responses to the TRC's language of reconciliation combined local values and human rights. Survivors used human rights procedures to pursue their own agendas without necessarily taking on human rights values and many local actors were resistant to restorative human rights, preferring a retributive model instead. Wilson argues that human rights institutions exist within a concurrent web of centralizing and pluralizing strategies. The TRC adopted a purely religious-redemptive definition of reconciliation and so it was unable to engage with or even transform emotions of vengeance. Despite the existence of the TRC, South Africans continue to resort to alternative local channels for justice, reconciliation, and social order.

Conclusion

Though scholars have worked out a general framework for the goals, procedures, and expected outcomes of truth and reconciliation commissions, there has yet to be a practical example that meets these criteria and allows all victims to speak their piece and reconcile themselves with their perpetrators. Indeed, there is a risk that efforts to develop "best practices" can themselves end in the imposition of a single template on local communities. In the case of South Africa, a significant majority of scholars have identified various factors contributing to the shortcomings of the truth and reconciliation process. Political parties obstructed the work of the TRC through public attacks on its work and credibility. Religious institutions sought to dominate the language and hearings of the TRC and, as a result, were incapable of participating meaningfully in its proceedings. The mandate of the TRC included an unclear and contradictory understanding of the truth and reconciliation it sought, because its mandate was the result of negotiations between rival political parties, and so its work suffered. Finally, the perceived need for a unified procedure and narrative marginalized many victims who continue to seek alternative routes to reveal the truth and achieve reconciliation.

These problems are encountered by all truth commissions as they set out to accomplish a task that seems insurmountable. All of the authors discussed above acknowledge the value of the truth commission process, but the various obstructions and issues that plague the commissions must be addressed to improve the process and outcomes. With mixed success, this is what truth commissions, from Timor-Leste to Canada, have attempted to do.

Notes

1. Erin Daly and Jeremy Sarkin, *Reconciliation in Divided Societies: Finding Common Ground* (Philadelphia: University of Pennsylvania Press, 2007).
2. Johann Galtung, "After Violence, Reconstruction, Reconciliation, and Resolution: Coping with Visible and Invisible Effects of War and Violence," in *Reconciliation, Justice, and Coexistence: Theory and Practice*, ed. Mohammed Abu-Nimer (Lanham, MD: Lexington, 2001), 3–24.
3. Mark R. Amstutz, *The Healing of Nations: The Promise and Limits of Political Forgiveness* (Lanham, MD: Rowman & Littlefield, 2005).
4. Priscilla B. Hayner, *Unspeakable Truths: Facing the Challenge of Truth Commissions* (New York: Routledge, 2001).
5. Vasuki Nesiah, "Truth vs. Justice? Commissions and Courts," in *Human Rights & Conflicts: Exploring the Links between Rights, Law, and Peacebuilding*, ed. Julie A. Mertus and Jeffrey W. Helsing (Washington, DC: United States Institute of Peace Press, 2006).
6. Robert I. Rotberg, "Apology, Truth Commissions, and Intrastate Conflict," in *Taking Wrongs Seriously: Apologies and Reconciliation*, ed. Elazar Barkan and Alexander Karn (Stanford, CA: Stanford University Press, 2006), 33–49.
7. Onur Bakiner, *Truth Commissions: Memory, Power, and Legitimacy* (Philadelphia: University of Pennsylvania Press, 2016).
8. Ibid., 3.
9. Hayner, *Unspeakable Truths*.
10. Gillian Slovo, "Truth and Reconcilation in South Africa," *Maisonneuve*, 1 June 2003, http://maisonneuve.org/article/2003/06/1/crime-and-no-punishment/(accessed 10 February 2017).
11. Alex Boraine, "South Africa's Truth and Reconciliation Commission from a Global Perspective," in *Peace versus Justice? The Dilemma of Transitional Justice in Africa*, ed. Chandra Lekha Sriram and Suren Pillay (Scottsville, SA: University of KwaZulu-Natal Press, 2009), 138.
12. Boraine, "South Africa's Truth and Reconciliation Commission from a Global Perspective," 139.
13. Graeme Simpson, "'Tell No Lies, Claim No Easy Victories': A Brief Evaluation of South Africa's Truth and Reconciliation Commission," in *Commissioning the Past: Understanding South Africa's Truth and Reconciliation Commission*, ed. Deborah Posel and Graeme Simpson (Johannesburg, SA: Witwatersand University Press, 2002), 220–51.
14. Russell H. Botman, "Truth and Reconciliation: The South Africa Case," in *Religion and Peacebuilding*, ed. Harold Coward and Gordon S. Smith (Albany: State University of New York Press, 2004), 243–60.
15. Hugo van der Merwe, "The Role of the Church in Promoting Reconciliation in Post-TRC South Africa," in *Religion & Reconciliation in South Africa: Voices of Religious*

Leaders, ed. Audrey R. Chapman and Bernard Spong (Philadelphia, PA: Templeton Foundation Press, 2003), 269–81.

16   Hugo van der Merwe, "Reconciliation and Justice in South Africa: Lessons from the TRC's Community Interventions," in *Reconciliation, Justice, and Coexistence: Theory and Practice*, ed. Mohammed Abu-Nimer (Lanham, MD: Lexington, 2001), 187–208.

17   Hugo van der Merwe and Audrey R. Chapman, "Did the TRC Deliver?" in *Truth and Reconciliation in South Africa: Did the TRC Deliver?*, ed. Audrey R. Chapman and Hugo van der Merwe (Philadelphia: University of Pennsylvania Press, 2008), 241–79.

18   Paul Gready, *The Era of Transitional Justice: The Aftermath of the Truth and Reconciliation Commissions in South Africa and Beyond* (New York: Routledge, 2001).

19   Claire Moon, *Narrating Political Reconciliation: South Africa's Truth and Reconciliation Commission* (Plymouth, UK: Lexington, 2008).

20   Ibid., 1.

21   Philipa Rothfield, "Resistance and Reconciliation: Antimonies of Post-Traumatic Justice," in *Trauma, History, Philosophy*, ed. Matthew Sharpe, Murray Noonan, and Jason Freddi, 164-185 (Newcastle, UK: Cambridge Scholars Publishing, 2007), 164–85.

22   Ibid., 169.

23   Kay Schaffer, "Testimony, Nation Building and the Ethics of Witnessing: After the Truth and Reconciliation Commission in South Africa," in *Pathways to Reconciliation: Between Theory and Practice*, ed. Philipa Rothfield, Cleo Fleming, and Paul A. Komesaroff (Burlington, VT: Ashgate Publishing Company, 2008), 89–102.

24   Richard Wilson, *The Politics of Truth and Reconciliation in South Africa: Legitimizing the Post-Apartheid State* (New York: Cambridge University Press, 2001).

SECTION I

Memory, Truth, and Reconciliation in Timor-Leste

Memory, Truth, and Reconciliation in Timor-Leste

Mixed success, the note on which chapter 2 ends, characterizes most truth commissions. Our first case study, Timor-Leste (East Timor, in its English-language translation) held one of the world's more impressive commissions, but it has not lain to rest the legacies of mass atrocities under Indonesian rule.

The Democratic Republic of Timor-Leste was declared in November 1975, and regained its independence in May 2002. Between those years lay a bloody military invasion by the armed forces of neighbouring Indonesia; twenty-four years of Indonesian rule that never quite succeeded in overcoming local aspirations; a referendum on continued Indonesian rule or independence in 1999, resulting in a strong pro-independence vote and a wave of violence against independence supporters; and finally, after much international pressure, Indonesian withdrawal followed by an interim United Nations administration. 20 May 2002 is marked as "restoration of independence day," tying the emergence of the first independent country of the twenty-first century back to its original independence declaration. Here is an assertion that the Timorese nation is not a new state, not a creation of the UN, but a nation founded much earlier, and forged in resistance to foreign rule.

So issues of post-conflict reconstruction and transitional justice could never be plotted on a clean sheet of paper. Models from overseas could not simply be imported into newly free Timor-Leste. This is true of all post-conflict situations, of course: history's ghosts live on, and they haunt all efforts to reconcile post-conflict societies.

The sections of this book will move from historical background, to analysis of truth commission experiences, to personal accounts that draw out other lessons and other legacies. We begin with Timor-Leste because it offers the strongest truth and reconciliation model in the region, and because it grapples with key issues more visibly than many other places.

This section opens with a historical overview of Timor-Leste, noting the legacies of violence under Indonesian rule, the efforts to create a mechanism to hold the perpetrators accountable, and the compromises made by Timorese and international political leaders. Chapter 3 highlights the "legacies of violence" in the complex histories of Timor-Leste and the extent to which those legacies contributed to the Timorese experience of transitional justice. As Indonesian soldiers left and an international peacekeeping force entered, and as Indonesian authorities gave way to United Nations administrators, calls abounded from inside Timor-Leste and beyond for an end to impunity. There was real consideration of creating a formal tribunal that would hold accountable the perpetrators of mass atrocities.

Instead of a tribunal or other form of "retributive justice," however, Timor-Leste held a truth commission designed to reconcile Timorese with one another and to establish the facts about human rights violations committed on all sides, notably by Indonesia, its former colonial ruler. Global compassion and global will to enforce human rights norms was selective: there would in the end be no international tribunal for Timor-Leste, and indeed none anywhere after the pioneering international criminal tribunals for Rwanda and the former Yugoslavia. The Commission on Reception, Truth and Reconciliation (Comissão de Acolhimento, Verdade e Reconciliação, or CAVR), with a four-fold mandate to establish the truth about human rights violations; to help reconcile a divided society by receiving back Timorese who had perpetrated less serious crimes in 1999; to restore the dignity of victims; and to write a report that included findings on responsibility and recommendations to prevent any recurrence of this historical violence.

In this there were echoes of the pioneering South African truth and reconciliation model and clear links to the global truth and reconciliation industry, recounted in chapter 2. Yet the process was also driven very much by Timorese needs and Timorese politics. Chapter 4 offers a close examination of the CAVR experience—what the commission did, what was unique about it, and how its work has been carried forward in the years since it issued its five-volume report in 2005. The CAVR's report had choice words for the many governments that for twenty-four years quietly or full-throatedly supported Indonesian rule over Timor-Leste, with all its attendant deaths and human rights violations. Chapter 4 amplifies this international note, drawing connections across borders that echo the border-crossing aspects of chapter 3.

A truth commission report cannot answer all questions or resolve all conflicts. It is words on paper, and can only live when people act on it. What is done, or not done, with a commission's final report has repercussions all throughout post-conflict societies. Chapter 3 highlights a "failure of leadership" by the new elected governments of independent Timor-Leste.

Chapter 5 seeks the origins of this failure in the political methods of the independence struggle. Fighting a much stronger enemy requires secrecy, a clandestine approach, the use of *noms de guerre* and other underground strategies. But what happens when those methods continue after the triumph of the resistance struggle? How well does clandestinity serve independent Timor-Leste—and does it hamper prospects for truth, and for true reconciliation?

The same questions can be asked about economic development. Indonesian rule did not lead to a prosperous Timor-Leste, even though Indonesian governments often justified their rule by claiming it delivered development (*pembangunan*). The brief UN administration (1999–2002) also fell short in this department. Though it could point to some successes, there were also failures. Famously, the amount of money spent on bottled water for international consultants was more than the estimated cost of delivering safe drinking water to the entire country. Chapter 6 examines economic development strategies since 2002. It positions Timor-Leste in an interesting place between traditional development aid provided by Western governments and the increasingly important aid policies of China, the giant of eastern Asia. It asks whether development hopes are hampered by the legacies of conflict and the unhealed traumas of occupation.

Development also raises questions of the relations between government and the non-governmental organizations, many of them with international links and international funding, who must deliver many of the projects. During the occupation years, there was only one legal national Timorese institution outside the control of Indonesian authorities: the Catholic Church. During the occupation, Timorese accordingly embraced the church. From an elite institution linked to Portuguese colonial rule, the church became a Timorese institution embodying the hopes of the people. From a minority in 1975, church membership came to embrace the vast majority of the Timorese population. Chapter 7 describes the three-cornered relationship between church, state, and civil society, and examines how the church has navigated the transition to independence.

Church leaders were, unsurprisingly, central to reconciliation processes. Catholic doctrine treats reconciliation as a sacrament, absolving believers of sin through their sincere acts of repentance. Protestant teachings also place a high value on reconciliation. Members of both the Catholic Church and the much smaller Timorese Protestant Church informed

Timorese truth and reconciliation processes and served on the CAVR. In each case, they also drew on cross-border religious networks.

The church proved to be one institution pushing the government against any impulse to forget the occupation's human rights legacy as Timorese leaders forgave their Indonesian counterparts. There have also been voices in both parliament and civil society. Chapter 8 provides evidence of this in the form of a speech by one opposition politician that is one of the strongest statements of Timorese commitment to human rights. Respect for international human rights became central to Timorese resistance strategies during the occupation years, and independent Timor-Leste proudly ratified a huge basket of UN human rights covenants and treaties. Since regaining independence in 2002, it has held multi-round election campaigns (presidential first-round and run-off elections plus elections for the National Parliament) every five years. There have been two peaceful changes of government. Democratic forms are firmly in place. But sometimes government commitment to taking tough decisions informed by a commitment to human rights flags. When it does, Timorese advocates have hastened to call for a recommitment to the country's rights-respecting political culture.

While a human rights critique has come from political leaders, it has been most strongly grounded in civil society. One major reason that the truth commission report continues to be the subject of discussion and the charge of follow-up institutions is pressure from civil society. The commission's report is not the property of the government, rights advocates have insisted: it belongs to all the people of Timor-Leste. Both government and civil society have a role in "socializing" the report—disseminating its findings and advocating for its recommendations. The message has been carried most strongly by the NGO ACbit, an affiliate of the International Centre for Transitional Justice. Chapter 9 lets that group speak in its own voice, making the case that a truth commission is a "living document" that belongs to the nation, not a simple report to government to be filed and forgotten. It explains the concept of "socialization" in ongoing civil-society work for truth and reconciliation. And it speaks against impunity, against allowing perpetrators of mass atrocities to carry on as if they had no guilt.

It is with the problem of impunity that the next chapter opens: specifically with impunity for the Suai massacre, remembered in the circle of stones with which this book began.

3

East Timor: Legacies of Violence[1]

GEOFFREY ROBINSON

On 30 August 2009, East Timor's prime minister, the former resistance leader Xanana Gusmão, quietly authorized the release of a man directly implicated in one of the country's most notorious massacres. Maternus Bere, a commander of the pro-Indonesian Laksaur militia group, had been indicted for his role in the September 1999 killing of as many as two hundred unarmed supporters of independence who had taken refuge in the Catholic church in Suai. Of the forty victims whose identities could be determined, three were priests, ten were under the age of eighteen, and more than a dozen were women. The Suai church massacre was part of a shocking campaign of violence that followed a United Nations–organized referendum in which Timorese had voted overwhelmingly for independence from Indonesia.

Like many others responsible for serious crimes committed in 1999, Bere had escaped unscathed to Indonesia in the orchestrated chaos that followed the referendum. Then, in August 2009, he had made his way back to East Timor, where he was captured and handed over to police. Gusmão's decision to release Bere to Indonesian authorities—a move that circumvented the judicial process and effectively guaranteed that he would not be prosecuted—passed without comment from the foreign dignitaries who had gathered in Dili for ceremonies marking the tenth anniversary of the 1999 referendum, but it provoked deep anger among East Timorese.[2] Coming ten years to the day after they had risked their lives to vote for independence, it also sullied what many had hoped would be a joyful celebration of a defining moment in the country's history.

Viewed more widely, Gusmão's decision offers a glimpse of some of the problems that continue to plague East Timor. Chief among these are the deep and lasting legacies of decades of violence and misrule; serious failings on the part of East Timor's own leaders, especially in the areas of justice and the rule of law; and a marked lack of commitment by key players in the international community and the UN to the cause of accountability for past serious crimes.

Some History

Indonesian forces invaded East Timor in early December 1975, just one week after a nationalist party, Fretilin, declared the territory's independence from Portugal. The Indonesian invasion and subsequent occupation resulted in the death of at least 100,000, and possibly as many as 200,000, of a pre-invasion population of about 650,000. The scale of the killing in the first four years of the occupation was such that many scholars have described it as genocide.[3]

Those best placed to prevent this tragedy—notably the United States, the United Kingdom, and Australia—instead actively lent their support to Indonesia. In a meeting one day before the December 1975 invasion, US president Gerald Ford and secretary of state Henry Kissinger gave President Suharto repeated assurances that the United States would "understand" if Indonesia deemed it "necessary to take drastic action" in East Timor. Kissinger also offered Suharto some advice: "It is important that whatever you do succeeds quickly. ... We would be able to influence the reaction in America if whatever happens, happens after we return. This way there would be less chance of people talking in an unauthorized way."[4]

Over the next twenty-four years, powerful states largely turned a blind eye to Indonesian atrocities, and lavished its staunchly anti-communist leadership with economic and military assistance. Despite a growing chorus of criticism from human rights and church groups at home and abroad, Indonesia steadfastly rejected any suggestion that it should withdraw from East Timor—and largely got away with it. All of this started to change in May 1998, when President Suharto was forced to resign in the face of a deepening financial crisis and widespread street protests. His resignation opened the door for renewed negotiations between Portugal and Indonesia, and to a political solution in the form of a UN-supervised referendum on independence.

The referendum took place on 30 August 1999, amidst mounting intimidation and violence by supporters of continued Indonesian rule. Despite the threats, almost 80 per cent of East Timorese voted in favour of independence. Sadly, within hours of the vote, Indonesian forces and the local militias they had created launched a coordinated campaign of violence against real and presumed supporters of independence, including Catholic clergy and local UN staff. Over the next few weeks, some 70 per cent of all buildings in the country were destroyed, 400,000 people were forcibly displaced from their homes, and at least 1,500 were killed.

Responding to widespread revulsion and protests at this one-sided violence, key powers including the United States and Australia pressured Indonesia to accept help in restoring order, and the UN Security Council authorized the swift deployment of a multinational force. That force landed in late September and by the end of October the violence had ended. After a period of transitional UN administration, East Timor formally became independent in May 2002.

Some years after independence, there are legitimate grounds for celebration. The country has so far defied predictions that it would sink quickly into civil or "tribal" war following Indonesia's withdrawal, or that it would prove to be economically unviable. In fact, East Timor has now conducted four rounds of parliamentary and presidential elections in a manner largely free of violence or fraud. No single party has monopolized political power, the idea of civilian rule appears to be widely accepted, and there is a reasonably free press. Thanks to its success in securing rights to large offshore oil reserves, moreover, it now has a substantial source of government revenue, as well as opportunities for future economic growth.

East Timor is not, then, the "failed state" or economic basket case that many feared it would be. In fact, considering that the entire country was laid to waste and half the population forcibly displaced from their homes in 1999, East Timor's current strength and stability ought to be seen as something of a success story. Nevertheless, there are problems. These include, most obviously, high unemployment, especially among youth, allegations of corruption fueled by large oil revenues and cronyism, a lack of professionalism in the security forces, and weaknesses in the rule of law.

Together, these problems have had the effect of generating impatience with the country's political leaders, and a general frustration that independence has not brought the benefits many had hoped it would. Less obviously, East Timor's future is threatened by the deep and lasting legacies of past violence and misrule.

Legacies of Violence

In the years since independence, political conflicts and rivalries that date to the occupation period and earlier have re-emerged, sometimes in new and surprising forms. Likewise, models or repertoires of violence inherited from earlier periods have reappeared, leaving an unmistakable mark on East Timor's political and social life. These legacies have been at the heart of some troubling incidents of violence, most notably between 2006 and 2008 when, according to some observers, the country came close to civil war, and they may well resurface in the years ahead.

One of the most resilient of these legacies has been the tradition of mobilizing irregular armed groups for political ends. Such groups, referred to at the time as militias, were the main perpetrators of the violence in 1999 when they operated with the support of the Indonesian army, and especially Kopassus (Special Forces Command), an elite army command specializing in covert operations and with a reputation for brutality. Since 1999, a wide variety of new groups, including martial arts clubs, criminal gangs, veterans' organizations, and quasi-religious sects, have emerged across the country. Like the militias of 1999, many of these new groups have been involved in small-scale criminal activities, but also in political violence.

The similarities with the militias of 1999 have led to speculation that the new groups have been bankrolled by Indonesia as part of a strategy of destabilization. While some do trace their roots back to the Indonesian occupation, most are led not by former advocates of Indonesian rule, but by past supporters of independence who have become dissatisfied with the fruits of freedom. It is also clear that many of these new groups are funded, mobilized, and sometimes supplied with weapons not by Indonesia, but by competing political and military factions within East Timor.

None of this should come as much of a surprise. Armed civilian groups have a very long history in East Timor, having been mobilized and trained by a succession of colonial powers, including Portugal, Japan, and

3.1: Burned-out building, Dili, Timor-Leste, 1999. Photo: Jess Agustin.

Indonesia. That long history has helped to make them an integral part of the country's social and political fabric. It also means that the distinctive repertoires of violence used by these groups—house burning, beatings, terror, rape—are likely to survive long after the departure of their original patrons. That is all the more likely if East Timor's leaders continue to mimic their Indonesian, Japanese, and Portuguese predecessors by mobilizing such civilian groups for political ends.

Another of the enduring legacies of East Timor's history of violence has been the friction it created between those who supported or acquiesced in Indonesian rule and those who actively opposed it. Since 1999, that tension has appeared within and between the two national armed services, the army (Falintil-Forças de Defesa de Timor-Leste) and the police (Policía Nacional de Timor-Leste). Many members of the police previously served with the Indonesian police in East Timor, while many in the army are former Falintil guerrillas who fought for more than two decades against Indonesia's security forces. That historical tension has been compounded by the fact that since independence the respective roles of the police and the army have not been clearly delineated. Against that background, the Fretilin government's decision in 2003 to establish three new paramilitary police units and to supply them with large quantities of modern weapons fueled anti-government anger on the part of elements of the army and some veterans' groups.

Within the army itself, there has also been tension between soldiers from the eastern and western parts of the country. These tensions are a reflection of a wider conflict that dates to the period of the Indonesian occupation, when the western districts gained a reputation as pro-Indonesian strongholds, while those in the east were considered to be more steadfast in their resistance. The fact that most of the former Falintil guerrilla fighters in the new army come from the east while most of the new recruits come from the west has helped to fuel claims on the part of the westerners that they have been unfairly treated—among other things in the matter of rank and promotion—by those from the east who have occupied most command positions.

The frictions between and within the different services have been exacerbated—though in some instances also complicated or crosscut—by close bonds of personal and family loyalty, again dating back to the Indonesian occupation and earlier. Such bonds have served to link individuals and groups to powerful civilian and military figures, creating networks of patronage outside the formal chain of command. Those tendencies have been further compounded, and have been tipped in the direction of violence, by the willingness of some civilian and military leaders to unlawfully distribute weapons to their followers.

Finally, there have been conflicts among former resistance leaders based, at least in part, on strategic and political differences that date back to the 1980s. One of the more serious lines of tension has been between a group of senior Fretilin figures, like Mari Alkatiri, who spent the years of Indonesian occupation in exile, mainly in Mozambique, and those, like Xanana Gusmão, who remained in East Timor and/or Indonesia. These tensions resurfaced after 1999 as leaders from both camps returned to Dili and began to compete for political office. The expatriate group, sometimes dubbed the Maputo mafia, quickly asserted control of Fretilin and won a majority in the first parliamentary elections in 2001, with Alkatiri as prime minister. On the other side, Gusmão pinned his political hopes on the new CNRT,[5] and was elected to the less powerful position of president in 2002. Since that time, the rivalry between these two groups has been at the heart of much of the political competition and conflict in East Timor.

This cluster of lingering tensions and conflicts came to a dramatic head in 2006, in a cascading cycle of violence that left up to 38 people dead, destroyed some 6,000 houses and forced more than 150,000 people to flee their homes.[6] While the number of casualties was small compared to 1999, by some accounts the violence came close to escalating into a full-blown civil war, and it led to the forced resignation of the prime minister, Mari Alkatiri, the interior minister, Rogerio Lobato, and the defence minister, Roque Rodrigues. The crisis also triggered a decline in support for Fretilin in the following year's elections, opening the door for Xanana Gusmão to become prime minister as the leader of a new multi-party coalition known as the AMP (Alliance of the Parliamentary Majority).

The crisis began in January 2006, when a group of soldiers, angered by what they saw as unfair treatment by the army leadership, presented a petition to President Gusmão. Members of the group, who became known as "the petitioners," went on strike in February to press their demands but were ordered back to their barracks. When they refused to do so, they were summarily dismissed from the army. In April the petitioners organized a large demonstration in Dili, which was joined by a fringe group named "Colimau 2000" and a large number of unemployed youth who had their own grievances against the government. When the demonstration turned violent, Prime Minister Alkatiri called in the army to restore order. The army's intervention that day resulted in the death of five protesters and allegations of the deaths of many more.

These events became a lightning rod for simmering tensions within the army, and between the army and the police, leading to a breakdown in the normal chain of command and the formation of makeshift alliances based on political, personal, and regional loyalties. Soldiers sympathetic to the petitioners and demonstrators left their posts to join police units that had likewise taken the side of the petitioners. Among the most important of these "rebel" soldiers was Major Alfredo Reinado, the commander of the military police, who deserted his post on 3 May with seventeen men and a large amount of ammunition, and joined up with some of the recently formed paramilitary police. By the end of May 2006, these tensions had degenerated into open conflict, with different elements of the security forces and their allies engaging in firefights in Dili and elsewhere.

The violence was exacerbated by the decision of leaders on both sides to distribute firearms to those, including members of veterans' and civilian groups, whom they considered sympathetic to their cause. Particularly egregious were the actions of Interior Minister Rogerio Lobato, who illegally distributed arms to gang members and to police units sympathetic to him, while disarming some "eastern" police units. On the other side, the commander of the army is said to have distributed weapons to sympathetic veterans' groups and others, encouraging them to join the fight against the rebels and the police. The violence was further fueled by a popular perception, encouraged by some political leaders, that the conflict was between "easterners" and "westerners"—with the army representing the east and the petitioners and police representing the west.

The immediate crisis was defused through the direct intervention of international forces between May and June of 2006. But the underlying tensions that fueled the violence had not been resolved. For one thing, the crisis had raised serious questions about the capacity and professionalism of East Timor's security forces, leading the country's government to agree to give UN police operational command, with the national police in a secondary role.[7] Meanwhile, rebel soldiers and police under the command of Major Reinado remained in the hills with some armed civilian groups and sympathetic police units. Charismatic and armed, Reinado and his followers came to be seen as heroes by many East Timorese frustrated by the lagging economy and high unemployment. Various efforts to arrest or negotiate with Reinado proved fruitless, and he remained in the bush with a substantial armed force through 2006 and 2007. This period, which coincided with campaigning for the 2007 elections, was also marked by continued insecurity and violence as local communities, mistrustful of the army and the police, turned increasingly to martial arts groups, gangs, and veterans' groups to provide security.

The dramatic final act in this crisis came on 11 February 2008 when, in disputed circumstances, rebel troops (led by Lieutenant Gastão Salsinha and Major Reinado, respectively) attacked Xanana Gusmão, who was now prime minister, and President José Ramos-Horta. While Gusmão somehow escaped unscathed, Ramos-Horta was critically wounded and had to be rushed to Australia for medical care. Reinado himself and one of his men were killed in the attack, and several rebel figures were later arrested.

Since then, the security situation has been outwardly calm, and some measures have been taken to address it. In 2008, for example, the AMP government briefly integrated the police and army into a joint command, and in early 2010 a court sentenced about two dozen of the rebels to between nine and sixteen years in prison. But the underlying problems that gave rise to the crisis have changed very little. Armed civilian groups continue to operate, tensions between and within the armed services persist, and old differences between former resistance leaders have not abated.

Meanwhile, there are signs of a growing impatience with the current leadership, especially over allegations of corruption and cronyism. There is a real possibility that these problems will resurface, and that renewed violence will be the result.

A Failure of Leadership

One way to disrupt such patterns of violence, human rights experts argue, is to ensure that those most responsible for serious crimes, including crimes against humanity and genocide, are brought to justice. The failure to do so can lead to a cycle of impunity, a lack of respect for the rule of law, and continued violence. Regrettably, not a single Indonesian military officer or government official has been successfully tried for the crimes committed in 1999. A similar pattern is evident for the crimes, including murder, committed between 2006 and 2008. Despite abundant evidence linking certain individuals to those crimes, those recognized as most responsible remain free. Meanwhile, the handful of suspects who were convicted in 2010 have since been released after serving only a small fraction of their sentences.

Surprisingly, perhaps, among the main obstacles to the search for justice have been East Timor's own leaders—notably José Ramos-Horta, Xanana Gusmão, and Mari Alkatiri, who since 2002 have all served either as prime minister or president, or both. For several years now, they have argued strenuously against what they call "punitive justice," against an international criminal tribunal, and in favour of "restorative justice" and "reconciliation." Gusmão and Ramos-Horta have also been strong proponents of amnesty for those accused or convicted of serious crimes, and have issued pardons and commutations to some of the country's most notorious criminals. Their argument, in essence, is that reconciliation with Indonesia, and among East Timorese, is essential to the country's stability and security, and that justice must therefore take second place.

That position undoubtedly reflects the country's profound political and economic vulnerability, compounded by continued pressure from Indonesia, whose leaders will not countenance any attempt to prosecute members of its armed forces. It may also reflect genuinely held beliefs. The ideal of national unity was, after all, central to Gusmão's political vision long before independence, and lay at the heart of the impressive nationalist coalition, the CNRT, he and Ramos-Horta formed to achieve that goal.

And yet, coming from these men, the argument that justice must take second place to national stability and security is an extraordinary one—particularly when one considers that in their long struggle for independence, they relied so heavily on claims about the universality of human rights, and routinely castigated Indonesia for seeking to justify systematic human rights violations in East Timor with almost identical arguments about stability and security. Those similarities may also explain why their appeals to reconciliation and unity over and above justice sound a decidedly discordant tone among many East Timorese.

Whatever the reasons for it, their position has been reflected in a series of troubling official decisions and statements in recent years. In March 2005, for example, then President Gusmão agreed to establish a joint Commission on Truth and Friendship (CTF) with Indonesia, ostensibly to establish the "conclusive truth" about the events of 1999—but with the clear understanding that the commission's goal would be reconciliation and *not* justice. Indeed, the CTF was self-evidently an effort to deflect demands for justice and in particular an international criminal tribunal. As an expression of their contempt for the new body, which was also known by the acronym TFC (Truth and Friendship Commission), some East Timorese began to call it "Timor Fried Chicken." When the commission's final report was made public, it surprised critics by stating clearly that crimes against humanity had indeed been committed by Indonesian forces and their local allies. As feared, however, it was silent on the question of justice, and the government welcomed it warmly in the name of reconciliation.[8] Since then, it has come to be widely accepted that the report "was a tacit declaration that, as a result of private discussions between the two governments, there would be no further prosecutions."[9]

In that regard it was telling that in May 2008, shortly before the CTF report was made public, President Ramos-Horta pardoned dozens of prisoners, again in the name of reconciliation and unity. Among those released was Joni Marques, a former commander of Team Alfa, a pro-Indonesian militia group based in Lautem. Marques had been sentenced to thirty-three years and four months in prison in 2001 for his role in organizing the ambush and murder of nine people, including five Catholic clergy, in late September 1999.[10] According to testimony at trial, one of those killed in the ambush, Sister Erminia, had knelt down by the roadside to pray during the attack. As she prayed, a militiaman slashed her with a machete. Another testified that he had yelled "Don't kill a Sister!" but that Joni Marques had replied "Kill them all! They are all CNRT!" A militiaman then picked up Sister Erminia and threw her in the river, before shooting her twice.

Then, as described above, on 30 August 2009, the tenth anniversary of the referendum, Prime Minister Gusmão controversially approved the transfer to Indonesian custody of Maternus Bere, the notorious former militiaman who had been indicted—though never tried—by East Timor's Prosecutor General Office for crimes against humanity.[11] The mood of celebration was further dampened by President Ramos-Horta's public comments during the ceremony and over the next several weeks. With dozens of foreign dignitaries in attendance, including Bill Clinton, the president told East Timorese that they should forget about the past, and set aside idle demands for justice.[12] At about the same time, Ramos-Horta strongly advocated a policy of complete amnesty for all serious crimes committed between 1974 and 2008.[13]

The government assault on the idea of accountability gained further momentum in 2010. In an address to the UN's Human Rights Council in March of that year, Ramos-Horta ridiculed Amnesty International, whose support he had routinely courted—and which countless East Timorese had looked to for support—during Indonesian rule, as a "fringe group" because it had called for an international criminal tribunal for East Timor.[14] In an even more controversial move, in August 2010 the government granted a full amnesty to Gastão Salsinha and twenty-two others who had been sentenced for their involvement in the 2008 assassination attempts just a few months earlier. Though it was portrayed by Ramos-Horta as an act of generosity and reconciliation, the decision was met with incredulity by many East Timorese. Why, they asked, do those who have threatened the very integrity of the state go free, while petty criminals remain in jail?[15]

Throughout this period, government leaders also poured cold water on the findings of the country's own truth commission, the CAVR (Comissão de Acolhimento, Verdade e Reconciliação, or Commission on Reception, Truth and Reconciliation), whose comprehensive final report, *Chega!*, was presented to the president in late 2005.[16] Among other things, the report called for those responsible for crimes committed between 1975 and 1999 to be brought to justice, if necessary before an international criminal tribunal. To date, little action has been taken by the government or by parliament on the report's many detailed recommendations.

In addition to undermining efforts to see that justice is done, the actions of East Timor's leaders have alienated many ordinary citizens, particularly those who lost loved ones in the periods of violence. The problem was neatly summed up by a man from Viqueque: "I have doubts about reconciliation. My father was murdered. Do you think I can reconcile with the person who killed him? I suggest that the offender be punished."[17] More generally, the contempt shown by East Timor's leaders for the very idea of the rule of law—and their embrace of the idea that justice must be sacrificed for stability—threatens to weaken the country's already fragile judicial system at a critical juncture in its history.

International Responsibility

It would be a mistake, however, to lay the blame for these failings solely at the feet of the East Timor's own leaders. The truth is that, for better or worse, East Timor's fate has been, and continues to be, profoundly shaped by the actions, attitudes, and interests of powerful states and international bodies like the UN.

Despite the terrible bloodshed and destruction that preceded it, the multinational intervention of late September 1999 has generally been regarded as a model of what the UN might do when it has the support of major powers. After all, this was a rare instance in which timely intervention stopped what some observers thought might become a genocide. It certainly compared favourably to the record of the previous twenty-four years, during which the United States and its allies aided and abetted Indonesia as it conducted a destructive war of occupation in East Timor. Likewise, the international community has sometimes played a positive role since 1999 as well, most notably through its timely and effective action in the crisis of 2006–8.

Unfortunately, during this same period, a handful of influential states—notably the United States and Australia—have reverted to an earlier mode in which narrow ideas of national interest, and Indonesian preferences, have been routinely accommodated at East Timor's expense. Over the past few years the UN's failings in East Timor have also become increasingly obvious, leading to calls for a prompt end to its mission there (the UN finally withdrew at the end of 2012).[18] Much of that criticism is well deserved. Particularly in its later years, the UN Mission in East Timor (UNMIT) was a disappointment. Through a combination of incompetence and poor management it has arguably complicated the job of establishing a well-functioning state, while angering many East Timorese who once held the UN in high regard. Nowhere perhaps have the failings of the international community been more evident than in the area of accountability for past crimes. The need to punish the perpetrators of serious crimes in East Timor has been clearly articulated in no fewer than six expert reports and reviews issued since 1999.[19] At the same time, key powers and the UN Security Council have been unwilling to back the cause of justice in any meaningful way. As a consequence, the demand for accountability has effectively been derailed, and the idea of an international tribunal has been shelved.

This basic pattern emerged just a few months after the violence of 1999 ended. Eager to mend relations with Indonesia, and in particular with the Indonesian National Army (TNI), the Clinton and Bush administrations sought to restore military ties that had been cut in mid-September 1999, and began to soften demands for an international inquiry.[20] That position was rooted in a general reluctance to support international criminal tribunals, partly for reasons of cost, and partly out of a concern that United States citizens might easily be brought before them. The priority of restoring good relations with the TNI was given added impetus after 11 September 2001, and the declaration of Southeast Asia, including Indonesia, as a "second front" in the "war on terror."

Needless to say, the lack of support for an international tribunal among key states, and also within the UN, emboldened Indonesian resistance to the idea. Indonesian authorities set about, usually without resorting to evidence, to challenge the most basic conclusions reached by all previous investigations and to deflect demands for an international judicial process. In 2001 Indonesia established the Ad Hoc Human Rights Court to try cases arising from the events in East Timor. Of the eighteen people charged with crimes against humanity committed in 1999, twelve were acquitted in first instance trials, and six were later acquitted on appeal, including the notorious militia leader Eurico Guterres. No Indonesian officers or officials were ever jailed, and some were actually promoted and appointed to sensitive command positions.

While Indonesia was staging show trials that some expert observers believe were designed to fail,[21] East Timor's fledgling judiciary, with UN assistance, was starting to conduct something closer to a serious investigative and judicial process. In 2000, the UN Transitional Authority in East Timor (UNTAET) enacted a statute establishing the Special Panels for Serious Crimes to try serious crimes including crimes against humanity. UNTAET also established a Serious Crimes Unit with a mandate to investigate and prosecute serious crimes committed in 1999. By early 2005, indictments had been filed against a total of 391 individuals and of those more than 80 were eventually tried and sentenced. Given the fact that East Timor had no functioning judiciary in 2000, this was a remarkable achievement—an example of effective and meaningful international co-operation and assistance.

Yet the picture was not all rosy. For one thing, as the Serious Crimes Unit's UN mandate expired in May 2005, the vast majority of those indicted, including several senior military officers, remained at large in Indonesia, effectively beyond the court's jurisdiction. In the years since, the UN Security Council has shown a lack of commitment to pursuing further prosecutions. When the Security Council took up the issue again in 2006, for example, it created a unit[22] with a mandate to continue investigating serious crimes, but with no authority to ensure their prosecution. As a consequence, the only cases that have been tried in East Timor to date are those of local militiamen; and since 2006 only three serious crimes cases have been heard.[23]

This situation has led to growing frustration among East Timorese, who have noted with dismay that it is only East Timorese of lowly means who are being caught up in the judicial net, while the big fish go free. That view has been expressed on many occasions in East Timor after 1999, most memorably at a public hearing on massacres held by the CAVR in November 2003. "It is wrong," one speaker said, "for the courts to try only low-level East Timorese militiamen, when it is well understood that the crimes they committed were part of a plan conceived and coordinated by Indonesian authorities."[24]

Against this backdrop, in January 2005 the UN secretary-general appointed a commission of experts to assess the progress made by the judicial processes in Jakarta and Dili, and recommend measures to ensure that the perpetrators would be held accountable. In its May 2005 report, the commission concluded that the Jakarta process "has not achieved accountability for those who bear the greatest responsibility for serious violations."[25] On the basis of these findings, it recommended that, unless Indonesia took prompt measures to remedy these shortcomings, the Security Council should "adopt a resolution under Chapter VII of the Charter of the United Nations to create an ad hoc international criminal tribunal for Timor-Leste, to be located in a third State." Those conclusions and recommendations found further support in the final report of the CAVR, completed in late 2005, and a report commissioned by the UN Office of the High Commissioner for Human Rights, published in 2006.[26]

Despite this growing consensus on the urgent need for justice, no meaningful action has since been taken to bring those responsible to account. Indeed, governments that once advocated accountability and justice now speak instead of the need for reconciliation. The change in attitude was poignantly captured in the silence of foreign dignitaries and governments when East Timor's leaders agreed to transfer the indicted militiaman, Maternus Bere, to Indonesian authorities in August 2009.

The shift away from justice has been further reinforced in recent years by continued US efforts to restore cordial relations with the Indonesian military. A crucial move in that direction came in July 2010 with the announcement in Jakarta by US defence secretary Robert Gates that the United States would be resuming ties with Indonesia's notorious Kopassus after a twelve-year hiatus. Aware that the decision was controversial, Gates stressed that Kopassus training would not begin immediately, and that future co-operation would be contingent on "the continued implementation of reforms within Kopassus" and the military as a whole.[27]

The proponents of this move have sought to justify it on the grounds that Indonesia and its military have changed since 1999; that as a vital partner in regional security and the fight against Islamist extremism Indonesian forces must receive US backing; and that the best way to influence those forces is to train them. These are familiar arguments. In some form they were used by Indonesia's supporters at various stages during the regime of General Suharto—with the exception that the enemy to be fought then was global communism rather than global terror. But these arguments are no more convincing now than they were then. While it is certainly true that Indonesia has become more democratic since 1999, and there has been modest reform within the country's military and police, to date there has been no meaningful reform within Kopassus. Indeed, Kopassus stands out as the military institution in which reform is both most urgently needed and most deeply resisted. Senior Kopassus officers routinely dismiss concerns about the unit's human rights record as overblown and demands for justice as unwarranted. No Kopassus officer has been tried and convicted for any of the crimes against humanity committed in East Timor from 1975 to 1999, and many suspected of such crimes in East Timor and elsewhere have been promoted to senior positions inside and outside the military. There is little reason, moreover, to believe that United States ties with and training of Kopassus will lead to reform as the advocates of restoration claim. Indeed, the historical record shows that the only time the United States and other states have managed to influence the Indonesian military in a positive way has been by *cutting* ties, as they did briefly in 1999.

In making the decision to restore ties with Kopassus, then, the US government may have given too much room to considerations of regional security at the expense of concerns about justice and accountability for serious crimes. That decision could have profound consequences in East Timor and in Indonesia, where the institutions of justice and respect for the rule of law are still struggling to recover from decades of violence and authoritarian misrule.

Notes

1. This chapter was previously published as "East Timor Ten Years On: Leagacies of Violence," *The Journal of Asian Studies* 70, no. 4 (November 2011): pp. 1007-1021, copyright 2011 The Association for Asian Studies, Inc. Reprinted with the permission of Cambridge University Press.

2. For reactions to Bere's release, see *Tempo Semanal* (blog), 10, 25, and 28 September 2009, http://temposemanaltimor.blogspot.com (accessed 30 April 2011).

3. There is, of course, debate about whether the massive violence of this period constitutes genocide as defined in the UN Genocide Convention. Nevertheless, a growing number of scholars and human rights professionals maintain that at least in the colloquial sense of the word, and arguably even by its strict legal definition, this was genocide. See Geoffrey Robinson, *"If You Leave Us Here, We Will Die": How Genocide Was Stopped in East Timor* (Princeton, NJ: Princeton University Press, 2010), chapters 1 and 3.

4. Ibid., 59–60.

5. The new CNRT (Congresso Nacional da Reconstrução de Timor, or National Congress for the Reconstruction of Timor), established in 2007, is distinct from the original

CNRT (Conselho Nacional de Resistência Timorense, or National Council of Timorese Resistance), the broad nationalist alliance that led the final push for independence in the 1990s.

6 *Report of the United Nations Independent Special Commission of Inquiry for Timor-Leste* (Geneva: October 2006).

7 East Timor's police resumed overall responsibility on 27 March 2011. International Crisis Group, "Timor-Leste: Reconciliation and Return from Indonesia," *Asia Briefing* 122 (2011): 8.

8 Indonesia–Timor-Leste Commission on Truth and Friendship, *Per Memoriam Ad Spem: Final Report of the Commission on Truth and Friendship (CTF)* (Denpasar, ID: CTF, 2008). The report was made public on 15 July 2011.

9 International Crisis Group, "Timor-Leste," 6.

10 For an account of these murders, see Geoffrey Robinson, *East Timor 1999: Crimes against Humanity. A Report Commissioned by the UN Office of the High Commissioner for Human Rights* (Jakarta: Elsam and Hak, 2006), 201–2.

11 While acknowledging that the transfer circumvented the law, Gusmão vehemently defended the move in parliament, saying that it was in the "national interest" to place good relations with Indonesia ahead of due process. Likewise, in televised comments, Ramos-Horta said that "not all legal measures support the national interest." International Crisis Group, "Timor-Leste," 8.

12 See *Tempo Semanal* (Dili), 30 August, 3, 6, and 25 September, and 6 October 2009.

13 International Crisis Group, "Timor-Leste," 16.

14 See *Tempo Semanal* (Dili), 3 September 2009.

15 See *Tempo Semanal* (Dili), 29 August 2010.

16 The CAVR was established under UNTAET regulation 10/2001 (13 July 2001). Its final report, *Chega!*, is available at http://www.cavr-timorleste.org/en/chegaReport.htm.

17 Cited in Robinson, *"If You Leave Us Here, We Will Die,"* 224.

18 In a recent article, a former UN official cited eight studies that had made that case since 2008, and drew the same conclusions. Edward Rees, "Time for the UN to Withdraw From East Timor?" *Atlantic Monthly*, 21 December 2010.

19 These were: United Nations, *Situation of Human Rights in East Timor* (New York: December 1999); United Nations, *Report of the International Commission of Inquiry on East Timor to the Secretary-General* (New York: January 2000); KPP-HAM, *Laporan Penyelidikan Pelanggaran Hak Asasi Manusia di Timor Timur* (Jakarta: January 2000); United Nations Security Council, "Summary of the Report to the Secretary-General of the Commission of Experts to Review the Prosecution of Serious Violations of Human Rights in Timor-Leste (then East Timor) in 1999" (New York: May 2006); CAVR, *Chega!*; and Robinson, *East Timor 1999*.

20 Kofi Annan also argued at this time that before an international mechanism was set up, Indonesia should first be given an opportunity to hold perpetrators to account through its own judicial system. See "UN Secretary-General Briefing to the Security Council on Visit to Southeast Asia," speech, New York, 29 February 2000.

21 David Cohen, *Intended to Fail: The Trials before the Ad Hoc Human Rights Court in Jakarta* (New York: International Center for Transitional Justice, 2003).

22 These came before the Serious Crimes Investigation Unit or SCIT.

23 International Crisis Group, "Timor-Leste," 5.

24 Cited in Robinson, *"If You Leave Us Here, We Will Die,"* 224.

25 United Nations Security Council, *Summary of the Report to the Secretary-General of the Commission of Experts* (New York: May 2006), 6.

26 See the *Chega!* report and Robinson, *East Timor 1999*.

27 Quoted in *Jakarta Globe*, 23 July 2010.

4

Shining *Chega!*'s Light into the Cracks

PAT WALSH

In his song "Anthem," Leonard Cohen sings: "Ring the bells that still can ring / there is a crack in everything / that's how the light gets in / that's how the light gets in."[1]

Canadians have long spent time and energy working with Timorese people to find the cracks, enlarge them, and let the light in. That lonely, often frustrating, but heroic hard work by a dedicated few was acknowledged to wide acclaim in 2015 with the award of the Order of Timor-Leste to the East Timor Alert Network (ETAN/Canada). Some of this extraordinarily gritty work is recorded in the report of the Timor-Leste Comissão de Acolhimento, Verdade e Reconciliação (Commission for Reception, Truth and Reconciliation, or CAVR) entitled *Chega!* ("enough" or "no more"). Thanks to the Timor-Leste government and the Indonesian Gramedia publishing house, this report is now available in hardcover in English.[2] In addition to ETAN, one of the few organizations anywhere to address the human rights responsibilities of the private sector, *Chega!* credits the Canada-Asia Working Group, the Indonesia-East Timor Program, and a number of creative individuals for speaking truth to power and ensuring that Timor-Leste's distant voice was heard in Canada. The challenge confronting us now is how to put this monumental report to work for the good of Timor-Leste, including Timorese victims, Indonesia, and humanity in general.

Due to limitations of space in this already long report, the references to Canada in *Chega!* are sparse. Canadians, Timorese, Indonesians, and others should consult other sources for the full story which, like Australia's, is an object lesson in the subordination of principle to pragmatism and the failure of political imagination.

In brief, Canada did not support Timor-Leste during the Indonesian occupation. It voted only once for Timor-Leste during the period 1975–82, when the territory's status was discussed in the UN General Assembly, and it gave de facto recognition to Timor-Leste's forced annexation by Indonesia. In its detailed review of the great famine that devastated Timor-Leste in 1978–79, *Chega!* mentions that Canadian ambassador Glen Shortliffe, though he was one of eleven senior diplomats who visited the disputed territory at the time and saw the cruel impact of the famine, said little about this appalling war crime. Famine, *Chega!* concluded, was used as a weapon of war by the Indonesian military in violation of its obligations under the Geneva Conventions. *Chega!* also concluded that this famine—and not direct killing, as many assume—was the major cause of the massive death toll in Timor-Leste.

It is impossible to read the account of this famine in *Chega!* without reeling with shock and disbelief. And yet Canada maintained a program of military co-operation with Indonesia, along with Australia, France, the United Kingdom, and particularly the United States. The Canadian government would probably deny that any of its matériel was used directly against the Timorese, but it is surely safe to say that the Indonesian military took Canada's support as a green light for its Timor campaign, the unchecked humanitarian impact of which is graphically detailed in *Chega!* Suharto, Indonesia's president from the late 1960s until 1998, had ultimate command responsibility for the campaign and is named by the CAVR for crimes against humanity and war crimes in Timor-Leste. He visited Vancouver for the Asia Pacific Economic Co-operation (APEC) summit in 1997, not long before his resignation.

The CAVR proposed a number of ways in which international governments might respond to *Chega!* The commission called for the report to be given the widest possible distribution domestically; for states that had military co-operation programs with Indonesia during the illegal, UN-condemned occupation of Timor-Leste, whether or not this assistance was used directly in Timor-Leste, to apologize to the people of Timor-Leste; for

4.1: Entry to *Chega!* exhibit, Dili, Timor-Leste. Photo: David Webster.

corporations who profited from the sale of weapons to Indonesia to contribute to a reparations program for victims; and for Indonesian officers indicted by the UN-sponsored Serious Crimes Unit and named in *Chega!* to be denied visas and subjected to other sanctions until their innocence has been credibly established by a court of law.

Canada has contributed to the postwar reconstruction and development of Timor-Leste. The Canadian International Development Agency also provided US$200,000 to the CAVR, and Canada's Truth and Reconciliation Commission on residential schools studied the CAVR process. These, as well as expressions of interest in the *Chega!* report by a number of Canadian institutions, including universities and NGOs, are welcome developments. They do not, however, amount to an official admission of responsibility or an acknowledgement of the needs and rights of victims to reparations.

What was this CAVR that made the findings and bold proposals mentioned above? Addressing some of the salient features of this commission will also allow me to clear up some misunderstandings about it and to comment briefly on a few of the issues to which the CAVR's findings and recommendations have given rise.

The Chega! *Report: Some Misconceptions*

First, it is important to state that the CAVR was a Timorese institution. Because the commission was established during the UN interregnum that followed Indonesia's withdrawal, some have concluded, erroneously, that it was a UN body and that *Chega!* is a UN report. Like a number of institutions from that period, the commission benefited from the support of the UN, donors, international advisers, and the experience of others—in this case, truth commissions in South Africa and various Latin American countries. But it was not a foreign import or clone of South Africa's famous commission.

The CAVR was established following a unanimous request by the Timorese resistance under Xanana Gusmão, and it enjoyed the support of the community and historic Timorese political parties such as Fretilin and the Timorese Democratic Union (UDT), despite their misgivings that truth-seeking might reflect adversely on them.[3] Great care was taken to consult Timorese stakeholders and to create a body and processes appropriate to Timor-Leste's cultural and other circumstances, including reviving and utilizing the country's local conflict-resolution customs and locating the commission in a former political prison. The commission was led by seven Timorese commissioners, each of whom was nominated by the community. It was staffed mainly by Timorese and all its senior advisers had been closely involved with the Timor-Leste issue prior to joining the commission. The CAVR is acknowledged in the Timor-Leste constitution, was endorsed by Timor-Leste's parliament, and throughout its life collaborated closely with Xanana Gusmão, Timor-Leste's first post-independence president. The CAVR, in short, was made in Timor-Leste.

Second, consistent with its mandate to restore victims' dignity, the CAVR set out to be victim-focused. Valuing victims and acknowledging their experiences was critical to the commission's peace-making and healing mission. A process that alienated or angered Timor-Leste's many victims or that failed to pre-empt potential outbursts of local revenge and payback would have compromised peacebuilding at the local, grassroots level during the critical first days of the newborn nation.

The CAVR used its extensive truth-seeking process, which involved individual debriefing, public hearings, and community mapping to give thousands of ordinary Timorese in all parts of the country a chance to share their experience, to be listened to and honoured, and to have their stories recorded in the CAVR's archives and the *Chega!* report for the benefit of future generations. Victims also participated actively in hundreds of community reconciliation ceremonies and some of the most vulnerable benefited from a reparations program and related services provided by the commission.

The CAVR was proud of its innovative community reconciliation process. The commission undertook some 1,400 reconciliation ceremonies across the country between low-level perpetrators of the 1999 violence and the families and communities they had offended. Had time permitted, an estimated 3,000 additional cases could have been addressed. The CAVR felt, however, that it had achieved critical mass and done enough to settle local communities. Most offenders were young men recruited into pro-Indonesian militias by the Indonesian military. Participation in these reconciliation ceremonies was voluntary; though painful and resulting in a sanction, they offered perpetrators what they treasured most—namely, acceptance back into their communities and immunity from future prosecution—not to mention what the community needed and wanted most: peace at the grassroots. Victims actively participated in ceremonies and insisted on full accountability to the truth and genuine remorse on the part of offenders.

Two elements, inter alia, contributed significantly to the effectiveness and sustainability of the process. One was the CAVR's use of familiar customary methods, such as the laying out of the big mat (*biti bo'ot*), developed by the Timorese over time to settle internal conflicts, and the sanctioning presence of traditional elders. The other was the opportunity for all parties to listen to each other and understand for the first time the background to the crimes and their shocking impact on communities. An excellent detailed review of the process can be found in volume 4 of the *Chega!* report.

The CAVR was mandated to restore victims' dignity. To this end, the commission made a determined effort to listen to victims and to ensure their voices were heard publically and officially. The *Chega!* report documents their distressing experiences in graphic detail. It also identifies the individual and institutional perpetrators of the crimes they suffered and the factors and policies responsible, and it proposes dozens of recommendations designed to address the rights and needs of victims and to ensure non-recurrence (these can be found in volume 4 of the report). Though legally and morally incontestable, the CAVR's findings and recommendations have been outweighed by political calculations that have tacitly benefitted perpetrators, not victims.

This victim-centric approach differentiated the CAVR from Timor-Leste's bilateral commission with Indonesia, the Commission for Truth and Friendship, and it informs the extensive recommendation for reparations to victims found in volume 4 of *Chega!*

In anticipation of political and administrative objections, the CAVR recommended that reparations be aimed at those who are still most vulnerable as a result of the human rights violations they suffered, such as torture and sexual violence. It also avoided mention of financial handouts in favour of service referral and other forms of reparation. Nevertheless, this recommendation has so far failed to win official support in Timor-Leste.

The government has not offered a formal explanation for its aversion to reparations, but a mix of factors appears to be at work. These include fears of a cost blowout, of social jealousy and division, of a repetition of the troubled veterans program, of double-dipping, and of a culture of dependency and entitlement. Some decision-makers probably also object to the idea of Timor-Leste offering reparations when those most responsible for the harm, including Indonesia, are avoiding their obligations. The end result is that veterans of the armed resistance have done well while the most vulnerable of Timor-Leste's victims have not benefited from the reparations which are their due. This has also distorted retrospective perceptions of the CAVR, which the commission is no longer around to do anything about.

Third, it is important to state that *Chega!* is first and foremost a human rights report, not primarily a piece of formal historical research. There is a growing tendency, including at the highest levels of Timorese society, to rebrand the report as history and to promote it—particularly as an educational resource—for its information value only. This is welcome as far as it goes, but it is also a significant distortion of the CAVR's basic raison d'être and function. The CAVR engaged in serious research and fact-finding, but this was not done for its own sake. Rather, it was done primarily to identify what human rights violations had occurred during the twenty-five-year period from 1974 to 1999—who suffered, who and what should be held accountable, and what policy and programmatic measures should be taken to address these findings and to ensure non-recurrence. This is a very different agenda than that undertaken by a history textbook. Reducing *Chega!* to a teaching resource bypasses the significant moral, legal, and political issues that the CAVR was mandated to address. It allows the report to be used without offending the offenders (whether Timorese, Indonesians, or others), and without having to act on or even debate many of its key recommendations. It is a serious misrepresentation of the CAVR and disservice to the victims whose dignity the CAVR was asked to restore.

Volumes 2 and 3 of *Chega!* documents seven sets of human rights violations committed during the commission's 1974–99 mandate period. This disturbing litany starts with an assault on the Timorese people's right to self-determination, the fundamental principle of decolonization to which Western members of the international community in particular paid only lip service during the worst years of Indonesia's occupation. A long report on killings and disappearances follows. The *Chega!* index lists over a hundred massacres. The CAVR engaged Benetech, the independent California-based human rights data group, to research the death toll from the war. Using an innovative process, Benetech concluded that it could be scientifically established that at least 100,000 civilians had perished as a direct or indirect result of both the civil war and the war with Indonesia. It allowed that the total could have been as high as 180,000, but that the absence of reliable data and the passage of time made it impossible to be definitive. The CAVR's evidence on forced displacement and famine is particularly distressing. It documents the use of famine by the Indonesian military, in violation of the Geneva Conventions, to starve tens of thousands of Timorese into surrender. Harassed by the military as they sought "to separate the fish from the water," many elderly people and children starved to death like animals. The CAVR also documented detention and torture, unfair political trials, violations of the laws of war, violations of children's rights, and sexual violence, particularly against women. The latter is painful reading. *Chega!* also includes a review of the limited available literature on violations of social and economic rights, matters not generally addressed by truth commissions. Further research is needed but the study provides compelling evidence that top-down development, particularly when it is designed principally to serve security objectives, is inherently unsustainable.

Then there is the important matter of Timor-Leste's second, bilateral truth commission with Indonesia, the Commission on Truth and Friendship (CTF), and its impact on *Chega!*

Since 2009, when the CTF report, *Per Memoriam Ad Spem* (*Through Memory to Hope*), was released, I have argued that it should be embraced because, although it does not go as far as *Chega!*, and is especially weak on the fundamental issue of impunity, some of its findings and recommendations are very similar to those of the CAVR. Unlike the CAVR's report, however, the CTF's recommendations also enjoy the status of being officially endorsed by both governments—in Indonesia's case by president Susilo Bambang Yudhoyono, himself a former military officer in Timor-Leste.

The CTF was established by the presidents of Indonesia and Timor-Leste in 2005 as the CAVR was winding up. A bilateral body led and staffed by respected nationals from both countries, it mainly operated out of, and was controlled by, Indonesia. Not surprisingly, then, many concluded that its function was to override and neutralise *Chega!*, and that its mandate to focus only on specific periods in 1999, to offer amnesty, not to name names, and even to clear the names of those "wrongfully accused," was provocative and a patent whitewash in the making. It was effectively boycotted by the UN, NGOs in Indonesia and Timor-Leste, and the victims themselves. The CAVR did not oppose it a priori but called for any further truth-seeking to complement, not contradict, the CAVR's work and to strengthen, not weaken, the chances of criminal justice.

In some respects, however, the CTF belied these concerns. The CTF did not recommend anyone for amnesty or clear the names of any individuals and, like the CAVR before it, it concluded that crimes against humanity and war crimes were committed in Timor-Leste in 1999. Though it stopped short of naming names, it also affirmed that the Indonesian military and its militias were principally responsible for these excesses. Furthermore, the CTF recommended reparations for victims and the opening of Indonesian archives as part of a joint, long-term research project into the causes and impact of the conflict. As its title indicates, *Per Memoriam Ad Spem* represents a clear official commitment to remembering the Timor-Leste issue in Indonesia rather than having it swept under the carpet. It is an open invitation for joint examination of the issue that is waiting to be taken up. Unfortunately, few Indonesian researchers and intellectuals seem to be aware of the report. Neither government made it available on the Internet (though the Indonesia-based group Asian Justice and Rights, or AJAR, has posted an English translation of the report).[4] Meanwhile, responses to its recommendations have been subjected to in-house management by senior public servants on both sides. Indonesian-Timorese government negotiations remain focussed on border and pension issues, not recommendations concerning human rights or the broad joint interrogation of the shared history of both countries recommended by the report.

While some aspects of the CTF's work are to be welcomed, its contribution should not be overstated. The CTF did not claim, or even intend, to facilitate reconciliation between Indonesian perpetrators and their Timorese victims. It settled for "friendship." Arguably, even this is too big a claim, given the pragmatic self-interest at work on both sides: "marriage of convenience" might be a more accurate description of the outcome. Indonesian politicians are silent on the matter but the claim by some Timorese politicians that the CTF is a unique international model of reconciliation is an exaggeration prompted more by self-defence against erstwhile critics than by reality. It also does violence to the deeply sensitive concept of reconciliation, gives comfort to perpetrators over victims, and weakens the campaign against impunity across Asia.

What Does the Future Hold for the CAVR Report?

Given that more than a decade has passed since the report was handed over in 2005 and the Timor-Leste parliament has failed to complete its self-appointed task to address the report's contents and recommendations, it could be concluded that *Chega!* is a lost cause in Timor-Leste. The report also seems to be at odds with state-sponsored trends in Timor-Leste that favour, for example, a more intense community focus on development, an end to "mourning," and the prioritising of veterans over victims by promoting the narrative of military resistance and the rewarding of militant service. Ever closer relations with Indonesia at the economic, educational, cultural, diplomatic, and even military levels, and Indonesia's determination to delete its embarrassing Timor-Leste adventure from public consciousness, also appear to rule out possibilities for justice despite the patent legal and moral logic of the case for due process.

On the other hand, it can be argued that there is no reason to fear for *Chega!*: it is a gift to humanity, a testament of such quality and power that it will stand the test of time and the vagaries of politics. Advocates like Archbishop Desmond Tutu, who chaired South Africa's Truth and Reconciliation Commission, call for *Chega!* to be given "its rightful place in the international canon of human rights and conflict resolution literature."[5] Thai conflict resolution expert Surichai Wun'Gaeo of Chulalongkorn University believes that *Chega!* transcends politics and time. The events it recounts, he says, should be seen as a part of humanity's history, with universal lessons for all.[6] Others cannot understand why Timor-Leste's government appears to distance itself from the CAVR, the first commission of its kind in the region and said to be one of the most effective truth commissions to date anywhere.[7] According to this view, Timor-Leste's Ministry of Foreign Affairs and other government agencies should be marketing the CAVR and its report as achievements, analogous to the way in which Costa Rica makes capital out of its contribution to peace and energy renewables.

A number of favourable developments can be pointed to both in and outside Timor-Leste.

Many truth commissions lack any follow-up institution; this is a problem, for instance, in Solomon Islands, as Betty Gigisi and Terry Brown discuss in their chapters. For its part, the Timorese government has continued to fund the Post-CAVR Technical Secretariat, which was established as a short-term body after the final *Chega!* report in 2005. It has also financed both the publication and international dissemination of *Chega!* in English and Portuguese translations. This initiative has been positively received internationally. Scholars, specialists in conflict resolution, civil-society activists, and government officials engaged in facilitating peace in a number of countries have expressed their appreciation for the report and the methodologies and insights it offers.

Timor-Leste's Ministry of Education has also begun to make use of *Chega!* in its first ever homegrown school curriculum for the teaching of history and human rights in primary schools. In due course, this rollout can be expected to create a demand for the use and study of *Chega!* at the secondary and tertiary levels.

A further domestic development with significant potential is the interest of Timor-Leste's prime minister (from 2015 to 2017), Dr. Rui Maria de Araújo, in the idea of a follow-up institution to preserve memory and truth. Both the CAVR and the CTF made proposals for such an institution and have indicated a number of activities that a follow-up body might pursue. These include further statement-taking, archival and educational activities, memorialization, a targeted reparations program for the most vulnerable victims, and, based on a CTF recommendation, a co-operative program of research, archive-building, personnel exchanges, and shared learning with Indonesia. In 2010, the Timor-Leste parliament went as far as drafting a law for the establishment of an "institute of memory," but, after sporadic discussion, the initiative lapsed. It has not been revived by the current parliament.

The interest of prime minister Araújo, who also had responsibility for the best use of the government funding provided to the current Post-CAVR Technical Secretariat, may represent a needed breakthrough. In 2016 Araújo broke the stalemate by proposing a working group to review the status of the CAVR recommendations, to consult stakeholders, and to advise the government on issues of mandate, legal status, governance, and funding for a new body. It is to be hoped that it will build on the unique legacies of both commissions and result in a permanent institute of memory and human rights akin to those in Taiwan, Colombia, and other parts of the world, and that it will serve to deepen relations between Timor-Leste and Indonesia and contribute to a culture of human rights in both countries and in the region as a whole.

The Fate of Chega! *in Indonesia*

While Timor-Leste is making some progress in memorializing its past, Indonesia—joint authorship of the *Per Memoriam* report notwithstanding—remains set on the path of denial and obfuscation. This is characteristic of Indonesia's general attitude to past violence, most notably the extensive extra-judicial killings and detentions led by the military after Suharto's takeover in 1965–66, a few short years before the invasion of Timor-Leste and its rationalisation on the same grounds.

Inconvenient Truths, a recent study into the fate of both *Chega!* and *Per Memoriam Ad Spem* in Indonesia commissioned by AJAR, found that few educated Indonesians knew of either report; when asked for their views, these same individuals tended to default to Suharto-era propaganda.[8]

The study reports that the Indonesian government disingenuously dismisses *Chega!* as the document of a foreign country, one that is none of Indonesia's business. "*Chega!* belongs to Timor-Leste. So we don't have anything to do with it," a foreign affairs official told researchers with a straight face. The report also points out that Timor-Leste has been dropped from Indonesia's education curriculum and that self-serving memoirs are being published by ex-military "to correct history" (*untuk meluruskan sejarah*) and deny responsibility for human rights violations in Timor-Leste. In other words, Indonesians are either being told nothing about this chapter of their country's history, or are given the old official version: that their army's intervention in Timor-Leste was not an invasion and occupation in violation of international law, but instead a justified intervention in a local conflict that, it was falsely claimed, threatened Indonesia's national and political unity.[9]

However, cracks are appearing in the Suharto-era defences. During a lecture tour to present the *Chega!* report to university audiences in eight Indonesian cities, I was impressed by the openness of younger lecturers and students to the *Chega!* narrative and their interest in incorporating it into existing courses. The good will they showed is also evident in other areas, such as the publication by Gramedia of the *Chega!* report and the work being undertaken by AJAR to reunite Timorese children taken to Indonesia during the war with their families and culture. AJAR is also the driving force behind the development of a joint Timorese-Indonesian teaching course grounded in *Chega!* and the shared history of the two societies.

Several Indonesian think tanks are also open to revising their position and engaging further on the subject. For example, the Centre for Strategic and International Studies (CSIS), whose founders advised Ali Murtopo and Suharto on the issue in the mid-1970s, expressly committed to discuss *Chega!* and contribute to a review of Indonesia's narrative and its place in the school curriculum. In his memoir *Shades of Grey*, CSIS éminence grise Jusuf Wanandi acknowledges that he made mistakes on the Timor-Leste issue and laments the fact that, far from liberating Timor-Leste, Indonesia colonised the former Portuguese territory, imposing on the Timorese what he calls "much misery and abuse."[10]

These developments did not just happen by accident. They are the outcome of creative initiatives undertaken to make use of changes in Indonesia in particular. But, though important and promising, these developments are relatively small and leave much to be done.

Canada was once a player in the Timor-Leste issue but it has retreated to a seat on the sidelines. One hopes that one or more of its great institutions, whether in government, academia, church, or civil society, will find a way to respond to the CAVR recommendations mentioned earlier and that it will engage with some of the unfinished business that *Chega!* and *Per Memoriam Ad Spem* have identified, and that have universal relevance for humanity's efforts to build a better world.

On 31 October 2016, eleven years to the day after the CAVR submitted its *Chega!* report to the president of Timor-Leste, Prime Minister Rui Maria de Araujo's Timor-Leste government passed a law (Decree Law 48/2016) to establish the follow-on institution recommended by the CAVR.

The new institution will be known as *Centro Nacional Chega!: Da Memória à Esperança* (*Chega!* National Centre: Through Memory to Hope). The title reflects the names of both truth commission reports whose central thrust was *chega!* ("enough" or "no more")—that is, non-recurrence of the violence that blighted Timor-Leste and Indonesia for a quarter of a century. It also signifies that the best way to achieve this objective is to remember rather than forget.

The institution was formally budgeted for and was established in 2017. It aims to be a hub of post-conflict best practice and to reach out to Indonesia and the international community. Its principal mission will be to collaborate with government and other stakeholders to facilitate the implementation of the recommendations made by both the CAVR and the bilateral CTF. This includes ensuring that the most vulnerable survivors of past human rights violations are cared for.

The centre is based at the former colonial prison in Dili, itself a site of conscience, and it will replace the existing Post-CAVR Technical Secretariat.

A 2015 UN study on truth commissions concluded that many commissions fail to realize their full potential because their recommendations are not carried out. In breaking away from this mold, Timor-Leste's new centre also promises to set a precedent in the practice of international transitional justice.

Box 4.1 Centro Nacional *Chega!* is born

Notes

1. Leonard Cohen, "Anthem," on *The Future*, Columbia Records, 24 November 1992.
2. *Chega! The Final Report of the Timor-Leste Commission for Reception, Truth and Reconciliation (CAVR)* (Jakarta: Gramedia, 2015). This translates the original Indonesian-language report delivered in 2005. The English translation was edited by Pat Walsh. For tales of the editing process, see Pat Walsh, "Two Sharp Eyes," in *Stormy with a Chance of Fried Rice: Twelve Months in Jakarta* (Jakarta: Gramedia, 2015). Other CAVR publications are available at www.cavrtimorleste.org and www.chegareport.net.
3. Fretilin (Independent East Timor Revolutionary Front) and UDT (Timorese Democratic Union) leaders' testimony about their own records is summarized in *Timor-Leste Internal Political Conflict 1974–1976* (Dili, TL: Post-CAVR Technical Secretariat, 2009).
4. Indonesia–Timor-Leste Commission on Truth and Friendship, *Per Memoriam Ad Spem: Final Report of the Commission on Truth and Friendship (CTF)* (Denpasar, ID: CTF, 2008), http://www.chegareport.net/profil-of-ctf/ (accessed 28 October 2016).
5. Desmond Tutu, foreword to *Chega!*, xxi.
6. Remarks in Pat Walsh, "*Chega!* 10th anniversary Regional Roadshow," http://home.patwalsh.net/chega-10th-anniv-region-roadshow/ (accessed 28 October 2016).
7. Truth commissions expert Patricia Hayner lists the CAVR as one of the five strongest truth commissions. See Hayner, *Unspeakable Truths: Transitional Justice and the Challenge of Truth Commissions* (New York: Routledge, 2010).
8. Budi Hernawan and Pat Walsh, "Inconvenient Truths: The Fate of the *Chega!* and *Per Memoriam Ad Spem* Reports on Timor-Leste," *Asia Justice and Rights (AJAR)* (August 2015), http://home.patwalsh.net/wp-content/uploads/Inconvenient-Truths.pdf (accessed 28 October 2016).
9. The official version appears in Marwati Poesponegoro and Nugroho Notosusanto, *Sejarah Nasional Indonesia, VI: Zaman Jepang dan Zaman Republik Indonesia* (Jakarta: Balai Pustaka, 2008).
10. Jusuf Wanandi, *Shades of Grey: A Political Memoir of Modern Indonesia 1965–1998* (Jakarta: Equinox, 2012).

5

Politika Taka Malu, Censorship, and Silencing: Virtuosos of Clandestinity and One's Relationship to Truth and Memory

Jacqueline Aquino Siapno

>*Silence can be a plan rigorously executed*
>*the blueprint to a life*
>*It is a presence it has a history a form*
>*Do not confuse it*
>*with any kind of absence.*
>
>—Adrienne Rich, *Cartographies of Silence*[1]

>*Their history is to have none.*
>
>—James Scott, *The Art of Not Being Governed*[2]

>*Because it is a systematic negation of the other person and a furious determination to deny the other person all attributes of humanity, colonialism forces the people it dominates to ask themselves the question constantly: "In reality, who am I?" ... Once again the objective of the native who fights against himself is to*

> *bring about the end of domination. But he ought equally to pay attention to the liquidation of all untruths implanted in his being by oppression. ... Total liberation is that which concerns all sectors of the personality.*
>
> —Frantz Fanon, *The Wretched of the Earth*[3]

This chapter explores the paradox of being asked to examine "the truth" when the methods used during the clandestine period were to have no history of records (i.e., leave no trace behind)—a negation of the work of historians and historiography (while keeping in mind the paradox and irony that some of the clandestines were historians—both Timorese and "international").[4] What happens when memory fails? What if one remembers selectively? What if silence and having no history is not only a strategy, a plan—rigorously executed, the blueprint to a life—but an identity, even a kindred spirit network of being and belonging? Clandestinity was a method that worked so well during the resistance towards colonial occupation, but in post-independence, "free" and "democratic" Timor-Leste, senior ministers, MPs, and other key decision-makers remained virtuosos of clandestinity and refused to change and/or adopt new identities or new methods of learning, not to mention a so-called "free press" that is not really that free at all.[5] In some cases, the clandestine identity is stronger and more dominant than the "real" identity. In other cases, the clandestine identity and fictive name has become embedded into the "real" name. Some ex-clandestines even argue that transparency and honesty are "foreign/Western values," as some ex-Falintil-guerrillas-turned-MPs informed us when we interviewed them about their thoughts on civilian oversight of the military and police, and in relation to strengthening transparency in public financial administration and anti- corruption. What are the consequences of this *politika taka malu* (covering up for each other) for truth commissions and activists, for struggles of gender justice, access to basic services, the democratization process, anti-corruption initiatives, and accountability in public financial management and economic development?

5.1: Display from Archives and Museum of the Timorese Resistance, Dili, Timor-Leste. Photo: David Webster.

Clandestiny as Identity and Method

In music, a virtuoso is someone who isn't just technically proficient, but also spiritually gifted and talented, someone who embodies the music itself: the musician is the music (not something outside or separate). In war, the virtuoso of clandestinity embodies the same identity as the musical virtuoso. It is someone who doesn't just put on multiple masks for winning the war and running the resistance struggle in an instrumentalist kind of way, but someone who has embodied this way of knowing and being, someone with the unusual skill, gift, talent, even identity, to blend with one's worst enemies, and with the skill set for self-preservation and defending one's privacy from unnecessary and unwanted intrusion. It is a soft power by which the enemy is defeated not with violence, guns, or weapons, but by other means—including living with them close by, working behind the scenes, blending in so that they have no idea that you are even there, writing and using one's pen. Such were the survival skills of the clandestine virtuoso during the resistance against colonial occupation.

Paradoxically, in the post-independence, post-conflict era, some people who do not want to understand or appreciate this *longue durée* history dismiss clandestinity and secret identity as a weakness, a flaw, even a liability, possibly a crime; they mostly blame individuals, but not the structures, societies, and environments that engender this way of being, operating, and networking. Being duplicitous, hiding truths, operating in secret networks, protecting one's privacy from intense public surveillance are now considered by certain sectors as unacceptable, if not dangerous to nation-building and economic development. Publicly, some people condemn it as killing development ("hamate desenvolvimento") and not good for the nation ("laduun diak ba nasaun"), but at the level of everyday politics, something else happens.[6] What happens when war veterans who have never sought psychological support for unpacking and processing their old attitudes and methods of doing things are now suddenly being told that they have to throw away all their past history to begin a new life, to start telling the truth, to start doing "civilian oversight on their close friends in the military and police," and to open up? How might they react? Clandestinity is an ongoing *modus operandi*, a chosen identity especially in an environment that is riddled with brutal (but subtle, hidden) inter-party and intra-party violence (cloaked by a thin public veneer of "coalition" and "harmony") and a weak judicial system. Trust is the highest casualty. The importance of psychoanalysis in trying to comprehend the psychology of the state and its character and actors is both underestimated and under-studied.[7] One telling example is the rhetoric of doublespeak, if not hidden meanings: only other clandestines can figure out what is really being said (by analyzing the irony and the silence in the speech act—i.e., what is *not* being said). For example, a TV Timor-Leste interview with Fernando La Sama de Araújo, in Tetun, on how his "boss" makes solo decisions in government. Referring to Xanana Gusmão (president, subsequently prime minister), he captures in a quintessentially "clandestine style"—very funny, yet subtle, not really saying anything directly, but saying a lot (to those who can read the silences)—Xanana Gusmão's "art of governing."[8]

If one's identity for a long period of time is marked by clandestinity, what would it take for change and transformation to happen in one's psyche, one's methods and *modus operandi*, in the postwar context of a society full of other clandestine virtuosos? How does one go about "disarmament" if one had no "arms" in the first place—as compared to the ex-guerrillas who had to go through a precarious process of disarmament, demobilization, and reintegration (or DDR)—but only one's mind and pen? Shouldn't there be a different kind of DDR for clandestine virtuosos? In fact, one can argue that the unarmed clandestine method of infiltrating and collaborating very closely with the enemy was much more difficult that being an armed guerrilla in the isolated mountains. In the hierarchy by which the armed struggle, the clandestine front, and the diplomatic front is supposedly more "important" than the other, it is the armed struggle, led by the armed guerrillas, that is often held in the highest regard. In post-independence nation-building, former guerilla fighters get the most medals, along with other material and symbolic markers of honour.

If one reflects carefully, one can argue that it is the virtuosos of clandestinity, the secret identities with a pen, who had a much more difficult time, living and connecting very close to the enemy (physically and psychologically), against overwhelming odds, with no weapons. The capacity to survive in such an environment required extraordinary courage and skills that are very different from those acquired by someone who can use a weapon to simply shoot and kill. On the contrary, many of the virtuosos of clandestinity honed their writing, argumentation, rhetoric, and translation skills, and learned through a long process that the pen is mightier than the sword, or that rhetorical persuasion is much more effective than shooting your opponents. It would serve them well in the post-independence period, where they are able to "dialogue" with difficult opponents instead of just shooting them down. In comparison, the guerrillas from the armed struggle have had a much harder time in the transition to independence. One of the most revealing interviews we conducted for our DDR research[9] comparing former members of the Moro National Liberation Front in the southern Philippines with ex-Falintil members in Timor-Leste was with a Timorese guerrilla-turned-MP. He said: "One of the most difficult things for me in this transition from being a guerrilla to an MP is being told to learn how to dialogue. In the past, when we didn't like somebody, we just beat them up, or shot them. But now … apparently, we have to learn how to dialogue and communicate." He also added: "When we were disarmed, I literally felt as if my arm was cut off. I slept with my weapon for seventeen years. It was like my wife."

Clandestinity is a method. It was meaningful under a colonial occupation that suppressed dissent, opposition, and freedom of expression. But under a post-independence semi-democracy, it continues to be the predominant method. Why are ideas about clandestinity, leadership, hierarchy, social stratification, and gender inequality so resilient and persistent, even as governments, including the Timorese government, sign on to global human rights treaties, conventions, and co-operation agreements (including the Convention on the Elimination of All Forms of Discrimination Against Women, or CEDAW; civilian oversight of the military; human rights; and truth and reconciliation commissions), and global governance mechanisms on public financial administration (such as transparency portals; anti-corruption commissions; and investigative journalism)?[10]

Another thing about clandestinity as a method is that it is very suspicious of outsiders, even semi-outsiders, unless one has done a traditional, sacred "pact" with them. It is like a mafia—an organized group that is impervious and impermeable (except that in this case, we are talking about a state actor, not a non-state one). How does one unpack the paradox that the more "transparent" the Ministry of Finance's online budget portals, the more sophisticated the corruption?[11] The problem with clandestinity as an ongoing method of independent governance is that it is set up in such a way that if one is not part of an inner circle of an *ema boot* (big shot), whatever you need to get done doesn't get done unless an *ema boot* is approached and wants to, or learns how to, delegate. But what if one has no connections with such a figure?

The other problem with the culture of silence and clandestinity and personalistic politics is that people think it is best to change things by going through silent, informal channels instead of having an efficient public service that is easily accessible to "ordinary" people. Politically savvy Timorese think that clandestinity is the best way to expedite whatever it is you need to get done. In such an environment, the consequences for the work of grieving and mourning, for memory, truth, and reconciliation—especially for those who have a different definition of "normal"—can be devastating. Another problem is that it breeds an environment of paranoia. People are prone to put more trust in fabricated rumours and propaganda, than in "official truths" produced by the state and government, precisely because the nation, and the colonial occupation before that, were built on lies. An outside observer might find it shocking, for example, that most

Timorese consider various private websites more credible than official government sites, which they assume are propaganda. An additional problem with clandestine methods is that they have created a community of people with persecuted mentalities, especially among those in the higher echelons (one never knows if and when a fellow clandestine will finally act out against another, so one is always on edge). But the most tragic and violent consequences of clandestinity are those felt at the level of the family and household; it is what keeps husbands and wives awake at night, and children wondering about their fathers. Women become the signs of disorder.

International Advisers and Global Entanglements

At the end of the day, who, ultimately, should be and can be made responsible and accountable for these cultures of silence? Are the Timorese solely to blame? What about their former colonizers and the international organizations responsible for building this new nation-state? The only reason that the system of money, politics, corruption, and lack of accountability continues is that the internationals (the advisers, donors, consultants, and others) in Timor-Leste are complicit. Instead of being agents of change and transformation, some actively participate in perpetuating the system, mostly in order to keep their jobs and lucrative salaries as "advisers." One of them even told me: "You can't believe how much money they pay us! Imagine."

Some of the white Australians and Americans in Timor-Leste, the Indonesians, Filipinos, and members of other nationalities are, ironically, even more nationalistic than the Timorese. They defend everything the Timorese do. Instead of creating and supporting new spaces for dissent, opposition, and transformation, they are part of the problems of inequality and domination, acting as apologists for the dysfunctional state and corrupt government. Very few disengage, distance, let go, disconnect, or detach themselves to reflect on what their continuing engagement means in terms of ethical responsibility. Meanwhile, some "solidarity activists" are quite competitive with each other in their quest for resources (the "dark side" of giving and so-called solidarity). This is especially true for citizens of Timor-Leste's former colonial overlords: Indonesia and Portugal. While I have a lot of respect for some Indonesians and Portuguese who have gone through the painful process of examining their identity as colonizers, one cannot say that for many others, including those who are now still operating in East Timor as if it was "business as usual," those who work as advisers to the Timorese, seemingly without ever having to reflect on the history of violence first, and who have absolutely no interest, capacity, or willingness, to meditate on that violent history, and their ethical responsibility as human beings.

In the larger geopolitical context, whose "ethical politics," whose "transparency," whose "justice," and whose "democracy" are served when highly paid international consultants find it so easy to dump on and mock the Timorese without examining their own complicity? Apparently, it is all the fault of the Timorese. But what about all those advisers from the UN, the World Bank, and other multinational organizations? What could they possibly have been advising? Was it all just very expensive bad advice? Huge mistakes were made that contributed to the disillusionment in the nation-building process. Are we even willing to listen, to study history so as to avoid repeating the same mistakes? Are we equipped to listen? Do we have the capacity? Or are people, institutions, and countries condemned to make exactly these same mistakes over and over? What can the West Papuans possibly learn from the processes that unfolded in Timor-Leste? Or is politics, in general—whether an independence movement or post-independence government, and regardless of where we sit (whether in Quebec or West Papua)—an environment riddled with clandestinity?

Writing about India, Sankaran Krishna contrasts two opposing views of politics:

> a simplistic view of politics as, at some level at least, the exercise of power for the sake of the betterment of the nation and the people, versus an understanding of politics as a domain constituted by crime, corruption, illegal and unethical activities. Understandings of the political were split between a covert and real economy of power, on the one hand, and an overt and rhetorical economy of ideas and idealism on the other. Naive people, media and leaders believed the latter while insiders knew reality to be the former.[12]

Continuities of Violence and Clandestinity

If we act on the above understanding of politics, what comparative studies and analyses can be drawn for political sociology (e.g., psychology of the state), conflict, post-conflict reconstruction, democracy and democratization, coalition formation, voting behaviour and party competition, government structures and institutional reform, peacebuilding in postwar societies, the role of the UN and other international organizations in humanitarian interventions, comparative public policy, and nation-building processes? What could possibly be useful for West Papuans from the Timorese experience? It's not enough to remain independent geographically or symbolically only. One has to decolonize one's mind, which, as Fanon writes, is a program of complete disorder.[13] It's also not enough to decolonize one's mind. The post-colonial society might need another social revolution and new methods of learning. That's why critical educators are important. Get rid of old violent methods of "solving problems" like distributing guns; this one, especially, has to go. Get rid of "politika taka malu" on corruption. But when you have ex-guerrillas dominating the institutions of power, these—not dialogue and accountability—seem to be the default mechanism that we turn to whenever there is a "problem" or "disorder."

I have argued that in the case of the Indonesian occupation of East Timor, the use of clandestinity and secret identity was a condition of survival under colonial occupation. In the post-1999 independence period, however, it has turned into a politics of ruling cliques. My reading weighs more on finding out the "why" of such a persistence of clandestinity, in a post-independence era of alleged "freedom of the press" and "freedom of speech and expression." While secrecy during the anti-colonial struggle was often a precondition for survival, it loses its reason to exist after 1999—unless, of course, the new state's leadership continues to operate in clandestinity in order to remain "untouchable" and "unchallenged."

Critical investigative reporting on politics in East Timor and the formation of a vibrant and dynamic opposition has not been possible for various reasons. Nevertheless, since 1999 there have been some political and economic developments that are relevant to the discussion of memory, truth, and reconciliation. The second half of the 2000s saw the re-entry of the old Indonesian business network whose presence was so significant during the occupation years. Some of these businesses were connected in the past to the Indonesian military. In light of this development, the scrutiny of the peculiar form of politicking among members of the ruling class should be contextualized in such an evolving development and "relationship" (too much friendship, not enough truth). When did these clandestine relationships become the noticeable rule for those in the central government's "inner circle"? What does it entail, really—apart from contributions to election funds for certain political parties and personalities? Cronyism in the face of postwar belligerence among military factions? A necessary tactical level of maneuver for the ruling group, in response to the inter- and intra-party competition and violence in the new electoral politics? Or is it a new oligarchy in the making, not unlike the bureaucratic corruption in Indonesia? If so, what then was the point of becoming independent? What was the point of so many people, including Fernando La Sama de Araújo, sacrificing their lives for an "independent" East Timor?

The Role of Scholars

The truth is that even with the so-called free press in East Timor, there is actually a lack of a space for opposition and dissent. What is our role as scholars? We become scholars, I hope, not just to interpret the world, but also to solve problems and tensions, to transform and change society. If we spend all our time studying, researching, and teaching, but we still cannot change anything when it comes to the problems of corruption and the disempowerment of marginalized peoples, then we are bad students, researchers, and teachers.

While the discussion above focuses on the Indonesian and Timorese governments, I would add that we also act as critics of the power of international organizations, including the United Nations and its missions and agencies, and other global governance outfits, rather than apologists, which some scholars tend to be. Some, but not all of the *malae* (outsiders or internationals who are in Timor-Leste as advisers, activists, consultants, and business people) are complicit with, and indeed sometimes the cause of, the new forms of domination and inequality that impact knowledge production. Others are sycophantic, incestuous, ingratiating themselves to the powerful and dependent on the state for their salaries. These individuals and groups comfortably accept the culture of silence, censoring themselves in order to keep their jobs. Instead of embracing the critical possibilities inherent in the status of outsider, they are so desperate to belong, to be part of insider circles, that they are willing to forego moral clarity, integrity, and ethical responsibility.

"True Colours": Clandestines—From the Perspective of a Child

My son and I are in the process of rebuilding again, after my husband's death. This time, it is a lot more challenging, as we are rebuilding our lives in a country where my son is a new immigrant. We can empathize with those who have fled regime change, especially those from Eritrea, as the similarities and parallels are troubling. Recently, my son wrote a short narrative piece called "True Colours," which is about the true colours of clandestine war veterans like his father and the differences in their behaviour in public and at home. Even though he was only eleven when he wrote it, he was able to capture the tensions and transformations in so many societies—in Southeast Asia and in North America—especially those relating to the impact and long-term consequences of the wars on children. I hope that I can share it someday with other Timorese. But for now, that space does not exist. It has to be created and built—a space where it is all right to be truthful and honest about the veterans of the war, the national heroes of the anti-colonial struggle for independence, from the perspective of a child. Children are the greatest teachers of life's most mysterious lessons. And yet, in Timor-Leste, we hardly listen to their voices. Like poor youth, and poor women, hardly anybody listens to them.

Notes

I wish to thank Hendro Sangkoyo, David Webster, and "mica" Barreto Soares for careful reading and sharp and insightful comments on this paper. The title of this paper was inspired by an interview by *Tempo Semanal* with my late husband, Fernando La Sama de Araújo, who passed away on 2 June 2015, on Anti-Corruption day, at https://www.youtube.com/watch?v=LhmU6rcORBc (accessed 29 June 2017). Fernando La Sama de Araújo was a former clandestine activist and political prisoner in an Indonesian jail, then leader of the Democratic Party (PD) in independent Timor-Leste, serving in a number of positions including speaker of parliament and acting president.

1   Adrienne Rich, "Cartographies of Silence," in *Collected Poems: 1950-2012* (New York: W.W. Norton & Company, 2016).

2   James Scott, *The Art of Not Being Governed: An Anarchist History of Upland Southeast Asia* (New Haven: Yale University Press, 2009), 34.

3   Frantz Fanon, *The Wretched of the Earth,* preface by Jean Paul Sartre, translated by Constance Farrington (New York: Grove Weidenfeld, 1963), 250.

4   Clandestinity and secret identity were by no means limited to the Timorese. Scholars from other countries, who empathized with and supported the Timorese cause, wrote articles against the violence of the Indonesian colonial occupation under pseudonyms. See for example Aloys Smith [Rodolphe de Koninck], "Timor Oriental Devant la Conscience de l'Humanité," *Le Devoir* (Montreal), 20 December 1991. A kind of excavation or archaeology of knowledge would be required in order to uncover and determine the depth and expansiveness of the clandestine struggle (including new archives coming out of Japan, Canada, Australia, the Philippines, the UK, and other places) and evidence that "the pen is mightier than the sword" (despite current discourses of militarized masculinity arguing that it was militarized men who won the war).

5   For example, some Timorese ambassadors, members of parliament, and some government ministers continue to use clandestine names on Facebook and other social media sites. During the day, they work for the state and government, and at night and weekends they "activate" their clandestine identities.

6   Since first writing these reflections on "virtuosos of clandestinity" in August 2015, three months after my late husband's death, some interesting, unexpected transformations at the institutional level have occurred in Timor-Leste's dysfunctional system. See for example: www.tribunais.tl, especially the section on *"Camara de Contas"* and "Auditorias," for eye-opening, thought-provoking reads. It is possible that untimely deaths and collective national mourning, possibly even "Desluto Nacional" (translated in their official website as "National Mourning-End" celebration; see http://timor-leste.gov.tl/?p=13180&lang=en) in all their paradoxes and contradictions can perhaps be a cathartic opening for critical self-reflection and institutional transformation and change. My sincerest gratitude to former virtuosos of clandestinity, themselves "insider/outsiders" in the state, for sending me the recent information on "transformations" in anti-corruption mechanisms. It just goes to show that the state and government is porous and permeable and not as able to "put a lid" on its everyday secret activities as it may wish.

7   For one example of a psychosocial needs assessment in Aceh, see International Organization for Migration, "Indonesia: A Psychosocial Needs Assessment of Communities in 14 Conflict-affected Districts in Aceh": http://reliefweb.int/ report/indonesia/indonesia-psychosocial-needs-assessment-communities-14-conflict-affected-districts (accessed 29 June 2017).

8   See "Steitementu Fernando Lasama," 27 January 2015, https://www.youtube.com/watch?v=ygBoH9NrnUY (accessed 29 June 2017). For those who understand Tetum, this is a very revealing statement on Xanana Gusmao's random, authoritarian, personalistic governance style.

9   Some of this research is taken from a 2008 study commissioned by the Timor-Leste National Commission on Planning, in co-operation with the Ministry of Defense, focusing on engendering the security sector. The study was commissioned by Ms.

Milena Pires and her team at the National Commission on Planning, with the author as principal investigator. The intention and idea of the state-sponsored research was to open up the discussion on civilian oversight of the military, and uncover the dynamics of civilian-military-police relations, in order to link research and policy, and transform Timorese society from a zone of "commando style" militarized masculinities to one of more open, inclusive, egalitarian, democratic, an pluralistic dialogue. The findings were presented in a public seminar entitled "Security Sector Reform: Gendered Perspectives" in Delta Nova, Dili, attended by representatives from the military, police (including commanders from the rural districts), the former minister of defense and former minister of interior during the Fretilin government, international security forces (including the UN and the ISF), Atul Khare, the former UN special representative of the secretary-general, and his wife Vandna Khare, and former UN police commissioner Rodolfo Tor. See also Jacqueline Aquino Siapno, "De guerilléros à soldats, civils et membres du parlement: L'intégration des femmes et des ex-résistants Timorais dans l'Administration et la Societé Civile," in *Timor-Leste Contemporain: L'émergence d'une nation*, ed. Benjamim de Araújo e Corte-Real, Christine Cabasset, and Frédéric Durand (Bangkok: IRASEC, 2014); and Jacqueline A. Siapno, "Brave Women Warriors, Unfinished Revolutions: Political Subjectivities of Women Ex-Falintil and Falintil-FDTL Combatants in East Timor," in *Women Warriors in Southeast Asia*, ed. Vina Lanzona and Tobias Rettig (New York: Routledge, forthcoming).

10   For one useful explanation, see Thomas Nail, "The Politics of the Mask," 11 December 2013, http://www.huffingtonpost.com/thomas-nail/the-politics-of-the-mask_b_4262001.html (accessed 29 June 2017).

11   Again, please refer to www.tribunais.tl and read the interesting comments on "contradictions" in the "camara de contas" section.

12   Sankaran Krishna, "The Moral Economy of Political Assassinations," paper presented at "Political Violence in South and Southeast Asia," Colombo, LK, April 2007 and Kuala Lumpur, MY, August 2007.

13   Franz Fanon, *The Wretched of the Earth* (New York: Grove Press, 1963), 250.

6

Development and Foreign Aid in Timor-Leste after Independence

Laurentina "mica" Barreto Soares

State-building and development is a continuous process. Timor-Leste has been engaged in this endeavour since the restoration of its independence in 2002, following a period in which the United Nations helped lay the groundwork for institutional development from 1999 to 2002. Many have acknowledged Timorese development is a difficult process, especially given the fact that it started almost from scratch. Timor-Leste has achieved some remarkable progress. However, efforts so far have placed more emphasis on economic development than human development. This continuing focus is evident in the state budget allocation for the past five years, in which the bulk of funds have gone to infrastructure while allocating limited funds to other sectors—particularly agriculture, tourism, health, and education programs.

This leads us to ask: when we talk about development, what do we mean? What is development? Are we talking about cultural development, economic development, political development, or social development?

In 1996 the United Nations Development Programme defined development as a process that not only focuses on economic growth—although that is crucial—but also on human development, on health, education, and the environment.[1] This is important because when most capitalist governments talk about economic growth, they do not necessarily emphasize what such growth means for the people.

During its attempts at state-building and development, Timor-Leste received foreign aid from multiple donors, including the Canadian government. The largest contributions came during the United Nations Transitional Administration (1999–2002) and the early years after independence in 2002. According to the local NGO La'o Hamutuk, from 1999 to 2009, donors gave an estimated US$5.2 billion to Timor-Leste.[2] The major part of these funds, however, went to pay for the salaries of so-called international advisers and for other overhead bureaucratic costs; only one-tenth of it entered into the country's economy.[3] Donor contributions slowly decreased after 2009 due to donor countries' changing priorities and perhaps also donor fatigue and Timor-Leste's increased ability to generate its own resources. Despite reducing their assistance, a significant number of donors continued to engage in Timor-Leste. These included the European Union, the World Bank, the Asian Development Bank, United Nations specialized agencies, Australia, Germany, the United States, Portugal, and Japan. The People's Republic of China is also among the current crop of donors to Timor-Leste. China's assistance is comparatively small in quantity, but its presence and engagement is on the rise and it is seen, particularly by Timorese leaders, as a significant contribution to the country's state-building and development efforts.

This chapter will focus on state-building, development, and foreign aid in Timor-Leste after independence. The first part will provide an overview of Timor-Leste's development over the past fourteen years by highlighting some of the progress it has made and the challenges it has faced. The second part will discuss foreign aid and state-building with a focus on China's engagement in Timor-Leste's state-building and development. It will conclude by linking Timor-Leste's development with reconciliation; given Timor-Leste's past experience of atrocities committed by the Indonesian military between 1975 and 1999, as well as the internal crisis of 2006, these two aspects are closely linked.

Overview of Timor-Leste's Economic Development: Progress and Challenges

In May 2002, Timor-Leste restored its independence after two years under UN transitional administration. From the start it was plagued by many troubles. In 1999, after the Timorese voted for independence, pro-Indonesia military and paramilitary groups destroyed about 70 per cent of public buildings, homes, and schools. The violent last days of Indonesian rule also saw 75 per cent of Timorese people displaced from their homes.[4] In 2006, Timor-Leste was tested again as it went through an internal crisis in which more than a hundred thousand people were displaced, mostly to the capital, Dili.[5] Many houses in the city were burned, both in 1999 and in 2006. This crisis led to, in 2008, the attempted assassination of José Ramos Horta and Xanana Gusmão, at the time the president and prime minister, respectively. Ramos Horta was seriously injured and had to be hospitalized in Australia.

Despite these problems, Timor-Leste has witnessed remarkable progress over the years since independence. On the political front, after 2008, Timor-Leste enjoyed relative political stability. At the 2017 presidential and parliamentary elections, the country held its fourth round of peaceful democratic elections. In February 2015, a new prime minister took office in a peaceful transfer of power, although some have questioned what they perceive as a lack of transparency and consensus within the members of the coalition government led by then prime minister Kay Rala Xanana Gusmão from the CNRT. The new prime minister came from the opposition Fretilin. Many regarded his appointment as part of power-sharing executive and "political reconciliation," especially between the two leading figures, Xanana Gusmão and Marí Alkatiri of Fretilin. After the 2017 elections, Alkatiri became prime minister and Xanana went into opposition.

In 2011, Timor-Leste came up with a new strategic development plan (SDP) that set its vision for development over the period of twenty years (until 2030). This twenty-year strategic development plan covers four main pillars: social capital; infrastructure development; economic development; and institutional framework. While this plan intends to mirror Singapore's development preference, many observers view it as overly ambitious for Timor-Leste and are critical of its tendency to privilege economic infrastructure goals, particularly in the first two decades, over human development objectives. Critics have also pointed at the absence of clear strategic guidelines for the implementation of the plan and milestones of achievable results. In addition, it has been revealed that the new SDP failed to reflect the previous development plan that was established in 2002 (and which was slated to last until 2020). There was no evaluation of the previous SDP, which was drafted with assistance from the international community. Timor-Leste created a petroleum fund based on the Norwegian model, a fund to save the revenues coming from its main natural resource, oil and gas. This fund has been widely regarded as a strong example of a sovereign wealth fund for managing petroleum resources in a fragile or post-conflict setting.[6] However, its successful management is highly dependent on institutional strength. Compared to the Norwegian model, with its well-established institution and over forty years of experience, the Timor-Leste petroleum fund, though it appears resilient, remains untested.[7] Nonetheless, it is a major income source for the state budget: indeed, about 90 per cent comes from oil and gas revenues. Another significant development has been the creation of a transparency portal, which aims to increase transparency, building trust and good governance. Although it has yet to be further developed, the system has so far housed information on Timor-Leste's state budget, donors' contribution, electronic procurements, and development results.

Timor-Leste has been able to lay the foundations for state institutions, gradually strengthening them with international support. Women's role in the public sphere has slowly increased despite the country's predominantly patriarchal culture. For example, Timorese women's representation in the National Parliament is 27.69 per cent, the highest in the region. This has been made possible because of a quota system in which every political party is required to have one woman for every three candidates they field. And yet, while women's participation in politics is high, Timor-Leste has yet to demonstrate evidence of the quality of women's participation and what women of Timor-Leste have produced so far in order to be mirrored by other countries. The situation still leaves many things to be desired, including better communication.

In social-sector development, an increased number of children have access to education. As of 2013, 91.9 per cent of children were enrolled in primary school.[8] Timor-Leste has increased the number of health facilities as well: the government has clinics in many areas, with a good structure from the national to the village level. Again, the quantity looks promising, but the quality of the health-care system is still far from adequate. The Cuban government established a scholarship program and almost a thousand Timorese medical students studied in Cuba. After they graduated, these Cuban-trained Timorese doctors were deployed to the villages, but they cannot do much because there is not enough medication, facilities, or transportation. In Timor-Leste, most people are treated with simple analgesic and antibiotics due to lack of proper medication.

Timor-Leste has also been active in international forums. The country is now a party to many international treaties, but it experiences issues when applying for these agreements due to various factors, including its human-resources capacity. The government has in particular signed most international treaties related to human rights issues. Timor-Leste also plays a leading role in the g7+, a group composed of countries that have recently emerged from conflict. It is a member of the Community of Portuguese Speaking Countries, an observer in the Pacific Development Forum, and is in the process of joining the Association of Southeast Asian Nations (ASEAN). Timor-Leste was one of ten countries given responsibility for the implementation of the UN Special Development Goal 16, concerning peace, justice, and strong institutions.

Significantly, Timor-Leste has assisted other countries as well. It has done so as a soft power, one that has advanced its diplomatic currency to promote its global image as a responsible member of the international community. In 2013, it successfully led the voter registration process in Guinea-Bissau. The United Nations had estimated a large budget for Guinea-Bissau's needs. The Timorese government was then invited to do its own calculations, coming up with a lower cost and providing figures to justify it. The Timorese government then contributed to the US$63 million budget for Guinea-Bissau's government to register voters for their elections.[9] Similarly, since 2005 Timor-Leste has been a humanitarian aid donor, providing aid for natural disasters to, among others, the United States after Hurricane Katrina in 2005, to Cuba and Haiti after the 2010 earthquake, and to Portugal, most recently in 2016 after a spate of forest fires.

Yet Timor-Leste can also be viewed as a petro-state because the majority of the state budget comes from oil and gas. The country does not yet have many programs to diversify the economy, except for an initial attempt at creating two megaprojects: the Tasi-Mane project for a supply base in

Suai district, on Timor-Leste's south coast, and a special economic zone called ZEEMS (Zona Espesial Ekonomia Merkadu Sosial, or Social Market Economy Special Zone) in Timor-Leste's exclave district of Oecusse. The supply-base project and special economic zone are still in their early stages of development and they have yet to deliver revenue, and both projects face domestic criticism. Already some experts say that these sources of income will be depleted in five to seven years. At the time of writing, Timor-Leste was involved in a dispute with Australia over maritime boundaries, with the government seeking to determine the future exploration of oil and gas in the Greater Sunrise field. This is a major prospect for Timor-Leste to generate future income to run the country. Timor-Leste is calling for Australia to resubmit to the maritime boundary jurisdiction under the International Court of Justice.

Timor-Leste also has high youth unemployment. Roughly 70 per cent of the country's population is below thirty and about 54 per cent is below working age.[10] Some 13,000 to 15,000 people enter the job market every year, but there are very few industries available in the territory to provide jobs to these people. In the meantime, Timor-Leste still has very poor quality education. As a result, while there are many people available, the country does not have the ability to educate them.

Furthermore, Timor-Leste has a poor health-care system. At one point, the entire country was dependent on warehoused supplies in Dili to provide medication but these supplies ran out and shipping issues have caused further medication to arrive late. Some of the medicine that was already purchased was unusable because of these shipping issues. There are also issues with the allocation of money to buy medication.

Another challenge is the rate of malnutrition: according to one recent study 47 per cent of children under the age of five are malnourished.[11] The government denied this statistic, but many still cite it. Statistics are hard to obtain in Timor-Leste, but according to civil-society groups, there has not been much improvement. There are gaps in economic opportunity because everything is centralized in the capital. Dili is the centre of the country's prosperity at the moment. The city has seen the increased presence of migrants and sojourners from Indonesia, the Philippines, China, Portugal, and Vietnam, many of whom are involved in various economic activities or are seeking jobs. For example, small kiosks run by Chinese traders abound all over the country, but local Timorese people run far fewer. The presence of these new Chinese traders has created a sense among some that Timor-Leste is being taken over by the Chinese.

Timor-Leste also faces a high rate of population growth, with current levels projected to double in seventeen years.[12] Currently, Timor-Leste has 1.2 million people; this is a very rapid increase from the population of 1999, which was only around 800,000 people.

Finally, there is the challenge of institutionalized, systemic corruption. One hot topic among activists and students is a protest movement against the national government regarding one specific law: No.1/2007, called Pensão Mensal Vitalícia dos Deputados e Outras Regalias (Lifetime Monthly Pension and Other Benefits for Members of Parliament). As its title suggests, the law creates a lifetime pension for former members of the government and parliament. Protesters call it a disaster for the future because it provides benefits only to certain people, not to the entire population—many of whom are still living on one or two dollars per day. The law was then revised by the National Parliament and repromulgated by the president in 2017. Nonetheless, a majority of the people continue to demand its total abolition. Similarly, without any public discussion, following a public protest through social media against a large payment of national advisers at the Office of Prime Minister—it was higher than the president's US$5,000 monthly salary—the government created a decree law aimed at securing and protecting advisers' assigned salary scale. Some international advisers earn more than US$10,000 monthly. This issue has profound implications for budget sustainability.

Foreign Aid and State-building

Foreign aid remains an important part of Timor-Leste's state-building efforts. Over the last sixty years, state-building has emerged as a key practice in international relations, generating different outcomes and fuelling debate amongst scholars, key actors, and practitioners. The central debates focuses on the relationship between state-building, democracy, peace, and security in weak states, as well as issues of power and national ownership—particularly in the context of traditional donors' agendas—and ultimately, sovereignty. The key schools of thought on state-building include the realist, liberal, post-structuralist, and post-colonial perspectives. Realists view external players' state-building actions as overriding the traditional principle of Westphalian sovereignty, while liberals see it as imperative for maintaining global democratic peace through the establishment of democratic institutions, the rule of law, human rights, and free-market economics.[13] Post-colonial analysts view externally led state-building as a form of colonialism because the arrangement is imposed upon the targeted people and is therefore considered "exploitative."[14]

Among different approaches to state-building, most traditional donors within the Organization of Economic Co-operation and Development (OECD) and its Development Assistance Committee (DAC) adopt the liberal approach as a guidance paradigm for their policies and programs.[15] There are, however, a growing number of scholars who criticize the liberal approach to state-building. Their critique focuses on the method by which proponents of state-building operate in the field.[16] For example, David Chandler outlines critiques of the liberal approach based on power relations, concepts and ideas, and critical consensuses about policy intervention.[17] Chandler criticizes the liberal approach to state-building, arguing that the international community lacks "transformative aspirations," demonstrates a lack of accountability, creates a sense of dependency on international supervision, and denies local capacity for self-government.[18] Oliver Richmond's critique focuses on the liberal approach to state-building, which he argues has a tendency to neglect local concerns about identity and culture.[19]

Julien Barbara offers an alternative approach to state-building. His critique of the neo-liberal approach is focused on the "constitution of free markets" as undermining the consolidation of effective and strong states, maintaining that it has been "ineffectual" in boosting the economic growth of states in need.[20] Inspired by the successful state-building approach of East Asian countries (notably Taiwan, South Korea, and Singapore), Barbara argues for a "developmental state" to address the development and economic challenges of countries in need. Such an approach would require the international community to acknowledge the failures of the neo-liberal approach to state-building. On the other hand, Marquette and Beswick argue for a state-building agenda with a need for building state institutions and ownership, as well as politics and legitimacy.[21] In this case, the authors stress the need to consider "whose" state-building agenda is implemented, not only "what" has been built. Thus the authors argue that the issues of ownership in the state-building process are of paramount importance.

I side with the authors who argue for the importance of considering the social, political, and cultural aspects of states in need as well as the importance of inclusiveness for state-building in order to create a sense of local ownership and legitimacy in the state-building process for post-conflict societies. In post-conflict states, while most of the state apparatus is either absent or weak, it is important to emphasize the agenda of building a strong and effective institutional framework to be able to provide service delivery for human development as well as economic rules and regulations to contribute to the stimulation of economic growth.

Case Study: China and State-building in Timor-Leste

The international community's engagement in state- and peacebuilding efforts in fragile or weak states is no longer dominated by the DAC countries such as the United States, Australia, the United Kingdom, and France. Instead the significant role played by the BRICS (Brazil, Russia, India, China, South Africa) countries and others such as Kuwait, Thailand, and South Korea, as non-traditional donors in these efforts has been on the rise.[22] A key new development-assistance actor is the People's Republic of China. China does not employ the term *state-building*, preferring to speak of non-intervention in other countries' internal affairs. A number of governments have welcomed this approach. In Timor-Leste, China's assistance is relatively small, but is highly visible through its focus on strategic infrastructural development, including major government buildings in Dili, such as the foreign ministry and presidential palace. Chinese assistance is on the rise through grant aid for public infrastructure projects, technical and economic co-operation through trade, and investment and military training programs. From 2002 to 2011, China contributed more than US$55 million to Timor-Leste.[23] In 2015, during Timorese president Taur Matan Ruak's state visit to China, the Chinese government pledged to provide another US$13 million.[24]

China's international engagement has increased since the end of the Cold War, and it has followed a different aid model than most traditional donors. Chinese assistance prioritizes physical infrastructure projects in an attempt to gain access to contracts and resources.[25] China argues that, as a non-traditional donor and a developing country itself, it has a distinctive approach and objective in providing its international assistance.

As stated in its foreign aid policy, Chinese assistance aims to promote recipient countries' self-development through a South-South co-operation framework of self-reliance, non-interference, non-conditionality, and equal and mutual benefit.[26] In recent years, some observers, such as Richmond and Tellidis, have noted that China has adjusted its engagement in a general sense towards embracing some aspects of the liberal peace approach to state-building, such as a desire for a stable bureaucratic state with control of the means of violence and varying degrees of capitalism.[27] Within the BRICS countries, India, Brazil, and South Africa have stressed democracy, the rule of law, human rights, and a robust civil society as elements of liberal peace while continuing to be critical of some aspects of the state-building approach advocated by the traditional donors, particularly the "interventionism" aspect.[28]

As China has gradually moved towards embracing some aspects of the liberal peace approach to state-building, however, its engagement has continued to emphasize the policy of "non-interference" in foreign relations. It traces this doctrine to the Five Principles of Peaceful Coexistence between China and India in the 1950s and the Ten Principles of the Bandung Conference adopted by twenty-nine Asian and African countries in 1955.[29] China argues that the main purpose of its policy of non-interference is to gain greater "understanding, trust, and co-operation for the betterment of all." China's stated non-interference policy in international engagement is parallel to the realist view of international state-building approaches in that it is critical of the interventionist approach, which tends to override the traditional principle of Westphalian sovereignty. This is in contrast to the liberal view of international state-building as imperative for maintaining global democratic peace.[30]

China's policy application, however, is subject to question. I argue that in reality China has not always followed its stated norms and principles. Increased Chinese aid to Timor-Leste serves as an example. Timorese leaders in both the current government and the opposition parties have welcomed Chinese aid as a pivotal part of the country's state-building process. In a speech during the inauguration of the Chinese-built defence ministry building in 2012, then prime minister Xanana Gusmão praised China's assistance in "the development and consolidation" of the state of Timor-Leste.[31] This statement was echoed by President Taur Matan Ruak during his visit to Macao in 2012: "Our relations with the People's Republic of China are excellent ... co-operation between our governments has been intense and fruitful."³²

China's donor relationship with Timor-Leste is indicative of power dynamics in the region, and it has broader relevance for debates about emerging power constellations in the region. The visit of US Secretary of State Hillary Clinton to Dili in 2012 sent a "clear and unmistakable message" about the United States' role and interest in the region.³³ China's growing presence in the region is significant to Australia, which has been regarded as the "big brother" or "viceroy" of the Pacific region.

At the signing of the diplomatic communiqué between China and Timor-Leste in 2002, the policy of non-interference was stressed. Timor-Leste has respected the One-China policy and been unswerving in its support of China in dealing with the issues of Taiwan and Tibet.³⁴ However, it is important to ask whether China's non-interference policy really applies to Timor-Leste. China has departed from its non-interference policy on multiple occasions. In the early years of the Indonesian occupation of East Timor, China provided support in the form of money and small arms to the Timorese resistance led by Fretilin.³⁵ During Timor-Leste's twenty-four-year independence struggle, the People's Republic of China was a strong supporter of Timorese independence. Diplomatically, China was the only permanent member of the UN Security Council to consistently vote against the Indonesian invasion and occupation of Timor-Leste. In this context, Timor-Leste regarded China as a "true friend" during difficult times.³⁶ China's support was a far cry from Western governments' acceptance of Indonesian rule over East Timor.

In 1999, China voted in favour of the UN Security Council resolution authorizing the UN peacekeeping mission to Timor-Leste—a gesture that many observers saw as an indication of China's active involvement in international affairs through multilateral arrangements. In the post-independence period, through its embassy in Timor-Leste, China has continued to be tacitly involved in Timorese affairs. In 2012, the state-run company China Nuclear Industry 22nd Construction Company (CNI22) allegedly provided financial support to one of the parties in the coalition government, the CNRT, during the election campaign. Chinese representatives gave political speeches at Timorese political party events, such as in 2001 during the launch of the Democratic Party and at a Fretilin event in 2006.

While China presents its non-interference policy as a way to gain trust from countries that it engages with, it is China's direct and indirect *interference*, through a soft-power approach, that has gained Timor-Leste's trust. Timor-Leste now considers China to be an important development partner. As Timor-Leste embarks on a pilot megaproject worth more than US$4 billion to build the ZEEMS special economic zone in Oecusse, the need for private-sector investment is crucial.[37] China has expressed interest in participating in the development of the zone.[38]

China's engagement in Timor-Leste's state-building and development has generated some discomfort among other donors. Most of these concerns address the form and location of Chinese engagement and the strategic position of Timor-Leste. On the strategic issue, a report from Norwegian Co-operation in Timor-Leste concluded that China's presence in Timor-Leste shows a desire for strategic competition for influence over Timor-Leste's natural resources and strategic position in the region.[39] Molnar also argues that Timor-Leste's natural resources and geopolitical position influenced donors' strategic considerations beyond their stated goals of providing assistance to Timor-Leste's state-building process.[40] So far, China has not publicly addressed the criticism from other donors regarding its engagement in Timor-Leste. China's confidence perhaps has been boosted by the government of Timor-Leste's high regard for China's role as a partner in the state-building and development process.

The China-Timor-Leste relationship offers rich insights into both state-building and new power relations in the region. China's stated approach to state-building leans towards the realist view, particularly the sovereignty aspect. Its stated policy of non-interference, however, has not always been reflected in practice. As Timor-Leste's state-building process continues to take shape, China's involvement will continue to be important. China may continue to argue the importance of its non-interference policy in dealing with the international community, but the actual application of such a policy is dependent upon pragmatic concerns, specifically its contemporary political and commercial interests.

Development and Reconciliation

Timor-Leste is still in the earliest stages of independence, and economic development is still in its infancy. There are certainly many lessons to be learned. The country must focus on achieving economic growth in parallel with inclusive human development. One concrete action would be to balance the allocation of the state budget and spend it sensibly and effectively across the country. The looming end of oil revenues makes the role of outside development partners crucial for the future. However, Timor-Leste should be mindful of its past, since much of the foreign aid it has received has been contingent on events and the bulk of foreign aid contributions have not gone towards Timor-Leste's development. While donor assistance remains important for Timor-Leste's future, this assistance must reflect the needs of Timor-Leste, rather than simply being spent in Timor-Leste.

As the country moves forward with its strategic development plan for 2030, both Timor-Leste and the international community should be aware that the role of development and state-building strategies are vital in considering reconciliation. Indonesia once justified its occupation of Timor-Leste as a contribution to the territory's economic development (*pembangunan*). Increasingly, Timor-Leste's post-independence government also relies on development strategies coming from outside the country.

The *Chega!* report addresses the years from 1974 to 1999, a period of violence that was the responsibility of another country, Indonesia, with the support of major Western powers. The internal political crisis of 2006, on the other hand, took place among "us"—that is, among Timorese. With international peacekeepers gone, Timorese leaders turned against each other and there was violence and massive displacement of people. Though the immediate crisis has been resolved, and displaced people have returned home, internal conflict and the memories of the 2006 crisis still represent a major challenge for both Timor-Leste and the international community.

Development and reconciliation should be closely linked; after all, there can be no proper development, let alone human development, without seriously addressing the wounds left behind from past atrocities. Those wounds are a barrier to development, to moving forward. Internal conflict also "un-develops" by destroying past progress. On a personal level, my parents' house was set on fire and burned down twice. In 1999 it was completely burned down by the pro-Indonesia militias. It was partly burned down again in 2006 during the internal crisis.

It is much more difficult to deal with issues when they involve our own people, our neighbours or our friends. I have discussed with my friends and family the importance of avoiding a victim mentality; we need to move on. We experienced crisis, but so what? This kind of philosophical thinking actually helps us to carry on living. Although we acknowledge that things have happened that were utterly unjust, there will be a time to deal with all these things. We as Timorese people have faced atrocities but life must continue!

Notes

1. United Nations Development Programme. *Human Development Report 1996*. New York: Oxford University Press, 1996.
2. La'o Hamutuk, *The La'o Hamutuk Bulletin* 11, no. 1–2 (2010), http://www.laohamutuk.org/Bulletin/2010/Feb/bulletinv11n1-2.html#donor (accessed 10 September 2015).
3. Ibid.
4. Geoffrey Robinson, *Timor-Leste 1999: Crimes against Humanity. A Report Commissioned by the United Nations Office of the High Commissioner for Human Rights*, revised version, published as volume 5 of *Chega! The Final Report of the Timor-Leste Commission for Reception, Truth and Reconciliation* (Jakarta: Gramedia, 2015).
5. International Crisis Group, "Stability at What Cost?" *Asia Report*, no. 246 (2013): http://www.crisisgroup.org/en/regions/asia/south-east-asia/timor-leste/246-timor-leste-stability-at-what-cost.aspx (accessed 15 December 2015).
6. Alastair McKechnie, *Managing Natural Resource Revenues: The Timor-Leste Petroleum Fund* (London: Overseas Development Institute, 2013).
7. Jennifer Drysdale, *Sustainable Development or Resource Cursed? An Exploration of Timor-Leste's Institutional Choices* (PhD diss., Australian National University, 2007), 82–83.
8. Education Policy and Data Center, *Timor-Leste: National Education Profile Update 2014*, http://www.epdc.org/sites/default/files/documents/EPDC%20NEP_Timor%20Leste.pdf (accessed 5 October 2015).
9. Government of Timor-Leste, "Guinea-Bissau: 'Thanks for the Support and Help of Timor-Leste,'" press release, 8 April 2014, http://timor-leste.gov.tl/?p=9942&lang=en (accessed 5 October 2015).
10. Fidelis Magalhaes, "Past, Present, and Future: Why the Past Matters," in *A New Era? Timor-Leste After the UN*, ed. Sue Ingram et al. (Acton: Australian National University Press, 2015), 10.
11. Oxfam Australia, "Childhood Malnutrition in Timor-Leste," 2015, https://www.oxfam.org.au/what-we-do/health/food-and-nutrition/childhood-malnutrition-in-timor-leste/ (accessed 20 July 2016).
12. United Nations Population Fund, "Timor-Leste, Democratic Republic of," 8 February 2010, http://countryoffice.unfpa.org/timor-leste/2009/11/02/1482/timor-leste_democratic_republic_of/ (accessed 5 October 2015).
13. David Craig and Douglas Porter, *Development beyond Neoliberalism? Governance, Poverty Reduction, and Political Economy* (New York: Routledge, 2006); Oliver

Richmond and Jason Franks, "The Emperor's New Clothes? Liberal Peace in East Timor," paper presented the Centre for Peace and Conflict Studies, University of St. Andrews, UK, 30 March 2007, http://www.academia.edu/1144446/The_emperors_new_clothes_Liberal_peace_in_East_Timor (accessed 20 April 2014).

14   Ralph Wilde, "Colonialism Redux? Territorial Administration by International Organizations, Colonial Echoes and the Legitimacy of the 'International,'" in *State-Building: Theory and Practice*, ed. Aidan Hehir and Neil Robinson (New York: Routledge, 2007).

15   Heather Marquette and Zoe Scott, "Marrying State-Building and Aid Policy: Civil Partnership or Irreconcilable Differences?" paper presented at the SGIR 7th Pan-European International Relations Conference, Stockholm, SE, 9–10 September 2010; Julien Barbara, "Rethinking Neo-Liberal State-Building: Building Post-Conflict Development States," *Development in Practice* 18, no. 3 (2008): 307–18.

16   Roland Paris, *At War's End: Building Peace after Civil Conflict* (Cambridge: Cambridge University Press, 2004); Barbara, "Rethinking Neo-Liberal State-Building"; David Chandler, "The Uncritical Critique of Liberal Peace," *Review of International Studies* 36, Special Issue S1 (Evaluating Global Orders) (2010): 137–55.

17   Chandler, "Uncritical Critique of Liberal Peace."

18   David Chandler, *Empire in Denial: The Politics of State-Building* (London: Pluto Press, 2006).

19   Oliver P. Richmond, *Peace in International Relations* (London: Routledge, 2008).

20   Barbara, "Rethinking Neo-Liberal State-Building."

21   Heather Marquette and Danielle Beswick, "State-Building, Security and Development: State Building as a New Development Paradigm?" *Third World Quarterly* 32, no. 10 (2011): 1703–14.

22   Oliver P. Richmond and Ioannis Tellidis, "The BRICS and International Peacebuilding and Statebuilding," *Norwegian Peacebuilding Resource Centre*, 1 February 2013, http://www.peacebuilding.no/Themes/Emerging-powers/Publications/The-BRICS-and-international-peacebuilding-and-statebuilding (accessed 10 July 2016).

23   Laurentina Barreto Soares, "Foreign Aid for State-Building: A Comparative Study between Australia and Chinese Aid Programs in Timor-Leste" (MA thesis, Ohio University, 2011).

24   "Xina apoiu miliaun 13 ba dezenvolvimentu Timor-Leste," *Timor-Post* (Dili), 15 September 2015.

25   Chaldeans Mensah, "China's Foray into Africa: Ideational Underpinnings and Geo-Economic Interests," *African Journal of Political Science and International Relations* 4, no. 3 (2010): 96–108.

26   "China's Foreign Aid," *Xinhuanet*, 21 April 2011, http://news.xinhuanet.com/english2010/china/2011-04/21/c_13839683_5.htm (accessed 10 July 2016).

27   Richmond and Tellidis, "The BRICS and International Peacebuilding and Statebuilding," 2.

28   Ibid.

29 Ministry of Foreign Affairs of the People's Republic of China, "China's Initiation of the Five Principles of Peaceful Co-Existence," 2014, http://www.fmprc.gov.cn/mfa_eng/ziliao_665539/3602_665543/3604_665547/t18053.shtml (accessed 15 May 2013).

30 Richmond and Tellidis, "The BRICS and International Peacebuilding and Statebuilding."

31 Government of Timor-Leste, "Address by His Excellency the Prime Minister and Minister of Defence and Security Kay Rala Xanana Gusmao at the Inauguration of the Building of the Defence and F-FDTL Headquarters," 3 April 2012, http://timor-leste.gov.tl/wp-content/uploads/2012/04/Inauguration-of-the-MD-and-F-FDTL-Headquarters-3.4.12.pdf (accessed 10 December 2015).

32 Helder Baja, "Timor Embraces China," *Macao Magazine*, http://macaomagazine.net/china/timor-embraces-china (accessed 10 December 2015).

33 "Hillary Clinton's First Visit to East Timor Sends 'Clear Message,' " *Australian* (Surry Hills), 6 September 2012, http://www.theaustralian.com.au/news/world/hillary-clinton-makes-first-visit-to-east-timor/story-e6frg6so-1226466468359 (accessed 10 July 2014).

34 Embassy of the People's Republic of China, "Bilateral Relations," http://tl.chineseembassy.org/eng/sbjx/ (accessed 10 December 2014).

35 Awet Tewelde Weldemichael, *Third World Colonialism and Strategies of Liberation: Eritrea and East Timor Compared* (Cambridge: Cambridge University Press, 2013); Loro Horta, "Timor-Leste: The Dragon's Newest Friend," *IRASEC Discussion Paper* 4, no. 18 (May 2009): 1–18.

36 "White Papers: China's Foreign Aid," *Xinhuanet*, 10 July 2014, http://news.xinhuanet.com/english/china/2014-07/10/c_133474011.htm (accessed 10 July 2014).

37 Government of Timor-Leste, "Guinea Bissau."

38 Antonio Sampaio, "Chineses Querem Comprar Todo o Projeto de Oecussi," 2015, *Platforma Macau*, http://www.plataformamacau.com/lusofonia/timor-leste/chineses-querem-comprar-todo-o-projeto-de-oecussi (accessed 15 January 2016).

39 Susan Soux et al., *Review of Development Cooperation in Timor-Leste: Final Report*, Norwegian Agency for Development Cooperation, October 2007, https://www.norad.no/globalassets/import-2162015-80434-am/www.norad.no-ny/filarkiv/vedlegg-til-publikasjoner/review-of-development-cooperation-in-timor-leste-.pdf (accessed 24 April 2014).

40 Andrea Katalin Molnar, *Timor-Leste: Politics, History, and Culture* (New York: Routledge, 2010).

7

Reconciliation, Church, and Peacebuilding

Jess Agustin

Surreal is the word that I always use when I describe my experiences in East Timor. It is a tiny country, a tiny territory, but it has everything, both the negative and the positive. It is surreal in the sense that Canadians can now meet with the heroes and heroines of the independence movement. It is hard to believe that this is true when the Canadian government said for many years that East Timor was a lost cause, unrealistic, an illusory dream. Yet here we are: there is a country called East Timor.

This chapter provides some context to understand the role of the Catholic Church in East Timor and in international support for East Timor. The church's role has been very complex, and it is full of paradoxes, tensions, and contradictions.

My aim is to capture and describe the tools, the strategies, and the means by which the church played its role in the Timorese struggle. It was an institution that was part of a broad-based social movement, but one that also interacted both with the state and state actors, and with civil society and the market. I illustrate with references to my own experiences coordinating East Timor work for the Canadian Catholic Organization for Development and Peace (henceforth Development and Peace), beginning in the 1980s.[1]

I came into Development and Peace totally ignorant of East Timor. Then, when Elaine Briere, founder of the East Timor Alert Network, came all the way from Vancouver to meet me in Montreal, she insisted that my first mission should be in East Timor. It was worse than Cambodia, she insisted. I thought then that this must be an exaggeration.

In the early 1980s only a couple of NGOs operated in East Timor. The country was isolated and foreigners were restricted. Development and Peace was among the first that set foot in East Timor. It was easy for me to enter the territory because I look Indonesian, but then later, on my third or fourth day in East Timor, I was followed by Indonesian agents. I tried to meet with Catholic bishop Carlos Ximenes Belo, who had just recently been appointed as apostolic administrator, but he refused to meet with me. Eventually on my last day, the late Bishop Ricardo, who was then the vicar general, met with me in an almost clandestine way. He apologized and told me that Bishop Belo suspected that I was an Indonesian intelligence agent. For about a couple of hours he narrated to me the horror of Indonesian military abuses and pleaded with me to spread the word to the world.

In Development and Peace, I am sometimes called Forrest Gump because every time I go to East Timor, something significant happens. During the first Bali bombing, I was there. When the pro-Indonesia militia launched their first attack in the Timorese capital of Dili in 1999, I arrived while they were having a blood ceremony in front of the governor's house, drinking the blood of a dog. Then they started attacking those former pro-integration figures who had betrayed them. I, along with Father Domingo, who had attempted to rescue some people, was almost killed by the militia. We witnessed the fact that the attack was not simply the work of a rogue militia with machetes and homemade guns, as was often depicted by Indonesian newspapers, but in fact the Indonesian military directing the Dili rampage while discreetly supplying heavy weapons later during the night. I was also there when General Wiranto came to sign the agreement on the cessation of violence. Bishops Belo and Basilio do Nascimiento asked me to be there. I felt that it was surreal to see Wiranto, who had so much blood on his hands, there in the bishop's house. The church, still quite innocent, wanted to sign an agreement for the cessation of violence, so we contacted experts on canon law. Immediately we were told, and advised Bishop Belo: "Don't sign it because you cannot enforce it if one of the parties violates the agreement."

7.1: Jess Agustin (right) with Bishop Carlos Belo, Dili, Timor-Leste. Photo courtesy of Jess Agustin.

East Timor is still in transition and the church is definitely still in transition, but when it comes to peace and reconciliation, Timor-Leste is much farther ahead compared to the Philippines or Indonesia. There was no truth and reconciliation in the Philippines after the end of the Marcos dictatorship and the same is true of post-Suharto Indonesia. There were some reparations, and some of the money stolen by the Marcos dictatorship was returned, but there was no recovery of the memory of exactly what happened during the period of martial law. No wonder members of the Marcos family are still in positions of power.

The best way to explain the church's delicate and even complex role in East Timor is to locate it within three wider circles: the institutional Catholic Church; pro-independence and pro-integration movements in East Timor; and finally the nexus of state, civil society, and market.

We can locate the Timorese Catholic Church in the wider institutional church, including the Vatican and the Indonesian Bishops' Conference (KWI). Bishop Belo, like Bishop Martinho da Costa Lopes before him, was an apostolic administrator. They were not bishops of East Timor in name, but only administrators of the diocese. Technically, Bishop Belo was the bishop of an obscure town in Italy called Lorium, and in Dili, he was an apostolic administrator on behalf of the pope, whose titles included Bishop of Dili. Part of the reason for this was to neutralize the KWI. A number of bishops then accepted as a fait accompli the Indonesia occupation of East Timor and the fact that the church in East Timor was part of the KWI. Due to the Vatican's decision to administer the East Timor diocese directly, the bishop in Dili would attend the KWI gatherings, but only as an observer.

During the struggle for independence the Timorese church was still rather feudal. Since they were isolated, many priests acted like they were lords. This is why in East Timor priests are called "Amo," meaning "my lord." Even with the reforms of Vatican II in the 1960s, priests remained dominant figures in East Timor. But gradually the Timorese church became an important part of the Timorese self-determination movement. It represented a space for dissent, a shield against human rights violations, and a voice for the people. Its role was not only to promote independence, but also to play a behind-the-scenes role to try to uphold the people's rights, not just in terms of being pro-integration or pro-independence, but also in the actual reconciliation process, to try to bring various people and leaders together. It played this role within the Timorese independence movement, seeking to reconcile its various factions, and later searching for a balance between reconciliation and justice. Just before the 1999 referendum, the church initiated an All-inclusive Intra-East Timorese Dialogue, followed by the Dare 1 and Dare 2 dialogue processes supported by the international community. Development and Peace was very much a part of this initiative to bring the pro-integration, pro-autonomy, and pro-independence groups together in a low-profile manner. To a certain extent, that process was succeeding until the sudden announcement that a referendum might take place, as it did in 1999.

It was the church and Bishop Belo who actually framed the whole discussion, saying that it was not simply about Indonesia occupying East Timor, with all the brutality the occupation entailed, but also a matter of offering the people a democratic option in the referendum. When Bishop Belo called for a referendum, the counter offer was for a gradual transition: releasing political prisoners, then establishing an autonomous government, and finally holding a referendum. With the downfall of Suharto, however, the whole process was accelerated.

The church had also been very much a part of Timorese social movements. There was a sense that after decades of isolation, Timorese were part of an international community. Bishop Belo articulated concerns over human rights in 1989 in a letter to the secretary-general of the United Nations. Timorese, including the Timorese church, were able to communicate with solidarity movements all over the world. There was an informal committee, mostly solidarity supporters within the international church, that operated very discreetly in Australia, in Canada, in Europe and elsewhere. We had our own lobbyist in Washington, DC, Arnold Kohen, who went on to be Bishop Belo's official biographer.[2]

The church was attempting a balancing act between the idea of Christendom, where the church is leading the people and very much part of the state, and the idea of the church as completely outside the secular world. There is a tension between the idea of the church as a revolutionary force (expressed in Latin American liberation theology), and the church as purely concerned with morals, uninvolved in politics, and exclusively religious. The Timorese church was able to sustain this balancing act during the Indonesian occupation. However, after the restoration of independence in 2002, and the emergence of a new and well-funded civil society, the church underwent a crisis of identity as it suddenly ceased to be the leading institution in the country.

Because I was seconded to work for Caritas Australia for two years, I was very much part of the reflection within the church as it tried to discover its proper role between being a servant church or a dominant institution, directing and leading the transition to a new country. What would be the role of the church in terms of the new constitution and the structure of the new government? There was a suggestion to create a council to advise the president, with the church as a permanent member of that council. Again the advice was that the church could not be part of the state, that it could not lead another strong movement as it had during the independence struggle. It should be a servant church, and the church should accompany civil society in the consolidation of democracy and peace and in building a just society, and in supporting the growing movement rather than being a principal institution promoting its own agenda. This was the view provided by Cardinal Orlando Quevedo when we invited him to share his experience from the Philippines, where the church had played a key role in the overthrow of the Marcos dictatorship and the subsequent transition to democracy.

A collection of Bishop Belo's speeches and lectures from the period right after the referendum outlines exactly what the church's role is, even today.[3] During the period of the restoration of independence, the Timorese church became more of a traditional church, pushing the new state not to remove Catholic elements from the education system. There was a push to ban abortion, and the church stood against reproductive health and family planning. Many people attributed the Timorese church's sudden decision to stress "moral" issues and to de-emphasize the social aspect to the pervasive conservative tendencies within the Catholic hierarchy in the Vatican. Development and Peace was a victim of that global shift: it was accused of being too progressive and it eventually had its funding cut by Stephen Harper's Conservative government, which affected its East Timor program.

The Timorese church's historic position within social movements affected its response to the *Chega!* report. In East Timor, there was a lukewarm reaction to the report. Right after the restoration of independence, Bishop Belo decided to resign as bishop of Dili. One reason was that he was very disappointed that the Vatican did not immediately open an apostolic nunciature, the Vatican equivalent of an embassy, in East Timor. (It decided instead that it would continue its representation in Jakarta.) It took a further nine to ten years for the Vatican to decide to establish an apostolic mission in East Timor. There was also a clear order from the Roman Curia of Pope Benedict XVI not to be involved in politics and to focus more on moral issues. Ironically, this provoked widespread distress within the church and among the Timorese population: the church was no longer speaking about issues of justice and peace at a time when political leaders were debating the socio-economic direction of the new country. When the church suddenly withdrew from social debates and became more concerned with selective moral issues, the people, especially women's groups, started to assert themselves. They were less afraid of the church hierarchy and they openly challenged the church's policies, particularly on the issue of women's rights. Timorese civil society's disappointment in the church's shift represents a tension on the part of the Timorese church as the country consolidates its democratic institutions and its people become more aware of their rights.

The Timorese church is highly influenced by the Vatican. Pope Francis's impact on the Catholic Church in general has tended to bring it back towards greater involvement in issues like poverty, corruption, inequality, and violence, and a greater engagement with movements for social change. Pope Francis's reform of the church will definitely have an impact in East Timor, creating a space for the local church to push more for the implementation of some of the *Chega!* recommendations. With Pope Francis at the helm, this is an excellent opportunity to follow up on truth and reconciliation in East Timor.

We should look at *Chega!* not so much as a report, but as the culmination of a process. The Timorese church played a leading role in peacebuilding over the last few decades by trying to create a culture of peace, especially among pro-Indonesian Timorese and the various political factions vying for power. It has been a long process, and it will take more time still. The violence that broke out in East Timor in 2006, creating many internally displaced people, is a heartbreaking reminder that peace is still fragile in this new country. East Timor still suffers from poverty and it is one of the world's most traumatized countries. The healing process takes time. They say that to be considered traumatized you have to experience at least three traumatic events. The Timorese have suffered many more than that. A healing process in which the church—itself also deeply wounded—can continue to play a key role, is still a pressing need. Creating a culture of peace, after all, is a significant part of the healing process.

Notes

1. On the work of Development and Peace in East Timor, see David Webster, "Canadian Catholics and the East Timor Struggle, 1975–99," *Historical Studies* 75 (2009): 63–82. On the role of the Timorese church under Indonesian rule, see Patrick A. Smythe, *"The Heaviest Blow": The Catholic Church and the East Timor Issue* (Münster, DE: LIT Verlag, 2004).

2. Arnold Kohen, *From the Place of the Dead: The Epic Struggles of Bishop Belo of East Timor* (New York: St. Martin's Press, 1999).

3. Carlos Filipe Ximenes Belo, *The Road to Freedom: A Collection of Speeches, Pastoral Letters, and Articles from 1997–2001* (Sydney: Caritas Australia, 2001).

8

Human Rights and Truth

FERNANDA BORGES

This chapter is the text of a speech by former Member of Parliament Fernanda Borges, delivered on the occasion of United Nations Human Rights Day, 2010. Borges was at the time a member of the Timorese National Parliament and president of Parliamentary Committee A, responsible for justice and constitutional issues.

I must begin by saying that through our struggle for Timorese independence, human rights have become an integral part of our identity.

As a people and a state we are remembered around the world as the small island that persistently fought for our rights to self-determination and to national sovereignty. This trademark was acquired through the sacrifice of blood and bones, by the persistent and creative ways in which we tried to awaken the world to the human rights violations taking place then, and by the insistence that international law establishing human rights, norms, standards, and principles established by the international community, is implemented to protect the East Timorese people's human rights.

As recorded magnificently in our CAVR *Chega!* report, history depicts the great suffering and aspiration of the people, our capacity to unite, and the international community's struggles and efforts to fulfill the universally recognized value system of human rights.

With our independence, it all culminated in the Timorese people achieving civic and political rights, what is sometimes referred to as "first generation rights." That alone is not enough. We must turn our human rights trademark into a real competitive advantage for the people and take positive action to achieve our social, economic, and cultural rights, or "second generation rights," so that the people are finally free from "fear and want." Free from fear because the Democratic Republic of Timor-Leste is also free from fear to provide access to justice for the people in national and international courts, and to ensure that the implementation of the rule of law is applied equally for all citizens. The people are free from fear because they can be certain that the state will fulfill its role to protect the people from gross human rights violations and hideous crimes against humanity. There can be certainty that accountability will ensure non-repetition of past atrocities.

Unfortunately for us, the "fear factor" is still with us as the state has not taken all the positive actions under the obligation to respect, fulfill, and protect human rights. We have all the international and national laws in place, but with little goodwill to implement them. The "fear factor" has pushed us to compromise on justice, and in some ways shy away from the very words *human rights* and from having a frank reflection on what the real situation is and its deep causes.

As chair of Committee A in parliament, I was often asked to justify the cost and financial sustainability in implementing a reparations program in Timor-Leste. I would like to take a little time to explain this concern, which has become a key factor in the postponement of the debate in the National Parliament for two very important human rights laws. They are the law that establishes an institution to continue to implement the recommendations of the CAVR *Chega!* report, and a reparations law.

First of all, promoting human rights should not be seen as a cost but an investment in the people's well-being and in the newly established state of Timor-Leste, founded on the principles of human rights and the rule of law. The state also has a moral and ethical obligation to provide assistance to victims, which cannot be measured in economic or monetary terms. Cost should be viewed from the perspective of the harm that these vulnerable victims will bear if we deny them the assistance they rightly deserve in accordance with the law.

Further, reparations are an investment because the finite number of vulnerable victims between the age group of thirty to sixty-five years old, to be determined through a registration process, will not grow in the future in terms of monetary burden to the state. In front-loading the costs of a reparations program now, we would effectively cap the costs to this finite group of vulnerable victims. This may save us a lot in service needs and financial support in the future.

Appropriate measures should be taken now to help vulnerable victims address the traumatic experiences of the past, and provide them with the confidence to be able to participate in the development process. This investment will also affect the next generation of East Timorese who are family members of these victims. If the individual vulnerable victims are provided with assistance, their children and their families will contribute to a healthier society. Naturally there will be more people capable of participating actively in the economy.

On the other hand, if we do not make this investment, studies also reveal that victims of violence remain traumatized and unable to work. Perpetrators used to violent behaviour can also reoffend if there is no accountability. The neglect of these groups of vulnerable victims may assist in the people losing confidence in the state to protect their human rights, which can then lead to further violence. In denying victims' rights to truth, justice, and reparations, the state is also not guaranteeing non-repetition of past atrocities. Economic sustainability will be better guaranteed if we can assist the victims to put the past behind them and help break down the poverty traps in order to chart a path to sustainable economic development based on people's rights.

If we are going to do justice to human rights in a post-conflict setting, it is important to acknowledge and understand that human rights cover all aspects of life, that they are indivisible and interdependent. In this sense, addressing poverty by meeting the United Nations Millennium Development Goals is important, because it is part of human rights. Our past success in achieving our human rights is really attributable to the total commitment, sacrifices, and risks that many brave people made. Our future success in implementing human rights will depend on a renewed total commitment from the state in the long-term interest of the nation and the well-being of the people.

There are great opportunities for Timor-Leste to deliver on human rights. The current state of the nation requires real concerted effort to promote and protect people's social, economic, and cultural rights in a holistic way. People's right to land ownership and security in property rights is a determining factor in economic development. To be able to make a real impact on development, we must double our efforts and budgetary resources for education, health, and agriculture. Human development and sustainable food security will go a long way in ensuring that people are freed from the poverty trap.

Finally, I am proud that Timor-Leste was successful in gaining a seat on the CEDAW (Convention on the Elimination of All Forms of Discrimination Against Women) committee and then in winning a seat at UN Women. We can certainly now speak up to stop discrimination at the international level. On a local level we must swiftly act to end the plague of domestic violence and child sexual violations and incest. The National Parliament will need to make proposals to strengthen the budget for the implementation of the domestic violence law.

9

Chega! for Us: Socializing a Living Document

MARIA MANUELA LEONG PEREIRA

This chapter is based on a spoken text by the director of ACbit (Chega! for Us Association), translated by Laurentina "mica" Barreto Soares.

The Asosiasaun *Chega!* Ba Ita (ACbit, the "*Chega!* for Us Association") aims to promote the values and principles that underlie the work of the Commission for Reception, Truth and Friendship (CAVR), including human rights, justice, and reconciliation. We are committed to bringing the lessons of the past to guide our decisions and choices as individuals and as a society, working towards the fulfilment of the promise for a better future for all.

ACbit has four major programs. These are to facilitate outreach, education, and policy debate on the CAVR findings and recommendations; to conduct innovative research and training using participatory methods; to carry out advocacy and community organizing on the implementation of the CAVR recommendations, particularly on gender justice; and to support victims in asserting their rights though access to assistance programs from the Ministry of Social Solidarity and other relevant institutions.

ACbit receives funding from international donors and the government of Timor-Leste. Current and past international donors are the United Nations Trust Fund (UNTF); the Dutch development organization HIVOS; and the Indonesia-based group Asia Justice and Rights (AJAR). We also receive funds from the Timor-Leste Ministry of Social Solidarity and the Fund for Civil Society Organisations of the Prime Minister's Office.

Our major task is the socialization and dissemination of the *Chega!* report. Since 2010, we have organized a school visit program to bring students to the *Chega!* exhibition site. To this end, we have facilitated about twenty-five to thirty students on each visit, which last about one hour. In this school visit program, apart from showing and explaining the *Chega!* report to students, we also organize small discussions and reflections to find out the students' understanding of the history of conflict in Timor-Leste and to what extent they are aware of the *Chega!* report and what they think about it.

We organize "*Chega! Ba Ita* mobile" programs to facilitate the socialization and dissemination of the *Chega!* report in the districts and some subdistricts. The target groups include students, youth, women, and the community in general. In the districts and subdistricts, the exhibitions normally remain about three to four days and attract many visitors.

In 2013, we organized and facilitated training programs for youth groups to become guides for the *Chega! Ba Ita* mobile activities in the districts and for them to learn and understand Timor-Leste's history and the impact of the conflict on their lives. Their feedback showed the training program was not entirely successful because the youth asked to be paid for their time spent guiding the exhibition. ACbit did not have enough financial capacity to address such issue and we considered it a failure. To fill the vacuum, staff from ACbit were and are the ones directly in charge of all the exhibitions so far. There might be a possibility to resume the training program in the future but it depends on the availability of funds.

With the help from the ICTJ (International Center for Transitional Justice), we developed a simple and short version of the *Chega!* report to help readers reach a quick understanding of the content. This short version was completed, printed, and distributed in 2013 to all the secondary schools in Timor-Leste. We then worked together with school teachers and developed a guide to help them educate their students about Timor-Leste's history and conflict.

For us, socialization is important. The report belongs to everyone in Timor-Leste. Since 2010, we have been campaigning on the findings and recommendations of the CAVR using the slogan, "*Chega!* Ba Ita," or *Chega!* For Us, the Timorese people. This refers to our deep conviction that the people of Timor-Leste have had enough of conflict and injustice, and need to genuinely implement the recommendations of the truth commission to ensure that these violations are never repeated. The saying "*Chega!* Ba Ita" also underlines our belief that the CAVR report was written based on the experiences and voices of the people, for the people. It is not a document that should be shelved and forgotten. It is a living document to be understood, debated, and reinvented for generations to come.

Socializing and disseminating the *Chega!* report was supposed to be the responsibility of the Post-CAVR Technical Secretariat because that is part of their mandate and they have funds for that activity. In ACbit, our advocacy department is in charge of the socialization and dissemination of the *Chega!* report. Our primary target groups for this activity are the secondary and university students, community groups, and the members of victims' associations. Whenever we organize exhibitions on the *Chega!* report, we always invite these target groups to visit the site and we hold discussions and reflection sessions with them after the visit.

In Dili alone, under the school visit program, we have organized thirteen school visits for secondary-school students, one for university students, and nine for youth groups. In total, we have helped 1,792 students and youth (931 girls and 861 boys) to visit the exhibition and attend discussion and reflection sessions. We brought in visitors from all the thirteen districts in Timor-Leste. The school visit program started in 2011, but the above-mentioned statistic only covers visits from 2013–15.

Our biggest constraint or obstacle is a lack of human resources and financial capacity. We are not able to cover all the subdistricts, *sucos* (villages), and *aldeias* (hamlets) due to inadequate funding and a shortage of human resources. Demands for exhibitions and opportunities to learn about Timor-Leste's history are quite high, but people do not take the initiative to voluntarily visit the site unless we organize the visit for them and provide transportation to and from the location. In the districts, our problem is the limited means of transportation to bring the exhibition materials to districts, subdistricts, and *sucos*.

In terms of information and people's awareness about the *Chega!* report, we observe that so far, many people, especially the younger generations, do not have good knowledge about the history of conflict in Timor-Leste. And many people are still not aware of the CAVR's *Chega!* report. It is ACbit's mission to change that, to bring the report and the people together.

SECTION II

Memory, Truth-seeking, and the 1965 Mass Killings in Indonesia

Memory, Truth-seeking, and the 1965 Mass Killings in Indonesia

Out of the shadows, into the light of public debate: this is a call that applies as much to Indonesia as it does to Timor-Leste. The chapters above speak of campaigns for truth and reconciliation that spill over Timorese borders into the country's former colonial ruler, Indonesia. Although there was an innovative bilateral truth Commission on Truth and Friendship (CTF) between the two countries, it has done little to change the general climate in Indonesia of denial or indifference towards the legacy of mass atrocities in Timor-Leste.

Indonesia grapples with its own troubled past, too. It is far from the only country that has experienced a dictatorship implicated in sustained human rights violations. But Indonesia's New Order regime was both especially long-lived (it lasted thirty-two years) and especially bloody in its path to power. In 1965, left-wing army officers kidnapped some of the country's top generals. The surviving army command struck back quickly and took control of the state apparatus of power. Blaming the large Indonesian Communist Party (Partai Komunis Indonesia, or PKI), the army launched a wave of mass killings that engulfed most of the country. The death toll is impossible to estimate: the army placed the number at 78,500, while other estimates run as high as 2 million. Another million left-leaning Indonesians faced detention and in some cases long prison terms. The army's net was cast far beyond the PKI's members to encompass numerous popular movements; the anti-communist violence also aimed to stamp out potential challengers to army power and to depoliticize what was then a highly mobilized Indonesian society.

The army blamed the PKI for trying to stage a coup. Virulent images of PKI savagery flared up as mass killings went on, and they were ritually repeated in government accounts and in a film shown annually to Indonesian students. And yet, the response to the mass killings that followed the attempted coup and counter-coup was a state command to the people: forget. A five-volume official history of Indonesia gave the killings one sentence. Otherwise the killings were not discussed, and debate on their meaning and consequences was forbidden. National memory was to be erased, the trauma of national suffering denied.

When the "1965 events" did merit discussion, the New Order insisted on the absolute truth of its own narrative. It blamed the now-banned PKI, even while using its memory as a means of controlling dissent, by labelling dissenters from the government agenda as communists. Anti-communism was a key basis of legitimacy for the New Order, which recalled 1965 only to bolster its self-proclaimed role as the nation's saviour in the face of communist subversion. The death of six generals formed the central memory of these events. The many deaths of civilians that followed were eliminated from the record.

In 1998, the New Order finally collapsed amidst an economic crisis and popular pro-democracy protests. President Suharto was out after three decades in power. His vice president succeeded him and lost the subsequent general election. Indonesia has had four democratically elected presidents since then: liberal Muslim teacher Adburrahman Wahid; Megawati Sukarnoputri, daughter of the founding president and a former opponent of Suharto; general-turned-reformer Susilo Bambang Yudhoyono; and Joko Widodo, a popular non-ideological figure who rode his record of competent administration as mayor of Solo and then Jakarta into the presidency. Jokowi, as he is known, is the first president not linked to the old elite, and his accession to the presidency seemed to augur a more open reflection on the past. Yet, like its predecessors, the Jokowi presidency has done little to change the government's reluctance to discuss the 1965 events. The New Order's official narrative has loosened, but it has not given up its grip as the dominant view in government circles.

Chapter 10 provides an exploration of clashing historical narratives. It pictures the official narrative as a wall that blocks light and words, a hegemonic view of the past that denies other views. At the same time, it describes efforts of non-government voices half a century later to break through that wall. Victims' groups, friends and families of those who died or suffered in the 1960s and after, historians and other academics, non-governmental organizations dedicated to supporting victims and telling their stories—all are challengers to the official narrative. Two historical narratives—unequal but nevertheless in contention—emerge from this picture, with the non-government narrative seeking to break silences, speak through the wall, and start, perhaps, to make it crumble.

In this account the role of civil society is clear. There have been calls for a truth commission, amongst other calls for truth-seeking and truth-telling about the past. A new law authorizing a truth commission even passed in 2004, but the government soon dropped the plan over objections from civil-society organizations. The voices calling for truth emerge here in an adversarial relationship to the apparatus of state power, which still prefers to forget the violent past. We can consider the period since the New Order's fall in 1998, with the emergence of civil-society voices challenging the silence, as a pre–truth commission period: these are calls from outside government for truth-seeking. Whether they will succeed or not remains to be seen.

The government's reluctance to debate the past has its border-crossing counterpart in the reluctance of other governments to reveal their own role in the 1965 coups and killings. Suharto and the other army commanders acted for their own reasons, but they did not act in isolation. They blamed Communist China, a country whose role in the 1965 events remains unclear. They were encouraged to act—and to kill—by US officials keen to see communism snuffed out in Indonesia as they waged a full-scale war in Vietnam. Other Western governments also lined up to encourage the army to overthrow President Sukarno and eradicate the PKI. It is impossible to fully understand what happened in 1965 without also looking at the global setting and the actions of major governments outside Indonesia.

This international dimension is discussed in chapter 11, which concentrates on the United States and China and considers what an eventual truth commission might look like. An effective commission would have to go beyond Indonesia's borders. There is a precedent in the joint Indonesian-Timorese CTF. There is precedent for opening archives in the United States to truth commissions in Central America. Just as the events of 1965 were in part international, so, too, must a truth commission be, with archives opened in several countries.

Continued silence, these chapters argue, extends the violence committed in 1965 and prevents Indonesian society from reconciling with its violent past. Forgetting has not brought healing: remembering might. Chapter 12's presentation of poignant writing by one of the victims of 1965 personalizes these issues through one man's experience, a story not previously published. It ends abruptly, in rupture. The 1965 coup also presents itself as rupture, followed by imposed forgetting. It is to a closer look at that rupture that we now turn.

10

Cracks in the Wall: Indonesia and Narratives of the 1965 Mass Violence

BASKARA T. WARDAYA

If we were flowers
You were the wall
But in the wall we have planted seeds
One day we will grow together
With the conviction: you have to crumble
In our conviction
Everywhere tyranny has to crumble

—Wiji Thukul, "Bunga dan Tembok" (Flower and Wall)[1]

When, in the early hours of 1 October 1965, six top Indonesian generals were abducted and killed in the capital city of Jakarta, most Indonesians were taken by surprise. Of course, the events did not come out of the blue.[2] But thanks to the scarcity of media and the censorship that was soon imposed, it was difficult for the general public to monitor developments from one moment to the other. Only later did they learn that in addition to the generals who were violently murdered, a lieutenant was also killed, along with the daughter of one of the generals. Three of the generals were killed in their homes, while the other three were still alive when they were brought to the southern outskirts of the capital before eventually also being killed. Their bodies were then dumped in an unused well in a village called Lubang Buaya, not far from Jakarta.

As it was not immediately clear who actually masterminded these bloody events, a variety of information, rumours, and speculation circulated in the first days following the violence. One group, which called itself the September 30th Movement, claimed responsibility, declaring that its main intention was to save President Sukarno from a government takeover that they believed was about to be launched by a council of generals in the Indonesian National Army (TNI).[3] The September 30th Movement's main members were three army officers—Lieutenant Colonel Untung, Colonel Abdul Latief, and Brigadier General Soepardjo—but others may have been directly or indirectly involved, including the top leaders—but not the rank-and-file members—of the Indonesian Communist Party (PKI).

Before it was clear who was responsible for these killings, a group of army officers under the control of Major General Suharto—who was then the commander of the Indonesian army's Strategic Command—declared that the PKI, the army's political archrival, was the mastermind of the bloody events. Suharto and his group then waged a propaganda campaign saying that the PKI had not only plotted the kidnapping and killing, but also planned to launch a *coup d'état* and abandon the reigning political ideology of Pancasila (or Five Principles) in favour of "godless" communism. The propaganda campaign also spread the rumour that women members of the PKI mutilated the bodies of the generals while dancing erotically around their dead bodies.

Though it was at best half true, the campaign was effective in spreading anti-communist sentiment among Indonesians, especially on the islands of Java, Bali, and Sumatra (particularly North Sumatra). Under the leadership of Lieutenant General Sarwo Edhi Wibowo, of the army's Special Forces Command (then known as RPKAD, now Kopassus), military units were dispatched from Jakarta to other parts of Java. Their goal was to transform anti-communist sentiment into collective violence against those accused of being members of the PKI or of being communist sympathizers. Under the provocation and coordination of army units, civilian groups apprehended, arrested, tortured, and killed those who were thought to have played a role in the killings of the generals in Jakarta—although most of them never personally set foot in the capital city.

The mass violence against alleged communists started in Central Java around the third week of October 1965. In November it spread to East Java, and in December similar violence took place on the island of Bali.[4] The violence also occurred on a smaller scale in other parts of the country, continuing until 1968. In the end, it is estimated that somewhere between 50,000 and 1 million civilians were killed in the violence, mostly in the last three months of 1965. Many more were tortured, imprisoned, exiled, and discriminated against.

Beginning in early 1966, a phased takeover of national leadership took place in Jakarta, in which the left-leaning President Sukarno was gradually pushed from power. Slowly but surely he was replaced by none other than General Suharto. Suharto gave himself the responsibility not only of maintaining order, but of presiding over political matters as well. To this end, he made himself acting president and then, in 1967, president.

Suharto's ascension to power was soon followed by militaristic and authoritarian-style government. Moreover, Suharto's government implemented policies favourable to foreign investment. During Suharto's presidency, many major Western corporations did business in Indonesia, exploiting the country's rich natural resources and favourable market potential as one of the most populated nations on earth. Suharto would rule Indonesia for the next three decades, before he himself was pushed out of power in 1998 in the midst of social, economic, and political upheaval.

Viewed in a broader context, the gory events of 1 October 1965, and the mass violence that took place afterwards, were not simply a matter of crime and punishment. Realizing that the mass violence against suspected communists did not only involve mass killings but also torture, incarceration, destruction of property, exile, and even the revocation of citizenship, it was clear that the violence was more than a spontaneous act of revenge, as was often claimed by the Suharto government.

Despite common claims, especially in the West, that the violence was part of the Indonesian custom of "running amok," it was clear that the violence was actually carried out in stages, each of which involving planning, coordination, and control, especially by the army's Special Forces Command.[5] As historian John Roosa writes, "the typical pattern was for the victims to be detained first, taken out at night, trucked to an isolated spot in the countryside, shot, stabbed or bludgeoned to death, and then left in unmarked mass graves or dumped in a river. ... Cold-blooded executions, not frenzied mob attacks, accounted for most of the deaths."[6] Such a pattern in no way indicated that the acts of killing and torture were simply expression of spontaneous traditional customs.

Douglas Kammen and Kate McGregor argue that attacks on the PKI were only the first stage of a plan to reorganize Indonesian society from the people-oriented and anti-foreign-investment regime of Sukarno to an elite-oriented society with close ties to Western business interests. In their words, the mass violence that spanned from the second half of 1965 to the end of 1968 was a "counter-revolution" that aimed "to curtail the mass mobilization and popular participation unleashed by the national revolution; to destroy the social bases of Sukarno's left-leaning political system, called Guided Democracy; and to establish a new pro-Western military authoritarian regime."[7]

In a still broader context, the 1965 violence in Indonesia had strong international dimensions. Bradley Simpson, for instance, demonstrates that, more than just national political upheaval, the 1965 mass killings in Indonesia and their aftermath "were a form of efficacious terror, an indispensable prerequisite to the overthrow of Sukarno, to Indonesia's reintegration into the regional political economy and international system, and to the ascendance of a modernizing military regime." In Simpson's words "the mass violence against the Indonesian Left ... had a political and economic logic apparent to officials in London, Washington, Tokyo, Kuala Lumpur, Moscow and elsewhere."[8]

The Narratives

Despite the complexities of the events of 1965 and what followed afterwards, the Suharto government's official narrative was rather simplistic and self-serving. The government essentially said that the PKI solely masterminded the generals' abduction and killing on 1 October 1965 and planned to change the state's ideology from Pancasila to communism. As a result, this narrative implies, the PKI deserved the harshest punishment possible. It also implies that any harsh measures taken against suspected communists in the wake of the 1965 events were justified, even necessary.

With regard to the massacres that took place after the killing of the generals in Jakarta, the government simply stated that they were part of "spontaneous" acts of revenge by patriotic Indonesians against the

Communist Party. In other words, the government's narrative suggested that the mass killings were not coordinated but were necessary in order to save the country from the nefarious forces of communism.

Throughout its reign, the Suharto government also tried to perpetuate the notion that the PKI remained the main danger to the nation. Because of this perceived danger people were asked to be vigilant, regardless of the fact that the Communist Party had been annihilated. But the alleged threat was continuously reiterated as if the PKI had returned to life to haunt and influence the people. The Suharto government then used every method available to reproduce this notion, be it through monuments, rumours, radio and television programs, names of public spaces, propaganda films or books[9]—all with the intention of supporting the official narrative of the 1965 events and to justify the authoritarian rule of President Suharto and his supporters.

One of the propaganda films used by the Suharto government to promote its version of the 1965 events was a docudrama called *Penumpasan Pengkhianatan G30S/PKI* (or *Suppression of the Treacherous Plot of the September 30th Movement/the PKI*). Produced in 1984, the film portrayed in visual form the official narrative that the PKI was indeed behind the brutal abduction and murders of the generals in the early hours of 1 October 1965. It also showed Sukarno as an unreliable as president because of his dubious attitudes toward the PKI. Beginning in 1985, students were required to see the film every year on 30 September; it was also shown on national television.

Meanwhile, the official narrative was enshrined in a 1967 book by government historian Nugroho Notosusanto called *40 Hari Kegagalan "G-30-S" 1 Oktober–10 November* (*The 40-Day Debacle of the September 30th Movement from 1 October–10 November 10*). Another official book was called *Gerakan 30 September: Pemberontakan Partai Komunis Indonesia: Latar Belakang, Aksi, dan Penumpasannya* (*The September 30th Movement: The Attempted Coup of the Indonesian Communist Party: Its Background, Actions and Eradication*).[10] It was published by Indonesia's State Secretariat as late as 1994, and was widely known as *buku putih* (the white book) pertaining to the official (read "true") history of the 1965 events.[11] In sum, these books, official proclamations, and repeated film screenings created an official narrative—a "wall," if you will—bolstering the Suharto government.

The Wall of Political Taboo

Under the rule of President Suharto and his self-proclaimed New Order government (1966–98) the official narrative of the 1965 events was closely guarded. The production and interpretation of the history of this period were backed by the Indonesian military.[12] Gaining access to the relevant military documents was difficult if not impossible. At the same time, it was also difficult to ask potential informants to share their knowledge or experiences about 1965 for concerns of personal safety.[13] Any criticism of the official narrative was met with pressure either from the government or government supporters. Any open and critical public discourse on the period became a political taboo. As Mary Zurbuchen puts it, "divergent perspectives, controversial events, and critical voices were not allowed to compete alongside the official record."[14] Like an impenetrable wall, this well-guarded taboo stood firm. In the midst of such a situation it was almost impossible for Indonesians, and even foreigners, to talk critically about the violence of 1965–68.[15]

As reflected in the title of the propaganda film mentioned above, the government insisted that people mentioning the term *G30S* (the September 30th Movement) add the suffix *PKI*. This was considered an important aspect of strengthening the claim that the PKI was the sole mastermind of the abduction and killing of the generals on 1 October 1965—and therefore deserved harsh punishment.

Under Suharto any discussion of the 1965 events that deviated from the official narrative was either banned or discouraged. These included victims' and witnesses' testimonies, as well as any critical scholarly accounts. Among the latter was a 162-page paper written by Cornell University professors Benedict Anderson, Ruth McVey, and Frederick Bunnell, and published under the title *A Preliminary Analysis of the October 1, 1965 Coup in Indonesia* (also known as the "Cornell Paper").[16] In the wake of its publication, Anderson was banned from entering the country for twenty-six years. During the same period, any forum intended to publicly discuss the 1965–66 events was prevented from forming.

Meanwhile, the manufactured fear of *bahaya laten komunis* (the "ever-present danger of communism") was reproduced and circulated among the Indonesian population. This was done by stigmatizing former political prisoners; for example, the government placed special identifying codes on the identity cards of people who were taken prisoner in 1965. Such measures, in turn, made it difficult for these former individuals to live as regular citizens or ordinary members of society.

Many questions about the 1965 events have gone unanswered. These include questions about General Suharto's true role in these events, especially in the planning of the events of 1 October 1965 and in the purging of its key organizers; the roles played by foreign business interests; and the fact that many non-communists were also subjected to violence by the army and its civilian supporters.

The Fall of the Wall?

All this began to change when, in 1998, President Suharto was forced out of power in disgrace. The Asian economic crisis of 1997 was followed by economic instability in Indonesia and the onset of socio-political upheavals. Widespread student demonstrations against Suharto's authoritarian rule ensued. As a result, in May 1998 the president was forced to resign. He was succeeded by his vice president, B. J. Habibie, who served as acting president until 1999.

Under the Habibie transitional government, the official narratives of the 1965 events appeared to tremble and break. As authoritarian-style government was succeeded by a more open-minded presidency, the public, as well as academics and former political prisoners, began to talk openly about the events of 1965 and what followed. As Mary Zurbuchen puts it, during this period "a flood of relief and euphoria inundated the landscape of public awareness."[17]

The compulsory annual screenings of *Penumpasan* stopped in 1998.[18] In 2001 then president Abdurrachman Wahid (1999–2001)—on behalf of his fellow-members of the Muslim organization Nahdlatul Ulama—apologized for the organization's involvement in the 1965 violence. In 2004 a law regarding the formation of a truth and reconciliation commission (which went under the title Undang-undang Komisi Kebenaran dan Rekonsiliasi) was enacted by then president Megawati Sukarnoputri (2001–04), the daughter of the first Indonesian president, Sukarno. A growing number of people—especially among academics and human rights activists—began to openly speak of the G30S without adding *PKI*.

Non-governmental organizations were established to address the 1965 events, including demands for truth-seeking and truth-telling initiatives and the rehabilitation of wrongly accused political prisoners. Grassroots initiatives regarding truth and reconciliation were introduced. In 2005, for instance, in the town of Surakarta (Solo), Central Java, one initiative began promoting the idea of reconciliation among survivors of the 1965 events. Every once in a while members of these groups gather together to hold a seminar, a workshop, or a film screening. The main purpose of these NGOs is to connect the survivors while promoting reconciliation at the local level.

To use and to underline such momentum in the post-Suharto period, a conference on 1965 and related issues was held at the University of California, Los Angeles, in April 2001. The conference was intended "to pursue research interests in how the past is being revisited and re-interpreted in the Indonesian present."[19] One of the questions being addressed during the conference was: "Why is it ... that we have seen in Indonesia since 1998 so few thorough investigations, commissions, trials, textbooks overhauls, rehabilitation, or other examples of 'getting to the bottom of' any one of the host of dimly understood incidents *(peristiwa)* that so many believe to have taken place?"[20]

A similar conference took place at the National University of Singapore in 2009. Viewing the mass violence that started in 1965, the aim of the conference, according to its organizers, was to further understand "the counter-revolutionary violence in Indonesia between 1965 and 1968." The conference was also aimed at understanding "the broad contours of the attack and the regional peculiarities of the violence" in a broader context.[21]

The Wall Re-erected

In spite of the progress outlined above, the once hegemonic anti-communist interpretation of the 1965 events gradually returned. In the early 2000s, as initiatives for dealing with Indonesia's legacy of violence were taking shape, so, too, were countermeasures aimed at discouraging people from talking about these issues. Rumours that communism was re-emerging began to be spread among the people. Public discussions on 1965 began to be discouraged or simply attacked. In other words, the anti-communist "wall" was being re-erected, and as a result the political taboo on talking about 1965 slowly returned.

Although they were heads of state, the country's presidents had only very limited political space (and will) to change this situation. President Wahid's apology to the victims of 1965 violence, for instance, was not widely supported by fellow members of the Nahdlatul Ulama organization, and it was generally ignored. To the surprise of many, in 2006 the law regarding the formation of a truth and reconciliation commission was annulled, less than two years after it had been enacted by President Megawati. In the same year, the Indonesian government decided that in all history textbooks the suffix *PKI* would once again be added to the term *G30S*.[22] Any textbooks that did not respect this rule were banned. Officials of district attorney's office in many cities burned the books in public. One such event took place in the town on Depok, just outside Jakarta. It was witnessed by the town's mayor, who was also a former State Minister of Research and Technology.[23]

In 2012 the government-sanctioned Commission on Human Rights (Komisi Nasional Hak Asasi Manusia, Komnas-HAM) presented a report—based on three years of research—to the government: it was simply ignored and has never been followed up. Earlier that year, there were reports that President Susilo Bambang Yudhoyono (2004–14) would apologize to the victims of the mass violence, but the apology never materialized. The was in part because of pressures from politicians and members of anti-communist groups.[24] But at the same time it was also due to the fact that President Yudhoyono himself is married to the daughter of the late Sarwo Edhi Wibowo, who was—as mentioned above—the commander of the army's Special Forces Command, which led the anti-communist purge in 1965 and afterwards.[25] Any apology, or any serious efforts to look into the 1965 violence, it was feared, might implicate Yudoyono's own late father-in-law. As a result, no serious action was taken. This situation continued until the very last day of President Yudhoyono's government in October 2014.

Cracks in the Wall

With the accession, in October 2014, of President Joko "Jokowi" Widodo, the Indonesian government's attitude to 1965 began to change. During the election campaign, Widodo promised that finding solutions to past human rights abuses would be one of his priorities if he were elected president. When he was indeed elected president, and as his government was relatively more accommodating to the wishes of the people, there were signs that the president wanted to be more open in discussing the 1965 issues and looking for a lasting solution. As *Time* magazine noted, "President Joko Widodo, the first leader of Indonesia to have no ties to the military or political elite, has repeatedly expressed his commitment to settling past human-rights violations, including the 1965–66 mass killings."[26] In May of 2015, Widodo's attorney general announced a government-backed reconciliation committee with the task of dealing with the 1965 mass violence along with other past human rights abuses, though this has not yet been formed.[27] There were also reports that the president would apologize to the victims of past human rights violations and their families.[28] In his state address to members of parliament on 14 August 2015, the president repeated his intention to find solutions to lingering human rights issues related to the 1965 anti-communist pogroms.[29]

Meanwhile, forces opposed to any reckoning with the 1965 events remain influential.[30] Leaders of certain military and civilian (especially religious) groups have continued to argued that the PKI had truly been guilty of a coup attempt, and that any form of apology to the 1965 victims would be seen as a call for the return of communism in Indonesia. Indeed, one minister in the president's own cabinet—a retired army general—declared that it was not proper for the government to offer an apology for the suppression of the PKI.[31] When the International People's Tribunal was held in The Hague in November 2015, a number of Indonesian government officials were critical. Some forums and events called to discuss 1965 were also attacked, including one in West Sumatra on 22 February 2015 and another in Solo, Central Java, two days later. In October 2015, in the midst of uncertainty over government pressures and self-imposed censorship, panels on 1965 at the Ubud Writers and Readers Festival in Bali were cancelled.[32] In February 2016 a forum at Gadjah Mada University in Yogyakarta, at which a guest lecturer from the Netherlands was going to talk about 1965, was also cancelled because of pressure from Indonesia's national intelligence body.[33]

Yet despite the strong opposition, numerous initiatives to address the 1965 events continued at the grassroots level. While some public forums were disrupted, others were held without any difficulty. In Central Java, for example, a number of government officials held dialogues with 1965 survivors. In Central Sulawesi, a city mayor publicly apologized to the victims of the 1965 mass violence residing in his jurisdiction. In East Nusa Tenggara, church groups encouraged former victims to speak up and tell their stories.[34] Through initiatives like Komnas-HAM and the Witness and Victims Protection Body, the Indonesian government provides health services to the victims of the 1965 violence. The Ministry of Culture and Human Development even provides funds for income-generating skills training to survivors and their families.

When, in November 2015, some young human rights activists held an event called Museum Bergerak (Museum in Motion), at which they displayed artefacts belonging to the survivors of the 1965 violence, the event went ahead undisturbed.[35] In the same month a choir group consisting of women survivors successfully performed Sukarno-era patriotic songs at the opening of an international arts festival in the city of Yogyakarta. Around the same time, at the state-run Gadjah Mada University, academic forums on 1965 convened, again without any interference. In early December 2015, a number of young Indonesian artists held a major arts exhibition with the 1965 events as its main theme in a prominent cultural centre in Jakarta. Despite some initial worries that it was going to be the target of protests, the exhibition received positive public reaction and media coverage.[36] Meanwhile, books that challenge the New Order government's official story can now be published, distributed, and discussed freely.[37]

Reasons to doubt that Indonesia will ever have the courage to seriously address the mass violence of 1965 abound. At the same time there are also many reasons for optimism. Despite political bickering among members of the political elite in Jakarta, at the grassroots initiatives—especially those aimed at restoring survivors' place as inseparable members of Indonesian society—are flourishing. Like small cracks in the wall of political taboo, local and national initiatives to tackle the issues of 1965 are spreading.

Closing Note

As expressed in the poem quoted at the beginning of this chapter, people have been planting seeds of hope. They hope to see them grow in the wall of tyranny established by the Suharto government. "One day we will grow together," the poet Thukul wrote. "Everywhere tyranny has to crumble."[38] Whether or not the cracks in the wall of 1965 mass violence will someday make the wall crumble, we do not know. But we can always hope. Indeed, we share the conviction that everywhere tyranny has to crumble.

Notes

1. This is a quote from a poem called *"Bunga dan Tembok"* (Flower and Wall), written by anti-Suharto poet-activist Paulus Wiji Thukul during the final years of President Suharto's rule. Thukul later mysteriously disappeared. See "Puisi-puisi Wiji Thukul," *Kumpulan Fiksi* (blog), 3 September 2011, https://kumpulanfiksi.wordpress.com/2011/09/03/puisi-puisi-wiji-thukul/ (accessed 26 January 2016).

2. Douglas Kammen and Kate McGregor, eds., *The Contours of Mass Violence in Indonesia, 1965-68* (Singapore: National University of Singapore Press, 2012), 13.

3. Asvi Warman Adam, *Seabad Kontroversi Sejarah [The Age of Historical Controversy]* (Yogyakarta, ID: Ombak, 2007), 65–66.

4. Robert Cribb, ed., *The Indonesian Killings of 1965-1966: Studies from Java and Bali* (Melbourne, AU: Centre of Southeast Asian Studies, Monash University, 1990). See also Geoffrey Robinson, *The Dark Side of Paradise: Political Violence in Bali* (Ithaca, NY: Cornell University Press, 1995).

5. Kammen and McGregor, *Contours of Mass Violence*, 7.

6. John Roosa, "The September 30th Movement: The Aporias of the Official Narratives," in ibid., 47.

7. Ibid., 4.

8. Bradley Simpson, "International Dimension of the 1965–68 Violence in Indonesia," in ibid., 51. See also Bradley R. Simpson, *Economists with Guns: Authoritarian Development and U.S.-Indonesian Relations, 1960-1968* (Stanford, CA: Stanford University Press, 2008).

9. Roosa, "The September 30th Movement," 25.

10. *Gerakan 30 September: Pemberontakan Partai Komunis Indonesia, Latar Belakang, Aksi dan Penumpasannya* (Jakarta: Sekretariat Negara Republik Indonesia, 1994).

11. Roosa, "The September 30th Movement," 31.

12. Mary S. Zurbuchen, ed., *Beginning to Remember: The Past in the Indonesian Present* (Singapore: Singapore University Press, 2005), 4.

13. Kammen and McGregor, *The Contours of Masse Violence*, 6.

14 Zurbuchen, *Beginning to Remember*, 5.

15 M. C. Ricklefs, a well-known scholar on Indonesian history who was based Australia, wrote a five-hundred-page book on the history of Indonesia. And yet he dedicated only one page to the 1965 events. See Kammen and McGregor, *Contours of Mass Violence*, 5. Other Western Indonesianists also avoided being overly critical for fear of losing access to the country.

16 Benedict Anderson, Ruth T. McVey, and Frederick P. Bunnell, *A Preliminary Analysis of the October 1, 1965 Coup in Indonesia* (Ithaca, NY: Cornell University Modern Indonesia Project, 1971).

17 Zurbuchen, *Beginning to Remember*, 3.

18 Asvi Warman Adam, "September Affair in History Courses," paper presented at "The 1956-1966 Indonesian Killings Revisited," Singapore, 17-19 June 2009.

19 Zurbuchen, *Beginning to Remember*, xv. The papers from this conference form the basis of Zurbechen's edited book collection.

20 Ibid., 13.

21 Kammen and McGregor, ix–x.

22 Adam, "September Affair in History Courses," 3.

23 Ibid., 5.

24 Anwar Siswadi, "SBY Diminta Tak Minta Maaf Pada Korban 1965," *Tempo*, 5 August 2012, https://nasional.tempo.co/read/news/2012/08/05/078421412/sby-diminta-tak-minta-maaf-pada-korban-1965 (accessed 26 January 2016).

25 "No Inquiry Into 1965 Killings on SBY's Watch," *Jakarta Globe*, 2 March 2014, http://jakartaglobe.id/news/no-inquiry-into-65-on-sbys-watch/ (accessed 26 January 2016).

26 Yenni Kwok, "The Memory of Savage Anticommunist Killings Still Haunts Indonesia, 50 Years On," *Time*, 30 September 2015, http://time.com/4055185/indonesia-anticommunist-massacre-holocaust-killings-1965/ (accessed 27 January 2016).

27 Hasyim Widhiarto, "Govt Forms Team to Settle Past Rights Abuses," *Jakarta Post*, 22 May 2015, http://www.thejakartapost.com/news/2015/05/22/govt-forms-team-settle-past-rights-abuses.html (accessed 26 January 2016).

28 Kwok, "The Memory of Savage Anticommunist Killings."

29 Danu Damarjati, "Pemerintah Bahas Permohonan Maaf ke Korban G30S/PKI dan Pelanggaran HAM," *DetikNews* (Jakarta),18 August 2015, http://news.detik.com/berita/2994968/pemerintah-bahas-permohonan-maaf-ke-korban-g-30spki-dan-pelanggaran-ham (accessed 26 January 2016).

30 Kwok, "The Memory of Savage Anticommunist Killings."

31 Indra Wijaya, "Ryamizard Tak Senang Jokowi Minta Maaf Soal PKI, Ini Sebabnya," *Tempo*, 20 August 2016, https://m.tempo.co/read/news/2015/08/20/078693495/ryamizard-tak-senang-jokowi-minta-maaf-soal-pki-ini-sebabnya (accessed 25 January 2016).

32 See http://www.pen-international.org/10/2015/the-ubud-writers-and-readers-festival-bans-the-last-in-a-long-line/ and http://mojok.co/2015/10/ubud-writers-readers-festival/ (accessed 25 January 2016).

33 See http://ruangtempur.blogspot.co.id/2016_02_01_archive.html (accessed 25 January 2016).

34 See Mery Kolimon, et. al., *Forbidden Memories: Women's Experiences of 1965 in Eastern Indonesia* (Melbourne, AU: Monash University Publishing, 2015).

35 The idea of setting up a "moving museum" came from the fact that in Indonesia it is almost impossible to build a stationary or permanent museum on the 1965 events that are not in line with the government's official narrative.

36 M. Agung Rajasa, "Museum Rekoleksi Memori untuk Tolak Pengaburan Sejarah," *Tempo*, 8 December 2015, https://m.tempo.co/read/beritafoto/36904/museum-rekoleksi-memori-untuk-tolak-pengaburan-sejarah/2 (accessed 26 January 2016).

37 Adam, *Seabad Kontroversi Sejarah*.

38 See https://kumpulanfiksi.wordpress.com/2011/09/03/puisi-puisi-wiji-thukul/ (accessed 26 January 2016).

11

The Touchy Historiography of Indonesia's 1965 Mass Killings: Intractable Blockades?

Bernd Schaefer

On the morning of 30 September 1965, a handful of members of the Communist Party of Indonesia (PKI) and sympathetic army officers orchestrated a coup against the leadership of the Indonesian army, only to be crushed by surviving army leaders that night. In the aftermath, the Indonesian army took bloody revenge with the encouragement and support of Western countries. Nevertheless, some surviving communist cadres, inspired by the rhetoric of Chinese Communist leader Mao Zedong, still dreamed of a successful armed revolution. Over a period of many months, the army and its political supporters organized the killing of hundreds of thousands of real and alleged communists across the country. An even higher number of Indonesians were imprisoned, lost their employment and possessions, and were discriminated against by government authorities for decades to come. In 1967, General Suharto officially deposed President Sukarno, who had not been involved in the 30 September coup attempt, and replaced him with a military junta that ruled Indonesia in a dictatorial fashion until 1998.[1]

At the time, Western political observers identified Indonesia as "the West's biggest success" of the Cold War; the political and economic course of an officially non-aligned but "communist-tilting" major country was reversed to "pro-Western."[2] As can be demonstrated, the 1965–66 events also had significant international origins and dimensions. The US and its various Western allies, the People's Republic of China, the Soviet Union, and others, had major interests at stake and were each involved to various extents.[3]

The violence of 1965–66 is both a domestic and an international issue. It cannot just be reduced to the fact that Indonesians were killing Indonesians, and therefore labelled an Indonesian affair and an Indonesian tragedy. That is only part of the story. It is also an international story: many countries bear responsibility, particularly the United States and its various allies at that time, first and foremost the United Kingdom, but also Australia, West Germany, Canada, France, and others.

Telling an Indonesian Story

On 23 July 2012, the Indonesian National Commission of Human Rights (Komnas-HAM) publicly presented a report on the results of its investigations into "grave violations of human rights during the events of 1965/1966." It called the events of those years "a human tragedy, a black page in the history of the Indonesian people." It also stated that the "events occurred as the result of a state policy to exterminate members and sympathizers of the PKI, which was deemed to have conducted resistance against the state. This state policy was accompanied by acts of violence against citizens who were accused of being members or sympathizers of the PKI on a truly massive scale, which took the form of inhuman acts resulting in loss of life and injuries."[4]

The current state of research on the domestic dimension of the 1965–66 events can be described briefly. For most of the last forty-six years, official Indonesian narratives of "the events" and their contexts remained distorted, misleading, or incomplete at best. Only a combination of sources that are now available in Indonesia and other countries, including painstaking oral history research with Indonesian perpetrators and survivors, have cleared up much of the history of "the events." The now-established scholarly narrative debunks the propaganda of the military junta, which began with the latter's assumption of control over the Indonesian media on 2 October 1965 and has dominated ever since. Yet it also casts doubts on communist retellings. In addition, it contests various conspiracy theories involving Indonesian president Sukarno and his successor, General Suharto, in different scenarios before, during, or after the aborted coup attempt of 30 September.

In 1965 a simmering conflict reached its peak, with the PKI and army leadership vying for dominant political power and influence over the country. Both forces simultaneously worked with and cajoled the ailing President Sukarno into siding with them. Both sides hoped to succeed him in power during his foreseeable last years in office or after his death. Both political antagonists vied for complete dominance, and both suspected each other of plotting to decide the political struggle through a coup during Sukarno's lifetime. The army longed for a pretext to attack the PKI, but apparently made no efforts to act first. However, it did not deny rumours of an imminent right-wing coup. In any case, the PKI and some of its supporters in the military expected a rightist army coup, regardless of the rumours. Thus they made efforts to "pre-empt" this through a coup of their own. Some PKI leaders and their military supporters planned to humiliate the army leadership through kidnappings, meant to force Sukarno into their political boat. They struck first, but seriously blundered; they killed the kidnapped generals and significantly altered their political message between the morning and afternoon of 30 September. The surviving army leadership swiftly retaliated. Over the coming months, in alliance with anti-communist political forces it relentlessly used this pretext to eliminate the PKI, its sympathizers, and untold others once and for all. In March 1966, the army sidelined Sukarno and basically established direct military rule.

This newly emerged, complex narrative conflicts with the elaborate but simplistic anti-communist version officially told and propagated for generations by the Indonesian military, its political supporters, and by thousands of educators and media outlets. However, the new narrative also contradicts widespread conspiracy theories, as well as leftist refusals to acknowledge any communist hand in the events of 30 September.

The murders of 1965–66 must be placed in the contemporary Cold War context of global American-Soviet rivalry, the fierce intra-communist Sino-Soviet split, and Indonesia's grandiose global ambitions under Sukarno. This is not about diminishing, or even exculpating, the Indonesian actors, especially those involved in organizing and committing mass murder. To the contrary, the international dimension adds to the picture and exposes some stunning international complicity, compliance, and shared responsibility.

Telling a Cold War Story

The Western anti-communist rollback, in particular the active role played both by the US embassy in Jakarta and the CIA, is well known due to the declassification of American records and subsequent publications based on them.[5] There is no doubt that the support given by American and British, and to a lesser extent Australian, French, and West German intelligence services were helpful to the Indonesian army in tracking and killing many real or alleged communists in the country.[6]

The role of the international communist movement provides the other side of this story of foreign involvement. By 1965, the communist world was split between the Soviet and Chinese camps. As the world's third-largest communist party, the PKI openly opted for and sided with Chinese communism during the Sino-Soviet split, to the point of insulting the Soviet Union and its allies. The inclusion of this international dimension clarifies why it was more important for the Soviet Union and its allies to denounce Chinese-inspired strategies than to engage in a sincere humanitarian appeal against the mass killings. The laudable declassifications of documents leading up to 1965 by the Chinese Foreign Ministry still left certain questions unanswered; now the archive has been shut down completely for an unforeseeable length of time due to reasons unrelated to Indonesia. Maoist China undeniably had a major ideological impact on the PKI's political and military strategies from 1963 until well into 1968.[7] In September 1965, for example, it was privy to the PKI's planning. But China has been extremely careful not to release material dealing with Chinese reactions to briefings by PKI leader D. N. Aidit. The Sino-Soviet split rendered the pro-Chinese PKI helpless without any foreign intervention or assistance during the Indonesian military's anti-communist campaign in 1965–66. In the face of mass violence against the PKI, China could do nothing. The Soviet Union and its allies, meanwhile, were largely silent as the PKI was annihilated. The attitudes and (non)actions of the Soviet Union and its Eastern European allies with regard to unfolding events in Indonesia are intriguing. To phrase it provocatively: would the Indonesian army and its Western supporters have dared to launch such deadly and persistent attacks on the PKI and others had the latter been pro-Soviet and supported by Moscow?

Recent studies have clearly debunked the former belief that the United States was just a sympathetic bystander rather than an actor.[8] It is also worth considering China's role. The army and the Suharto government justified their actions for decades by saying that they had to react to a communist coup. On the leftist side, this is seen as military propaganda, a pretext to kill communists. But while this was certainly used as a pretext, it also had some grounding in reality because part of the PKI leadership—not the entire party, but the leader and others—did consider staging a coup because they were convinced at some point in 1965, with Sukarno being ill, that the army would carry out a coup to eliminate them. In order to pre-empt the army, then, the PKI leadership considered its own coup to take out the army leadership and establish some sort of new regime. This was quite elaborately planned by some members of the PKI. As we now know, they went to China and shared their thoughts with Chinese leaders. A Chinese government document from this period released in the 1990s to some Chinese scholars without an archival citation reveals that there was a meeting between Aidit and Mao in 1965 at which the PKI leader outlined a coup plan. This document does not detail the Chinese reaction; the Chinese archives did not release that information. From the Chinese perspective today, the document does not officially exist; it is not declassified, and none of the scholars who have seen it are allowed to quote it.[9]

In the meantime, China has completely closed down its Foreign Ministry archive. Even when the archive was open, it painstakingly checked that none of the files on Indonesia contained any evidence on Chinese government reactions. Those reactions can be deduced, however, based on the record and the huge personality of Mao Zedong, who tended to lecture revolutionaries from all over the world. It was not a case of revolutionary leaders coming to Mao, discussing their plans, and Mao sitting silently. Usually he said a great deal, making recommendations and providing guidance.[10] This is one of the problems behind getting to the truth of 1965; what, after all, was China's role?

The international context also mattered in 1965–66, beyond the domestic rivalry between the PKI and the army leadership. President Sukarno's ambitious foreign policy earned the wrath of both Western powers and the Soviet Union. During his policy of *konfrontasi* (confrontation, or low-level conflict short of full war) with Malaysia from 1963 to 1965, Sukarno openly sided with China and its communist allies in Asia to build a global movement of under the Conference of Newly Emerging Forces (CONEFO) for the Third World guided from Jakarta and Beijing. This simultaneously challenged the Western capitalist powers, the Soviet bloc, the Non-Aligned Movement led by India and Yugoslavia, and even the United Nations, which Indonesia had left in 1965. Sukarno also confronted the International Olympic Committee, which had expelled Indonesia in the lead-up to the 1964 Tokyo Olympics. In response, Indonesia and China organized the Games of the Newly Emerging Forces (GANEFO) in Jakarta. This globally ambitious Indonesian foreign policy, undertaken in cahoots with China, was one of the most daring challenges to global superpower bipolarity during the Cold War. On top of it lay nuclear ambitions and efforts by Sukarno to acquire nuclear weapons with Chinese help.[11]

In the showdown year of 1965, this placed the country in the crosshairs of international attention and the global Cold War struggle. Moreover, it explains many of the actions and reactions from both the American and Soviet camps.

In the future, political, economic, ideological, and cultural reasons will have to be further explored as to why the bloody 1965–66 massacres in Indonesia were ignored, condoned, or supported by international actors around the world. Attempts to answer these questions, which frequently arise in Indonesia today, will reveal an array of ideological, geopolitical, cultural, and racial motives. They will also show the extent to which Indonesia under Sukarno had become internationally isolated by 1965, and why Chinese protests against the massacres had no effect. Furthermore, they demonstrate how eagerly leading Western countries promoted and furthered the physical elimination of communists, even to the point of expressing serious concerns that the Indonesian army might leave some communist networks and structures intact.

The economic promises made to the Indonesian army by Western intelligence officials and diplomats in Jakarta were a major factor in explaining the large scope of the killings in 1965–66. Only by completely eradicating real and alleged communists, and ultimately deposing Sukarno, did the Indonesian army garner Western support and sympathy that the military junta deemed necessary for the development of the country. Though perpetrated domestically, the killings in Indonesia were committed under the auspices of international actors that viewed Indonesia as a vital pawn in the Cold War. The organizers of the massacres also complied with Western expectations in order to receive promised economic and financial support.

It is still difficult to discuss the "events" of 1965 in Indonesia today, as Baskara Wardaya's chapter recounts. In 2011, when the Goethe Institute sponsored a conference on 1965 in Jakarta, it was met by demonstrators who portrayed the gathering as an attempt to restore the Communist Party.[12] This is usually the general mantra of those who have tried to attack anything that was related to 1965. However, the conference continued and produced a book.[13]

Can there be a Truth Commission on 1965?

The following section will discuss the major intractable barriers that currently stand in the way of an Indonesian truth commission and then try to address them from the perspective of what a truth commission might do. It would have to take the form of a historical commission because many witnesses, actors, and perpetrators are no longer with us, so a truth and reconciliation commission (which is usually formed pretty close to the actual events) would be more difficult. A historical commission is not directly related to the actual date of the events in question and can potentially establish a wider scope.

The intractable barriers begin with access to information. To do something substantial on this issue, Indonesian archival records from the period are needed, but these archives are not being opened. Elite groups block access to ensure that Indonesian files are not open to research—even though they are available in the archives, and some Indonesian archivists would be willing to share them. Another issue is the Chinese files, which would provide valuable information to understand the 1965 events more fully.

If there was a commission to address these events, it should seek a broad scope so as to prevent either side from dismissing the inquiry. This means a commission should look into the period of 1963–65, the last two and a half years of Sukarno's time in power, and the policies of those years. Consequently, it could examine in detail those two very fateful days in 1965, 30 September and 1 October. After 2 October, the military seized power, which led to the formation of a military dictatorship. Beyond that, there are the atrocities committed over more than a year and the systematic massacres, the total victims of which we still do not have precise numbers, but which were likely between five hundred thousand and a million. Each of these periods is important.

The period between 1963 and 1965 establishes the international context—the extent to which Indonesia was at the crossroads of the Cold War, and why the events of 1965 became an international issue. This was a period in which for the first and only time the Indonesian government, in alliance with China, was a global player with a clear political and ideological agenda. It had a huge communist party, the world's third-largest (after the Soviet and Chinese parties) in terms of membership, with hopes of succeeding Sukarno in power. Meanwhile, the Indonesian army was also waiting to determine the post-Sukarno future. While Sukarno was still in power, numerous international events made Indonesia a country of focus for the United States in particular and for its Western allies in general. Sukarno was believed to be seeking a close alliance with China and trying to establish a third global centre of geopolitical gravity alongside the Western world and the Soviet bloc. This putative third bloc was essentially the anti-Soviet communist bloc, led by China, seeking other Asian governments as allies. The PKI was very much in the Chinese camp, which turned out to be one of its greatest strategic mistakes. In this period Sukarno's policies increasingly antagonized the West, starting a conflict with Malaysia and its British allies. China and Indonesia also moved towards an alliance, a horrifying prospect for the United States. These years are vital if we are to understand what followed.

After the fateful days of 30 September and 1 October, the army took power, initiating a series of massacres. Western governments' archival files from the time, and even Western media reports, hailed the military takeover as the biggest Cold War success of the Western camp because it succeeded in transforming Indonesia from its previous pro-communist leanings to a pro-Western orientation, thereby laying the groundwork for the permanent eradication of the PKI and thus any prospect of communism coming to power. Many confidential documents from Western sources reveal a concern that after Suharto established his regime in October he might fail to seize this great "opportunity" to destroy the Communist Party. Indeed, there were concerns that the army did not kill enough communists, and that Suharto might not deliver the final blow to the

PKI. Of course this is a case of stunning international complicity, actively supported by US, British, and other intelligence forces. This international complicity is a vital part of the story.

The question is whether there is a chance to establish a commission, which must be primarily Indonesian. This cannot be imposed from the outside, although foreigners may consult or be involved in some marginal way. If a commission broadened its scope by looking into the events in their context, rather than leaving things out on the grounds that it might offend one side, and if it was able to consult Indonesian archival records, it could address the conspiracy theories that still abound in Indonesia about the roles of Sukarno and Suharto, Chinese and Soviet involvement, and American agency. This is a huge challenge, one that begins with the co-operation of Indonesian elites and those in the still-powerful Indonesian army. Otherwise, we risk being stuck in the situation where there are meetings of survivors, where there is internal discussion, but those who take part in it are in danger of reprisals. International involvement could help reduce that danger. One thing is certain: only the recognition of historic facts and truly sincere respect for the suffering and dignity of countless Indonesians will beget understanding and, perhaps, steps toward reconciliation.

Notes

1. See John Roosa, *Pretext for Mass Murder: The September 30th Movement and Suharto's Coup d'Etat in Indonesia* (Madison, WI: University of Wisconsin Press, 2006) and Robert Cribb, ed., *The Indonesian Killings of 1965–1966: Studies from Java and Bali* (Clayton, AU: Monash University Centre of Southeast Asian Studies, 1990).

2. For the role of the United States, see Bradley R. Simpson, *Economists with Guns: Authoritarian Development and U.S.-Indonesian Relations, 1960–1968* (Stanford, CA: Stanford University Press, 2008).

3. Bernd Schaefer and Baskara T. Wardaya, eds., *1965: Indonesia and the World / Indonesia dan Dunia* (Jakarta: Gramedia, 1965).

4. "Statement by Komnas-HAM (National Commission for Human Rights) on the Results of its Investigations into Grave Violations of Human Rights during the Events of 1965–1966," TAPOL translation, 23 August 2012, http://www.tapol.org/sites/default/files/sites/default/files/pdfs/Komnas%20HAM%201965%20TAPOL%20translation.pdf (accessed 5 March 2016).

5. Edward C. Keefer, ed., *Foreign Relations of the United States, 1964–1968, Volume XXVI, Indonesia; Malaysia-Singapore; Philippines* (Washington: United States Government Printing Office, 2000).

6   Bernd Schaefer and Baskara Wardaya, *1965: Indonesia and the World*, contains chapters on some of this assistance.

7   The so-called Interkit meetings organized by the Soviet Union and its Eastern European allies to coordinate its ideological struggle against China are obviously biased but also reveal much information on Chinese global activities. The January 1969 meeting in Berlin in particular looked at Indonesia and the ties between China and the PKI. Its lengthy transcript is still available in German only; for an English summary, see http://digitalarchive.wilsoncenter.org/document/113294.

8   Simpson, *Economists with Guns*.

9   See Taomo Zhou, "Ambivalent Alliance: Chinese Policy towards Indonesia, 1960–1965," CWIHP Working Paper (August 2013), 20, https://www.wilsoncenter.org/sites/default/files/CWIHP_Working_Paper_67_Chinese_Policy_towards_Indonesia_1960-1965.pdf (accessed 5 March 2016).

10 Odd Arne Wested et al., eds., "77 Conversations between Chinese and Foreign Leaders on the Wars in Indochina, 1964–1977," CWIHP Working Paper (May 1998), https://www.wilsoncenter.org/sites/default/files/ACFB39.pdf (accessed 5 March 2016).

11 See various documents from 1964–65 on Sino-Indonesian nuclear issues at http://digitalarchive.wilsoncenter.org/collection/105/chinese-nuclear-history/2. See especially the following Chinese report from 21 September 1965, about the visit of an Indonesian delegation to China a few days before cataclysmic events unfolded in Indonesia and changed the equation: http://digitalarchive.wilsoncenter.org/document/121566 (accessed 5 March 2016).

12 "Conference on 1965 Tragedy Overshadowed by FPI Threat," *Jakarta Post*, 19 January 2011, http://www.thejakartapost.com/news/2011/01/19/conference-1965-tragedy-overshadowed-fpi-threat.html#sthash.Blh8o9Z2.dpuf (accessed 1 March 2016).

13 Schaefer and Wardaya, *1965: Indonesia and the World*.

12

Writings of an Indonesian Political Prisoner

GATOT LESTARIO

The following excerpts come from the diary of Gatot Lestario, and from letters he wrote to supporters overseas. They are taken from unpublished material in London, courtesy of Carmel Budiardo, who also translated the diary excerpt. The text of letters remains in the English original, with grammar untouched. Accused of being an activist in the East Java branch of the Indonesian Communist Party, Gatot Lestario was arrested and charged. He conducted his own defence at his trial in Blitar in 1978. He was executed by firing squad in 1985.

On Prisoners

Dear Mark,

Prisoners are just like people everywhere. There are tall and short, good and bad. ...

I have received your letter and the First Certificate in English Practice with key and the First Certificate in English Course also with key. Thank you very much.

Also many thanks for your Oxford paperback dictionary and the magazine "National Geographic." The handwriting of the address is the same as yours? Is it true?

I am happy with the study books, dictionary and magazine. I enjoy them and forget for a while that I am a lonely prisoner.

On Survival

Dear Mark,

It is hard to keep your mind alive in prison. … I know I am living in the midst of a totally abnormal society, where survival is the first duty and where too much tenderness or sentiment or resentment or rage would sap my strength and perhaps affect my judgement.

I have begun to understand there are certain costs you have to pay for survival and you had better accept them and not fight them.

No temptation is too strong and no temptation is irresistible. We know that life of sweetness is of pain and sorrow born.

On Our Experiences

Dear Patricia,

The account of a prisoner's feeling in a "South African Prisoner's Journey" has the similar aspects but there were some essential different experiences as ours.

Here, we were imprisoned after passing through the notorious massacre. … Anyone can kill us without any accusation and years long persecution.

The ironical side was that relating to the imprisonment, we got another oppressive feeling—the possibility after being imprisoned, we would be brought before the Court.

On Waiting

Dear Patricia,

I am still waiting for the further development of the rejection of my request for pardon to the President.

We are feeling fairly well, so don't worry about us.

The Lord gave us great assurance and boldness to witness for Him.

The Saviour will never leave us in the lurch, not in that respect either.

We are not afraid.

Dear Doreen,

Did I thank you for your nice calendar with Kipling's poem "If'"?
It hangs over my pillow.

Your "Pilgrims Progress" has arrived already but it can't be delivered yet. It is still in the Security Office.

So Many Letters

Dear Eloise,

I've told Doreen that the correspondence becomes too much, too many letters to answer. I've written to some friends, mostly teachers. Well all my correspondence is helping to improve my English and my Dutch.

To my Dutch friends, I explain that writing letters is a form of therapy or self help, as when one writes about one's feelings, one's anger, one's frustrations, just writing helps one to feel better.

By Accident

Dear Eloise,

I've received safely the two paper clippings you sent me, for they were not in the knowing of the Security Officer.

Accidentally I've met the censor one day and I've known your letter on his box, but he hadn't censored it. So I've asked him to read it your letter without his knowing. I've put the paper clippings in my pocket, for I know it is not allowed to receive your paper clippings containing of political matters. I've returned the letter to him without the clippings. After censored and registered, I got your letter some days later.

The Crime

Dear Mark,

I was sentenced to death according to the Indonesian law and jurisdiction owing to the rejection of my cassation by the High Court on 25th November 1982.

I have made a request for mercy to the President as a last stage on the month of March 1983. If this chance is also rejected by the President, of course I must stand for the firing squad.

To be said, the main conclusion is, we both, my wife and I, are both imprisoned for only having differences of political views with the ruler.

At Pamekasan, November 1984

Dear Diane,

There are 22 prisoners here and about 480 criminals

5 - death sentence
6 - life long
2 - sentence to 20 years.

2 - sentenced to 19 years
2 - sentenced to 17 years
2 - sentenced to 15 years
2 - sentenced to 13 years
1 - sentenced to 10 years

All without deduction of their pre-trial detention which in general between 10 and 12 years long.

Next year we will remain 18 prisoners. The four will be released.

We stay now in a block separated from the criminals. Our condition are relative better.

Sad News

Dear Patricia,

Roderick wrote: "I do hope the lawyer who visited you, was able to do something effective to help your case."

But I am very sorry I have news that is very hard to write to you.

My friend, the lawyer, Pamoeja S. H. (55 years) who helped me to make my second appeal to the President, died on the 15th February 1985 because of cerebral haemorrhage and hyper-tension. It was a sudden death.

Dear Friend (Patricia)

5th August 1982

I am now 57 years old. I was born on 25th November 1925. My birthplace is Trenggalek, a small town surrounded by mountains in south-east Java.

My wife was born on the 8th August 1929 in Semarang, the capital of Central Java. We had been teachers in TAMAN DEWASA, a secondary school, an educational institution being established by the well-known

Indonesian pedagogue, HADJAR DEWANTORO like Rabindranath Tagore of India.

I taught history, my wife English and Indonesian.

Final Page of the Diary: The News from Pamekasan

At 11pm, 30th June '85 the meeting began, Gatot still smiled as usual. To his mother, he gave no messages.

1st July 1985, they were brought to the killing fields (SEKIP PAMAKESAN)

Three warriors were falling down with many bullets of Great Fascis inside their body.

In one hole they were buried (Gatot, Djoko and Rustomo).

Their remains were transferred to Pamekasan Prison Cemetery on 2nd July, 1985.

—The End of the Diary—

SECTION III

Local Truth and Reconciliation in Indonesia

Local Truth and Reconciliation in Indonesia

Mass graves abound in Indonesia. The hole into which Gatot Lestario's body was lowered is one of many sites, marked or unmarked, where the victims of 1965 lie buried.

Mass graves are not of the past alone. Indonesian nationalism has had remarkable success in knitting together a diverse society. The accomplishment of Indonesians from many different faiths, ethnicities, and religions should not be underestimated. Yet unity has come at times with a high cost in human life. Timor-Leste, annexed after the 1975 invasion and never part of the Dutch East Indies, was finally and with great difficulty able to gain its independence. For the rest of the Indonesian national space, its frontiers defined by the Dutch-drawn borders of their Indies colony, "territorial integrity" is sacrosanct.

This is not for lack of challenges. West Papua, the subject of the next section, has never been entirely reconciled to the Indonesian rule that began in the 1960s. At the far end of the archipelago, Aceh was wracked from 1976 to 2005 by an armed conflict between the Indonesian government and the Free Aceh Movement (Gerekan Aceh Merdeka, or GAM). And "horizontal conflicts" painted as ethnic struggles span large areas of Indonesia.

The end of the New Order brought hopes that human rights would improve, that democracy would take hold, and that different groups across the country might gain more control over their own lives. To a large extent this has happened. In most of Indonesia, human rights violations are no longer an everyday affair. Democratic elections are entrenched and parliamentary contests have replaced much of the former dictatorship's ways of ruling. Non-governmental organizations are mostly free to organize and to campaign. The country has decentralized much of its administration, offered special autonomy packages to some provinces, and even allowed some minority groups to secede from one province and form their own new province (eight of them since 1998).

The creation of possible truth commissions has been mooted since the New Order's demise, and promised in writing to the two "autonomous areas" with active armed independence movements (Aceh and Papua). These talks and pledges went nowhere. Meanwhile, the end of the New Order regime took the lid off local tensions, with contesting factions—including the Indonesian army—becoming involved in local conflicts in the Molucca

Islands (Maluku), parts of the large islands of Sulawesi and Borneo (Kalimantan), and elsewhere. These conflicts have cooled in many regions, with communities managing to reconcile with each other. In other regions, however, reconciliation efforts have failed.

This section takes a close look at two regions of past or present conflict: the special autonomous region of Aceh and the *kabupaten* (regency or district) of Poso in Central Sulawesi province. Both experienced lengthy pre-truth commission periods, with civil society mobilizing with demands for some form of transitional justice but no institutional response in place.

In Aceh, this phase ended in 2016 when the provincial government, run mostly by former GAM fighters, authorized its own Truth and Reconciliation Commission (Komisi Kebenaran dan Rekonsiliasi, or KKR). Chapter 13 describes the campaign to form a commission, outlines the form this embryonic commission is taking, and assesses its prospects and structure.

Aceh has a special place in Indonesian history. As an independent sultanate, it was fiercest in its resistance to Dutch colonial rule, fighting off Dutch attacks for many years. Some Acehnese still insist their land was never conquered by the Dutch. It was a stalwart of independence during the Indonesian national revolution against Dutch rule in 1945–49. After Indonesian independence, Aceh fought hard for autonomy within the Indonesian Republic. With a reputation as the most fervently Islamic region of a mainly Muslim but pluralistic Indonesia, Aceh was one of the centres of the Darul Islam (House of Islam) rebellion in the 1950s. That rebellion ended in 1959 with the Indonesian government agreeing to grant Aceh the status of an autonomous province. But tensions simmered on. Meanwhile, the discovery of natural gas brought an inflow of wealth to Aceh but created enclave economies rather than enriching local people. Aceh finally felt the full force of international capitalism in its new role as resource exporter, but few people felt better off. Instead, growing income inequalities sparked resentment and continued tensions in Aceh.

In 1976, the Free Aceh Movement declared independence. It never controlled large areas, but the GAM insurgency helped to militarize Aceh as the Indonesian army struck back with brutal force, often against civilians. Non-governmental organizations were often branded as "separatists" and then repressed—a theme common in Indonesia's *daerah operasi militer* (military operation zones): Aceh, Timor-Leste, and Papua. Economics and politics combined in a toxic brew that cost many Achenese lives, shattered Acehnese civil society, and polarized the province.

Boxing Day 2004 saw a huge tsunami strike Aceh, along with other areas bordering the Indian Ocean. Close to the epicentre of the earthquake that caused the tsunami, Aceh was especially hard hit. Thousands died; half a million people were left homeless. The disaster drove GAM and the Indonesian government to the bargaining table, where, through the mediation of a non-governmental organization based in Finland, they struck a deal to end the war. Indonesia's government was able to end the secessionist rebellion and maintain unity at the cost of granting Aceh new powers as an autonomous region. GAM was allowed to form a political party which dominates provincial politics. Both the first and incumbent governors of Aceh are former GAM members.

Post-conflict Aceh was home to a highly active civil society. It was voices within that civil society that called for a truth commission, seeking to end silences and impunity. In 2016, the provincial government agreed to form one. Though the new truth commission lacked a national government mandate, it had a strong mandate from the local governing authority. It clearly drew on outside inspiration, too. Its name reflected global trends, translating directly the TRC title that has been used in South Africa and many other places since then, from Solomon Islands to Canada. It drew also on the Timorese experience of truth and reconciliation.

Uniquely, as chapter 13 recounts, the Acehnese truth commission is to be permanent. It will not end with a bulky final report. It will continue indefinitely, with no post–truth commission phase at all. In this aspect, Aceh strikes out in a new direction not attempted by any previous truth commission.

In other words, there is hope in Southeast Asia's newest commission. Hopes are lower in another area where political and economic factors have formed a toxic brew: Poso, Central Sulawesi. This region, as chapter 14 explains, has long been divided between different religious communities. The eastern half of the Indonesian archipelago is majority-Muslim, but it is also home to a substantial Christian presence and to other religious communities, including followers of traditional Indigenous belief systems. Much of eastern Indonesia is seen as less developed, closer to the diverse Indigenous traditions of its diverse parts.

Despite religious division, there is little history of religious conflict in areas like Poso before 1998. The end of the New Order saw tensions increase, partly fueled by forces within the Indonesian army. Poso became one of the more intractable conflict regions. Insurgent forces there are increasingly linked to terrorist groups claiming to fight in the name of Islam. Local groups brand themselves with the names of global terrorist outfits. The Indonesian army fights back, often viciously, alienating still more local people through its harsh tactics. The reconciliation methods used in other conflicts have brought paltry results. Chapter 14 argues this is because reconciliation efforts have been top-down, largely driven by government. They have viewed the Poso conflict as a fight along ethnic or religious lines, and tried to solve it with a template drawn from other areas of ethnic or religious conflict. They have ignored social class, which may be the key line of division.

To put it another way, the assumptions on which these reconciliation efforts are based may be false assumptions. If tension in Poso is driven more by economic than religious factors—if income inequality and the workings of extractive capitalism are the key causes of conflict—then reconciliation has to be done differently.

Doing things differently is a common note to be found in the two diverse Indonesian case studies presented in this section.

13

Gambling with Truth: Hopes and Challenges for Aceh's Commission for Truth and Reconciliation

Lia Kent and Rizki Affiat

During a recent Sunday drive near Bener Mariah, in Central Aceh, to visit the district's famous lake, we pass thick mountainous forests where it is said that tigers and elephants still roam. Our friend, a local peace advocate, gestures out of the car window to the sites of several mass graves. "Here is a place where the military threw bodies over the edge of a cliff into the valley below. ... Over there is a place where there are many body parts lying, decomposed, in the jungle." We stop at one site, a dilapidated tourist lookout, and climb the chipped tile steps to the top. There is no memorial to the dead. The terrain below seems treacherous, steep and unforgiving. We ask if families are trying to recover and rebury the bodies of their dead. "It is too difficult," our friend replies, gesturing below to the trees tangled with vines. "And how would they identify the body parts anyway?"

This conversation was a stark reminder of the enduring legacies of several periods of violence and conflict in Aceh. Only ten years after the state-sponsored mass killings of 1965–66 that affected the lives of hundreds of thousands of Indonesians, Aceh experienced further violence in the form of a bitter, twenty-nine-year civil conflict between the Indonesian military (Tentara Nasional Indonesia, or TNI) and the Free Aceh Movement (Gerakan Aceh Merdeka, or GAM). The conflict, which followed

GAM's 1976 declaration of Acehnese independence, is thought to have claimed the lives of between 15,000 to 30,000 people[1]; many others were tortured, raped, imprisoned, and displaced from their homes. Yet there has never been a systematic documentation process. These truths reside in the memories and bodies of those who lived through these events, passed on through oral stories to the next generation.

Acehnese human rights activists have long lobbied for an official truth commission to establish the extent and nature of human rights violations committed during the conflict. In 2016, it seemed that a significant step forward had been taken. Seven commissioners for Aceh's locally mandated Commission for Truth and Reconciliation (Komisi Kebenaran dan Rekonsiliasi, or KKR) were selected by Aceh's provincial parliament. The commission is expected to begin its work in 2017, but its success, and the support of the government of Indonesia, is by no means certain. In this chapter, we draw on recent interviews in Aceh to highlight what is at stake, and for whom, in the KKR's truth-seeking and reconciliation processes, and outline some of the obstacles that lie ahead for the commission's advocates.[2]

Background to the KKR

Aceh's KKR has been a long time in the making. Both the Helsinki Memorandum of Understanding (MoU) that was negotiated between the Indonesian government and GAM in 2005 and the 2006 Law for Governing of Aceh (LoGA) provided for a Truth and Reconciliation Commission (TRC) in Aceh as part of a national Indonesian TRC. Yet, the national TRC has been in legal limbo since late 2006 when the constitutional court ruled that the 2004 law under which it was to be established was invalid. A key issue was that the law contained provisions that would allow for "amnesty and hence legal immunity for perpetrators of gross human rights abuses."[3]

This setback posed a challenge for Acehnese human rights activists, who debated whether to continue pushing for a national-level commission or to lobby their own provincial government and parliament to establish a local Acehnese TRC by way of *qanun* (provincial legislation). Although fully aware that the powers of a locally constituted KKR would be more limited than those of a national commission, they were disillusioned after years of lobbying, and believed that, by pushing for a local commission, they might have more chance of success. As one activist put it, "we are gambling now. If we don't push now [for a provincial TRC] we will be waiting for a long time."

Activists believe their lobbying efforts had some influence on the eventual passing of the *qanun* KKR by the Acehnese provincial parliament, which took place in 2013, after several delays.[4] Further delays then ensued and it was not until 2015 that the parliament formed a small committee to select commissioners. In early 2016, the committee selected twenty-one candidates based on potential applicants' performance on a test. It then provided these names to the provincial parliament, which selected the final seven names. Despite concerns that the parliament would politicize the process, human rights activists seem happy with the final selection of commissioners. Most are well-known activists with a long history of involvement in various human rights advocacy campaigns. Commissioners were inaugurated into their new roles in October 2016.

Mandate and Function of the KKR

Like most truth commissions, a key aspect of the KKR's work will involve "truth-seeking." To this end the commission is mandated to conduct systematic investigations into the causes and impacts of the conflict, including the role of state and non-state actors. After gathering information from government organizations and NGOs, and taking statements from victims and their families, the commission will present a final report of its findings to the provincial government, the provincial parliament, and the national government.

The KKR also has a mandate to design a reconciliation mechanism incorporating Acehnese *adat* (custom) dispute-resolution practices. This idea may well be informed by Timor-Leste's Commission for Reception, Truth, and Reconciliation (CAVR), which incorporated a similar *adat*-based reconciliation mechanism into its nationwide community reconciliation process (CRP).[5] Widely regarded as a factor that contributed to the CAVR's local legitimacy, the CRP hearings that took place at the *suco* (village) and *aldeia* (hamlet) level enabled thousands of Timorese to come together to debate and discuss the conflict, and resolve disputes using familiar methods. Panels comprising CAVR staff and local community leaders adjudicated these hearings, deliberated on cases, and requested that perpetrators repair roads, clean churches, and undertake other acts of community service to atone for their acts.

In Aceh, *adat*-based reconciliation mechanisms are expected to be established at the level of the *gampong* (village) and *mukim* (a customary unit that consists of several villages). As in Timor-Leste, these mechanisms will only be permitted to adjudicate cases that do not involve gross human rights violations.[6] Acehnese *adat*-based practices have already been utilized as part of the peacebuilding process that took place after the signing of the 2005 MoU. *Peusijuek* (cooling down) rituals, which involved "pouring sacred water, yellow rice or powder on those blessed after reconciliation of a dispute," were drawn upon to help reintegrate amnestied political prisoners and former GAM combatants.[7] While there is some (limited) evidence of the success of this experiment,[8] which bodes well for the KKR's *adat*-based reconciliation mechanism, as we discuss further below, the fact that it is now ten years on from the end of the conflict raises a set of new challenges.

It is also envisaged that the commission will recommend a reparations program after the reconciliation process is completed, although the establishment of this program will be the responsibility of both the national and Acehnese governments. The commission's mandate also allows it to provide urgent services to the "most vulnerable victims" in the short term. Again, this provision is likely to be informed by the Timor-Leste commission, which developed a similarly urgent reparations program that gave the CAVR the ability to respond to some of the immediate needs of conflict survivors.

While many of the features just discussed are common to truth commissions, the KKR has, in addition, two unusual features. First and most striking is the breadth of the temporal mandate for the truth-seeking process. While the period of the GAM insurgency, from 1976–2005, will be considered in the first truth-seeking phase, a second phase will delve into events that occurred before 4 December 1976, and it will not stipulate a starting date. This provides the scope to consider the 1965 anti-communist killings (Aceh was the first killing field of 1965), along with Dutch colonial crimes, the Cumbok Civil War, and the Darul Islam/Tentara Islam Indonesia (DI/TII) insurgencies. The rationale for such a wide temporal mandate is unclear and may well be unrealistic.[9] Yet, it is likely that this framing will resonate with popular narratives that place the period of

GAM resistance within a much longer history of Acehnese struggle and resistance to external powers, and for control over territory and natural resources, beginning with the Dutch War of 1873–1912. These narratives, carefully cultivated by GAM, emphasize strength, pride, and cultural and religious distinctiveness, and hark back to a once glorious civilization.[10] They have become an indelible feature of Acehnese identity.[11]

The second unusual feature of the KKR (and one that aligns with its open-ended temporal mandate) is that it is envisaged as a permanent body, although commissioners will be required to apply for re-election every five years.[12] This model, it seems, could have both positive and negative consequences. On a very practical note, compared to most truth commissions, the KKR will have ample time to build community trust. It can take many years to build community confidence in the work of a truth commission, particularly when it comes to encouraging perpetrators to come forward. In the case of Timor-Leste's CAVR, after the conclusion of the two-year community reconciliation program, there were thousands of perpetrators who wished to take part in the program who were no longer able to do so.[13] For these reasons, peacebuilding scholars Ray Nickson and John Braithwaite have recently made the case for permanent TRCs that keep "their doors open to assist with truth, reconciliation and justice at whatever point in time victims and perpetrators are emotionally ready."[14]

The permanent nature of the KKR might allow commissioners to develop a more expansive vision of their work. Most truth commissions have short time frames and tend to be confined to a particular phase of a peace process (a tendency that leads to the adoption of a "tool-kit" approach oriented towards producing "outputs" such as final reports). By contrast, KKR commissioners have the opportunity to approach their work as a long-term, locally grounded, and evolving process. Unlike the staff of most truth commissions, they would have the capacity to engage, in an ongoing way, in efforts such as lobbying political elites, supporting local commemorations, developing education materials, and fostering public discussions and debates.

A permanent commission is not without its risks, however. Commissioners could become bogged down in an ongoing, open-ended truth-seeking process, which could reinforce an ethno-nationalist agenda of legitimating Acehnese myths of lost greatness, rebellion, and cultural and religious uniqueness. This could also crowd out the experiences of ethnic minorities. On top of this, Aceh has a history of allowing permanent institutions to become moribund. The most prominent example is the Aceh Peace Reintegration Agency (Badan Reintegrasi Damai Aceh, or BRA), which was established in the wake of the Helsinki MoU to assist former GAM combatants to reintegrate, distribute compensation for victims of the conflict, and rehabilitate public and private property. While in its early years the BRA distributed a significant amount of compensation, it was also widely criticised for its poor performance and its lack of transparency and accountability.[15] Ten years after the Helsinki MoU, the BRA continues to exist, and is referred to by its critics as an "ATM machine" that now does little more than provide a salary to some one thousand staff, many of them former GAM. Careful monitoring will be needed by civil-society organizations to ensure that the KKR does not suffer a similar fate to that of the BRA.

Truth Commissions: Between Idealism and Political Reality

The KKR has had a galvanizing effect on Acehnese human rights activists. They have projected onto it a complex set of hopes concerning justice, truth, reconciliation, and prevention. They hope that the KKR will provide both recognition and practical support to conflict survivors that will assist them to rebuild their lives. They hope, too, that the KKR will provide the first comprehensive account of the myriad factors that produced the conflict, and the extent of human rights violations that took place, in a way that will counter official attempts to deny, obfuscate, or downplay what occurred.[16] A long-term hope of many activists is that cases of human rights violations revealed by the KKR in Aceh will be forwarded to a human rights court for prosecution. These hopes speak to their years of struggle for some form of official recognition of the magnitude of Acehnese suffering at the hands of the TNI. That these hopes are now invested in a particular institution, a *truth commission*, also speaks to the power of this globalized model, which is now imbued with the perceived capacity to assist both individuals and societies to "come to terms with" and "move on from" the violent past.

While the power of this hope should not be denied, it would be wise to temper expectations. Mounting evidence suggests we may be asking too much of truth commissions. The assumption that the public recounting of painful stories is redemptive, liberating, or healing for victims has been challenged by recent work which shows that much depends on the circumstances in which the telling takes place, the forms of material and psychological support available to the witness, and the response of political leaders to these stories.[17] These critiques are borne out in the Timor-Leste context, where many of those who told their stories to the CAVR were disappointed that there were no practical "results," by which they meant material support to assist their day-to-day lives.[18]

In addition, while truth commissions can establish impressive national records of past abuses, the question remains, to what extent are they authoritative? There is no guarantee that establishing the "truth" about past events changes beliefs, attitudes, or the pre-existing narratives of conflict held by conflicting parties.[19] The Timor-Leste case is again instructive here. The CAVR seems to have had little ability to change the narratives of the conflict promoted by the political elite. The CAVR's final report, *Chega!*, remains a neglected national resource that is rarely debated or discussed. East Timorese leaders continue to promote their own preferred narrative of the conflict and of the subsequent peace, a story that stresses the population's experiences of heroism and resistance rather than victimhood, and promotes reconciliation with Indonesia rather than prosecutions of the TNI. Civil-society organizations, rather than the state, have kept the findings and recommendations of the CAVR alive in the public sphere. They have developed education and oral history projects, encouraged local initiatives to remember the conflict, and provided financial and counselling support to survivors.[20]

In Aceh, any "truth" produced by the KKR will similarly confront powerful official narratives of the conflict and of *damai* (peace). Both the TNI and former GAM leaders have sought to shape collective memories of the conflict, claim ownership of the peacebuilding process, and steer the population towards a focus on the future. For its part, the TNI prominently displays the words "Damai itu Indah" (Peace is Beautiful) and "Bersama Rakyat TNI Kuat" (Together with the Community TNI is Strong) on its barracks across Aceh, in an effort to reinvent itself as a benevolent partner of the Acehnese people. GAM has similarly sought to reinvent itself as peacemaker, promoting its role as the author of the Helsinki MoU that has delivered a degree of peace and prosperity to the population, and further cementing its claim to power and its control over economic resources through reference to its leadership of the thirty-year-long struggle for Aceh's independence. [21] Given the extent to which GAM makes effective use of cultural symbols and resources to reinforce these narratives, they will not easily be dislodged.[22]

In addition to these challenges, which bedevil all truth commissions, several specific difficulties lie ahead for the KKR due to its basis in *qanun* law. Key among these is the fact that the KKR will not have the power to subpoena witnesses from institutions such as the TNI and the police, who are unlikely to co-operate. These institutions could even be a source of intimidation for witnesses.[23] And some commentators have questioned whether "true" reconciliation can occur in the absence of an acknowledgement and apology on the part of the TNI or the Indonesian government. Who, they ask, will be reconciling with whom? A similar question arises in relation to reparations. If the funding for reparations does not come from the Indonesian state, but from other sources (including the Acehnese government), can this really be understood as state reparations?

The absence of central government involvement or TNI co-operation raises other uncertainties about the nature of the "truth" that will emerge from the truth-seeking process. Without the capacity to gather detailed information about the TNI chain of command, will enough information come to light to clearly establish the circumstances under which human rights abuses were committed and the identity of those responsible? And will the truth that emerges be sufficient to serve as a basis for prosecutions? Even if it is, it seems highly unlikely, at least in the short term, that human rights violations uncovered by the truth commission will be prosecuted in a human rights court.[24] Many members of the TNI implicated in the violence remain in positions of power and influence, indicating that, as Aspinall and Zain put it, an "implicit political deal" has been reached in Indonesia by which "the military [has] eased itself out of politics in exchange for effective impunity for past abuses."[25]

For victims, perhaps the more important question is whether enough truth will come to light to enable the graves of the dead to even be located. For grassroots peace workers like our friend in Bener Mariah, the identification of the graves of the dead is seen as the most meaningful contribution that the KKR could make, as it is linked to the need amongst Muslims to commemorate and pray for their deceased relatives. As she put it, "the need to know the truth about the dead is about knowing the last resort of the lost lives. It helps to fulfil a deeply personal, and spiritual, need."

Finally, because of its basis in *qanun* law, not all of Aceh's political leaders are supportive of the KKR. The limited funding available for the first year of the KKR's operations is evidence of this: while commissioners requested 21 billion Indonesian rupiah (approximately US$750,000) for its 2017 budget, the Aceh parliament only approved 3 billion rupiah.[26] The fact that many political leaders are former GAM who, after the peace process, underwent a dramatic transformation from guerrillas to political players and successful business people, reinforces their equivocation.[27] Some now express concerns—for reasons that are both legitimate and self-serving—that the KKR will demonstrate "one-sidedness" by disproportionately focusing on the human rights abuses committed by members of GAM over those committed by the TNI. As Aspinall and Zain suggest, there are good reasons for many former GAM combatants to be wary of any process that seeks to uncover the truth.[28] GAM's own role in committing violent acts, not only against military adversaries but also against civilians, is a persistent shadow that lies over it.[29] And while the MoU provided "amnesty" for individuals associated with GAM, it seems unlikely that this amnesty would apply to those accused of human rights abuses.[30] These concerns seemed to be at the forefront of former governor Irwandi Yusuf's mind when he described the KKR as a "two-sided dagger" that will focus on GAM who have already been amnestied, thereby bringing these issues to life once again.

Community Expectations of Bantuan

Translating the goals of the KKR and garnering local support for them within the complex social and political reality of Aceh will be another key challenge for KKR commissioners. The extent to which the commission is able to respond sensitively to the population's high expectations of *bantuan* (assistance) will be a litmus test for its local legitimacy.

In a context where livelihoods have been severely disrupted by the loss of breadwinners, displacement, and the interruption of farming activities, many Acehnese look to the government for assistance to help them rebuild. The uneven forms of assistance provided to civilians affected by the conflict in the wake of the Helsinki MoU have only elevated these expectations. Local narratives of injustice are widespread in many conflict-affected communities, where ordinary people feel they were unfairly overlooked by the BRA's post-conflict assistance packages.

Part of the issue is that post-conflict assistance packages were implemented alongside a massive international humanitarian response to the 2004 Boxing Day Tsunami, which took the lives of approximately 165,000 people. There was a disparity between the generous assistance provided to tsunami victims (through an institution known as the BRR), most of whom were located in the coastal areas, and the far more limited assistance provided to conflict-affected populations, most of whom lived in the interior of the province.[31]

Of the support specifically designated for post-conflict reconstruction, high-ranking members of GAM were prioritized for BRA reintegration packages while civilians and less highly ranked members of GAM did not fare as well. While various forms of assistance were available for *korban konflik* (conflict victims), the process of beneficiary selection was "murky"[32] and, in a context where "there was a limited amount of post conflict assistance to go around," allegations also began to circulate that "various recovery plans were available to the highest bidder or the well-connected."[33] There is a pervasive sense amongst those who identify as *korban konflik*—a fluid category that includes low-ranking combatants, farmers, women, children, and others who are still suffering the effects of the conflict—that they have been excluded from the "spoils of peace" enjoyed by GAM commanders and elite leaders.[34]

Women—both combatants and civilians—fared particularly poorly in terms of post-conflict assistance. The exclusion of women from the peace-negotiation process contributed to a problematic gender blindness in the drafting of the MoU and LoGA which, in turn, led to the neglect of the Inong Balae (the women's combatant wing of GAM) in the reintegration packages for combatants.[35] Women were also sidelined in the BRA's compensation packages for conflict victims, despite the efforts of Acehnese women's organizations to promote their needs. Women's organizations describe how the BRA demanded "medical evidence" of violations that, in cases of sexual violence, was both insensitive and unrealistic, particularly as these violations had often occurred several years previously. Village leaders were also reluctant to advocate for women affected by sexual violence, in part because of the shame and stigma that attaches not only to female victims but also to their families and villages.[36] Further marginalizing women was the fact that village leaders and the BRA prioritized men over women for assistance because male "heads of households" and male combatants were perceived to have a greater need.

Amid this legacy of unevenness and gender bias, data about who has received assistance (and how much), and who has not, is not easy to come by. Designing an urgent reparations program in this context, and making recommendations for a more substantive reparations program, will undoubtedly be a fraught task for the KKR. More generally, the KKR will need to take care not to raise expectations of *bantuan*, particularly as it will not have a mandate to deliver a comprehensive reparations program, only to make recommendations to the provincial government. The KKR will be heavily reliant on the perseverance of its commissioners, working groups, and human rights NGOs to put pressure on the parliament and state institutions in this regard.

Opening Old Wounds

Ten years have now passed since the signing of the Helsinki MoU and many ordinary people are preoccupied with the needs of the present and the future, with some expressing the view that they have already "forgotten" the past. In this context, another key challenge KKR commissioners will face is that of negotiating narratives of concern about "opening old wounds" that circulate amongst the Acehnese population.

These concerns seem particularly potent in some parts of the province, such as the district of Bener Meriah, where the conflict played out in distinctive ways. Human rights and peace activists commonly describe the violence that occurred there as "horizontal" as it was deeply entangled in the complex relations between local communities rather than a simple case of "TNI against GAM." Indeed, while during the 1970s and '80s the population—which is of mixed Acehnese, Gayonese (Indigenous), and Javanese ethnicity—was relatively protected from the conflict, this changed rapidly in the late 1990s, when GAM launched a massive recruitment effort. The Indonesian government responded by launching its own counter-insurgency measures, which involved TNI support for anti-separatist militia groups, primarily recruited from Javanese transmigrant communities.[37] Given the ethnic mix of the community, levels of communal inter-ethnic violence soon escalated, leading to large-scale displacement throughout the district.[38]

In Bener Meriah, there remains much uneasiness about the idea of truth-telling. This uneasiness struck us in the course of a focus-group discussion among conflict survivors, in which those who spoke of their past experiences and their hopes for the future narrated their stories in general terms, avoiding names and paying careful attention to subject positioning. Many were reluctant to speculate as to whether the perpetrator of a past incident was a member of the TNI or GAM, and instead made use of the euphemism OTK (*orang tak dikenal*: an unknown assailant). Those who spoke of having taken up arms to "defend their village" (in some cases, it seemed, as members of anti-separatist militia groups) took care to position themselves as *korban konflik* who had no choice. After the discussion, our friend and local peace advocate told us that if the KKR expected people to publicly reveal the names of perpetrators, the result would be "like throwing oil on fire."

The uneasiness expressed about "opening old wounds" highlights the degree to which peace, in Bener Meriah at any rate, seems to have a fragile quality. While a tentative peace exists amongst Gayo, Javanese, and Acehnese communities, and in many cases people are forming new connections through inter-ethnic marriages, there is a sense that the public airing of accusations and counter-accusations of violence could unravel this peace, and that hostilities and revenge could re-emerge. Among the Gayonese and Javanese communities, where support for GAM was relatively low, there is also, perhaps, a feeling of continued vulnerability. A complicating factor is the district's political volatility; no political party has a majority here, and a number of prominent former militia figures who were closely affiliated with the TNI during the conflict hold positions in the district legislature (one of whom is running for the position of Bupati, or district administrator, in the 2017 district election). For these figures, it is clearly not desirable to open up a discussion of the past.

Against this backdrop, we often heard people in Bener Meriah describe how their desire to "forget" was reinforced by aspects of Gayonese and Javanese culture, which do not favour direct forms of confrontation or public confession. We heard of how Gayonese people could express their sadness and loss through subtle, and less direct, idioms such as music, singing, and dance.[39] Many spoke of how they sought solace in religious practice. In the focus-group discussion, for instance, we were told by one participant that that "Javanese and Gayonese don't want to remember. They focus on the future. They easily forgive and forget. They surrender to God."

The frequent references people made to religious practices also underscores the power of Islam in the Acehnese context, which has provided many local residents (whether of Acehnese, Javanese, or Gayonese ethnicity) with a framework for coping with losses, "forgetting" the past, and focusing on the present and the future. As well as providing spiritual solace, the *ulama* (Islamic leaders) are a powerful political force in Aceh, one that exerts a behind-the-scenes influence upon political leaders and among the population generally through the *dayah* (Islamic community schools). While some religious leaders are supportive of the KKR, many others seem to have mixed opinions, and it appears that there has been limited consultation with these leaders thus far. It is not known how religious leaders will respond to the KKR's efforts to encourage women to reveal experiences of sexual violence, or whether women themselves will be prepared to speak publicly about these experiences in a context where sharia law treats cases of adultery harshly.[40] Nonetheless, in order to resonate with the spiritual beliefs of much of the population, and to avoid backlash from powerful religious leaders, it will be critical for the commissioners to find ways of "translating" the goals of the KKR in ways that resonate with Islamic discourse and teachings rather than secular-liberal human rights discourses.[41]

Conclusion

There is obviously much at stake—for political leaders, conflict victims, and human rights activists—in the KKR's "gamble" with truth. Well aware of these stakes, Acehnese activists are working closely with each other, and with KKR commissioners, to strategize how best to build a foundation for a strong truth commission in the context of significant political constraints. Perhaps the best that can be hoped for is that the KKR will help to paint a more accurate picture of the contours of the conflict. Even if this truth will not be as complete, definitive, or "agreed to," as many Acehnese would like it to be, it might at least create a crack in the official story, through which bottom-up narratives might begin to challenge this story.[42] The KKR's efforts might also provide a springboard for the development of educational materials, help catalyse local forms of memorial culture, and provide a useful set of recommendations around which advocacy efforts can coalesce.

Perhaps the biggest danger is that the KKR's capacity to deliver truth, justice, reconciliation, and reparations will be "oversold" to the community, which will encourage high expectations that it is unable to meet. It is not difficult to foresee that conflict victims may experience truth-telling as another form of injustice if they are expected to tell their stories in exchange for limited personal benefit. It might be possible for commissioners to minimize some of these risks by undertaking "socialization" in ways that are modest and respectful, that acknowledge the diversity present within the Acehnese community, and acknowledge the commission's possibilities *and* its limits. Part of the challenge will be to listen carefully to community fears about "opening old wounds" rather than downplaying them or assuming that, for victims, speaking out is always a positive or therapeutic experience.

Finally, it seems to us that one of the KKR's key strengths is its unique permanent status. For all its potential problems, this gives commissioners the possibility of conceiving of their work as part of an ongoing process of negotiating the legacies of the conflict rather than as a short-term project aimed at producing a definitive output in the form of a final report. It might enable them to engage with communities over the long haul, and to find ways to ground the commission's work in the continuing efforts of Acehnese to rebuild their lives.

Notes

The authors would like to thank David Webster and John Braithwaite for comments on an earlier version of this chapter.

1. On the 1965–66 killings in Aceh, see John Roosa, "The State of Knowledge about an Open Secret: Indonesia's Mass Disappearances of 1965–66," *The Journal of Asia Studies* 75, no. 2 (2016): 281–97. On the GAM-TNI conflict, see Edward Aspinall, "Aceh: Democratization and the Politics of Co-option," in *Diminishing Conflicts in Asia and the Pacific: Why Some Subside and Others Don't*, ed. Edward Aspinall, Robin Jeffery, and Anthony J. Regan (New York: Routledge, 2013), 51; Amnesty International, *Indonesia: New Military Operations, Old Patterns of Human Rights Abuses in Aceh* (London: Amnesty International, 2004).

2. Interviews were conducted by Lia Kent and Rizki Affiat in March and November 2016 with human rights activists, KKR commissioners, political leaders, and ordinary

people in Banda Aceh, Bener Meriah, and North Aceh. Fieldwork was funded by the Australian Research Council (ARC DE150100857).

3   Edward Aspinall and Fajran Zain, "Transitional Justice Delayed in Aceh, Indonesia," in *Transitional Justice in the Asia-Pacific*, ed. Renee Jeffery and Hun Joon Kim (New York: Cambridge University Press), 94.

4   See Aspinall and Zain, "Transitional Justice Delayed," for a detailed background.

5   There have been many discussions and exchanges between East Timorese and Acehnese human rights activists, so this is very likely to be the case.

6   This may be both a strength and a weakness. On the one hand, it seems likely that some Acehnese would not accept an *adat*-based mechanism for cases involving killing. See Leena Avonius, "Reconciliation and Human Rights in Post-Conflict Aceh," in *Reconciliation Indonesia: Grassroots Agency for Peace*, ed. Birgit Brauchler (New York: Routledge, 2009). On the other hand, as in the case of Timor-Leste, it may be difficult to separate discussions of less serious crimes from more serious ones, and if the perpetrators of serious crimes are not prosecuted (which seems highly likely) both victims and perpetrators of minor crimes may perceive this as unjust. See Lia Kent, *Unfulfilled Expectations: Community Views of the CAVR's Community Reconciliation Process in East Timor* (Dili, TL: Judicial Systems Monitoring Programme, 2004).

7   John Braithwaite et al, *Anomie and Violence: Non-truth and Reconciliation in Indonesian Peacebuilding* (Canberra: Australian National University Press, 2010), 389–90; see also Avonius, "Reconciliation and Human Rights," 125.

8   Braithwaite et al., *Anomie and Violence*, 389.

9   One activist described this as a "political compromise." While activists wanted to limit the time frame, Partai Aceh politicians wanted it to extend as far back as 1873, when the war against the Dutch took place.

10 See, for example, Malik Mahmud's speech at his inauguration as Wali Nanggroe, December 2013, which speaks of the need to "weave back the once glorious Acehnese civilisation." Transcript of the Indonesian speech available at http://lintasgayo.co/2013/12/16/ini-pidato-pertama-wali-nanggroe-aceh-malik-mahmud-al-haytar.

11 Jesse Hession Grayman, "Official and Unrecognized Narratives of Recovery in Post-Conflict Aceh, Indonesia," *Critical Asian Studies* 48, no. 4 (2016): 538; Anthony Reid, "War, Peace and the Burden of History in Aceh," *Asian Ethnicity* 5, no. 3 (1020): 301–14; Edward Aspinall, "Democratization and the Politics of Co-option," 53.

12 This permanent status is implied rather than specifically defined in the *qanun*, as no time limit is set for the KKR to complete its activities.

13 Spencer Zifcak, "Restorative Justice in Timor-Leste: the Truth and Reconciliation Commission," *Development Bulletin* 68 (2005): 53.

14 Ray Nickson and John Braithwaite, "Deeper, Broader, Longer Transitional Justice," *European Journal of Criminology* 11, no. 4 (2014): 454.

15 Christine Beeck, *Repaving the Road to Peace: Analysis of the Implementation of DD&R (Disarmament, Demobilization and Reintegration) in Aceh Province, Indonesia*, (Bonn, DE: Bonn International Center for Conversion Brief 35, 2007); International Crisis

Group, "Aceh: Post-Conflict Complications," Crisis Group Asia Report 139, 4 October 2007.

16   Up until now, these efforts have been patchy. The most comprehensive effort was conducted by The Indonesian National Human Rights Commission (Komnas-HAM). Although its report was widely criticised for limiting the state's liability for past violence, Komnas-HAM did document thousands of cases of violence and recommended that five be the immediate priority of prosecutors. Its recommendations were ignored however. See Renee Jeffery, "Amnesty and Accountability: The Price of Peace in Aceh, Indonesia," *International Journal of Transitional Justice* 6, no. 1 (2012): 70. NGOs have also conducted their own documentation processes, and activists hope the first step of the KKR will be to integrate this already existing work.

17   Brandon Hamber, "Does the Truth Heal: A Psychological Perspective on the Political Strategies for Dealing with the Legacy of Political Violence," in *Burying the Past: Making Peace and Doing Justice after Civil Conflict*, ed. Neil Bigger (Washington: Georgetown University Press), 131–48; Brandon Hamber and Richard Wilson, "Symbolic Closure through Memory, Reparation and Revenge in Post-Conflict Societies," *Journal of Human Rights* 1, no. 1 (2002): 35–53.

18   Lia Kent, *The Dynamics of Transitional Justice: International Models and Local Realities in East Timor* (New York: Routledge, 2012), 168–72. Research in other contexts has drawn similar conclusions. See, for example, Simon Robins, "Whose Voices? Understanding Victims' Needs in Transition," *Journal of Human Rights Practice* 1, no. 2 (2009): 320–31: Rosalind Shaw, "Memory Frictions: Localizing the Truth and Reconciliation Commission in Sierra Leone," *International Journal of Transitional Justice* 1, no. 2 (2007): 183–207.

19   Erin Daly, "Truth Skepticism: An Inquiry into the Value of Truth in Times of Transition," *International Journal of Transitional Justice* 2, no. 1 (2008): 23–41.

20   See Lia Kent, Naomi Kinsella, and Nuno Rodrigues Tchailoro, *Chega! Ten Years On: A Neglected National Resource* (Canberra: State, Society and Governance in Melanesia Report, July 2016). See also the chapters by Pat Walsh and Manuela Leong Pereira in this collection. Nonetheless, the newly approved Centro *Chega!* does offer a ray of hope.

21   GAM as an insurgency group officially dissolved after the Helsinki MoU. However, as a political force it never disappeared. GAM reorganised itself into the Aceh Transitional Committee (KPA, or Komite Peralihan Aceh) and many former GAM members formed and joined Aceh's main political party, the Aceh Party (Partai Aceh).

22   For instance, the Aceh parliament approved 2.4 billion Indonesian rupiah in 2013 to pay for the inauguration of former GAM "prime minister" Malik Mahmud as Wali Nanggroe (guardian of the state). This symbolic position is said to be responsible for revitalising and preserving Acehnese traditions, culture, and identity. See http://aceh.tribunnews.com/2013/12/13/pengukuhan-wali-tetap-16-desember (accessed 1 June 2017).

23   Some interviewees also raised concerns about the national government's capacity to starve the commission of funding. Funding for the KKR is expected to come from the provincial budget, although there are also provisions for the institution to receive funding from national and district budgets, as well as other legitimate and non-binding sources—for example, national and international donors.

24 In addition to providing for a TRC, the Helsinki MoU and the LoGA mandates the establishment of a human rights court in Aceh that should be established within twelve months of the law being passed, although this has still not happened and even if the law passed, it would not be retroactive. See Aspinall and Zain, "Transitional Justice Delayed," 97. A more promising avenue is national Law No 26/2000 on human rights courts, which establishes a number of human rights courts across Indonesia, including one in Medan, North Sumatra, with jurisdiction over Aceh. This court has not yet heard any cases relating to Aceh. See Jeffery "Amnesty and Accountability," 78; Aspinall and Zain, "Transitional Justice Delayed," 98.

25 Aspinall and Zain, "Transitional Justice Delayed," 93.

26 See http://www.ajnn.net/news/anggaran-minim-pemerintah-aceh-dinilai-tak-serius-terhadap-kkr/index.html (accessed 1 June 2017).

27 Edward Aspinall, "Combatants to Contractors: The Political Economy of Peace in Aceh, Indonesia," *Indonesia* 87 (2009): 1–34.

28 Aspinall and Zain, "Transitional Justice Delayed," 95.

29 Ibid.

30 Edward Aspinall, *Peace Without Justice? The Helsinki Peace Process in Aceh* (Geneva: Centre for Humanitarian Dialogue, 2008), 6; Renee Jeffery, "Amnesty and Accountability", 61. This provision provided amnesty for individuals associated with GAM who were under investigation for crimes committed during the course of the civil conflict or who were already in detention, as well as those who fought under the auspices of the group.

31 Katrina Lee-Koo, "Gender at the Crossroad of Conflict: Tsunami and Peace in Post-2005 Aceh," *Feminist Review* 101 (2012): 66–67.

32 For a detailed background, see International Crisis Group, *Aceh: Post-Conflict Complications*; Braithwaite et al., *Anomie and Violence*, 380–88.

33 Jesse Hession Grayman, "Official and Unrecognised Narratives," 540.

34 Ibid., 541.

35 Only one woman, Shadia Marhaban, an Acehnese activist, was involved in the GAM delegation and, of the three thousand ex-GAM combatants listed in the MoU, there was not a single woman. See Lee-Koo, "Gender at the Crossroad," 70–72; See also Jaqueline Aquino Siapno, "The Politics of Reconstruction, Gender, and Re-Integration in Post-Tsunami Aceh," in *Tsunami in a Time of War: Aid, Activism and Reconstruction in Sri Lanka and Aceh, Indonesia*, ed. Malathi de Alwis and Eva-Lotta E. Hedman (Columbo, LK: International Center for Ethnic Studies, 2009), 163–90.

36 Lee-Koo, "Gender at the Crossroad," 73.

37 Grayman, "Official and Unrecognised Narratives," 528.

38 Ibid.

39 For instance, we were told that a popular song was recorded in Gayonese after the conflict, which recounts the story of a woman mourning the loss of her child and searching for her.

40   The KKR has a working group specifically focused on women which, one activist suggested, will need to be integrally linked to the other working groups.

41   According to one activist, the best strategy would be to reach out to the more moderate and less high-profile members of the *ulama* first, and frame the work of the KKR with reference to concepts such as human dignity and participation rather than "human rights."

42   See David Webster's introduction to this collection, "Memory, Truth, and Reconciliation in Timor-Leste, Indonesia, and Melanesia."

14

All about the Poor: An alternative Explanation of the Violence in Poso

Arianto Sangadji

In December 1998, a violent conflict thought by some to be "ethno-religious" in nature erupted in the *kabupaten* (regency or district) of Poso in Central Sulawesi province, an eastern part of the archipelago of Indonesia.[1] Unlike most other regencies in the country, Muslims and Christians each formed about half of Poso's population of 400,000 prior to the violence. The two groups fought along religious lines. Murder and the burning of property (houses, mosques, churches, public buildings, and vehicles) were common. As a result, around 1,000 people were killed and hundreds were wounded during the first three years of hostilities (1998–2001). Some 79,000 Christians and Muslims were displaced from their villages and around 8,000 houses burned.

In 2001, a government-led reconciliation process began, at which point the violence took on new forms. Until 2006, it took the form of sporadic deadly attacks on mostly Christian targets. Kidnappings, shootings, and bombings were common during this time. Since 2007, Poso has been engulfed in deadly tensions between the Indonesian security forces and Islamic militia groups; both sides have suffered losses. The militias are officially reported to have links with global or regional terrorist groups such as Jemaah Islamiyah, al Qaeda, and the Islamic State of Iraq and Syria (ISIS).

Why has Poso suffered violence? This chapter lays the groundwork for an alternative to mainstream interpretations that highlight ethno-religious affiliation as the major feature of the conflict. I argue that in order to gain a better understanding of the violence, we need a class analysis. For this reason I will look at the violence in the wider context of the historical development of capitalism.

The Context: Capitalism, its Crisis, and the Fall of the Suharto Regime

Like other outbreaks of communal violence across Indonesia in the past decade, the violence in Poso should be situated alongside the historical development of capitalism in the country. This is important because the vast majority of studies have ignored the link between violence and this modern system of exploitation.

First, I would argue that a major characteristic of capitalism's growth in the archipelago is its unevenness. Historically speaking, this unevenness means that some regions have more highly developed capitalist social relations than others. Java, for instance, was well developed under Dutch colonialism compared to the outer Indonesian islands. This unevenness can also be considered from the view of the comparative development of economic sectors. For example, the vast majority of the population remains engaged in agriculture, with manufacturing and other modern service sectors lagging behind. This implies that the bulk of the population is best characterized as part of a reserve army of labour, since the agricultural sector is mostly associated with a subsistence economy and low productivity. The "reserve army of labour" simply means people who are working outside capitalist social relations but who are subordinated to the capitalist system. The active working population is limited. However, under the law of uneven and combined development, despite the fact that there is unevenness, capitalism determines the shape of any given society as a whole, regardless of the uneven development within it.

A second context is the development of the economy under the Suharto regime (1966–98). After the deaths of between 500,000 and 1 million alleged members and sympathizers of the Indonesian Communist Party in the 1960s, Western support for Suharto accelerated, generating the country's state-led capitalist development. During his thirty-year tenure,

Suharto was successful in promoting capitalist development measured by national economic growth. However, this system created victims. Its rapid growth relied on ruthless exploitation of low-wage workers, involuntary displacement of poor farmers, and forced eviction of the urban poor. For the sake of this capitalist development, the regime employed an effective control over entire segments of society, especially workers and farmers. The class politics of the pre-Suharto period was effectively undermined. This was the necessary condition that underpinned the accumulation of capital during the Suharto dictatorship.

Since the system is prone to crisis, the depression in East and Southeast Asia at the end of the 1990s damaged the Suharto regime's legitimacy. The value of the Indonesian rupiah against the US dollar sunk to 18,000 to 1 in January 1998 (compared to 2,400 to 1 six months before). The country's GDP dropped by 13.6 per cent in 1998, compared to its average 5 per cent annual growth prior to the crisis. The government statistical bureau reported that the poverty rate skyrocketed from 11.3 per cent in 1996 to 39.1 per cent in 1998. International Labour Office projections pegged the poverty rate in December 1999 at 66.3 per cent.[2] This economic downfall caused a deterioration of the living conditions of the working class as a whole. The World Bank estimates that 20 million people were unemployed in 1998. The capitalist business cycle thus created a reservoir of people whose labour was idle.

Third, the worsening economic crisis in this, the most populous country in the region, led to political crisis. The authoritarian Suharto regime, one of the West's major Asian allies during the Cold War, was under pressure. Student protesters spread across the country demanding political reform. Unaware that the internal contradictions of the system were the underlying root of the crisis, various segments of the urban poor, such as the unemployed, the informal working class, and the lumpenproletariat, spontaneously turned to anti-Chinese rioting, which served as an outlet for resentment in multiple cities, including Jakarta. Suharto then stepped down in May 1998, leaving the country with economic, political, and social vulnerabilities. The so-called ethno-religious violence that followed in regions like Ambon, Kalimantan, and Poso,[3] is best understood from this viewpoint.

The Class Features of Violence in Poso

Capitalism's presence in the country can be traced back to Dutch colonialism—a system to which Central Sulawesi (including Poso) was marginal. The Dutch arrived in Poso and asserted territorial claims by the early decades of the nineteenth century as a part of the "pacification" of the outer Indonesian islands. After successful wars against the locals, the Dutch replaced traditional slash-and-burn techniques with permanent cultivation, as happened on the shore of Lake Poso. Although the Dutch were also interested in resources, there was no capital investment during colonialism. Since then, the population in Poso has been predominantly engaged in an agriculture-based economy. However, this society was not homogenous at all, and as Albert Schrauwers notes, there was differentiation among peasants. One of the historical achievements of the Dutch was the conversion of upland people from paganism to Christianity.[4]

After Indonesian independence, Poso remained one of the less-developed regions of the country. The vast majority of the population remains engaged in subsistence agricultural production on small holdings. In the countryside the old structure of tribal relations of production has merely been replaced by new forms. It includes the presence of independent agricultural producers with small-scale plots who rely on the labour of family members. There are also relatively rich peasants who either employ daily wage workers or contract their land out to landless sharecroppers. Since forest products like rattan and resin have been commoditized, this also constitutes class-based relations of production between forest-product collectors and intermediary merchants. For poor peasants who live around forest areas, the collection of forest products is an important way of generating cash. Since most of the poor are in debt, merchants can generate significant profits after paying peasants low prices. In addition, although incoming migration is not a new phenomenon, the growing of export-based commodities—cocoa, for example—during the last two decades has enhanced inter-province migration to Poso. This has led to the significant transfer of land in the countryside, where new migrants have been able to buy land from the local population.[5] In short, it can be concluded that rural society around Poso clearly has a class character. What needs to be stressed is that the existing class relations in the countryside are characterized by peasant differentiation: not all rural people are equal.

It also needs to be stressed that the development of a modern capitalist sector in the region is associated with resource-based industries. Logging companies operated around Poso from the 1960s onward, before the government banned the export of unprocessed logs in the 1980s and '90s. Since the early 1990s, palm oil plantations have started to operate. These include PT Tamaco Graha Krida (TGK), owned by Indonesian magnate Liem Sioe Liong, and the state-owned company PT PN XIV. This industry has recently expanded to include the subsidiaries of the major palm oil giants such as Sinar Mas and Astra Agro Lestari. These companies generate significant profit by employing cheap labour, mostly from casual employees working in precarious conditions. This kind of cheap labour is semi-proletarian in character since the workers also work in their own fields during breaks. In addition, since 2010, the nickel mining industry has significantly expanded, especially in the countryside throughout Morowali Regency and North Morowali Regency. It is true that a modern working class is forming in this sector. However, since this industry requires labour-saving technology, only a handful of the rural population has become mineworkers. Furthermore, because many skilled mineworkers come from other provinces, the vast majority of local people remain as an under-employed labour reserve.

In the town of Poso, since large-scale manufacturing has never been present, the vast majority of the working population comprises a non-industrial working class. The most interesting and the most permanent jobs belong to civil servants, while the remaining jobs are in small-scale commercial and service enterprises. The informal sector dominates and, as a result, there is a sizeable informal proletariat. In short, the active working population is tiny, while most people form the reserve army of labour. In the latter I include the informal working class, the unemployed, and *preman* (petty criminals). Of course, the reserve army of labour as a whole also includes traditional or subsistence peasants (i.e., small-holder producers and seasonal wage earners). The sheer size of this working population underpins the specific way in which capitalism developed in Poso and in Indonesia as a whole.

The Series of Violent Conflicts

The nearly two decades of violence in Poso can be described on three levels: clashes among people, sporadic attacks by militias, and clashes between the militias and security forces.

First, clashes among people erupted in December 1998 following the economic crisis and the collapse of the Suharto dictatorship. After escalating in the following years, especially up to mid-2000, a local conflict led to the killing of around 246 people.[6] "Revenge" for these killings later became the principal justification for the presence of Muslim militias in Poso. Despite widespread battles among local people, the major factor that contributed to the death toll was the Indonesian security forces: the Indonesian National Army (TNI) and the Indonesian National Police (PNI) each tolerated the war; indeed strong evidence indicates that they did nothing to prevent widespread mass mobilization. A massacre in Sintuvulemba village, in which hundreds of peasants were killed, provides a striking example. Instead of preventing the violence, members of the security forces tolerated the clashes and supported parties to conflict.[7] As a result, the scale of violence escalated, both in terms of the geographical distribution of violent attacks and the number of victims. Following the Deklarasi Malino (Malino Accord), the government-led ceasefire established in 2001, and the subsequent deployment of huge numbers of security forces (both police and army), direct clashes among the people drastically declined.

On the face of it this was a success. Yet the violence soon entered a second phase in which sporadic but deadly attacks by well-organized militias became common. In spite of their sporadic nature, however, these attacks showed a marked increase of violence in terms of methods used and targets chosen. Among the militias, it was Jemaah Islamiyah (JI) that was officially believed to have been clandestinely involved in bloody assaults. These targeted attacks took the form of mysterious shootings or killings, bombings, and bus attacks. One major strike orchestrated by this group was the bombing of a traditional market in Tentena District on 28 May 2005 that killed twenty-two people, including a three-year old boy, and wounded more than fifty others. The assaults also included the beheading of three Christian schoolgirls in October 2005 in Poso. Attacks were not confined to Poso, though, but were extended to Palu, Central Sulawesi's capital city. By the end of December 2005, a bombing at a traditional pork market in

Palu killed seven people and wounded several others. Later, Indonesian authorities charged and sentenced to jail some local members of the militias for these organized assaults. The most common interpretation, derived from official police investigations, is that the perpetrators were members of terrorist networks, especially JI.[8]

It is important to note that the scale of violence in Poso has significantly changed, with the growing presence of what have been characterized, in the context of the US government's "war on terror," as terrorist organizations. Poso has frequently been described as a base for transnational terrorist groups like JI and al Qaeda. Some claimed that these organizations set up military training camps not just for locals but also for people from other parts of Indonesia. Several key figures in the organizations are believed to have entered Poso in 2000–2005. Many who have been involved in terrorist attacks in Indonesia since the early years of the century spent time in Poso either as military trainers or trainees. This tells us that the violence in Poso cannot be isolated from national and global debates on terrorism.

A third phase has seen intensified clashes between the Indonesian security forces and the militias, mostly since 2006. One of the major gunfights between Indonesian police and militia groups took place in January 2007 in the heart of the town of Poso and resulted in the defeat of a group that was officially believed to have close ties to JI. Some members of the group were killed and others arrested, while one police officer was killed. Recently, a new group called Mujahidin Indonesia Timur (Eastern Indonesia Mujahedeen, or MIT) has arrived in the area. Santoso, or Abu Wardah, is listed as the leader of this militia. The MIT is also represented as an Islamic State–linked terrorist cell believed to have engaged in various attacks since 2011.[9] In May 2011, this group was responsible for shooting dead two police officers and injuring another officer in front of the Bank Central Asia office in Palu. On 20 December 2012, the group shot and killed four soldiers of the Indonesian police's Mobile Brigade (Brimob) and injured three others in the village of Kalora. This armed group is also reportedly responsible for the brutal killing of two low-ranking police officers in Tamanjeka village in October 2012. In mid-2013, in a six-minute propaganda video posted to YouTube, Santoso called on Indonesian Muslims to wage war against the police's anti-terror unit (Densus 88). In March and April 2015, the Indonesian military mobilized thousands of troops for a two-week incursion into the jungles of Poso in an attempt to surround Santoso's base. After evacuating hundreds of poor peasant families, troops employing missile launchers, fighter jets, and attack helicopters struck targets in the jungle and announced that MIT was no longer present in the area. On 3 April 2015, one of the militia's most prominent leaders, Daeng Koro, was killed during a forty-five minute battle with Densus 88 in Parigi Regency, close to Poso. The anti-terror unit also found an M-16 rifle owned by this militia.[10] However, Santoso's group immediately returned to the jungle following the military's withdrawal. On 19 August 2015, a Brimob officer was killed in a battle with the militia. In another battle in a mountainous area called Auma, one of Santoso's members was also killed.[11] In early February 2016, a gunfight between the police and MIT in Sangginora village left three dead, including one Brimob officer and two jihadists.[12] Since the group has employed guerilla tactics in the jungles of Poso, the Indonesian authorities have repeatedly deployed combat troops against Santoso. Indonesian authorities ordered renewed troop deployments in 2016, mobilizing twenty-five hundred police and army personnel, including the Special Forces Command (Kopassus), under the name Operation Tinombala.[13]

All about the Poor

Whatever the causes and effects of the violence since 2000, the dominant view holds that it was an ethno-religious contest. Most, if not all, religious organizations use this language, as do pundits and media personalities. According to this view the fighters on the street are being divided along religious and ethnic lines. Most importantly, the Indonesian government and security forces believe the violence was the direct result of inter-religious conflict. Therefore attempts to resolve the violence have relied on ethno-religious approaches. The 2001 Malino Accord was a striking example of the view that violence can only be ended through a peace agreement between religious and ethnic parties. In short, there is a widely accepted consensus that the violence is a matter of identity.

This explanation is not sufficient. Acts of violence cannot be understood as mere voluntary human action. Rather, they should be viewed within the prism of material conditions. As Marx rightly asserts, "Men make their own history, but they do not make it as they please; they do not make it under self-selected circumstances, but under circumstances existing already, given and transmitted from the past."[14] In this regard, we should not underestimate the class features of local society that dialectically determine human actions in violence. In this respect, when we take the example of those who were the victims and perpetrators, the class nature of the violence is immediately evident. Despite their ethno-religious divisions, to some extent the people who fought each other in the early phase of the violence came from the same class background. They were the unemployed, poor peasants, precarious seasonal workers, the informal proletariat, and the lumpenproletariat. They were all relative-surplus populations displaced under the objective conditions of capitalism's uneven development.

The members of this reserve army of labour had one thing in common: poverty. Because of the economic crisis some lost their jobs and, under current conditions, are constrained to enter certain jobs. What they do not have in common is a class consciousness that could potentially enable them to overcome the unequal conditions created by capitalism. Only from this view is it possible to properly analyze the principal factors that have generated violence in Poso.

In this light, I will elaborate by looking at the subjects who either took part in violent attacks or who became victims. Most people who died by the middle of 2000 were traditional peasants. Around two hundred peasants died in an event related to the massacre at the Javanese transmigration village of Sintivulemba, approximately nine kilometres from Poso. The people accused of masterminding the killing were Fabianus Tibo, Dominggus Da Silva, and Marinus Riwu, all characterized as poor. In spite of pressure from human rights organizations, Indonesian authorities executed the trio in 2006.[15] The three Catholics were basically semi-proletarians who owned small plots and were engaged as seasonal workers in rubber estates. They came from Nusa Tenggara Timur, one of the poorest provinces in the archipelago. Tibo arrived in the Regency of Banggai, Central Sulawesi, in 1973, where he worked for a logging company for some years. In 1978 he moved to Beteleme village in Poso (now Morowali) and became a seasonal rubber tapper for a state-owned company, PTPN XIV, in Beteleme. Dominggus arrived in 1991 and lived in Beteleme. He was an ex-worker (a driver for heavy equipment) for (probably a subcontractor of) PT Inco, a subsidiary of the Canadian nickel mining company Inco (itself now owned by Brazilian conglomerate Vale). He then worked for PTPN XIV until the outbreak of violent conflict. Lastly, Marinus arrived in Poso through the transmigration program by which the Suharto regime sought to relocate surplus populations to other areas with a need for labour. He lived in Molores village and worked as a seasonal worker in PTPN XIV as well. Considering their backgrounds, it is inaccurate to blame these poor men for being the masterminds of the violence. They were victimized.

The same logic can be applied to the Muslim side. What followed from the outbreak of the Sintuvulemba massacre was the increased attention of people outside Poso. Later, this killing became the principal pretext for the presence of Muslim militias in Poso. The groups included local and national organizations such as Laskar Jundullah and Laskar Jihad. They also included the supranational group JI, which has operated in Indonesia, Malaysia, the Philippines, Singapore, and Thailand. Moreover, JI is also identified as a "regional" partner of al Qaeda.[16] All these groups came to Poso and recruited local young people. Unlike other groups that seemed to operate on a clandestine basis, Laskar Jihad operated in the open. It recruited young people mostly from the informal proletariat, the unemployed, and from poor families. Some members of this group who came to Poso in the name of defending local Muslims, whom I interviewed in 2002, were unemployed. Some lost their jobs in the manufacturing industry during the crisis and then joined the jihadists, leaving their families behind in Java. Other groups mostly recruited their members from local people. The locals were basically from the reserve army of labour or poor families whose already difficult existence was exacerbated by the ongoing violence. Losing jobs, property, and even family members pushed these people to join jihadist organizations.

While the class feature of the violence is ignored by most studies, the present analysis suggests the need for a special attention to class. Like the trio discussed above, the perpetrators of violence after the Malino Accord were mostly local young men who were initially unemployed, and some who lost family members during the violence. Basri, for example, who was characterized as the commander of Tanah Runtuh in the fight against the police in January 2007, came from a poor family. He stated that he lost around twenty members of his extended family during the clashes in 2000. He did not complete secondary school and, prior to 1998, he might be best characterized as a member of the lumpenproletariat since he was involved in petty criminal activity in the town. He has covered his body in tattoos and since getting married in 2000 he has become a farmer, working in his parents' small plot. He and his friends were recruited into local militia groups after the outbreak of violence. They were well trained in using machine guns and in making homemade bombs, learning from jihadist trainers who were mostly from outside Poso.

Santoso, the MIT leader who subsequently proclaimed himself commander of the Islamic State group's forces in Indonesia, had a similar background. His parents arrived in the village of Lembontonara, an upland region of Poso (now a part of the Regency of North Morowali), in 1967 under the Indonesian government's transmigration program. Finding only wasteland unfit for cultivation, his parents then moved to Mayakeli village, near Lake Poso, where the family found more fertile agricultural soil. In order to attend secondary school, his parents sent their young boy to live with an acquaintance in Poso. Between 1995 and 1998, Santoso was a street vendor. Since the outbreak of violence in Poso the family has moved to Tambarana village in the coastal area of Poso.[17] The former police chief of Central Sulawesi (2006–8), Badrodin Haiti, who is currently the chief of the Indonesian National Police, stated that at that time Santoso was not involved in a terrorist network, adding that Santoso had a kiosk in Tambarana.[18] These stories show that the subjects are, in short, marginalized in various ways under the existing system of exclusion that is the capitalist order.

One should not isolate the subjects who have taken part in the violence in Poso from the global context of violence related to capitalism. Some jihadist trainers in Poso had experience during the Soviet-Afghan War, where they joined the US-backed Mujahedeen. For instance, Natsir Abas, a Malaysian citizen, was a veteran of the Afghan Mujahedeen who spent some years around 2000 in Poso, training locals and setting up the JI cell known as Mantiqi III. In addition, it should be stressed that the US invasion of Iraq immediately generated a growing negative sentiment in Poso's Muslim community. They characterized the invasion as a war against Islam and argued that it was therefore necessary to take action against the West. Although this was a misrepresentation, the global face of class tension contributed to violence in remote regions like Poso.

Violence in Poso and Reconciliation

The notion of ethno-religious clashes has dominated the mainstream narrative of violence in Poso. Rather than ignoring this ethno-religious investigation, the approach employed here seeks to tie the subject of ethno-religious violence to the objective conditions of capitalism and their role in the violence in Poso. It is important to consider the more than seventeen years of violence in Poso under the prism of systemic social exclusion deriving from the existing capitalist order in Indonesia. This lens permits a better understanding of the violence, which is best viewed as a war of the poor. The failure to understand the underlying face of capitalist contradiction brings the poor to act against one another. They do not fight against the capitalist system of exclusion, but against the victims of the system. They strike against themselves.

Given the failure to understand this context, efforts to end the violence that has occurred since the implementation of the Malino Accord have failed. The state-led reconciliation process has ignored the key issues described above, leading to ceaseless violence. The Malino initiative itself reflected an elite-based strategy, which is also widely criticized among the population of the region. Many complaints come from the grass roots. This is illustrated by a local joke: "the failure of the Malino Accord was due to the approach based on *toko-toko* (shops or retailers) without inviting *kios-kios* (small kiosks) to take part." The words *toko-toko* sound similar to *tokoh-tokoh* (leaders) and refer to the elites in a community, while *kios-kios* means all grassroots members of the community. The joke indicates that the reconciliation initiative excluded the voices of the "street fighters" or the poor from the process. The fact that Poso has been balkanized based on the division of Muslim and Christian settlements reflects the difficulties in bridging these two communities.

The fact that the escalation of violence is in a state of qualitative flux, with more recent violence associated with the war between militias and security forces, leaves us to question what kind of reconciliation should be endorsed. Since Indonesia has no experience at the national level in exercising a model of reconciliation that deals fairly with state violence (e.g., the 1965 pogrom) it is also necessary to speak of the state as one party rather than a mediator for the other parties in reconciliation.

Notes

1. See Lorraine V. Aragon, "Communal Violence in Poso, Central Sulawesi: Where People Eat Fish and Fish Eat People," *Indonesia* 72 (2001): 45–79, and Aragon, "Elite Competition in Central Sulawesi," in *Renegotiating Boundaries: Local Politics in Post-Suharto Indonesia*, ed. Henk Schulte Nordholt and Gerry van Klinken (Leiden, NL: KITLV, 2007), 39–89. By "Poso violence," I mean the violence that took place in the original regency of Poso, which has since been divided into four regencies: Poso, Morowali (created in 1999), Tojo Una-Una (2013), and North Morowali (2013).

2. Hal Hill, *The Indonesian Economy* (Cambridge: Cambridge University Press, 2000).

3. See Gerry Van Klinken, *Communal Violence and Democratization in Indonesia: Small Town Wars* (London: Routledge Contemporary Southeast Asia Series, 2009).

4. Albert Schrauwers, " 'Let's Party': State Intervention, Discursive Traditionalism and the Labour Process of Highland Rice Cultivators in Central Sulawesi, Indonesia," *Journal of Peasant Studies* 25, no. 3 (1998): 112–30.

5. Tania Murray Li, "Local Histories, Global Markets: Cocoa and Class in Upland Sulawesi," *Development and Change* 33, no. 3 (2002): 415–37.

6. Dave McRae, *A Few Poorly Organized Men: Interreligious Violence in Poso, Indonesia* (Leiden, NL: Brill, 2013), 6.

7. Arianto Sangaji, "The Security Forces and Regional Violence in Poso," in *Renegotiating Boundaries: Local Politics in Post-Suharto Indonesia*, ed. Henk Schulte Nordholt and Gerry van Klinken (Leiden, KL: KITLV, 2007), 255–80.

8. International Crisis Group, *Jihadism in Indonesia: Poso on the Edge* (Jakarta/Brussels: International Crisis Group, 2007) and *Indonesia: Jemaah Islamiyah's Current Status* (Jakarta/Brussels: International Crisis Group, 2007).

9. Devina Heriyanto, "Q&A: Introducing Santoso," *Jakarta Post*, 8 April 2016, http://www.thejakartapost.com/academia/2016/04/08/qa-introducing-santoso.html (accessed 28 June 2017); Marguerite Afra Sapiie, "The Hunting Party," *Jakarta Post*, 1 April 2016, http://www.thejakartapost.com/longform/2016/04/01/the-hunting-party.html (accessed 28 June 2017).

10. Ruslan Sangadji, "Wife confirms dead terrorist is Daeng Koro," *Jakarta Post*, 5 April 2015, http://www.thejakartapost.com/news/2015/04/05/wife-confirms-dead-terrorist-daeng-koro.html (accessed 10 March 2016).

11. Ruslan Sangadji and Ina Parlina, "Police Officer Killed in Shootout with Terrorists," *Jakarta Post*, 21 August 2015.

12. Ruslan Sangadji, "Two suspected terrorists, police officer killed in Poso shootout," *Jakarta Post*, 9 February 2016, http://www.thejakartapost.com/news/2016/02/09/two-suspected-terrorists-police-officer-killed-poso-shootout.html (accessed 10 March 2016).

13. Ruslan Sangadji, "High hopes for police generals to capture most-wanted Santoso," the *Jakarta Post*, 18 March 2016, http://www.thejakartapost.com/news/2016/03/18/high-hopes-police-generals-capture-most-wanted-santoso.html (accessed 30 March 2016).

14. Karl Marx. *The Eighteenth Brumaire of Louis Bonaparte*, 1852, https://www.marxists.org/archive/marx/works/1852/18th-brumaire/ch01.htm (accessed 28 June 2017).

15   McRae, *A Few Poorly Organized Men*.

16   International Crisis Group, *Jemaah Islamiyah in South East Asia: Damaged but Still Dangerous* (Brussels: International Crisis Group, 2003).

17   Nur Soima Ulfa, "Memburu Santoso di Gunung Biru," *Beritagar* (Jakarta), 14 February 2016, https://beritagar.id/artikel/laporan-khas/memburu-santoso-di-gunung-biru (accessed 10 March 2016).

18   Juwita Trisna Rahayu, "Badrodin akui pernah dekat dengan teroris Santoso," *Antaranews*, 9 March 2014, http://www.antaranews.com/berita/423032/badrodin-akui-pernah-dekat-dengan-teroris-santoso (accessed 10 March 2016).

SECTION IV

Where Indonesia Meets Melanesia: Memory, Truth, and Reconciliation in Tanah Papua

Where Indonesia Meets Melanesia: Memory, Truth, and Reconciliation in Tanah Papua

The Indonesian state cannot successfully mediate conflicts to which it is a party. As we saw in the previous chapter, this is true at the local level in Poso. It is truer still at the provincial level, in Tanah Papua, to which we now turn. The Indonesian government has tried to resolve its longest-running conflict through a "security approach" by cracking down with military force. It has tried to resolve it through a "development approach" by offering the promise of economic gain to win Papuan hearts and minds. It has tried, most recently, by granting "special autonomy" within the Indonesian national fold. But it has never accepted the need for dialogue between the Indonesian state and Papuan nationalists. Most relevant to the themes of this volume, it axed the commitment to a truth commission that was promised as part of the autonomy law.

What is Tanah Papua? Part of the problem for observers is that there are as many names as there are sides to the conflict. The colonial name was West New Guinea or Netherlands New Guinea. Indonesians demanding the colony be handed over to them called it West Irian. Then for many years it became the Indonesian province of Irian Jaya. Nationalists seeking an independent state referred to it as West Papua. In a move to conciliate rising pro-independence sentiment in 2000, the Indonesian government agreed to rename the province Papua. Just to add confusion, the western third of the province was snipped away (with questionable legality) to form a new province, officially called West Papua to distinguish it from the rest of the island—still called Papua. Here we use the term *Tanah Papua*, the "Land of Papua," to recognize the term's growing acceptance among Papuans and to avoid the politics of choosing another name.

The territory was part of the Netherlands East Indies. When, in 1949, the Dutch recognized Indonesian independence, they retained control of Papua. Since Indonesia also claimed the territory, that meant confrontation between the two governments, alongside Papuans' mobilizing for independence. We often think of colonization, decolonization, and sometimes *recolonization*, as processes that happen in sequence. In the Papuan case, all three things were happening at once, as simultaneous, linked processes. Indonesia began to prepare for a military invasion. To prevent that, the United States intervened to mediate a resolution to the dispute, and the territory was transferred in stages to Indonesia in 1962–63. The handover was formalized in an "act of free choice" organized by Indonesian authorities in 1969, in which 1,022 carefully picked electors delivered an unopposed verdict in favour of integration. Indonesia's success in adding Papua to its territory marked the completion of decolonization for the Indonesian government, but the beginning of recolonization for Papuan elites who had thought they were about to receive their independence. Thus an independence movement continued and indeed gathered force under Indonesian rule. After the Suharto regime was toppled in 1998, Papuan nationalism came out of the forests and into the open with renewed vocal calls for independence. Although Indonesian authorities were forced to accept an independent East Timor after 1999, and inked a peace deal with separatist fighters in Aceh province in 2005, they have maintained a harder line against independence sentiment in Papua.

Indonesian and Papuan nationalists deploy very different versions of this history. The two clashing historical narratives are not simply different ways of *representing* the past; these different perceptions of the past are a root cause that helps to *constitute* the current conflict. Historical dialogue is needed if there is to be any prospect of resolving the conflict. The Indonesian state has deployed a historical narrative of completing national unity by annexing and retaining control of Tanah Papua. Papuan nationalists counter with a narrative of a people on their way to self-determination until outside interference forced the handover of their country to foreign Indonesian rule. These clashing narratives have become tools in the diplomatic arsenals of two competing nationalist movements. They remain so today, in ways that continue to fuel conflict.

Conflict in Tanah Papua is spurred by a wide range of factors. Papuans feel at risk of being reduced to a minority in their own homeland as more and more Indonesian settlers arrive and dominate local economies. There are complaints that a resource-rich land is looted to feed the national treasury, while poverty and AIDS among Papuans are well above the national average. Human rights violations and cultural clashes continue to enflame tensions. Indonesian security forces continue to tag any dissent as "separatist" and to treat that label as sufficient reason for repressive tactics.

The democratic governments that emerged in Indonesia after the fall of Suharto offered special autonomy for Papua, a move with the potential to resolve the conflict. In avoiding the symbolic aspects and refusing to engage in a dialogue of historical narratives, however, it failed to do so. The Special Autonomy Law of 2001 granted a greater share of natural resource revenues and political autonomy, but rejected the symbolic claims and thus ignored the emotive force behind calls for independence. The issue was still framed in terms of uneven economic development, so the solution remained development-oriented. The autonomy law did mandate a truth commission, but no such commission has been formed.

These dilemmas are explored in chapter 15, which opens with the issues of clashing views of history and highlights troubles with state-led reconciliation efforts that parallel those in Poso (described in Chapter 14). Tanah Papua is very much in a pre–truth commission phase, a period in which calls for truth are embodied in the demand from some civil-society groups to correct the historical record (*pelurusan sejarah*). What might an eventual Papuan truth commission look like? The question, when asked for Indonesia with respect to the mass killings of the 1960s, suggests that any truth-seeking must also be international. The answer here turns on a respect for Papuan Indigenous reverence for the natural world: a truth process would need to include careful consideration of the living environment (*lingkunan hidup*), ravaged by resource-extraction capitalism.

Indigenous aspects of peace-seeking shine through in chapter 16, which shows the extent to which Papuan cultural identity has rejected assimilation into Indonesia's "unity in diversity." Papuan nationalism does not always look like other forms of nationalism. It often sings rather than shouts—not an uncommon theme when nationalist aspirations face a repressive government. It sings not just against a government, but against a system of rule in which multinational mining companies are experienced as colonizers and despoilers. As in Aceh, extractive industries based outside Indonesia exacerbate conflict and a local sense of dispossession.

The implication is that reconciliation will also have to include international actors—the same conclusion we reached in previous sections. Chapter 17 spells this out with a close examination of the human rights discourses used by what is still the dominant outside power, the United States. The US role in forcing Tanah Papua into Indonesian hands, along with the American headquarters of the key mining company in Tanah Papua, imply that the United States has a particular responsibility to resolve a conflict it helped to create. Especially important here is that Western human rights discourses—chapter 17 highlights annual human rights reporting by the US State Department—must make space for Papuan and other Indigenous understandings that embrace human rights but expand our understanding of rights.

Clashing historical narratives represent different claims to what is true about the past. Different understandings of human rights also make the notion of truth a sometimes contested concept. In Tanah Papua, truth-seeking has to contend with a multitude of barriers. Among them is the challenge of "non-truth" peddled by the Indonesian state, which the next chapter begins to explore.

15

Facts, Feasts, and Forests: Considering Truth and Reconciliation in Tanah Papua

TODD BIDERMAN AND JENNY MUNRO

In this chapter we are interested in what sorts of "truths" are included in "truth and reconciliation" and from whose perspective. We also consider what sorts of reconciliation are already taking place in Tanah Papua, even amid ongoing violence. In Tanah Papua we have the problem of a multi-dimensional conflict and a state that is very dedicated to controlling what is said about that conflict. It is worth considering how "non-truth" plays out in local reconciliation attempts and who or what institutions are defended or marginalized in this dynamic.

Tanah Papua has been the site of low-level, endemic conflict since the 1960s. Despite Indonesia's efforts to eradicate Papuan nationalism, Indigenous aspirations for independence have persisted. The Free Papua Movement (Organisasi Papua Merdeka or OPM), a network of poorly armed fighters based in remote areas that has staged sporadic attacks on Indonesian forces, has gained much attention from Indonesian authorities. However, the OPM is only one of many groups that criticize Indonesian rule and draw attention to social injustices and human rights abuses. The vast majority of Papuans do not participate in any OPM-related activities and most are not in favour of violence as a means of achieving independence. More recently, organizations such as the West Papua National Committee (Komite Nasional Papua Barat, or KNPB) have put forth a vocal critique of

Indonesian abuses, while the United Liberation Movement for West Papua (ULMWP) seeks to bring attention to political conditions in Papua on an international stage.

Politics in Tanah Papua is not reducible to the historical context by which Indonesia came to govern. Rather, Papuans critique the social, economic, environmental, and political conditions that have emerged under Indonesian rule. The Indonesian state, especially the police and military in Papua, has been intolerant of such criticisms. Criticism of Indonesian governance is branded as "treason," suppressed through violence, murder, and intimidation, and often punished through arbitrary detention and imprisonment. There is denial about the actions of the military and police in Papua at the highest levels of Indonesian governance, and human rights violations have not been addressed. Indeed, truth, denial, secrets, and impunity are at the heart of the political conflict in Papua. Indonesian non-truth is central to Papuan experiences and grievances. Yet scholars have argued that non-truth is exceedingly common in approaches to conflict resolution throughout Indonesia, including in Papua, and even for community actors drawing on local understandings.[1] Still, for Papua, one question that arises is how non-truth as an approach is valued or enforced in response to incidents of state violence, even as Papuans and their supporters continue to criticize non-truth as a broad political practice of the Indonesian state because it denies history, rights, and current conditions.

In looking at the concept and practice of truth and reconciliation in Papua, we first acknowledge that Papuans and their supporters have been doing work that reflects the principles of truth and reconciliation in spite of ongoing conflict. Their work, as we discuss later, is mainly of local inspiration and derivation, but also reflects international connections and experiences.

Papua's diversity provokes questions about how international, national, or otherwise high-level processes can engage appropriately with local voices, world views, and cultural values. What, then, are Papuan approaches to reconciliation, and what is the role of truth? Because conflict is ongoing, the Papuan case also gives us an opportunity to ask what has to take place, or what conditions have to be created, in order for reconciliation to occur and so that truth may be spoken.

There are three aspects to highlight about approaches to truth and reconciliation in Papua. The first aspect is the present landscape and state of Papuan approaches to conflict resolution. The second aspect, extending from that, questions what needs to be resolved and why. One area we highlight is the impact of economic development projects, namely resource extraction and land exploitation, on Papuan identity. Thirdly, given these points, and exploring some recent examples of small-scale reconciliation in the wake of state violence, we ask what truth and reconciliation processes in Papua might look like.

In this chapter we make use of secondary sources on the conflict and resolution-related actions, present some views from people we have worked with in Papua, and generally draw on over a decade of experience working with Papuans. Truth and reconciliation is a topic we have come to by way of a keen interest in inequalities in Tanah Papua and a commitment to community-based and Indigenous-led efforts to ameliorate inequalities. Todd Biderman comes from a development and social- and ecological-justice background, largely in Indonesia. Over the last eight years he has been working with Papuan civil-society groups and communities. Jenny Munro is an anthropologist who works on gender, health, and education in Papua, particularly in the central highlands of Papua province. We have also collaborated on developing an Indigenous-led HIV prevention strategy for Tanah Papua.[2]

Understandings of the Conflict in Tanah Papua

Before we can discuss what approaches have been taken towards resolving the political conflict in Papua, it is important to note that there is disagreement about the nature of the conflict itself, and therefore what needs to be resolved, by whom, and why. This situation partially underpins Papuans calls for truth, or "straightening history" (*pelurusan sejarah*), described in more detail later. In general, there are dominant Indonesian and dominant Papuan perspectives on the conflict. The Indonesian perspective is mainly represented and put forward by government officials and some commentators. The Papuan perspective includes Papuan scholars, some political leaders and representatives, and everyday Papuans. There is also diversity within Indonesian and Papuan views.

INDONESIAN VIEWS

The dominant, official perspective in Indonesia is that there should be no question about the legitimacy of Indonesia's hold on Papua. In this view, Papua never should have been retained by the Dutch in the first place, as the Netherlands was obliged to return the entire former East Indies colony to the new independent government of Indonesia. From this point of view, Papua is critical part of a complete Indonesian nation, and indeed bringing Papua into its fold was an important emphasis of early Indonesian actions. Thus, one analysis of Papuan desires for independence suggests that the Indonesian agenda of generating a feeling of national belonging and common identity has failed. A less sympathetic view holds that "radicals" (the OPM and other groups that have been branded as terrorist organizations), who are presumed to represent a violent minority of Papuans, refuse to accept Indonesian authority, actively wage war on the state in order to achieve independence, and need to be eradicated through violent means.

Related to this, another dominant, official Indonesian viewpoint on the conflict holds that Papuans are aggrieved by conditions of underdevelopment and poverty. Not being part of the Indonesian national trajectory of economic growth and increased prosperity is in some ways another manifestation of exclusion. But more generally, this perspective suggests that the source of Papuan grievance is mainly economic. Papuans are also said to be envious of the economic achievements and dominance of Indonesian migrants. Thus, there is a social dimension to this economic understanding of the conflict. In this view, Papua is often said to be rich in natural resources that have not yet been exploited to advance the social and economic conditions of the Indigenous inhabitants.

Researchers have also described how some Indonesians hold related, but unofficial views of Papua as a land of riches to be exploited, a frontier economy where profits can be made quickly and easily. These perspectives were present twenty years ago,[3] and are probably even more prevalent today. Slama and Munro for example, describe conversations with Indonesian businessmen in Jakarta who were eager to gain access to lucrative development, construction and other sorts of *proyek* (project) in Papua.[4] These ambitions suggest Indonesian (and other) entrepreneurs, managing agencies, and contractors are angling to capture some of the trillions of rupiah that make up decentralization funds in Papua.

Papuan Views

Dominant Papuan views of the conflict tend to diverge from Indonesian understandings, though certain understandings are shared with progressive actors and agencies in Indonesian society. From a historical perspective, Papuans find Indonesian control illegitimate, noting that their leaders declared independence in 1961, and that their right to self-determination was obliterated in the sham referendum of 1969.

Where the Indonesian view holds that Papuans ought to feel a sense of belonging in a diverse nation, some Papuans argue that their cultural and ethnic distinctiveness from the rest of Indonesia undermine Indonesia's right to govern. Related to this, Papuans have also increasingly been drawing attention to experiences of stigmatization, racism, and discrimination that challenge those who claim that Papuans are valued as equal cultural citizens. Papuan critiques also draw attention to the in-migration of Indonesians and other practices related to "Indonesianization" as proof that notions of national belonging are little more than political rhetoric.[5]

There is a perception that Indonesian claims of nationalistic feelings or the desire to develop Papua are false claims that cover up true intentions. For example, a key element of Papuan understandings of the conflict is that Indonesia wanted Papua in order to develop and profit from newly discovered gold deposits.[6] Many Papuans suggest that Indonesia is not interested in improving Papuan lives and would rather Papuans were eliminated to make access to resources easier. State violence, neglect of health and welfare issues, including a burgeoning HIV epidemic, the in-migration of Indonesians (particularly Muslim Indonesians) that has reduced Papuans to a minority in cities, and the birth control agenda are held up as examples of how Papuans lives are not valued. Leslie Butt has analyzed what might be called a "conspiracy theory" among Indigenous highlanders that argues that Indonesia has deliberately introduced HIV-infected sex workers to decimate the Indigenous population.[7] Through her research she demonstrates that the term *conspiracy theory* is misleading because highlanders have good reason to question what they are told by Indonesians about HIV based on observations and rational assessments. For example, sex work is illegal, and yet highlanders can see that it occurs with the acknowledgement of government authorities and the involvement of military protection.

Understandings of the conflict also draw attention to local situations. In the highlands, for example, Indigenous leaders frequently lament the chaos in the Indonesian system, and that their previous strategies for leadership, land issues, and social and economic needs are in disarray.[8] The Indonesian system has normalized corruption, the role of money in politics, and poor governance, and this continues to permeate local governance. Thus locals also express frustration that members of parliament fail to represent their constituents' interests and that democratic processes are allowed to be openly flaunted. This leads to a deepening of resentment towards Indonesian rule and Indonesian migrants, as well as tensions among Papuans.

State Approaches to Conflict Resolution

Generally speaking, Indonesian governments have taken two approaches: those of "security" and "development." The security-led approach was based on the idea that the conflict is being generated by particular armed groups, and is being inflamed by those who report on human rights abuses and other forms of repression. Indonesia usually claims that these reports are false and are just being made to increase support for Papuan independence, both among locals and among foreign audiences. Foreigners are often accused of "false reporting," supporting banned groups, and otherwise promoting separatism. This has been the justification for both the earlier designation of Papua as a "military operations zone" (*daerah operasi militer*), which restricted access, and the persistent reluctance to allow access to both domestic journalists and observers and foreigners. The ostensible need to control these activities has been the justification for continuing to increase the presence of the military, police, and special forces.

Yet, as noted above, an increased military presence often means more restricted democratic social and political spaces, including restrictions on people's right to protest and communities' right to organize. This not only incites feelings of injustice among Papuans but for Indonesia it also necessitates the further surveillance on Papuans and the deepening involvement of security agents in policing everyday life as well as community, NGO, and other civil-society activities. Repression of civil-society expression and activism has also resulted in repeated abuses of human rights. The security approach to conflict resolution thus generates increased and deepening conflict. This has long been recognized by Papuans and others, leading to calls for peacebuilding, dialogue, and political solutions. Despite acknowledging that Papuan grievances might amount to more than just a few so-called terrorists who disagree with the historical conditions of incorporation, the Indonesian government continues to allow security forces to play a dominant role in managing conflict in Papua.

The security approach has been coupled with the "development" (*pembangunan*) or "prosperity" (*kesejahteraan*) approach to conflict resolution, which is derived from an understanding that conditions of underdevelopment, poverty, and lack of economic development contribute to Papuan desires for independence. However, the Indonesian state has a particular view on what sort of development is lacking in Papua, and what is therefore needed to improve "prosperity." No doubt there are differing opinions within this approach to conflict resolution, with some focusing more on Papuans' poverty, economic inequalities with Indonesians, and lack of services, while many others take the need for development to mean investment into Papua through capital projects, often funded by foreign aid. The Special Autonomy Law of 2001 reflected the view that profits from Papuan resources had been flowing to Jakarta with very little being retained in the way of development returns or outcomes. The central government thus saw the problem as one of unequal development, not of self-determination. It mandated transfer payments, through which billions of dollars have been poured into projects to improve governance, infrastructure, health, and education.

Special autonomy had some input from Papuan representatives, but at the time most Papuans saw it as an unwelcome alternative to independence, and many were opposed to it from the start: it was seen as Jakarta's solution, not theirs. There is very little evidence of how much money has remained in Papua and how much has flowed back out again to Indonesian contractors tasked with delivering development (especially infrastructure) projects.[9] Some critiques centre on the fact that the funds have contributed to the growth of a Papuan political elite, and have not been used to benefit Papuans more generally.[10] However, Papuan leaders have also criticized the implementation of special autonomy, declared it deceased, rejected it, and symbolically "returned" it to Jakarta. For example, in 2010 protesters carried a banner that said, "Special Autonomy (Otsus) has failed; Papuan peoples' right to life is threatened."[11] More recently, in

March 2016, the Civil Servants Association of Papua declared its support for "the Governor and Vice-Governor of Papua to return Special Autonomy to the central government."[12]

Beyond financial transfers, special autonomy was supposed to guarantee Papuan leaders some authority to increase the numbers of Papuans in government and to empower Papuans more generally. Richard Chauvel among others notes that Papuan policy efforts have been hampered by power dynamics in Jakarta.[13] Anecdotally, the presence of Papuans in government has increased, but there is no research to specify how and where this has occurred, and what effects it has had in terms of authority or decision-making power.

Along with special autonomy provisions there has been a decentralization program that aims to bring development outcomes for communities (in part through direct village development funds) and facilitate better access to government services. A new province, West Papua, was carved from the western tip or Bird's Head region of Papua province. Within that, further devolution has occurred through the creation of new regencies (*kabupaten*) and districts. In West Papua province prior to 2003 there were six regencies and now there are fourteen, with more on the way. Within that, there are districts that are also subdivided. The official logic behind the creation of new regencies and districts is that it brings services closer to people and makes large or rugged areas more manageable from a logistical and governance standpoint, but at the same time the division of these areas results in the fracturing of communities and cultural groups. Competitive angling among Indigenous people (mainly men) for funds and political power has led to new violence and marginalization. It has also fed into the narratives of those commentators who wish to blame Papuans for the failures of governance in the era of special autonomy.

In some ways, the development approach to conflict resolution in Papua also brings increased securitization, building on a tradition of military involvement (official or clandestine) in development. For the thirty years of Suharto's rule Indonesia was run by a military-backed dictatorship, with police and military tasked with implementing development. In Papua, the security sector continues to be heavily involved, both legally and illegally, in corporate activities, especially resource extraction and development projects in remote areas. President Joko Widodo (known as Jokowi) has expanded the role of the military as a development actor in Papua,[14] and signed off on far-reaching security policies that take the military into more regions of Papua/West Papua, in greater numbers, with permanent bases, and with less oversight from Jakarta[15]—exactly the opposite of what most analysts say is needed to overcome abuses of power. Jokowi also failed to address an incident that occurred in Papua mere weeks after he took his oath, when unarmed school students were reportedly shot by police in the highlands during a protest against military abuses.[16]

A controversial effect of decentralization and the creation of new districts is that these processes result in an influx of soldiers filling new command posts and bases at each level of administration.[17] Increased military and increased money is a dangerous combination that has historically led to conflict and rights abuses in Papua. At the same time, there is a lack of recognition of historical violence, ongoing violence, and heavy-handed support of that development program.

After years of Indonesia's "security" and "prosperity" approaches, the land of Papua still ranks among the poorest regions of Indonesia and is the least developed according to the UN Human Development Index. At the same time, there is a continued closure of democratic and civil-political space. There are, within the five-decade history of this conflict, obvious and well-documented cases of killings, rape, torture, of political disappearances, of gross violations against segments of Papuan society.[18] These are the obvious issues that will come to the fore of any truth and reconciliation process—if we get that far.

Papuan-led Strategies towards Dialogue, Acknowledgement, Truth, and Dispute Resolution

Papuan leaders have made initial steps to meet the Indonesian government on at least three occasions since 1998—the year of the fall of the Suharto dictatorship—to try and bridge the gap between independence claims and the Indonesian government. West Papuan leader Octovianus Mote describes 1999 and 2000 as "years of political victory which saw a Papuan leadership take strong direction. Two successive Papuan National Congresses established the Presidium Dewan Papua (Papua Presidium Council) and, in turn, set two paths to territorial independence." Mote continues:

> Following the fall of the New Order military regime … 100 representatives of the Papuan nation travelled to Jakarta to make their aspirations clear in a peaceful, open, and democratic way to the new President of Indonesia, B. J. Habibie. The whole Papuan nation had united and cast off the ropes of fear that had entangled them for so long. From mountain to coast, from north and south, whether Protestant, Catholic or even Muslim, whether illiterate villager or educated city-dweller— all united and shouted a single word: merdeka! or freedom.[19]

Thus, a hundred Papuan leaders (sometimes referred to as Team 100) advanced a claim to self-determination for the Papuan people. They hoped this might start a process of positive change in Papua, one that would shift away from the nearly forty preceding years of conflict. After the fall of Suharto, the notion of "straightening" false history, a re-understanding of the events that have happened since the incorporation of Papua into Indonesia in the 1960s, gained prominence among Papuans. Papuan leaders explicitly called for this truth-telling as part of their political activism. They also embarked on an "international political campaign to kick-start the independence struggle for the return and consolidation of basic rights of the Papuan people and nation."[20]

Within the Special Autonomy Law of 2001, space was encoded or legislated to ensure a process that would address Papuan calls for correcting history and truth-telling. In 2003, in response to a call from religious leaders in Papua to help them promote peace, justice, and human rights, several faith-based organizations formed a network committed to supporting the campaign of Papuan religious leaders to make Papua a "land of peace."[21] The group describes the initiative, which was established by leaders of the Catholic, Christian, Muslim, Hindu, and Buddhist communities in Papua, as follows:

> "Papua, Land of Peace" aims to establish a culture of peace. It builds communication ties between the different peoples and religions within Papua and between Papuans and the Indonesian Government. It intends to offer a free and just space, an arena for an open-ended discussion, and a frame for dialogue acceptable to all parties. "Papua, Land of Peace" recognizes

> Papua's *memoria passionis*: the remembrance of a history full of violence, neglect and broken promises against the Papuans. It believes that this history needs healing and recognition.[22]

Activists and leaders have also taken this agenda forward in various international forums, ranging from religious and civil-society groups who have dedicated their efforts to documenting violence, to calls for international human rights observers. The ULMWP recently called for the Melanesian Spearhead Group (MSG) and the Pacific Islands Forum to initiate human rights investigations in West Papua, and this has certainly gained traction among some members of the MSG.

Yet so far, little to no progress has been made towards Papuan calls for historical "truth," nor truth in response to acts of state violence that continue to occur. For example, human rights organizations continue to call for investigations into widespread patterns of violence but these calls have led to minimal, if any, response. It is worth noting that, broadly speaking, Indonesia has a very poor record of addressing historical human rights violations.[23]

In 2009 the Indonesian National Institute of Sciences (LIPI) released a report that outlined a "road map" for resolving conflict in Papua.[24] The road map listed four pillars of Papua's problems, including lack of recognition of historical wrongs and injustices, and offered four recommended solutions. The road map has been a reference point for peace advocates and activists in Tanah Papua, in particular the Papua Peace Network (Jaringan Damai Papua), which has strong backing from church leaders in Papua. Calls for dialogue have been met with reticence under all previous Indonesian administrations.

Under President Jokowi, there has so far not been any movement forward on political dialogue, changing atmospheres of repression and abuse, or truth-telling. To some extent the government has acknowledged that violence occurs in Papua, and that there have been human rights violations, but it considers these violations to be a thing of the past.

Post-Violence Resolution in the Central Highlands: The Honelama and Tolikara Incidents

In this section we discuss the efforts at resolution and reconciliation that took place after two separate incidents of security-sector violence in the highlands. Our objective is to draw out some details on what current, local, and Papuan approaches to resolving state-perpetrated violence look like and to reflect on how they engage with truth, cultural values, and local and government leaders. We invite you to imagine how a truth and reconciliation process or commission might address a fifty-year history of incidents like these.

Honelama, Wamena, 6 June 2012

On 6 June 2012, while Jenny was in Wamena, Jayawijaya regency, in the central highlands, two soldiers from Battalion 756, speeding down a village road in Honelama, struck and injured a child with their motorbike at about 10 am. The child was rushed to the hospital. His relatives, attending a funeral nearby, did not know the child's exact conditions, and began fighting with the soldiers. One soldier was stabbed and died on the roadside, while the other was injured and rushed to the hospital.[25] Then, around 12 pm, two truckloads of soldiers from the battalion attacked Honelama village, killing an Indigenous man and stabbing about a dozen people.[26] The village, including homes, buildings, and vehicles, was burned to the ground. People fled the area.

Indigenous NGOs, led by the Central Highlands Legal Advocacy and Human Rights Network (Jaringan Advokasi Penegakan Hukum dan HAM Pegunungan Tengah Papua) immediately formed an investigative team and began documenting injuries, deaths, and loss of property.[27] The NGOs involved were not specifically legal or political organizations, and included the Jayawijaya Women's Voice Foundation, Yukemdi (the leading HIV NGO), and the Catholic Youth Association. The report contained details of the incident, photos of injuries and eyewitness testimony. It was prepared and disseminated quickly. When it was released, for example, the authors did not know whether the child hit by soldiers was alive or dead. According to the report, the soldiers not only attacked Honelama but then continued rioting down the main streets of town, shooting at buildings, destroying the homes of both Papuans and non-Papuans, and burning vehicles.[28]

On 12 June, a group of leaders and officials (*pimpinan daerah*)—including the regent of Jayawijaya, the head of the local legislature (the DPRD) and other parliamentarians, the Jayawijaya representative from the Papua Peoples Assembly (Majelis Rakyat Papua, or MRP), several church and NGO leaders, and traditional leaders—met in Wamena. From the security side, there was the district military commander (Kodim), the head of the Jayawijaya police, and the commander of Battalion 756 (the unit to which the two soldiers belonged). Based on the available descriptions, the security representatives were all Indonesian, and the majority of the local government, NGO, and church representatives were Papuan.

The group developed a joint statement, which they referred to as a "peace agreement" (*kesepakatan damai*), to resolve the incident. It contained eight points (translated below):

1. Their deepest concern and regret at the stabbing incident between TNI Battalion 756 Wimane Sili and the civilians, which caused loss of life and property.
2. All sides agreed to resolve the situation and safeguard security and order in the Jayawijaya region and through the central highlands by respecting the reconciliation process undertaken by the government.
3. The civilian and military perpetrators and the soldier should be investigated and processed according to the law.
4. The circulation of alcoholic drinks by civilians and the security apparatus in Jayawijaya should be stopped to reduce criminal behaviour.
5. The government will document all losses associated with the actions of 6 June 2012 and give compensation to the victims.
6. If a similar incident occurred again, the security apparatus is requested to take a persuasive approach [i.e., not a violent response].

7. If a similar incident were to occur again, the parties to the conflict should not take matters into their own hands nor use weapons.

8. The community and members of the military and police are requested not to provoke one another regarding this incident in the days to come thereby prolonging the problem.

Representatives then signed the statement.[29]

News reports also state that a traditional feast (*bakar batu*) was held in Honelama. It involved statements and impromptu speeches from the military representatives as well as victims and villagers, and was mediated by church and traditional leaders. The victims requested that the perpetrators from Battalion 756 and the civilians who stabbed the deceased soldier be arrested and processed according to the law. They asked that the legal proceedings be conducted in a transparent manner so that the community at large could be informed. Lastly, they asked the government to compensate them for all of their losses pertaining to the incident.[30]

Another media report indicates that Battalion 756 provided money to the victims to cover the cost of treating their injuries, and that this occurred at the *bakar batu* in Honelama.[31] The Jawawijaya district commander expressed regret at the incident and for the injuries caused to civilians as well as the soldiers. The Battalion 756 commander expressed regret at the "emotional and spontaneous" actions of his soldiers who took vengeance on the community, noting that regardless their reasons they would be sanctioned according to the law. Statements of regret were also made by church leaders and representatives from the local Nduga group. Interestingly, they asserted that the civilian who killed the soldier was from Lanny Jaya and had fled into Honelama, causing the residents of the latter to bear the brunt of the violence. They asked that the Lanny Jaya community apologize to the TNI and the people of Wamena.

News reports suggest that the meeting also provided an opportunity to review the facts of what occurred and to correct misinformation. For example, it had been rumoured that the military shot a civilian, and that the regent had confirmed or asserted this information. At the meeting, it was clarified that the regent had not stated this and that the military had not shot any civilians.

Beyond this, however, the investigative team also heard that soldiers were claiming that they attacked civilians because a weapon had been stolen from the injured soldiers. The investigative team found no evidence that villagers had stolen a weapon, strongly opposed this view, and argued that this was being used to justify what had occurred. The team thus demanded that the "TNI Commander examine the actions of the soldiers and clarify again what really happened."[32]

The first part of this particular truth and reconciliation process was a community-led investigation that took place very early on in the incident. Their efforts potentially thwarted an attempt by the military to explain their actions by alleging that people had stolen a weapon. Data and truth were clearly an important part of this agenda. The investigators represented highly respected locals—albeit all men—with extensive community networks and experience mediating between grassroots society and government institutions. Political leaders then engaged in a formal reconciliation meeting that was also attended by church and community leaders to devise the joint statement on the incident. It contains various statements of regrets from both sides and it criticizes the actions of both the civilians who fought with the soldiers and the soldiers who took vengeance. It contains various broader statements related to conditions that might have led to this sort of violence and which could prevent something similar from happening again. It notes the need for compensation and calls for a de-escalation of tensions and the eschewal of any further violence.

Then, a village-level reconciliation, mediated by church and traditional leaders, focused on the military and the local victims and villagers. It centred on a traditional *bakar batu* feast and some forms of compensation were paid, or at least promised. *Bakar batu* is widely recognized as an important Indigenous custom in the highlands. Guests bring pigs, sweet potatoes, and greens, and this is traditionally organized depending on the relationships between the hosts and the guests. The food is covered in banana palms and steamed slowly under hot rocks. When it is opened the food is distributed by the hosts to the guests, who are usually sitting on the ground, grouped according to different kinship relations and families. Men sit and eat separately from women and most of the children.

Historically, *bakar batu* was the culmination of marriage and funeral ceremonies through which large-scale exchanges of pigs occurred among clans. Nowadays *bakar batu* remains central at funerals and weddings but is also common at holiday celebrations, birthdays, and other community occasions, such as church openings, political gatherings, or the inauguration of an official. It is mainly practiced among Indigenous locals, though large-scale celebrations (church events or inaugurations) might attract non-Papuans. Given that it is typically a meal of pork, which the majority of non-Papuans (who are Muslim) do not eat, non-Papuans' participation in *bakar batu* is often limited. *Bakar batu* is normally organized on egalitarian principles, and reflects the view that sitting and eating together generates and affirms social bonds. When *bakar batu* needs to cater for officials and non-Papuans, then sitting on the ground is not considered an option, and chairs and tables are provided. The atmosphere is distinctly less egalitarian, much more formal, and potentially awkward as people who do not normally mix or interact (and who are probably not relatives or neighbours) are brought together. It is unclear from the various reports how, exactly, the *bakar batu* took place in Honelama, whether all sides sat and ate together. But it is important to keep in mind when thinking about this example of reconciliation just how out of the ordinary close interaction between Indigenous locals and Indonesian security personnel is in Wamena, other than potentially negative interactions like surveillance or questioning. Most locals would not have had military officials visit and speak publicly in their village, let alone share in *bakar batu*.

During the ceremony, different groups made statements of regret and impact. Those that were ostensibly concerned with regret contained important, less-conciliatory subtexts, such as the commander's view that the soldiers' "spontaneous" violence was attributable to emotion rather than organized or condoned by their superiors, or the Nduga group's emphasis on the culpability of the people of Lanny Jaya. This assessment reflects tensions between groups from different parts of the central highlands that go beyond the incident.

The Honelama reconciliation process can be said to broadly represent typical reconciliation efforts after state violence in the highlands and perhaps beyond. There is a strong formal and institutional dimension, including the production of a statement for popular consumption, and also a more local or cultural dimension in the use of the *bakar batu* and reference to compensation. At both levels Indigenous representatives, ranging from elite political actors like the regent to more community-based NGO and customary figures, were main leaders.

Karubaga, Tolikara, 16 July 2015

On 16 July 2015, in the town of Karubaga—located in another part of the highlands—a slightly more complex scenario unfolded. A large gathering of Christians from the Evangelical Church of Indonesia (Gereja Injili di Indonesia, or GIDI), many from outside the area, were participating in a religious camp that coincided with the Muslim holiday of Ramadan. GIDI leaders had advised the authorities, including military and police, of their gathering, and requested that the mosque not use its loudspeaker for the call to prayers during the event.[33] Early reports said that, while the police had agreed to this request, this message was not received or was not passed onto the imam. However, later investigations suggest that the situation was more complicated, in part because the GIDI activities had been rescheduled after the request was agreed to.[34] There may have been poor communication about the nature and the timing of the request. When the call to prayer came over the loudspeaker, a group of youth from the religious gathering went to the military command post, where the soldiers and police were themselves conducting their morning prayers, to ask why the loudspeaker was being used. Some reports say that the youths were throwing rocks and shouting, "Disperse." A soldier fired into the air and then others opened fire on the crowd. A Papuan youth, fifteen-year-old Edi Wanimbo, was killed and ten people suffered gunshot wounds. A riot ensued in which a number of shops were set alight by Papuans. The fire spread to the nearby mosque, which was damaged.

Reports travelled around Indonesia that Papuans had attacked a mosque and devotees during Idul Fitri prayers. These reports were soon (ostensibly) accompanied by a copy of a letter from the local GIDI church leader requesting that a number of restrictions be placed on local Muslims, including the banning of the call to prayer and wearing of the head scarf. Reports circulated that Tolikara regency had passed a local law restricting the activities of non-GIDI denominations and religions, but this was discovered to be false. Such a law had been proposed by the regent but had not gained approval from the governor, the district parliament, or the national Ministry of Home Affairs.[35]

The speed at which these unverified reports spread over the Internet was incredible. News of the incident incited outrage, especially among Indonesian Muslims then celebrating the end of Ramadan. According to an analysis from researchers at the Centre for Cross Cultural and Religious Studies at Gadjah Mada University in Java, a number of media reports exaggerated (*menggoreng*, literally "fried") the incident.[36] Victor Mambor, a Papuan journalist, later commented that within about two hours the police had already issued a chronology of events, largely based on information from text messages, and without talking to any of the eyewitnesses.[37] The violence was described as an attack on Muslims by intolerant, "crazed" (*amuk*) Papuans.[38] The news quickly reached Jakarta, and even President Jokowi was asked to comment and take action against the Papuans. A panel of Jakarta-based church leaders (including GIDI) was convened to comment on television. To combat these representations, church and other Papuan leaders, such as Catholic priest and peace advocate Dr. Neles Tebay, soon weighed in, arguing that Muslims and Christians had lived in peace in Karubaga for the past few decades and that there had never been tension or violence. They argued against labelling the incident a religious conflict and requested that outsiders end their provocative statements. Popular opinion on social media further asserted that the matter should be left to locals in Papua to resolve according to their existing relationships and knowledge of the context.[39]

In response, on 24 July, the regent formed a Reconciliation Team (Tim Pemulihan, though later news reports also used the term *rekonsiliasi*[40]) comprised of Muslim and GIDI church leaders, local Indigenous leaders, government representatives, and members of the police and military. The team was to facilitate the distribution of donations that were coming in for those who lost property as well as those who were in hospital with gunshot wounds, to provide psychological support, and to mediate between Christian and Muslim congregations so as to ensure that the atmosphere remained peaceful.[41] On 29 July, high-level representatives from the religious groups issued a joint statement in Jayapura, the provincial capital, by which they conveyed their understanding of the incident (it was characterized a miscommunication, not a religious conflict), mutual apologies, and commitments to rebuilding.[42]

Prior to this, a team from the National Human Rights Commission also conducted investigations and noted four separate human rights violations related to the case, both on the part of local authorities, who tried to restrict others' religious practices, and on the part of military and police, who shot at the crowd.[43]

A number of Papuans were also arrested, and there were calls from the local religious leaders to settle the matter outside the formal legal system and according to custom. The police, however, insisted that the accused be dealt with legally. Two men were ultimately imprisoned for two months.

In early August, the regent described a number of efforts underway to aid with reconciliation.[44] This included shows of solidarity and support towards Muslims by the regent and other high-level political officials, disbursement of funds to rebuild the shops and the mosque, a community festival, and the establishment of a number of new military checkpoints in town. Thus, even though the regent had seemingly promoted religious intolerance (including of non-GIDI Christian denominations), he quickly backed away from this perspective for the sake of reconciliation when pressed by higher authorities.

There are some parallels here with the resolution arrived at in the Honelama incident, such as the quick formation of a formal group comprised of government, community, and religious leaders, the emphasis on rebuilding, de-escalation, apologies without blame, and yet also simultaneous efforts to seek facts and develop a balanced account of the events. It appears, however, that there was no traditional feast or compensation paid, as occurred in Honelama. There was no explicit focus on a village-level ceremony since the violence took place in the centre of the small town. While Papuans and human rights defenders were critical of the police and military response, the police and military offered no regrets or apologies, and clearly felt that Papuans were the culprits. Thus, what actually might be read as a military-civilian incident was construed as a Muslim-Christian conflict, notwithstanding the fact that some of the Muslims who were praying, and even some who were shooting, were in fact soldiers.

The above examples give some sense of the broad patterns and parametres of post-violence reconciliation in the highlands. These examples focus on the immediate aftermath, which is significant because, given the underlying tensions between Papuans and Indonesians and the high level of militarization in the area, events like these could easily trigger widespread violence. The longer-term view seems to be that incidents continue to happen, and military and police violence continues, if not necessarily in Karubaga or Wamena specifically. Thus these measures secure a modicum of peace for the time being. It is difficult to say how far these approaches to reconciliation address violence that could be construed as "religious" or ethnic, because such conflict is rare (and it remains unclear to what extent Papuans' actions in Karubaga were directed towards Muslims per se or towards soldiers and police).

The cases above press us to question what "Papuan" or "local" approaches look like while also noting the strong role played by politicians and military/state agendas that were asserted in both cases. Papuans clearly participated, and took leading roles in some aspects of these reconciliation approaches, but many other Papuans were highly unsatisfied with the sort of truth and reconciliation that was demonstrated through the ensuing community performances. There are different degrees and meanings of participation, and ownership is a different matter altogether. None of the broader questions about the actions of police and military or ethnic tensions have since been seriously addressed, and a cynical view may hold that reconciliation was swiftly performed to shut down and exclude an expanding chorus of critical voices demanding real discussions, answers, and responses.

Truth and Place: Integrating Ecological and Cultural Perspectives into Reconciliation

If the above cases give a sense of the standard reactions to violations that occur in local contexts (rather than violation writ large, as in the entire political conflict), this section focuses on asking what might be possible, and what else should be considered.

When we talk about a human rights focus and the individual focus within truth and reconciliation, we are positing relationships with people and places as they are understood in Western, Euro-American legal and civil ideas. Thus it is important to ask how other people, and other communities in other parts of the world, understand themselves. When we talk about ethnic Papuans, we are talking about people who would identify as Indigenous peoples. There are some three hundred distinct languages and communities within just the western part of the island. This is a region, then, known for its remarkable biological, cultural, and ethnic diversity. Culture and heritage are significant in everyday life and as identity markers, and would need to be reflected in approaches to truth and reconciliation.

In Tanah Papua, societies, languages, and ways of being and seeing reflect inter-connected relationships among people and place. These understandings foster identities that may challenge limited notions of "individual rights" commonly addressed through truth and reconciliation processes, even as many Papuans are also educated and versed in other notions of rights and may be dedicated to inherited legal traditions. Honouring the place-based perspectives of Indigenous Papuans, and the integrity of relationships with the natural environment, would require diving deeply into local world views and experiences. Looking at place-based aspects of Papuan communities, particularly the ones that are living in proximity to forests, would perhaps present novel considerations for meaningful truth and reconciliation.

To underline this point, consider the words of Neles Tebay:

> The forest, for indigenous Papuans from all tribes, has multi-dimensional meanings … it is first and foremost a member of the community. The Papuan community is composed not only of living people, but also the deceased, spirits, plants, animals, and the whole of nature. That's why community, both as a tribe and a community within a tribe, always has its own forest with a clearly defined boundary. Culturally speaking, a Papuan can never be separated from the forest. It would be a mistake if the Papuan forest was seen as an isolated thing from the Papuans themselves because the forest and the people form one community. The deeper sense of forest is expressed in the Papuan saying "hutan adalah mama" (the forest is our mother). The forest is respected as a mother who tirelessly cares for, protects and sustains all of the members of the community, including the animals. Papuans cannot imagine life without the forest; emphasizing the deeper meaning of forests they say … "our forests, our lives."[45]

Similarly, one of the Papuan communities where we have recently worked lies on the north coast of West Papua province's Bird's Head region. There, the Mpur people have a saying: "nek te eyen" (the land is our mother).[46] When Mpur people say that their land is their mother or that their lives and souls are one with the forests, what they mean is rooted in a way of seeing and being in which "the quality of intimate relations with non-human and human components of the environment is one and the same."[47] There would seem to be a sense of self and a sense of identity that extends beyond their own "individual" body to include the agency of other community members and the living environment around them. Therefore, in thinking about the impact of resource extraction and the exploitation of people and environment that comes with development that is imposed or conducted in conditions of fear, it is important to consider the perspectives on identity, agency, and community held by those who have been violated. These kinds of expressions of coupling between people and place, and the integral meanings which co-arise among them, indicate novel understandings of identity. Individuals are in relationship with community and the more-than-human cohabitants of a place in a holistic way.

Papuan civil-society colleagues emphasize that human rights, development, and environmental issues are integrated and cannot be separated. From working in these realms of ecological, social justice, and community development, it seems to us that development, human rights, and cultural values and experiences cannot be separated. The need to grapple with these interconnections forces us to try to extend the concept of truth and reconciliation and its processes.

Extending the Foundations of Truth and Reconciliation in Tanah Papua

It seems that reconciliation depends first on what sort of truth comes out and how it is facilitated, and what understandings underpin the notion of "truth"; similarly, who or what was reconciled in Honelama and Karubaga, and what has been silenced. What would be the scale at which a future process would operate: village or state? Local or national?

Reconciliation requires modes that capture the complexities of Tanah Papua. We have focused on violence and the violation of identity and place that often occurs in contexts of coercive resource development. But there are many more angles and scales to truth and reconciliation in Tanah Papua that need investigation and consideration. The daily social challenges of ethnic relations, racialized histories, and the day-to-day discrimination will need to be transcended in any meaningful truth and reconciliation process.⁴⁸ This will not be easy in a country that is reticent to talk about race and racism. In order to get to a place of truth, the Indonesian government—and Indonesian society at large—has to acknowledge wrongdoing. It has to break the pattern of denial, and external actors, like companies and development agencies, need to stop facilitating denials in the name of avoiding political sensitivities.⁴⁹ This is not possible as long as truth and reconciliation in Tanah Papua depends on the will or ability of any particular political leader, who is constrained by conservative and growing neo-nationalist elements.⁵⁰

Another layer of complexity concerns what consensus exists, or might be built, among people in Papua and beyond, given asymmetries of power, alliances, and political entanglements.⁵¹ These entanglements, built over the past several decades, blur the lines between victims and perpetrators, and reflect multiple layers and modalities of exclusion. Religious leaders, community leaders, Indigenous leaders, women, men, ethnic and religious minorities, businessmen and women, government, local elite, non-elite, poor, rich, Javanese, Papuan: all have their own politics, orientations, and perspectives. What are the common denominators and where are the centres of gravity that can serve as the meeting place for this diversity and the hierarchies within it? On this note we find that although a Papuan elite is certainly emerging, Papuan leaders have also demonstrated their ability to build consensus and, to a large degree, unity, despite decades of fractious governance and the current flash flood of cash and power. In our various activities and relationships with civil-society organizations in Tanah Papua, we have consistently found the values of community-building, a sense of justice and ethical practice, and a sustained critique of inequality in all of its local and distant guises. Local experience thus bodes well for an inclusive and meaningful truth and reconciliation process.

Approaches to truth and reconciliation in Tanah Papua would need to consider how to capture and resolve violations of selves (individuals, rights) as well as lived experiences that include connections to the natural world. Such efforts would also need to account for multiple and diverse perspectives. "Truth" itself would have to be seen as somewhat dynamic, given the potential diversity of experiences and priorities. A fact-finding mission or investigative report, while useful for certain purposes, would also not seem fit to reflect Indigenous understandings. Flexibility and creativity of expression, along with a degree of experimentation, would be important.

If we posit a truth and reconciliation process as a modality for positive social change in Papua, and for individual and collective healing, how do we do that in a way that engages local understandings, needs, and perspectives? How can efforts to do so integrate rather than flatten out all of the complex dynamics and layers? What would a holistic process look like that reconciles the whole spectrum of abuse and violence experienced by individuals and communities across Tanah Papua? Is a more homegrown solution possible? In seeking answers to these questions from a Papuan starting place, perhaps we shed light on global questions of truth and reconciliation.

Notes

The authors wish to acknowledge support for their work in Tanah Papua from the Canadian International Development Agency, now part of Global Affairs Canada (Biderman and Munro), the Canadian Institutes for Health Research (CIHR) Institute of Gender and Health knowledge translation grant, CIHR meeting grant, and CIHR postdoctoral fellowship (Munro), Pacific Peoples' Partnership (Biderman and Munro), and the Australian National University (Munro). We are also grateful to interlocutors and collaborators in Tanah Papua who have welcomed us into their organizations and communities.

1. John Braithwaite et al., *Anomie and Violence: Non-truth and Reconciliation in Indonesian Peacebuilding* (Canberra: Australian National University E-Press, 2010).

2. Jenny Munro, "'HIV is Our Problem Together': Developing an Indigenous-led Response to HIV in Tanah Papua," *In Brief* 5 (Canberra: State, Society and Governance in Melanesia Program, Australian National University, 2015).

3. Benedict R. O'G. Anderson, "Indonesian Nationalism Today and in the Future," *Indonesia* 67 (1999): 1–11.

4. M. Slama and J. Munro, "Exploring Papuan Temporalities, Mobilities and Religiosities: An Introduction," in *From "Stone-Age" to "Real-Time": Exploring Papuan Temporalities, Mobilities and Religiosities*, ed. Martin Slama and Jenny Munro (Canberra: Australian National University Press, 2015), 3, 12–13.

5. See D. Gietzelt, "The Indonesianization of West Papua," *Oceania* 59, no. 3(1989): 201–21.

6. See K. McKenna, *Corporate Social Responsibility and Natural Resource Conflict* (New York: Routledge, 2015).

7. L. Butt, "'Lipstick Girls' and 'Fallen Women': AIDS and Conspiratorial Thinking in Papua, Indonesia," *Cultural Anthropology* 20, no. 3 (2005): 412–42.

8   Yulia Sugandi, "The Notion of Collective Dignity among Hubula in Palim Valley, Papua" (PhD diss., Wilhelms Universität, Münster, DE, 2014).

9   Slama and Munro, "Exploring Papuan Temporalities."

10 C. Nolan, S. Jones, and Solahudin, "The Political Impact of Carving up Papua," in *Regional Dynamics in a Decentralized Indonesia*, ed. Hall Hill (Singapore: Institute of Southeast Asian Studies, 2014), 409–32.

11 John Barr, "A Veil of Silence is Killing Papua," *West Papua Media*, 22 December 2010, https://unitingworld.org.au/blogs/a-veil-of-silence-is-killing-papua-2/ (accessed 12 July 2017).

12 Maria Fabiola, "Solidaritas PNS Papua Dukung Gubernor Kembalikan Otsus," *Tabloid Jubi* (Jayapura), 9 March 2016, http://www.salampapua.com/2016/03/pns-dukung-sikap-gubernur-kembalikan.html (accessed 12 July 2017).

13 Richard Chauvel, "Policy Failure and Political Impasse: Papua and Jakarta a Decade after the 'Papuan Spring' " in *Comprehending West Papua,* ed. Peter King, Jim Elmslie, and Camellia Webb-Gannon (Sydney, AU: Centre of Peace and Conflict Studies, University of Sydney, 2011), 105–15.

14 Nani Afrida, "Army Join Efforts to Accelerate Food Sufficiency," *Jakarta Post* 9 January 2015, http://www.thejakartapost.com/news/2015/01/09/army-join-efforts-accelerate-food-sufficiency.html (accessed 12 July 2017).

15 J. Munro, "Jokowi in Papua: Powerless or Duplicitous?" *In Brief* 29 (Canberra: State, Society and Governance in Melanesia Program, Australian National University, 2015).

16 Human Rights Watch "Indonesia: Security Forces Kill Five in Papua," 10 December 2014, https://www.hrw.org/news/2014/12/10/indonesia-security-forces-kill-five-papua (accessed 12 July 2017).

17 The Indonesian army is organized hierarchically into territorial commands and combat units. Some territorial commands have their own combat units, but in some cases combat units stand independently. Territorial command is organized as follows: military regional command (*kodam*), military area command (*korem*), military district command (*kodim*), military subdistrict command (*koramil*), and village supervisory non-commissioned officer (*bintara pembina desa* or *babinsa*). See A. M. T. Supriatma, "TNI/Polri in West Papua: How Security Reforms Work in the Conflict Region," *Indonesia* 95 (2013): 93–124.

18 Budi Hernawan, "Torture as a Mode of Governance: Reflections on the Phenomenon of Torture in Papua, Indonesia," in *From "Stone-Age" to "Real-Time": Exploring Papuan Temporalities, Mobilities and Religiosities*, ed. Martin Slama and Jenny Munro (Canberra: Australian National University Press, 2015).

19 Octovianus Mote, "West Papua's National Awakening," *Tok Blong Pasifik* 55 no. 2 (October 2001): 4.

20 Mote, "West Papua's National Awakening," 4–5.

21 Faith Based Network on West Papua, "Papua Land of Peace," http://www.faithbasednetworkonwestpapua.org/papua_land_of_peace (accessed 12 July 2017).

22 Ibid; see also B. Hernawan, *Papua Land of Peace: Addressing Conflict, Building Peace in West Papua* (Jayapura, ID: Office for Justice and Peace, Catholic Diocese of Jayapura, 2005).

23 See Lembaga Studi dan Advokasi Masyarakat, *Pulangkan Mereka! Meringkai Ingatan Penghilangan Paksa di Indonesia* (Jakarta: Elsam 2012).

24 Muridan S. Widido, ed., *Papua Road Map: Negotiating the Past, Improving the Present and Securing the Future* (Jakarta: Lembaga Ilmu Pengetahuan Indonesia, 2008).

25 Amnesty International, "Indonesia: Investigate Military Attacks on Villagers in Wamena, Papua," 9 June 2012, https://www.amnesty.org/download/Documents/20000/asa210202012en.pdf (accessed 12 July 2017).

26 See International Coalition for Papua, *Human Rights in Papua* (Wuppertal, DE: International Coalition for Papua and Geneva: Franciscans International, 2013).

27 T. P. Hesegem et al., "Laporan hasil investigasi Wamena 6 Juni 2012: Penyerangan oleh Pasukan Batalion Yunif 756 Wimane Sili/WMS Wamena Kabupaten Jayawijaya," 2012.

28 Ibid. We use the term *Indonesians* to refer to non-Indigenous inhabitants of Papua. Some Indonesians are long-term settlers while some are recent migrants. Indigenous Papuans are "Indonesian" by citizenship but in local cultural-racial designations "Papuan people" are differentiated from "Indonesian people." These are not the only categories.

29 The signatories were: Wempi Wetipo (Bupati Jayawijaya), Eventus Teddy Danarto (Dandim 1702), Alfian Budianto (Kapolres Jayawjya), Dwi Lagan Syafrudin (Danyon 756), Timotius Tjemi (Ketua Pengadilan Negeri Wamena), Agustinus Walilo (Ketua I DPRD Jayawijaya), Pdt. Dorman Wandikbo (Ketua PGGJ Jayawijaya), Pdt. Esmon Walilo (Ketua FkKUB Jayawijaya), Kayo Hubi (Ketua lMA Jayawijaya), Nahemi Nibikon (Anggota MRP Perwakilan Jayawijaya), Pdt. Mesak Wakerwa (Perwakilan Masyarakat Lanny Jaya), and dan Eliaser Tabuni (Wakil Ketua II DPRD Nduga). See http://www.kompasiana.com/kwamkilama/terjadi-kesepakatan-damai-tni-dan-warga-masyarakat-di-wamena_551121838133117c41bc60a8 (accessed 11 July 2017).

30 Keagop, "Warga Honelama Kehilangan Rumah."

31 Ramli, "Bakar Batu Sudahi Pertikaian Wamena."

32 Keagop, "Warga Honelama Kehilangan Rumah."

33 Lalu Rahadian, "Menag Bantah Ada Perda Agama di Tolikara, Papua," *CNN Indonesia* (Jakarta), 20 July 2015, https://www.cnnindonesia.com/nasional/20150719232650-20-67198/menag-bantah-ada-perda-agama-di-tolikara-papua/ (accessed 16 July 2017).

34 Forum Kerukunan Umat Beragama (FKUB) Provinsi Papua [Papua Province Religious Harmony Forum], "Laporan Klarifikasi dan Fakta Insiden Tolikara (17 Juli 2015)," http://www.academia.edu/14857498/Laporan_Tim_FKUB_Papua_tentang_Insiden_Tolikara_2015 (accessed 16 July 2017).

35 Ibid.

36 Centre for Religious and Cross-Cultural Studies, "Tolikara, Idul Fitri 2015: Tentang Konflik Agama, Mayoritas-Minoritas dan Perjuangan Tanah Damai," 19 July 2015,

http://crcs.ugm.ac.id/news/3511/tolikara-idul-fitri-2015-tentang-konflik-agama-mayoritas-minoritas-dan-perjuangan-tanah-damai.html (accessed 16 July 2017).

37   Victor Mambor, "Kronologis Insiden Tolikara Versi Masyarakat Karubaga," *Tabloid Jubi* (Jayapura), 24 July 2015, http://tabloidjubi.com/2015/07/24/ini-kronologis-insiden-tolikara-versi-masyarakat-karubaga/ (accessed 16 July 2017).

38   Alfian Kartono, "Belasan Kios dan Rumah Warga Hangus Dibakar Massa Tak Dikenal," *Kompas* (Jakarta), 17 July 2015, http://regional.kompas.com/read/2015/07/17/09461561/Belasan.Kios.dan.Rumah.Warga.Hangus.Dibakar.Massa.Tak.Dikenal (accessed 16 July 2017).

39   For a discussion of Islam in Papua, see M. Slama, "Papua as an Islamic Frontier: Preaching in 'the Jungle' and the Multiplicity of Spatio-Temporal Hierarchisations," in *From "Stone-Age" to "Real-Time": Exploring Papuan Temporalities, Mobilities and Religiosities*, ed. Martin Slama and Jenny Munro (Canberra: Australian National University Press, 2015). For a discussion of fundamentalist Christianity and politics in Papua, see Henri Myrttinen, "Under Two Flags: Encounters with Israel, Merdeka and the Promised Land in Tanah Papua," in *From "Stone-Age" to "Real-Time": Exploring Papuan Temporalities, Mobilities and Religiosities*, ed. Martin Slama and Jenny Munro (Canberra: Australian National University Press, 2015).

40   "Inilah Sejumlah Strategi Pemulihan Insiden Tolikara," *GATRAnews* (Jakarta), 3 August 2015, http://www.gatra.com/fokus-berita-1/158698-inilah-sejumlah-strategi-pemulihan-insiden-tolikara (accessed 16 July 2017).

41   Yustinus Paat, "Pemda Bentuk Tim Pemulihan Insiden Tolikara," *BeritaSatu* (Jakarta), 24 July 2015, http://www.beritasatu.com/nasional/293380-pemda-bentuk-tim-pemulihan-insiden-tolikara.html (accessed 16 July 2017).

42   Ican Ihsanuddin, "Umat Islam dan Umat Kristen Tolikara Sepakat Saling Memaafkan," *Kompas* (Jakarta) 11 August 2015, http://nasional.kompas.com/read/2015/08/11/1537387/Umat.Islam.dan.Umat.Kristen.Tolikara.Sepakat.Saling.Memaafkan (accessed 16 July 2017).

43   Ambaranie Nadia Kemala Movanita, "Komnas HAM Temukan Dugaan Pelanggaran HAM dalam Peristiwa Tolikara," *Kompas* (Jakarta) 10 August 2015, http://regional.kompas.com/read/2015/08/10/11452461/Komnas.HAM.Temukan.Dugaan.Pelanggaran.HAM.dalam.Peristiwa.Tolikara (accessed 16 July 2017).

44   Cuning Levi, "Tolikara Pulih Ini Program Pemda untuk Rekonsiliasi," *Tempo* 3 August 2015, https://m.tempo.co/read/news/2015/08/03/078688688/tolikara-pulih-ini-program-pemda-untuk-rekonsiliasi (accessed 16 July 2017).

45   West Papua Advocacy Team. "West Papua Report November 2007," http://www.etan.org/issues/wpapua/0711wpap.htm#forests (accessed 16 July 2017).

46   Adriana Sri Adhiati, "Songs of Worries, Songs of Strength" *Down to Earth Special Edition Newsletter* 89–90 (November 2011): 23–25, www.downtoearth-indonesia.org/story/dte-newsletter-89-90-full-edition-download (accessed 16 July 2017).

47   Tim Ingold, *The Perception of the Environment: Essays in Livelihoods, Dwelling and Skill* (New York: Routledge, 2007), 47.

48 J. Munro, "The Violence of Inflated Possibilities: Education, Transformation and Diminishment in Wamena, Papua," *Indonesia* 95 (2103): 25–46, and "'Now we Know Shame': *Malu* and Stigma among Highlanders in the Papuan Diaspora," in *From "Stone-Age" to "Real-Time": Exploring Papuan Temporalities, Mobilities and Religiosities*, ed. Martin Slama and Jenny Munro (Canberra: Australian National University Press, 2015).

49 J. Munro and L. McIntyre, "(Not) Getting Political: Indigenous Women and Preventing Mother-to-child Transmission of HIV in West Papua," *Culture, Health and Sexuality* 18, no. 2 (2016): 156–70, and J. Munro and L. Butt, "Compelling Evidence: Research Methods, Politics and HIV/AIDS in Papua, Indonesia," *The Asia Pacific Journal of Anthropology* 13, no. 4 (2012): 334–51.

50 E. Aspinall, "The New Nationalism in Indonesia," *Asia & the Pacific Policy Studies* 3, no. 1 (2016): 69–79.

51 E. Kirksey, *Freedom in Entangled Worlds: West Papua and the Architecture of Global Power* (Durham, NC: Duke University Press, 2012).

16

The Living Symbol of Song in West Papua: A Soul Force to be Reckoned With[1]

Julian Smythe

"I am Papua (aku Papua)," three-year-old Dietrich Malenua sings on his grandmother's porch in Papua, Indonesia. He is singing the hit song of Papuan musician Edo Kondologit, "Aku Papua," and in his song, he carries a Papuan identity often threatened in Indonesia's easternmost province of Papua.[2] I will argue here that, in the midst of poverty, continued violence, and racial segregation in Papua, song has served and continues to serve as a lived symbol of collective identity through which liberation is daily practiced in the Land of Papua.

Shortly before his death at the hands of Indonesian security forces in April of 1984, Papuan musician and anthropologist Arnold Ap sang, "The only thing I long for is only ever freedom."[3] His song carries one of the few direct references to freedom found in Papuan music and signals a rare point of direct political engagement in song—perhaps justified by the performer's sense that his own death was imminent. Although direct freedom is rarely experienced in West Papua, music has been one symbol for a unified Papuan identity that protests the extensive violence against the Papuan people carried out by the Indonesian security forces, a lethal campaign that may qualify as genocide.[4] A number of authors, most notably Diana Glazebrook, address how music has served as a receptacle of identity and resistance in Papua.[5] It is sometimes hidden, and sometimes, as in Ap's last song, direct—but a space, nevertheless, in which freedom can be practiced and lived. Although the singers and writers of many of the songs discussed here have been killed, the songs of Papuan pride and identity have continued through over one hundred years of Dutch and Indonesian occupation, changing with time and responding to the constraints and inequalities that arise, but always, ever remembering freedom.

Within the context of West Papua, music serves as a vessel for resistance and identity through which a group can mobilize against an oppressive order.[6] Gandhi's doctrine of non-violence speaks of the need for a potent symbol around which a community can mobilize.[7] Music offers such a symbol within the sustained non-violent social movement for self-determination in West Papua. However, unlike static icons, such as a flag or even Gandhi's own symbol of a spinning wheel, music, particularly in societies with a strong oral tradition, can serve as a living symbol, a participative practice that invites the physical engagement of human vocal chords and bodies across distance and time through harmony and improvisation. This "creative consciousness" of shared song generated by interactions among people can serve as an empowering practice/space for participative liberation.[8]

Through engaging with the histories of two musicians (sung heroes!) in Papuan history, Angganeka Manufandu and Arnold Ap, as well as a number of current musical heroes, I argue that song is a participative symbol that renegotiates boundaries of Papuan identity previously defined by the Dutch and Indonesian states, and creates and maintains the daily liberational practice of sustaining the ideological "notion-state" of Papua.[9] I begin with an exploration of music that played a role in the formation of early Papuan collective identity and nationalism during the *Koreri* millennial movement of 1939–43 under the leadership of Angganeka Manufandu, and then move to an exploration of the role of the music of Arnold Ap in maintaining and sustaining Papuan identity during the years of Indonesia's "New Order" government under Suharto (1965–98). I conclude with a discussion of current musical encounters with the Indonesian state in a post-Suharto Papua.

The First Wor: Music in the Koreri Millennial Movement, 1939–43

Angganeka Manufandu and the Songs of Wor

"My Aunts were named Angganeka," Rachel tells me. "I never knew where the name came from until recently when I heard her story." The story Rachel speaks of is a story of the woman once known as the "Queen of Papua." In 1939, Angganeka Manufandu, a widow and plantation coolie in Dutch New Guinea, became ill. While on the island where she was sent to die, Angganeka was healed and received a supernatural visitation calling her to prepare her people for the promised time of prosperity and equality for the Biak people—an anticipated millennial event known as *Koreri*—during which the existing hierarchy of Dutch colonialism would be reversed.[10]

Hearing news of her recovery and the prophecy, many pilgrims began to visit Angganeka, seeking the promise of the new era that the *Koreri* myth described. She urged them to shed no blood, to follow a specific diet, and to engage in the traditional Biak rituals of *Wor* (initially banned by Dutch missionaries), songs celebrating the advent of *Koreri*. Angganeka mediated with *Manggundi* (a Biak term for the Supreme Being), receiving messages of liberation and holy living in her "radio room" and writing them into songs for her followers to sing.[11] One of the songs is "Neno, Neno," which includes one of the very first mentions of unified Papuan nationhood. It says, "Oh Lord, come down and live with us here in this land of *Mambesak* [bird of paradise], God of the sky, bless the nation of Papua and its riches."[12] In response to these messages of freedom, she and her followers (there were close to six thousand) established a Papuan flag (the Dutch flag upside down) and a statement declaring Papuan nationhood.[13]

Angganeka's music used the traditional Biak form of *Wor*, a form rooted in the foundational *Koreri* myth, a historically recurring myth of identity for many coastal Papuans, which anticipates the return of justice, equality, and material well-being through the return of the deity, Manarmakeri.[14] The songs are enacted by the community (rather than performed in front of an audience) in village communal spaces, with each clan playing its own role. Angganeka Manufandu and her followers used the traditional categories of *Wor* to imagine a new way of being in which the structures of taxation, colonialism, and church were contested both in song and symbolically (through the flag and the establishment of a Papuan government).[15] However, Angganeka's *Koreri* was not only a freedom whose idea was spoken—it was a freedom that was practiced in the participatory enactment of the song!

Music in oral cultures, Ben Sidran argues, serves not merely to convey a message but to offer a communal space in which the message is actually experienced. He further states that music in oral culture functions as a transformative experience that occurs the very moment it is sung.[16] So, too, the *Wor* of Angganeka Manufandu celebrated a moment in which change occurred, and this process involved not merely the telling of a renegotiated relationship with Dutch authorities, but an actual practicing of this new relationship, a relationship of equality and justice not only described in the myth of *Koreri*, but realized at the very moment of its singing. Freedom had already come, in the song and in the people who sang.

It was this lived freedom out of which Angganeka and her followers acted, firmly believing that their reality of justice, equality, and empowerment found in their *Koreri* myth would come and was, in fact, already present (eventually their belief in *Koreri's* liberating message would cause them to consider themselves powerful enough to resist Japanese bullets, resulting in massacre in 1943).[17] Arend Lijphart, F. C. Kamma, Danilyn Rutherford, and Richard Chauvel have noted that, following the *Koreri* liberation movement, Papuans' relationship with the Dutch colonists, although not resulting in independence, resulted in greater representation for Papuans in a number of fields.[18] Concrete results included the restructuring of the Dutch church in Papua, which eventually resulted in its independence from Holland in 1956, as well as Papuans' formal and institutional preparation for independence[19] (although, arguably, these shifts were also influenced by the growth of post-colonial movements across the globe in the postwar era). Thus, the *Koreri* millennial movement of 1939–42 helped trigger visible shifts in power relations centred in colonial conceptions of race and primitivism. Even more importantly, the movement showed Papuans that they could name and govern themselves.[20]

Between Wors: *Indonesian Repression, 1961–98*

Arnold Ap and the Songs of Mambesak

Following the *Koreri* millennial movement of 1939–42, the songs celebrating Papuan identity were shared and performed throughout the period of Dutch annexation following Indonesian independence (1945–61), UNTEA (United Nations Temporary Authority, 1961–62), the Indonesian occupation (1962–69), and incorporation into the Indonesian state (1969 to the present).[21] The one who carried the songs of West Papua most notably during this period was Biak musician and anthropologist Arnold Ap, who is known across Indonesia and internationally both for the quality of his music and the power of his political protest. "He was the John Lennon and Bob Dylan and the Aboriginal band Yothu Yindi, all rolled into one," writes journalist Jay Griffiths.[22]

The time of Arnold Ap was a time of repression across Indonesia, and well-known musicians such as Iwan Fals and Roma, as well as traditional musicians (using such forms as shadow puppets), sang both indirect and direct protests against state violence.[23] The state's responses to such music included censorship, bans, and sometimes the death of the artist. As the Indonesian nation constructed itself, much discussion ensued about the way in which its diverse cultural spheres would be managed. Economically, Indonesia was a centralized state. However, operating under the slogan "Unity in Diversity" (Bhinneka Tunggal Eka), Indonesia recognized the need for a narrative of the state that would maintain the state, but still be able to ideologically mobilize loyalty from outlying regions.[24] After considerable discussion, it was decided, and confirmed in clause 32 of the constitution, that "the government shall advance the national culture of Indonesia."[25] This statement caused considerable upheaval among the various participants in the formation of Indonesia (Papua was not yet present in the discussion), resulting in a detailed clarification by then president Sukarno on 15 July 1945, stating that the clause

> does not mean that we reject the existence of regional cultures. Javanese, Balinese, Sundanese culture—these are all Indonesian culture. They must be respected and revered. The clause

means that because we want to institute unification, we must, so far as we are able, create a national Indonesian culture.[26]

As a part of this attempt to reify the boundaries of the nation in order to gain cultural purchase—especially in areas where secessionist movements were present—the government, in the 1980s, embarked upon the task of "museumizing" Papua's culture and music, while still enacting military measures to obtain land and resources.[27] To head up the task, they chose Papuan anthropologist Arnold Ap.

Although he was killed more than thirty years ago, during an era marked by widespread government censorship of the arts and media, Arnold's is a household name for many Papuans. I first heard his name from Tula. Walking down the street in Papua, the sun pouring down on us, she asked me, "Do you know Arnold, Julian?"

"No," I said. "Who is he?"

"He was a musician," she said. "He sang songs from all around Papua."

Rachel, a seminary student, added, "At first he just gathered songs from the various regions in Papua, traditional songs [*lagu-lagu suku*]. But then he started writing songs that were too deep. And he got into trouble with the government."

"Too deep?" I asked.

"He sang of Sampari [the morning star]," Eva, also a student, jumped in to explain. Sampari is one of the most potent symbols of Papuan nationhood.

"His songs were too strong," Rachel continued. "They made Papua strong, so he was killed."

As I was a visitor to the island, the first thing that people spoke to me about was Arnold. "Ah, you know Arnold?" they asked, speaking as if he were still alive. And perhaps, in a way, he was. I sat with *Tete* [grandfather], on the porch of Palei's parents' house on stilts over the sea, with waves breaking against the coral reef not far away. It was midnight at the wedding feast, and under a tent on dry land, Palei's band was playing his songs and Arnold's songs, and the village was dancing. The one who danced the most strongly was Palei's great aunt. She danced to the music of a song by Arnold, "Asaibori," which commemorates a beach not far from the place where we were sitting. Her skin was wrinkled from the touch of sun and sea and age. Her eyes were closed, her feet shuffled, and her arms formed the movement of birds. She outdanced everyone. I sat with *Tete*. His knees were old, and my legs were ill-informed, so we just watched Palei's aunt dance, while he told me stories—of the war, and the bomber planes, and of American soldiers. And then he told me stories of Arnold as we watched the morning star rise.

Ap lives on in his village, in his songs, and in the songs being written that remember his songs. "Tanah Papua" and "Aku Papua" are odes to the land, connecting the vast land even more directly (in ways that are less subtly expressed) to a shared identity—Papuanness—than does Ap's music. These songs emphasize that even when a people cannot speak, the land never stops singing, laughing, flowing, whistling. Papua.

It was around this very land that Ap travelled while working for the government, gathering music from two hundred and fifty tribal groups, airing them weekly on a national radio show. That music would then be recorded and broadcast on the Indonesian state broadcaster, Radio Republik Indonesia.[28] Papuans from many different regions listened, hearing their songs drifting, no longer just on the waves of the wind and the sea, but on radio waves. Music that had been termed backwards and primitive in the Indonesian discourse was honoured under the auspices of the national project to build a larger Indonesian identity.[29]

Soon, Ap and his band, The Bird of Paradise (Mambesak), named after Papua's best-known icon and commodity, also the shape of the land, were being listened to with rising excitement, and other Papuan bands began to form, reviving cultural symbols of music and of dance.[30] The songs Ap gathered centred in the land and creatures of Papua, with birds often representing the Papuan people, and sea voyages speaking of an eventual journey towards freedom.[31] Lania Unumowak remembers the time when Ap's songs were played. Every Sunday afternoon, everyone would anticipate, waiting for his music to come on air. "There was something in his music," she said, "something that we knew. The music was ours."

Ap's endeavour to collect and broadcast this regional music was initiated by the Indonesian state in its attempt to manage the cultural categories of primitivism for the purpose of gaining increased Papuan loyalty to the Indonesian national consciousness. No one could have guessed at the results when the project began. Ap used the categories of Indonesian legitimacy and modern technology (radio and cassette recorder) to engage with the "primitive" categories of Papuan song and culture, creating a new consciousness, not focused around the Unified Republic of Indonesia (negara kesatuan Republik Indonesia), but around the Land of Papua (Tanah Papua).[32] What had been intended as a cultural symbol supporting the unification of the Indonesian state instead became, as Glazebrook states, a symbol of unification for the varying ethnicities of Papua.[33] To quell his popularity, which was, Juillerat writes, "inexcusable on the political level," the state imprisoned Ap for treason in 1984.[34] Two months later, on 24 April 1984, he was shot in the back by Indonesian Special Forces (Kopassus) along with his cousin Eddy Mofu.

With his death, Ap's song, which had reified the Papuan boundaries of identity, appeared to have been subsumed in the unified Indonesian melody. However, although Ap's death resulted in the silencing of the individual Papuan voice that had discovered these songs, the songs remained.[35] The transmission of the songs to a recorded medium indicated a potential shift of the music from the communal oral holding space of participative musical encounter—the oral holding space that had given Angganeka's music its power—to a space where music can be preserved, and replayed, through technology. Even though the songs had been recorded in the static medium of cassette tapes, these cassettes were exchanged through communal channels similar to the oral patterns of singing and interaction found in *Wor*. Reciprocity and connection—the interactions that build society—were lived through the underground exchanges of music. Writes journalist Jay Griffiths: "People tenderly cherish almost worn-out cassettes of his music; women sell their sweet potatoes to buy batteries for doddery cassette players."[36] Even though Ap's songs were not always sung communally, the physical cassettes became commemorative, communal items of exchange in which his songs could be held until greater freedom arrived.

Arnold's songs remain. Sung in choir festivals, on porches, at volleyball games, and on the night before Easter, when Papuans circle their parishes, holding torches made of bamboo. Appearing on YouTube, ringing from cell phones, and played by students newly arrived from Ap's own village, Arnold and his songs inhabit and imagine the physical and aural landscapes of West Papua.[37] As his songs play in the afternoon light, Mama Lis says, "There is something in his music which makes me weep. It touches me like nothing else." People young and old whisper his name, "Arnold," as they remember the land that he sings.

The Return of Wor

During the years of the New Order, although Papuan musicians did not break forth and trigger millennial movements on the scale of Angganeka's *Wor*, other forms of music provided and sustained a discursive space in which the relationships of Papuans were being played out. In a YouTube film of *Wor*, the announcer says, as the community dances and sings, "Here, we see the excitement, the passion! They *Wor* the whole night. They are not gentle. They use *Wor* as a tool for attack. *Wor*! Ba *Wor*!"[38] These words, along with aural sources, indicate that *Wor*, which in the past served to mobilize the Biak people to join Angganeka's movement, remains a source of a shared identity. Musicologist Philip Yampolsky reports that, in 1993, *Wor* remained present in Biak in its heterophonous splendour, and the growing diversity of this performance genre reflected the multiplicity of its uses in Biak society. Writes Yampolsky: "There was an extensive repertoire of song types and established texts and new texts were constantly being created, often spontaneously during performance."[39]

However, this very living and symbolic power of *Wor* invited intervention by the Indonesian state, and in the mid-1990s, *Wor* became one space where the Papuan consciousness was contested. Yampolsky writes that, by 1994, "the local government had got hold of *Wor* and sponsored a revival" through the department of culture.[40] This revival, Yampolsky argues, simplified *Wor*—changing its heterophony to a single "synchrony," and assigning categories of value based, not in communal action and relationship, but on the uniformity of song and movement. The simplification of the complexity of *Wor*, which was altered from a living form made from diverse communal acts of participation, to a medium performed in synchrony, exhibits the attempted unifying co-optation of a liberational form of music by the state. Yampolsky implies in his description that the state was effective in co-opting the efficacy of *Wor* for action. *Wor* and other Biak forms of music were performed for tourists at the airport when an international flight from Hawaii was established, and the songs began to change, sung no longer simply for communal edification, but for performance and for profit.

Though Yampolsky implies that the state's intervention effectively tamed *Wor*, the negotiation of meaning through the living symbol of *Wor* had not yet ended. *Wor*, and the *Koreri* movement of freedom and identity with which it has been intertwined, has remained in villages from before the time of Angganeka, to the present, with rituals and stories and songs passed down from elders to youth in the daily interactions in the village. These songs move to the city with youth coming from the village to the city for school, for these students bring with them the songs of *Koreri* and *Wor*, and their instruments, and perform these songs in their dormitories, in sun-drenched campus yards in the afternoon, and for church and community feasts and ceremonies. The very ordinariness and pervasiveness of these songs in Biak life, in particular, can be found in Danilyn Rutherford's account of the Biak independence declaration of 6 July 1998, in which she draws parallels between the use of music in the *Koreri* movement of 1939–42 under the leadership of Angganeka, and the use of music during the demonstrations of 1998 (known as "Biak Berdarah") led by Filep Karma. She writes:

> The demonstrators spent their days dancing around the water tower and singing Biak and Indonesian songs. While they performed a contemporary genre, fitting with the youth of many of the participants, the allusion to *Koreri* and the Biak feasting was clear.[41]

The traditional music of *Wor* had created a space of communal encounter in which the identities and values of the community were lived. During the Biak flag raising in 1998, as Rutherford describes, the new forms of music combined with the direct assertion of independence in a public space, and this was an attempt to expand the boundaries of the conversation regarding Papuan identity beyond the audience of the Indonesian state into the "transcultural" space of meaning-making.[42] "Raiding the land of the foreigners"[43] for the power that they might offer, the people of Biak attempted to expand the boundaries of identity beyond the Indonesian unified melody, which was centred in oppression. Says Reverend Sawer of Biak: "They wanted people from outside. I think it's a dream. They expect someone from outside to help them."[44] Yet these dreams were partially realized, for the movement did receive limited Australian attention. But the most notable—and deadly—attention it received was from Indonesia.

In the words of Reverend Sawer, commenting on the massacre, "There was no help, no mediator, only bullets."[45] Responding within the conventional practices of a totalitarian state, the Indonesian military repeated the rhythms that defined their sovereignty in Papua—the deep bass of gunfire, the pounding syncopation of rape, and the wail of bodily mutilation. Such actions, argues Tracy Banivanua-Mar, arise out of interactions centred in a colonial history of racism.[46] When Papuans attempted to renegotiate inequitable relationships grounded in this conception of race through symbolic protests involving music and flag-raising, they undermined the authority and sovereignty of the state. Indonesia acted forcefully to reinstate the status quo. But mere imprisonment or even simple executions—actions that accord recipients some dignity, or at least legal recognition—would not reinstate the ideological groundwork that allowed the Indonesian state to justify extraction of resources and the continued use of violence in Papua. Dehumanizing acts were required to maintain the ideological status quo based in a deep racism that denied the humanity of the "other." Just as Angganeka and her followers experienced and created freedom through the very act of *Wor*, so through the very act of torture, through mutilated human bodies and desiccated land, the Indonesian security forces recreated for themselves the symbols of inequality upon which their empire was built.[47] In the words of Reverend Saud, "Development [*pembangunan*] is the same as murder [*pembunuhan*]."[48]

However, true to the spirit of improvisatory music made in community, the interactions did not end. And although the state song of torture seemed to overpower the participative core of *Wor*, it served, in fact, to honour Biak dignity. Although many were silenced through death, and although most of the dead were disposed of at sea, depriving them of a martyr's voice, the very force of Indonesia's response indicated a growing equality in the interactions between the Biak people and the Indonesian state.[49] The very violence of the quelling, similar to the silencing of both Angganeka and Arnold, proved that their song had been heard and taken seriously.

Encouraged, the people of Biak shared their renewed commitment to the struggle through the film *The Biak Massacre*, prepared by ABC Australia. Of the 170 to 200 deaths, only one was acknowledged by the military. In response, the man's wife spoke the message of freedom, the cause her husband had died for, even though for her to speak on film could result in her death. "I will say," she says, "Papua Barat [This refers to all of West Papua] will still be free. For the children." In the film, she gestures to her children sitting around her. "Their father's blood has been shed. They must be free. We have suffered enough."[50] Through the single note of the one martyr who was given the dignity of a meaningful death, the symbol of Papuan liberation lives on.

The Living Symbol of Song in West Papua

Lunia Tutalia hands me her battered cassette. "Don't lose this, Julian," she says. Writes Rayfiel: "Scratchy songs are handed down from parents to children. Weather-beaten copies are carried on foot to the remote highland villages."[51] Although Papuans still live in fear of violence, the living interactive symbol of song representing the collective Papuan identity remains strong. This living symbol of song I define as a participative practice into which beings can enter through harmony and improvisation. This symbol has been sustained over years in the songs of *Wor* and through Arnold's songs, and it remains now, twenty years later, in the music of Papuan activist and musician Palei Warinuri,[52] who records and sings both Ap's songs and new songs of Papuan people and land. In his song "Mambruk ma Manyouri" he tells the story of two birds, forever free. These birds represent the musicians, Arnold Ap and Sam Kapissa, who, through their music, elicited a shared identity for the Papuan people, allowing the varied melodies of the diverse groups to merge into a harmony of freedom.[53]

Although constraints and violence remain in Papua, the examples above indicate that the participatory identity created and strengthened through musical interaction and expression lives on. The participative method by which Ap collected music from all corners of Papua and through which Angganeka and Karma made music, used existing cultural forms embedded in village life. These forms allowed the harmony of many voices to redraw the boundaries of identity so that they encircle, and focus on, the Land of West Papua, rather than the Indonesian (or Dutch) archipelago, as had been intended by both the Indonesian state and the Dutch colonial government.[54]

Why were Ap and Angganeka (and Karma as well) successful in creating and maintaining an identity of Papuanness, when Indonesia, using the same tools on numerous occasions, was not? Diana Glazebrook gives examples of ways that Arnold's musical and dancing metaphors invoked a symbolism of the land (I would argue that Angganeka's do as well, although not as explicitly).⁵⁵ This is a symbolism vital to the Papuan consciousness. West Papuans rarely speak of the "nation" of Papua; instead, they frequently refer to the "land" (*tanah*) of Papua.⁵⁶ Journalist Jay Griffiths notes that Papuan music traces journeys towards a freedom strongly grounded in the mountains and the seas of Papua.⁵⁷

Although the land of Papua is not institutionally owned or governed by Papuans, it can be and is sung by them, existing in the reality of the songs that remember it.⁵⁸ Says resistance leader Benny Wenda: "Since people are interconnected with the land, women will sing to the seed of the sweet potato as they plant it, so the earth will be happy."⁵⁹ So, for Papuans, song serves as a holding space for their land, because, as Australian musician and activist David Bridie states, "You cannot stop people from singing."⁶⁰ Singing of the land recreates the land and offers a trajectory to a place, both a physical and a musical/ideological place. Griffiths writes, "The song is a journey and singing about a place makes it wriggle into life."⁶¹ While the sweet potato seed in the highlands is sung to life, so, too, the human soul comes into being through singing, say the Beam people of the highlands. The soul is the "seed of singing."⁶² The songs grow the land and the songs grow the people, connecting the Papuan people to their land even when the establishment of a constitution or a self-governing institution would invite violent repercussions.

The connection of songs and the land described in Griffiths's article can also be found in the lyrics of songs penned by Ap. In "Nyanyian Sunyi," one of Ap's most popular songs, he describes how the land also participates in the expression of song, and how the land can carry a song.⁶³ In these verses, it is the land that sings:

Nyanyian sunyi

Puisi yang menawan, terjalin bersama

Oh nyanyian sunyi Tanah yang permai ...

Terhampar di sana, di timur merekah melara

Dan bunyi ombaknya

Dan siul unggassnya

Melagu bersama, oh nyanyian sunyi

Surga … yang penuh senyuman

Laut mutiara … dan sungai yang deras, mengalirkan emas

Melagu bersama, oh nyanyian sunyi

Quiet/lonely song

The poem that is captured [enchants], woven together

Oh quiet/lonely song

The beautiful land …

There, it is spread out, east of the sunrise

And the sound of its waves

And the songs of its birds

They make songs together, oh quiet/lonely song

The heavens … filled with smiles

The pearl ocean … and swift rivers that flow with gold

They make songs together, oh quiet/lonely song

Ap's image of the quiet, lonely song, of *nyanyian sunyi*, speaks (sings) to the song of his own life which, like this song of the land, never ceases, even after his death.

While "Nyanyian Sunyi" is remembered even now across Papua, there is a line within it that has become a part of the Papuan consciousness. It is the phrase "dan sungai yang deras mengalirkan emas" (and swift rivers that flow with gold). This phrase was borrowed by Yance and placed in her song "Tanah Papua" (The Land of Papua), recorded in 2003. Yance changes the line slightly, but the change is virtually undetectable. She writes: "Sungaimu yang deras mengalirkan emas" (Your swift rivers that flow with gold).[64] I first heard "Tanah Papua" while riding home with a community of women from the beach where we had spent the day. They had borrowed the bus from the husband of a parishioner who worked for the local government. And on the way home, in the waning light, with the sea behind us and the valley in front of us, the "mamas" began to sing Yance's song. Ap's songs, and even the songs of the Black Brothers, although often sung, are sung quietly and with caution due to their political implications. "Tanah Papua," however, while echoing Ap's "Nyanyian Sunyi," which also sings of the multitudinous beauties and agency of the land of Papua, does not have the political repercussions of Ap's song (or even of Papua's national anthem, "Hai Tanahku Papua," which carries an audaciously similar title). Because of this, and the song's seemingly innocent celebration of the land, "Tanah Papua" is sung freely, with an enthusiasm that calls to mind Papua's more risky anthem and Arnold's songs.

Like Ap and the people of Papua, Indonesia (and Holland), too, had a discourse of land. The rallying cry of Sukarno, Indonesia's first president, who "liberated" Papua from the Dutch, was also put to song in "From Sabang to Merauke" (dari Sabang sampai Merauke).[65] However, the metaphoric basis for Indonesian and Dutch claims on Papuan land differed significantly from the metaphors that have grounded the songs of Ap and Yance and Angganeka. For the colonizers, the land was not a living thing to be participated with in song, but static soil to be pounded by the rhythm of mining and large-scale agriculture. This fundamental difference in the way that land is viewed is exhibited in the Freeport mining company's extraction of gold from Puncak Jaya. After the resources were extracted, only half the mountain remained. But for the Amungme, who live on that mountain, the land is their mother, and the mountain is her head. She is now decapitated, or, as Yosepha Alomang puts it, she has been consumed.[66]

> The Nemankawi mountain—that is I.
>
> The Wanagong lake, that is my womb.
>
> The Ocean, that is my feet.
>
> The land between, this is my body.
>
> You have already consumed me.
>
> Show me which part of my body you have not consumed and destroyed.
>
> You as the government must see
>
> And be aware that you are consuming me.
>
> I dare you to value this earth that is my body.

Ap's singing of the land offered those who live on the land a way to hold onto their living mother. Indonesia's unifying strategy, its imposing song, did not.

Ap's and Angganeka's music could not be destroyed or suppressed by the state because it created a symbol of freedom grounded in land that Papuans could live in and practice. The non-violence of participation in the living symbol of song does not lessen its power as a tool of resistance. Diana Glazebrook quotes a West Papuan refugee as saying that "teaching performance art is like sharpening the blade of a knife."[67] She goes on to say that "cultural performance as a representation of nationhood is conceived as an activity of resistance."[68] What is ironic is that Ap's songs and many of Angganeka's songs are not political songs. They are everyday songs that, in their very ordinariness, sing a land and a life into being in which the Indonesian juggernaut does not exist. In this imagined place, routine violence and unexplained disappearances never happened. Challenging the hegemony of Indonesia's song, these musicians allow Papuans to sing the harmonies of the land using their many different voices, and, in their songs, they are already free.[69]

The power of resistance evident in the music of Ap and Angganeka was acknowledged by the severity of Dutch, Japanese, and Indonesian responses to Papuan resistance aspirations. Threatened by the living symbol that Ap and Angganeka had created, forces imprisoned and later executed these two musicians. However, the deaths of Ap and Angganeka only caused more people to sing, taking the dissonance of the individual deaths and weaving them into a harmony of a suffering symbol sung in community.

This communally sung symbol of suffering became a sign around which the Papuan community could mobilize. Theories of non-violent social movements assume that the potent symbols will have the power to mobilize people into collective action once cognitive liberation occurs.[70] However, this process depends both upon some degree of democratic government and a modicum of press coverage to frame the movement that is happening, so that when deaths occur, there will be a public with the resources to speak and thereby act as the conscience of the region.

Even when these conditions are not present—as is often the case in Papua—if a non-violent struggle is sustained under constant threat of retaliation by the state, I argue that the lived liberty regularly practiced through an interactive symbol of collective identity, such as songs, can create and maintain collective internal freedom, until the time comes for the greater political freedom. The theory of symbolically interacting song is strong because it allows for a living symbol. Songs create a shared dream people can enter into, in almost any place at almost any time. Singing late at night on the passenger ship that travels around Papua. Singing at the funeral of a young activist who "killed himself" in prison. Singing in the early morning from a broken plastic chair outside a house filled with the agony of violence turned inward. Singing on an afternoon hazy with heat in a dormitory garden while roads are closed and soldiers patrol the streets. This singing captures something, holds something, something not quite named, but something that is lived in the singing. Robyn Kelley describes it as a freedom dreamed. He writes, "In the poetics of struggle and lived experience, in the utterances of ordinary folks, in the cultural products of social movements, in the reflections of activists, we discover the many different cognitive maps of the future of the world not yet born."[71]

When there is no democratic government, and there are no outside witnesses to see and to speak of the suffering that occurs, the participative symbol of song strengthens participants into a collective soul force, offering a map, a dream to live in for a time. Marxist scholars may view an intangible source like music as an opiate because it maintains the well-being of heart and soul to the seeming exclusion of economic and political freedom. However, when people join together in performing music, stories, or dance, the very medium becomes the place where liberty lives, creating a freedom just as "real" as freedom found in the political self-determination of a nation-state. As Webster writes, "A nation-state is not yet in the offing, but the decolonization of the mind ... is complete: a West Papuan 'notion-state' already exists."[72]

After Wor: *Angganeka, Megawati, and Edo*

Even as I write this, the song continues, made manifest anew in as many ways as there are voices. To honour these voices, I would like to conclude with an unlikely trio who have entered into the living symbol of Papuan identity found in song: Angganeka Manufandu, Megawati Sukarnoputri, and Edo Kondologit.

Angganeka Returns

A new movement of *Koreri* has begun that harkens back to the power of Angganeka's and Ap's movements. Angganeka's music and voice were revived in 2010, to sing and to speak to the concrete experience of women in the context of post–Special Autonomy Papua. These experiences include continued violence and the loss of loved ones, and the responsibility of finding work for their children in an increasingly divided economy.[73] Hearing a silence—the absence of women's voices—in the harmonies of Papuan resistance in recent years, Lena Simanjuntak, the director and founder of a theatre group fashioned on Boal's theatre of the oppressed, engaged in deep "digging, listening, and fishing" to draw out and dramatize stories of the lives of Papua's women.[74] The "packaging" the women chose was Angganeka's story, and over a period of two months, the women participants "expressed, analyzed, explained, advised, decided, and planned" the various pieces of their stories to share through the melody of Angganeka's story. The story begins with "A group of women clothed in bark-cloth with *nokens* [string bags] around their heads, mourning, while dancing." A drum sounds, and to its rhythm, the women begin to sing Angganeka's song: "Oh Lord, come down and live with us here in this land of Mambesak, God of the sky, bless the nation of Papua."[75]

Few direct sources describing Angganeka's *Wor* remain, but her use of *Wor* to reinvigorate and animate and heal continues. In 2007, I witnessed a lonesome performance of *Wor* that Angganeka would have certainly grasped. The singer was mourning the loss of a political prisoner, Isa, the son of a Papuan leader. In February of 2007, Isa's mother, Mama Torabi, received news that he had taken poison in the prison bathroom. He was rushed to the hospital, but could not be revived, and he died soon after arriving at the hospital. Later that day, as I was walking with Lunia and Mama Lis up to his house, we heard a song calling from the hills. The singer sat overlooking the valley on the porch of Isa's house, just off the living room. Mama Torabi had put her money and care into this room. It was white-tiled, with orchids and *bunga sepatu* (hibiscus) just outside its screened windows. Mama Torabi held in her fingers the touch of life, the neighbours agreed. Any plant she touched lived! But this day, her yellow orchids were held by her son's dead hands, and her hands cradled his still face. Her body covered his, and as she wept, the *Wor* sung by her brother-in-law crawled through the room, gathering into its melodies the grief of her family and community. The song crept out the back door, down over the hills. "Isa! Isa! Isa!" his name cradled in his uncle's song, travelled down into the valley, finally reaching the sea. The other mothers, known as "mamas," sat just outside the living room, draped in scarves to ward off the night chill. Sitting in their teal plastic chairs, they sang songs in English, songs from the church, songs of *Wor*, funny songs, and Arnold's songs. Their melodies merged with Mama Torabi's weeping and her orchids and the evening light. They faced the silence of death with the strength of their collective voices.

The *Wor* of Angganeka's new followers, and the *Wor* performed by Isa's family and friends, express the historic and contemporary need for identity, dignity, and survival. Although their songs, like Angganeka's and Arnold's, do not directly address the state or issues of politics and violence, they continue to provide a space of historical continuity with the cultural traditions of Papua, expressing (although indirectly) to the Indonesian state that Papua remains.

MEGAWATI: THE EMPIRE SINGS BACK ...

Because the song of Papuan identity continues, there is space for participation and response by the Indonesian state. In keeping with this chapter's focus on music as a living symbol, by which identity is created and recreated through participation by many parties, it is fitting to recount here a musical interlude with Megawati Sukarnoputri, president of Indonesia from 2001 to 2004. Her mode of singing and the exclusivity of her song choice present a marked contrast between her attempt to attract and secure Papuan loyalty, and the participative efforts of the first "Queen of Papua" and her disciples, described above.

Sing and Kin Wah describe Megawati's song as follows. "On 25 December, 2002, President Megawati Soekarnoputri made a one-day visit to Papua. During a ceremony with three thousand people in Jayapura, the normally reticent Megawati announced that she would sing her favourite song as a Christmas present for the people of Papua. The song she chose was one popularized by Frank Sinatra, 'My Way.' "[76] Standing on stage suspended above a field of green grass, within sight of the sea, the wind, and the birds that so many Papuans sing of, into the silence of Theys Eluay and Aristoteles Masoka's deaths, Megawati gently crooned the song popularized by Frank Sinatra, 'I Did It My Way.' "[77]

Increasingly unpopular in Papua, Megawati attempted to "give a gift" to the Papuan people one year and one month after she allegedly ordered the death of the elected Papuan leader, Theys Eluay, and his driver Aristoteles Masoka.[78] In her song, she reiterates the discourse of the colonial state, which minimizes the Papuans' own agency and right to speak. Although not referring specifically to race, her actions and her song bring to mind the dismissal of Papuans and their collective voice, generally, demonstrated by US diplomats who referred to Papua as merely "a few thousand square miles of cannibal lands."[79]

EDO

Musical interactions with the Indonesian state continue, as evidenced by Megawati's Sinatra impersonation, but, in response, Papuans have expanded their resistance to the unified and nationalizing "my way" of the Indonesian state by merging their message of music into new technological mediums. While the military still controls much of the Papuan press (this can be seen in the recent stabbing of reporter Banjir Ambarita[80]), the Internet, accessible in outlying regions through cell phones, links Papuans with each other and with the international community, forming a space in which they can discuss a Papuan identity often kept hidden for safe-keeping.[81] David Hill and Krishna Sen have written, "The internet obviously does not guarantee the emergence of counter-hegemonic discourses, but it does facilitate the opening of discursive spaces within which they may be formulated and conveyed."[82]

Making use of what Habermas terms the "bourgeois public sphere" where "private people come together as public,"[83] a transnational community of largely anonymous individuals can engage in a communal process that generates a new understanding of Papuan identity through the medium of the Internet. While Megawati's "gift" was presented uni-directionally to the Papuan people and no direct response was possible at the time, the Internet music scene offers a space in which people may respond to such "gifts." This type of response can be found, for example, in the intense debates between Sungkawa and various Papuan supporters in their comments on David Bridie's song "Act of Free Choice," which documents Indonesia's annexation of Papua.[84] Other examples of musical participation in the living symbol of song through the Internet include Papua New Guinean artist George Telek's "West Papua," recorded in conjunction with David Bridie, and also music coming from within Papua, such as "Tanah Papua," and the re-recording of traditional Papuan songs in modern musical idioms, such as "Tugurere" by Papua Original.[85]

Although all of these songs are worthy of scrutiny, I invite you to dwell with me here in Edo Kondologit's "Aku Papua," which carries within its images, melody, and lyrics a vivid symbol of Papuan identity that strongly counters Megawati's "My Way." In the music video, Edo appears on the screen in jeans, T-shirt, and sunglasses. As he sings, images begin to appear: children smiling, sitting on the steps of a house on stilts over the sea; a man in goggles gathering seaweed; a young girl, her curly hair loose, smiling; two birds of paradise flitting in trees; and young men wearing T-shirts, bark and feather headdresses, and *tivas*, jumping up and down and making music in a village and later in a boat. All of these images are bathed in golden light. As the camera pans back to Edo, we see in the background the grass roof of a *honai* (grass hut from the highlands).[86]

In both its images and lyrics, "Aku Papua" takes symbols of Papuan identity—symbols both of the land, and tribal symbols previously used to identify the primitiveness of Papua—and uses them to communicate dignity instead. Unlike the previous colonial interpretations of these markers—black skin, grass houses, and little clothing—that identified Papuans as "primitive," denied their humanity, and reinforced genocidal practices, those making the film reinvest traditionally primitive symbols of Papua with pride. This is evident in the way that Edo lives the music with his voice and body. He begins quietly, his eyes closed, as the song begins, "The land of Papua is the land of my ancestors. The land where I was born. Together with the wind, together with the leaves, I was raised."[87] He croons at first, his words and relaxed body expressing memories of a peaceful childhood lived in and with the land, but when he reaches the chorus, the volume of his voice rises and, in almost a shout, he sings about the very symbols of Papua that have been used so long as a rationale for state and military suppression. With the volume and movement of his voice, fist in the air, Edo almost militantly reinvests these historic symbols of denigration with dignity as he sings the words, "Black is my skin, curly my hair, I am Papua. Even if the heavens should tear apart, I am Papua." As he sings, he begins to wail, his eyes squeezed shut, his body swaying back and forth, one arm across his abdomen, his voice rising in a cry almost of grief—reminiscent of *Wor*, a music that had been thought so powerful that it could raise even the dead—and he cries out once more, daring anyone to challenge him, "I am Papua!"[88]

Notes

1. This chapter was previously published as "The Living Symbol of Song in West Papua: A Soul Force to be Reckoned With," Indonesia 95 (April 2013): 73-91. This chapter begins by quoting personal communication with author. All names of private individuals noted in this chapter are pseudonyms. With special thanks to Rachel and Eva.

2. Edo Kondologit, "Aku Papua," by Stanley Neo and Franky Sahilatua, 2008, http://www.youtube.com/watch?v=Nad-VQT0dEw (accessed 15 August 2012).

3. Alex Rayfiel, "Singing for Life: Music is Still a Potent Source of Cultural Resistance in West Papua," *Focus on Indonesia* 78 (April 1, 2004), http://www.insideindonesia.org/singing-for-life (accessed 13 March 2011).

4. Tery S., "Stories and Music from Papua," unpublished manuscript (Winnipeg: Centre for Oral Culture and Creative Writing, 2011); Jay Griffiths, "Songs and Freedom

in West Papua," *Guardian* (London), 15 March 2011, https://www.theguardian.com/global/2011/mar/15/west-papua-singing-freedom-indonesia (accessed 1 April 2011); and *Strange Birds in Paradise: A West Papuan Story*, directed by Charlie Hill-Smith (Melbourne, AU: The House of Red Monkey, 2009). Three studies have attempted to establish that the occurrences in West Papua constituted genocide. An estimated 70,000–200,000 Papuans have been killed since 1961. See E. Brundige et al., "Indonesian Human Rights Abuses in West Papua: Application of the Law of Genocide to the History of Indonesian Control," paper prepared for the Indonesia Human Rights Network, 2004; J. Wing and Peter King, "Genocide in West Papua? The Role of the Indonesian State Apparatus and a Current Needs Assessment of the Papuan People," Centre for Peace and Conflict Studies, University of Sydney and ELSHAM, 2005; and S. Yoman, "Systematic Genocide of the Indigenous Peoples of West Papua under Special Autonomy," submitted to International Commission of Jurists Australia, 2005.

5   Diana Glazebrook, "Teaching Performance Art is Like Sharpening the Blade of a Knife," *The Asia Pacific Journal of Anthropology* 5, no. 1 (2004): 1; Rayfiel, "Singing for Life"; Griffiths, "Songs and Freedom in West Papua."

6   Ibid.

7   H. W. Jeong, *Peace and Conflict Studies: An Introduction* (Burlington, VT: Ashgate Publishers, 2000).

8   "Creative consciousness" is described in George Ritzer, *Sociological Theory* (New York: MacMillan, 1992), 163.

9   David Webster, " 'Already Sovereign as a People': A Foundational Moment in West Papuan Nationalism," *Pacific Affairs* 74, no. 4 (2001): 507–28; and Paul W. Van der Veur, "Political Awakening in West New Guinea," *Pacific Affairs* 36, no. 1 (1963): 54–74.

10 See also Freerk C. Kamma, *Koreri: Messianic Movements in the Biak-Numfor Culture Area* (Leiden, NL: Nijhoff, 1972).

11 Danilyn Rutherford, "Nationalism and Millenarianism in West Papua: Institutional Power, Interpretive Practice, and the Pursuit of Christian Truth," in *Social Movements: An Anthropological Reader*, ed. J. Nash (Malden, MA: Blackwell Publishing) 146–47.

12 Dorothea Rosa Herliany, "Teater Papua dan Manusia yang Berharap," http://pembebasan-sastra.blogspot.ca/2010/10/teater-papua-dan-manusia-yang-berharap.html (accessed 1 April 2011).

13 Rutherford, "Nationalism and Millenarianism"; Kamma, *Koreri*; Otto Simapiaref, "Dasar Dasar Perjuangan Kemerdekaan Papua Barat," (n.d.) www.antenna.nl/~fwillems/bi/ic/id/wp/dasar.html (accessed 25 March 2011).

14 For a discussion of *Wor,* see Philip Yampolsky, "Forces for Change in the Regional Performing Arts of Indonesia," *Performing Arts in Southeast Asia* 151, no. 4 (1995): 700–725; Kamma, *Koreri*.

15 See Rutherford, "Nationalism and Millenarianism."

16 Ben Sidran, *Black Talk* (New York: Da Capo Press, 1971), 151; see also Griffiths, "Songs and Freedom in West Papua."

17 Kamma, *Koreri*.

18 Arend Lijphart, *The Trauma of Decolonization: The Dutch and West New Guinea* (New Haven, CT: Yale University Press, 1966); Kamma, *Koreri*; Rutherford, "Nationalism and Millenarianism"; Richard Chauvel, *Constructing Papuan Nationalism: History, Ethnicity, and Adaptation* (Washington, DC: East-West Center, 2005).

19 Rutherford, "Nationalism and Millenarianism"; Lijpart, *The Trauma of Decolonization*; Van der Veur, "Political Awakening in West New Guinea."

20 Danilyn Rutherford, "Waiting for the End in Biak: Violence, Order, and a Flag Raising," *Indonesia* 67 (April 1999): 39–60.

21 For a detailed analysis of these turnovers of power, see John Saltford, *The United Nations and the Indonesian Takeover of West Papua* (New York: Taylor and Francis, 2006).

22 Griffiths, "Songs and Freedom in West Papua."

23 Craig Lockard, *Dance of Life: Popular Music and Politics in Southeast Asia* (Honolulu: University of Hawaii Press, 1998).

24 Yampolsky, "Forces for Change." See Antonio Gramsci, "Culture and Ideological Hegemony," in *Culture and Society: Contemporary Debates*, ed. Jeffrey C. Alexander and Steven Seidman (Cambridge: Cambridge University Press, 1990), 47–54.

25 Yampolsky, "Forces for Change," 702.

26 Cited in ibid.

27 Glazebrook, "Teaching Performance Art."

28 Bernard Juillerat, "La Mort d'Arnold Ap et la Destruction des Cultures de Nouvelle-Guinee Occidentale," *Journal de la Boclete des Oceanistes* 40, no. 78 (1984): 103–6; Glazebrook, "Teaching Performance Art."

29 Glazebrook, "Teaching Performance Art"; Benedict Anderson, *Imagined Communities: Reflections on the Origins and Spread of Nationalism* (New York: Verso Books, 1983); Rayfiel, "Singing for Life."

30 Rayfiel, "Singing for Life."

31 Hill-Smith, *Strange Birds*.

32 See Glazebrook, "Teaching Performance Art."

33 Ibid and Webster, "Already Sovereign as a People."

34 Juillerat, "La Mort," 105.

35 Hill-Smith, *Strange Birds*.

36 Griffiths, "Songs and Freedom in West Papua."

37 Julian Smythe, "Singing Ourselves Into Being: A Study of the Aural Landscape of West Papua" *Evangelical Missions Quarterly* 47, no. 4 (2011): 470–75.

38 See "Wor Traditional Dancing from Biak, Papua," http://www.youtube.com/watch?v=kvg0Ctf_V6s (accessed 2 April 2011).

39 Yampolsky, "Forces for Change," 713.

40 Ibid.

41 Rutherford, "Wating for the End," 56.

42 For a complete discussion of the Papuan movement and audience, see Rutherford's *Laughing at Leviathan: Sovereignty and Audience in West Papua* (Chicago: University of Chicago Press, 2012).

43 D. Rutherford, *Raiding the Land of the Foreigners* (Chicago: University of Chicago Press, 2005).

44 *Indonesia—Irian Jaya: The Biak Massacre,* directed by ABC Australia (Surrey, UK: Journeyman Pictures, 1998).

45 Ibid.

46 Tracy Banivanua-Mar, " 'A Thousand Miles of Cannibal Lands': Imagining Away Genocide in the Recolonization of West Papua," *Journal of Genocide Research* 10, no. 4 (2008): 583–602.

47 This analysis of the role of state torture is informed by William Cavanaugh's *Torture and Eucharist* (London: Blackwell, 1998).

48 *Indonesia—Irian Jaya: The Biak Massacre.*

49 Rutherford, "Waiting for the End"; and Simapiaref, "Dasar-dasar Perjuangan."

50 *Indonesia—Irian Jaya: The Biak Massacre.*

51 Rayfiel, "Singing for Life," 5.

52 Pseudonym used.

53 Rayfiel, "Singing for Life."

54 Glazebrook, "Teaching Performance Art."

55 See Glazebrook's description of the Pancar dance in "Teaching Performance Art," 5–6.

56 A notable exception is Angganeka's song, "Neno, neno," described above, which does refer to the "nation of Papua." Arguably, she was functioning in a pre-Indonesian Papua, in which the discourse of nation was not yet as dangerous as it currently is. See Webster, "Already Sovereign as a People," 520. See also Trio Ambisi, "Tanah Papua," by Yance, 2004; and Franky Sahilatua "Edo Kondologit-Aku Papua," 3 May 2011, http://www.youtube.com/watch?v=Nad-VQT0dEw (accessed 14 August 2012).

57 Griffiths, "Songs and Freedom in West Papua."

58 For a discussion of the re-constructing or "re-membering" of society through acts of collective memory in the face of the "dismembering" of terror, see Cavanaugh, *Torture*, 212.

59 Cited in Griffiths, "Songs and Freedom in West Papua."

60 In Hill-Smith, *Strange Birds.*

61 Griffiths, "Songs and Freedom in West Papua."

62 Ibid.

63 "Nyanyian Sunyi" was recorded by the Black Brothers, and lead singer Andy Ayamiseba came from the same island as Arnold, so the cross-pollination of the songs is possible. See http://vidgrids.com/nyanyian-sunyi (accessed 7 October 2012).

64 Trio Ambisi, "Tanah Papua," by Yance, 2004.

65 Greg Acciaioli, "Culture as Art: From Practice to Spectacle in Indonesia," *Canberra Anthropology* 8, no. 1–2 (1985): 148–72. See Also Webster, "Already Sovereign as a People."

66 In B. Giaiy and Y. Kambai, *Yosepha Alomang: Pergulatan seorang perempuan Papua melawan penindasan* (Jayapura, ID: ELSHAM Papua and European Commission, 2003), i, my translation.

67 Glazebrook, "Teaching Performance Art," 1.

68 Ibid.

69 See Kelley, *Freedom Dreams*.

70 As outlined by Gene Sharp and Joshua Paulson, *Waging Non-violent Struggle: Twentieth-Century Practice and Twenty-First Century Potential* (Boston, MA: Porter Sargent, 2005); and Robert J. Burrowes, *The Strategy of Non-Violent Defense: A Gandhian Approach* (New York: State University of New York Press, 1996).

71 Kelley, *Freedom Dreams*, 9.

72 Webster, "Already Sovereign as a People," 528.

73 Kelompok Kerja Dokumentasian Kekerasan and Pelanggaran HAM Perempuan Papua, *Stop Sudah: Kesaksian Perempuan Papua Korban Kekerasan dan Pelanggaran HAM 1963–2009* (2010), http://www.scribd.com/doc/50102676/new-buku-laporan-stop-sudah-papua-revisi-2010 (accessed 2 February 2011).

74 Herliany, "Teater Papua."

75 Ibid.

76 Daljit Singh and Chin Kin Wah, *Southeast Asian Affairs 2003* (Singapore: Institute of Southeast Asian Studies, 2003), 97.

77 Personal observation, TeleVisi Republic Indonesia (Television of the Republic of Indonesia), Jakarta, 2002.

78 Singh and Kin Wa, *Southeast Asian Affairs*; B. Giaiy, *Memoria Passionis* (Jayapura, ID: Sekretariat Keadilan dan Perdamaian, 2001).

79 Robert Komer to Rostow, 17 February 1961, White House. Quoted in Gregory Pemberton, *All the Way: Australia's Road to Vietnam* (Sydney: Allen & Unwin, 1987), 86.

80 "Papua Reporter: Mental Scars Remain, 'I am Traumatised,'" *Pacific Media Watch*, 29 March 2011, http://www.scoop.co.nz/stories/WO1103/S00983/papua-reporter-mental-scars-remain-i-am-traumatised.htm (accessed 2 April 2011).

81 See James C. Scott, *Domination and the Arts of Resistance: Hidden Transcripts* (New Haven, CT: Yale University Press, 1990), 14.

82 David T. Hill and Krishna Sen, *Indonesia's New Democracy* (New York: Routledge, 2005), 116.

83 Cited in Hill and Sen, *Indonesia's New Democracy*, 8.

84 See Sungkawa, "David Bridie—'Act of Free Choice,' " 2008, at http://www.Youtube.com/watch?v= CO2CgjIRr9E (accessed 2 April 2011).

85 George Telek, "West Papua," by David Bridie and Tim Cole, 2004; Trio Ambisi, "Tanah Papua," by Yance, 2004; Papua original, "Tugurere," http://www.Youtube.com/watch?v=i4X-nhuops8 (accessed 14 August 2012).

86 Franky Sahilatua, "Edo Kondologit-Aku Papua," http://www.Youtube.com/watch?v=Nad-VQT0dEw (accessed 14 August 2012), translation mine.

87 Sahilatua, "Edo Kondologit."

88 Ibid.

17

Time for a New US Approach toward Indonesia and West Papua

Edmund McWilliams

There are few places in the world where US human rights policy is as disingenuous as it is in West Papua. The bankruptcy of US posturing when it comes to respect for fundamental human rights, including protection of the physical security of civilian populations, human dignity, equal application of the law, and racial equality, is nowhere more evident than in West Papua. US advocacy for fundamental democratic principles such as self-determination, civil control of the military, and the accountability of security forces before the law simply does not extend to West Papua.

For decades the US government has consistently failed to address the widely acknowledged systematic abuse of human rights in West Papua. The US State Department's annual exercise of compiling human rights reports for every country is nowhere more lacking in candour and honesty than in Indonesia, where US interest in preserving military-to-military ties and in protecting opportunities for US corporations dictate the broad sanitizing of any genuinely critical commentary, especially with regard to West Papua. As a participant at a senior level of these annual exercises and as both a US government, and subsequently an independent, reviewer of the reports on Indonesia, I have been witness to the compromises with the truth that consistently shield the Indonesian government and especially its security forces from deserved criticism.

The genocidal policy of "transmigration," which has rendered the Papuan population a marginalized minority in its own land, was rarely broached and never seriously criticized in the US State Department reports. Moreover, these reports and statements by US officials consistently avoid language critical of the Indonesian military that might jeopardize expanding military-to-military co-operation between the American and Indonesian militaries. This sanitizing of the Indonesian government's record in West Papua, and especially the conduct of its security forces, was especially important during periods when US congressional scrutiny of such military aid raised the prospect that US military-assistance programs might be curtailed by congressional action. That prospect has faded as even congressional concern over human rights in Indonesia and especially in West Papua has diminished.[1]

In their testimony before Congress regarding West Papua in late 2015, two senior State Department officials misrepresented the human rights environment in Indonesia and especially in West Papua.[2] Scott Busby, deputy assistant secretary, Bureau of Democracy, Human Rights, and Labor, and James Carouso, acting deputy assistant secretary for Maritime and Mainland Southeast Asian affairs, spoke before the Senate Foreign Relations Committee Subcommittee on East Asia, the Pacific, and International Cybersecurity Policy. During their remarks on the region and in specific comments about human rights observance in Indonesia, the officials failed to address the brutalization of Papuan civilians and demographic policies, especially transmigration, that amount to genocide. Moreover, neither mentioned the many outstanding cases in which Indonesian security personnel have not been held accountable for egregious human rights abuses committed against Papuans, such as the Paniai massacre in December 2014, in which five Papuan youths engaged in peaceful protest were gunned down by Indonesian military personnel.[3] The same two officials also ignored continued restrictions on access to West Papua by the UN special rapporteur, international journalists, human rights monitors, and humanitarian assistance personnel.

Instead, the officials commended Indonesia for its "press freedom." These officials did note restrictions on press freedom in Malaysia and Vietnam, making their failure to note the same rights violations in West Papua all the more glaring. Moreover, their refusal to acknowledge the restrictions on press freedom in West Papua was in stark contrast to reporting by

Human Rights Watch (HRW). In a report entitled "Something to Hide," HRW detailed the many ways that Indonesia has hindered the media and others from monitoring the situation in West Papua.[4] Based on interviews with journalists, humanitarian workers, government officials, and others, the report found that "past restrictions have far exceeded what is permissible under Indonesia's international law obligations." The report summarized and added details to the instances when Jakarta hindered international NGOs, journalists, and human rights investigators from reporting on West Papua. It also provided an important service by providing details on the threats and other barriers local journalists face in carrying out their work. These include beatings, detention, and the placement of intelligence officers in newsrooms.

Underscoring the determined obliviousness of the US government to rights abuses in West Papua was a contemporaneous report by the International Coalition for Papua which descried West Papua as "one of the regions in Asia most seriously affected by human rights abuse violations and an unresolved, long standing political conflict. The living conditions of the indigenous Papuan peoples are in stark contrast to those trans-migrants from other parts of Indonesia."[5] Amnesty International, exhibiting candour absent from US State Department accounts, noted the arbitrary arrest of at least 264 Papuan political activists for "peaceful protests when President Joko Widodo visited the province."[6]

Pressure on US administrations and on the US Congress to minimize criticism of the Indonesian government and its security and intelligence forces has for years been mobilized largely by the US–Indonesia Society (USINDO), a Washington-based lobby organization comprised of US corporations with interests in Indonesia and retired senior US officials with Indonesian experience and interests. This cabal, originally formed to counter broad criticism of Jakarta, which developed after the 1991 Santa Cruz massacre in East Timor, has long since benefited from informal collaboration between current and former senior US officials and US corporations with interests in Indonesia. The US embassy in Jakarta, for example, has worked with USINDO to prepare travel for US congressional staff and even members of Congress, with the intention of building congressional support for policy initiatives that expand ties between the United States and Indonesia at the expense of human rights.

Corporate Influence over US Policy

US corporations, working through USINDO and sometimes unilaterally, have long exercised strong influence over US policy towards Indonesia. The protection and furtherance of these corporate interests in Indonesia, as elsewhere, are largely co-mingled with genuine US national interests so that US policy is developed in conjunction with and at the behest of American corporations. At times these corporate interests so dominate the formation of policy as to undermine broader US concerns and interests. This is seen most frequently when corporate interests are in conflict with human rights concerns, with the latter invariably getting short shrift.

The archipelago's vast natural riches have drawn the interest of American corporations. Among the corporations that early on developed interests in Indonesia were oil companies, notably the forerunners of Texaco, Chevron and Mobil, as well as other extractive industries.

US corporate interest in West Papua and more generally in the Indonesian archipelago is also extensive when it comes to the production of palm oil and other forest products. These industries have had a devastating impact throughout the archipelago, where logging and the creation of palm oil plantations have led to the destruction of virgin forest. While this has most severely affected other parts of the archipelago, notably Sumatra and Kalimantan, it is also becoming more common in West Papua, where the burning of virgin lands reached unprecedented levels in 2015. Indonesian military involvement in the harvesting of wood products (some of it illegal) is a matter of long-standing record in West Papua. The full impact of these activities on the livelihood and health of Papuans is not yet fully calculated. The US government has pressured its Indonesian counterpart to abandon these destructive practices, but these efforts have fallen short of those of various European governments such as Norway. It is unclear whether US corporate interest in palm oil and forest products has or will mitigate US policy to limit the impact of such destructive "development." It is noteworthy, however, that human rights concerns arising from the Indonesian government's drive to "develop" West Papua have not yet precipitated significant comment on the part of the US government.

Freeport and West Papua

By far the most dominant American corporate player in West Papua is the mining giant Freeport-McMoRan, which operates the world's largest copper and gold mine in south-central West Papua.[7] For decades Freeport's mining operation has been the focus of human rights abuses meted out by the Indonesian military and police and directed against the Amungme and Kamoro peoples, the traditional landowners in the upland and coastal areas, respectively, of the sprawling mining operation.

Freeport's displacement of the local population—especially the Amungme, who have lived in the area for generations—has generated periodic tension and protest. Freeport has long relied on the Indonesian security forces, especially the army's Special Forces Command (Kopassus), to repress and intimidate the local people.

Freeport's at times contentious relationship with the Indonesian military has long amounted to a corrupt bargain. In one instance in 1996, the relationship transformed into one of naked extortion as the military, unsatisfied with the level of "support" it had received from Freeport, organized violent demonstrations among Papuans that threatened Freeport personnel and property. Freeport informed the US embassy of the nature of this extortion, but diplomats failed to report this to Washington because they feared that the US government would take steps against the Indonesian military and the Suharto dictatorship, which depended on the Indonesian military to retain control in West Papua and elsewhere in the archipelago.

Generations of Papuans have suffered extrajudicial killings, torture, and incarceration without trial at the hands of the security forces, and at the behest of Freeport. US military-to-military ties with the Indonesia have enabled the Indonesian military, rendering the United States complicit in the abuse of Papuan civilians. In the 1980s, the US military provided air-to-ground combat aircraft, which were then deployed against remote Papuan villages with devastating effect. The same aircraft were also employed by the Indonesian military to suppress popular resistance in East Timor, which Indonesia occupied from 1975 to 1999.

In addition to persistent human rights abuses, Freeport's mining operation has been responsible for damaging the ecology of the region and presenting serious long-term health risks for Papuans. For decades Freeport's mining operation has polluted the region in which it operates and beyond. Its deposition of mining tailings in the Ajkwa River system, a previously free-running riverine system on which local people depend for fishing, bathing, and transportation, has transformed the river into a wasteland. Decades of such activities have created a delta of toxic waste that extends for miles to the Arafura Sea. That delta is virtually devoid of life and includes dangerous quicksand pits. Freeport has constructed some dikes to channel the tailings but they are periodically topped, allowing the tailings to flow into surrounding forest, where they smother extensive stretches of trees, notably the sago palm, which is an important food source for local Papuans. The tailings deposition extends to the sea coast, where tidal action pushes them west and east along the coast. As the tailings are deposited along the coast by the tides and coastal currents, they kill the mangrove forests that protect the coast and provide habitat for many aquatic species.

The mining operation, with its acid mine drainage, has also polluted ground water for miles at and below the mining site. Even the ground water in Timika, some twenty-five miles below the mine, has been polluted.

For many years the US embassy in Jakarta worked with Freeport to limit public awareness of the devastating impact its operation was having on West Papua and its people. US officials routinely refused to assist journalists, even American ones, who sought to travel to the Freeport site. They also worked with the Indonesian government to block travel to West Papua by an American lawyer seeking to represent Papuan clients in a US court in the late 1990s. Even travel by US embassy officers was tightly monitored by Freeport.

Concerned that reporting by the US embassy was revealing the plight of its Papuan victims, in the 1990s Freeport prevailed on the US ambassador to cease all reporting on the region. The resulting silence persisted for over a year, ending only when the American ambassador departed. Subsequently, as elements within the embassy sought to report on developments there, there were strenuous efforts by the Defense Attaché Office and the ambassador and his senior deputy to quash or refute this reporting. At the same time, as a new team of officers were transferred to the embassy, and it became clear that these officers were inclined to report on West Papua more candidly, the files made available to these officers were stripped of any records that revealed the years of collusion between the embassy, Freeport, and the Indonesian military.

US Administrations Pursue Similar Policies towards West Papua

Successive US administrations, despite their strikingly different foreign policy outlooks, have adopted effectively identical positions with regard to West Papua. The administrations of George W. Bush and Barack Obama each refused to acknowledge the genocidal dimensions of Jakarta's assault on Papuan human rights. Both ignored Jakarta's pursuit of transmigration, as well as its policy of malign neglect/marginalization of Papuans, including the persistent failure to provide minimal health, education, or other basic services. Both ignored the historic transformation, inherent in Jakarta's policy choices, that has rendered Papuans a minority in their own land. Rather than developing a meaningful policy to address this genocide, the Bush and Obama administrations confined their policy response to tinkering with Jakarta's failed "special autonomy" formulations, which manifestly do not, and have never, addressed the ongoing tragedy afflicting Papuans.

US government unwillingness to pursue policies or initiatives that might address Jakarta's genocidal policies vis-à-vis West Papua should not be perceived as simply a failure to act responsibly. Sadly, since the 1962 American-engineered New York Agreement, which effectively transferred an incipient independent West Papua to Indonesian control, the United States has conspired with Indonesian regimes, notably the Suharto dictatorship, to solidify Indonesian control in West Papua. The United States provided military equipment and training for Suharto's military for decades, and thereby facilitated the brutal military efforts to repress the two most serious challenges to its control, namely in East Timor and West Papua. American complicity in this repression is not in question.

That two such different American administrations would pursue policies that failed to reflect meaningful, effective concern for systematic human rights abuses in West Papua, the absence of accountability for the security forces and effective civil control of the military, the fettering of free media, and most importantly the genocidal implications of Jakarta's approach to ensuring control of West Papua, is perplexing. In particular, how could the Obama administration, which claimed to sympathetic to human rights and the promotion of democratic principles, fail to protect human rights and democratic values in West Papua? A meaningful assessment of the weight of human-rights-related goals and objectives in the formulation of the Obama administration's foreign policy awaits a comprehensive analysis.

Nevertheless, a review of US policy vis-à-vis West Papua, along with a consideration of US security co-operation with regimes ranging from those of the coup-birthed government in Honduras or the human-rights abusing regimes of Uzbekistan or Vietnam, suggests that human rights may sometimes have been sacrificed at the altar of realpolitik. In this, neither the Obama nor Bush administrations veered significantly away from the post–Second World War American model.

The Possibility of a more Enlightened US Approach to West Papua

Given this record of complicity, is there any conceivable hope that future US policy might be directed toward addressing Papuans' desperate plight?

The sense, shared by many Americans, that the United States constitutes the only remaining superpower, the "indispensable nation" and "leader of the free world," renders it unproductive to search the globe for models that US policy-makers might seek to emulate in devising an approach that would more genuinely promote human rights and democratic principles in West Papua. American "exceptionalism," for good or ill, has long dissuaded US policy-makers from applying to themselves the constraints of moral/ethical, or even legal, obligations which might govern other nations' policy-makers.

However, there is one model in the United States' own historical experience that might have some bearing on its policy vis-à-vis West Papua and Jakarta. In late 1991, Washington was confronted by a massacre carried out by a dictator who had for decades been a U.S. ally. Indonesian dictator Suharto's military murdered several hundred unarmed, mostly youthful, protesters in the streets of Dili, the capital of Indonesian-occupied East Timor. The horrified reaction in the United States, and most especially in the US Congress, meant that the government was forced to react in substantive ways. The administration of George H. W. Bush, and subsequently that of Bill Clinton, agreed to congressionally-imposed sanctions on the Indonesian military, which as we have seen had heretofore benefitted from very generous US military-to-military co-operation. While the Suharto regime remained a repressive dictatorship, and while the Indonesian military continued to be a brutal oppressor (notably in West Papua and Aceh), repression in occupied East Timor waned. The reduction of US military assistance had some limited beneficial impact, at least in terms of Indonesian military abuses in East Timor. Might not similarly targeted sanctions limiting US-Indonesian military-to-military co-operation have an ameliorative effect in West Papua?

Long-term American interests in Indonesia entail encouraging the emergence of that country as a stable, democratic state in which the military is no longer corrupt, is accountable to a civilian judiciary, and, crucially, is under civil control. Currently, the Indonesian military is a very corrupt institution with deep involvement in both legal and illegal businesses, notably including illegal operations in West Papua that range from logging to shaking down Indonesian and foreign corporations based in the region, including, periodically, Freeport-McMoRan. The Indonesian military's business empire throughout the country, but especially in West Papua, contributes to the environmental devastation that, in turn, adds to Indonesia's major contribution to global climate change.

The Indonesian military is also notoriously unaccountable for its past and current human rights abuses. Once again, this is most apparent in West Papua, a reality acknowledged even in the otherwise truth-challenged annual US Department of State human rights reports. And it is in West Papua where the Indonesian military most obviously continues to operate under the rules of the Suharto dictatorship, inter alia ignoring efforts by the ever more hapless Widodo administration to liberalize rules governing journalists' and other international observers' access there.

An enlightened US policy in Indonesia, one that seeks to advance prospects for the evolution of an Indonesian state neither dominated by nor subservient to a corrupt, unaccountable, human-rights abusing military, could be the basis of a new US approach to Indonesia. That new approach could engage policies that employ existing, significant US leverage, including US military and other forms of assistance, to press for genuine reform of the Indonesian military, and in particular its operations in West Papua. Specifically, continued US military co-operation with the Indonesian security forces could be conditioned on explicit reforms, especially those having to do with Indonesian military conduct in West Papua.

Moreover, US officials should engage with their senior Indonesian counterparts to encourage them to abandon the "security approach" that has long governed Jakarta's policies in West Papua, and instead pursue reconciliation with Papuans. Realistically, for any reconciliation process to move forward credibly, the Indonesian threat to Papuan security must be removed. A withdrawal of Indonesian military forces from West Papua is therefore essential to any genuine reconciliation. This would also entail the dismantling of the military's massive, and often illegal, business infrastructure in West Papua. Retention of military components should be specifically defined and limited to legitimate border defence. A similar drawdown of state intelligence operatives targeting Papuan dissenters is similarly essential to a credible reconciliation process.

Such reconciliation must entail engagement with Papuan civil society, and not simply empower Papuan officials whose power and authority is often derivative of the political power circuitry emanating from Jakarta. Also, as a vital good-faith gesture, Jakarta must also be prepared to include, within the scope of reconciliation discussions, the long-standing Papuan demand that the internationally recognized right of self-determination be extended to them.

To date, US policy toward Indonesia has been in the service of American corporate interests as well as the Pentagon's long-held intention that Indonesia should serve as a component in the United States' Pacific defence policy, especially vis-à-vis China. This narrow, realpolitik-based definition of US interests has rendered the US government complicit in the crimes of the Suharto dictatorship and its bastard son, the Indonesian military, which continues to threaten democratic reform in Indonesia and the survival of the Papuan people.

A broader understanding of what constitutes long-term US interests in Indonesia—i.e., the evolution of a stable and democratic Indonesia—is long overdue.

Notes

1   West Papua Advocacy Team, "West Papua Report July 2015," http://etan.org/issues/wpapua/2015/1507wpap.htm#State_ (accessed 30 March 2016).

2   Department of State testimony to US Congress, 19 Nov. 2015, http://www.state.gov/j/drl/rls/rm/2015/249788.htm (accessed 30 March 2016).

3   Benny Wenda, "Statement on the Massacre of Youths and Children in Paniai, West Papua," press release, 9 December 2014, https://www.bennywenda.org/2014/statement-on-the-massacre-of-youths-and-children-in-paniai-west-papua/ (accessed 30 March 2016).

4   Human Rights Watch, "Something to Hide? Indonesia's Restrictions on Media Freedom and Rights Monitoring in Papua," 10 November 2015, https://www.hrw.org/report/2015/11/10/something-hide/indonesias-restrictions-media-freedom-and-rights-monitoring-papua (accessed 30 March 2016).

5   International Coalition for Papua, *Human Rights in West Papua 2015* (Wuppertal, DE: International Coalition for Papua, 2015).

6   Amnesty International, "Indonesia: End Mass Arbitrary Arrests of Peaceful Protesters In Papua," 11 June 2015, https://www.amnesty.org/en/documents/asa21/1851/2015/en/ (accessed 30 March 2016).

7   On Freeport see Denise Leith, *The Politics of Power: Freeport in Suharto's Indonesia* (Honolulu: University of Hawai'i Press, 2003) and S. Eben Kirksey, *Freedom in Entangled Worlds* (Durham, NC: Duke University Press, 2012).

SECTION V

Memory, Truth, and Reconciliation in Solomon Islands

Memory, Truth, and Reconciliation in Solomon Islands

If a truth commission reports and the government tries to keep its findings secret, does its work still have value? That is what happened in Solomon Islands. In bringing truths to light and in carrying out its work, we argue that it does.

Where the problem in Tanah Papua has been lack of a truth commission and any dialogue between the two sides of the conflict, the problem in Solomon Islands is different. A truth commission formed in the wake of conflict. It researched the conflict, and then reported on what had happened and what might be done in the future. To date, it is the only truth commission to be held in Melanesia. But the government declined to publish its report or act upon its recommendations.

The Solomon Islands Truth and Reconciliation Commission (SITRC) used South Africa's TRC as its model. Founded by an act of parliament in 2008, it held public and closed hearings and carried out a number of interviews from 2009 to 2011, then presented its report in 2012. The SITRC was mandated to investigate the causes of "the tensions" between Malaitan and Guadalcanal militia groups and the role of those groups, the government, and external actors in human rights violations, as well as to contribute to victim healing through testimonies. The SITRC aimed to include Indigenous *kastom* (custom) and gender, and included a special focus on violations of the rights of children. It identified major violations of human rights under the headings of killings, illegal detentions, torture and ill-treatment, sexual violations, property violations, and the forced displacement of people.

The SITRC produced an impressive five-volume report with careful documentation of the conflict and human rights violations, followed by a series of careful recommendations touching on everything from memorialization to land tenure to the justice system. That report is in the public domain only because its editor, Bishop Terry Brown, published it online. Brown's account of the conflict, the commission, and his own role forms chapter 18 of this book.

Unlike Timor-Leste, there is no truth commission follow-up institution or NGO dedicated to carrying out the report's legacy. However, Solomon Islands does have an active civil society, much of it linked to church and women's groups. In a heavily Christian country, the Solomon Islands

Christian Association (SICA) was the prime mover in proposing and pushing for a truth commission. To this local push was added the international presence of the South African TRC commissioner, Archbishop Desmond Tutu. The commission itself combined the local and the international in its mixed make-up (three Solomon Islanders and two international members) and in its operating methods. It tried to make more space for women, for instance, as SITRC officer Betty Lina Gigisi recounts in chapter 19.

In these aspects, the SITRC may have broken ground. Solomon Islands is a small country, and it was governed by Britain until 1978. Its diverse peoples fall into the Melanesian islands, which span from Indonesian-ruled Tanah Papua to Fiji, and also include Papua New Guinea, Vanuatu, and Kanaky (French-ruled New Caledonia)—four independent countries and two territories still under outside rule. All six have some form of membership in the Melanesian Spearhead Group (MSG) and the Pacific Islands Forum. While Solomon Islands is not the only one to experience conflict, it did suffer a relatively short but extremely violent conflict around the turn of the century.

Ethnicity was one cause of what local people call "the tensions." Economic factors also played a role. While few outsiders could locate Solomon Islands on a map, some might recall the island of Guadalcanal as a Second World War battleground, one of the turning points at which the Japanese military advance was turned back. The major airfield of Guadalcanal became the site of the Solomons capital, Honiara, which attracted migrants from neighbouring Malaita Island. Economic change was unsettling the previous balance. In the 1990s, the increasing presence in much of Guadalcanal of migrants from Malaita led to conflicts over land ownership that turned violent as both groups formed militias. One of these militia groups even managed to topple the national government. A peace agreement was signed in Australia but conflict continued until the arrival of an Australian-led Regional Assistance Mission to Solomon Islands (RAMSI) in 2003. After ten years, RAMSI became a police training mission only, and its mandate ended in 2017.

Yet the causes of the conflict went unaddressed, leading to civil-society calls for a truth commission. Church voices were especially prominent in this push. This mobilizing phase led to a 2008 parliamentary mandate that formed the SITRC. The commission than carried out its work. But the government's failure to publish or debate the report led to a state-sponsored forgetting. Most truth commissions report with ceremony and fanfare, and then hope for governments to act on their recommendations. The SITRC report, by contrast, vanished into a void. There has been almost no "socialization" since the report's completion. The reasons for this remain cloudy, but the next chapter starts to look for an explanation and an assessment of the SITRC's work.

18

The Solomon Islands "Ethnic Tension" Conflict and the Solomon Islands Truth and Reconciliation Commission: A Personal Reflection

Terry M. Brown

From late 1998 through 2003, Solomon Islands, a small independent nation in the southwest Pacific, suffered a period of what is locally called "ethnic tension" or "the tension" between Indigenous people of two of the major islands, Guadalcanal and Malaita.[1] Since the end of the Second World War, people of the country's most populous island, Malaita, settled in and around Honiara, on the north coast of Guadalcanal, formerly a US military base but, since the close of the war, the colony's capital. This movement of Malaitans to Guadalcanal continued for the next half century—including after independence in 1978—largely for economic reasons, as Malaitans sought jobs in Honiara, in the oil palm and rice plantations on the Guadalcanal Plains and at the Gold Ridge goldmine east of Honiara. The Indigenous people of Guadalcanal sold customary land to incoming Malaitans and many villages named "New Mala" sprung up around Guadalcanal. The Malaitans were entrepreneurial and often flourished economically while local Guadalcanal people often pursued a more traditional subsistence lifestyle. Malaitan men often took Guadalcanal wives, thereby giving them access to local land through Guadalcanal's matrilineal and matrilocal land tenure system.

With time, this gradual colonization of Guadalcanal by Malaitans became a source of anger among many people on Guadalcanal, and in late 1998 a local militant group emerged from the remote Weather Coast (south shore) of Guadalcanal, variously called the Guadalcanal Revolutionary Army (GRA) or Isatabu Freedom Movement (IFM), and began harassing Malaitan settlers on north Guadalcanal. The violence increased dramatically in 1999, when some twenty thousand Malaitans were expelled from Guadalcanal back to Malaita via Honiara, as houses, businesses, and oil palm plantations were burnt or destroyed and lives and properties lost.

By the end of the year, a Malaitan militant group, the Malaita Eagle Force (MEF), had emerged in Honiara to protect Malaitans there and to fight the IFM. Both militant groups relied on weapons stolen from or provided by the police, who generally split along ethnic lines. The government tried to broker various peace agreements but neither militant group was satisfied and the conflict continued between the Honiara-based MEF and the IFM, who were spread across the rural areas of Guadalcanal. Checkpoints appeared between the two militant groups' territories and travel through them became very difficult, if not impossible. Only certain church organizations, such as religious communities, were allowed across.

One local peace agreement after another failed, and at midnight on 5 June 2000 the MEF and a group of Malaitan Police Field Force officers raided the central Royal Solomon Islands Police Force (RSIPF) armoury in Rove, Honiara, effectively disarming the police. They then placed the prime minister, Bartholomew Ulufa'alu, under house arrest, demanded his resignation (which he eventually gave), and declared all-out war on the IFM.[2] Ulufa'alu was replaced three weeks later by Manasseh Sogavare, who met the approval of the MEF.[3] The coup was quickly denounced by the international community, including Australia, which brought in a warship to evacuate its citizens. The country's economy collapsed as businesses and non-government organizations left the country and fighting between the MEF and IFM spread throughout Guadalcanal, and even to other provinces. (In Auki, Malaita, where I was the local Anglican bishop, the MEF took over the police station.) In the meantime, fearful of militant activities by Malaitans in the Western Province, another group of militants, the Black Sharks, were brought across the Papua New Guinea (PNG) border from

Bougainville for protection.[4] However, all these militant groups, especially the MEF, also attracted criminal elements that saw a good chance to steal trucks and other goods and settle old scores.

Australian politicians dubbed Solomon Islands part of the "arc of instability" that began with East Timor and West Papua and extended across PNG, Solomon Islands, Vanuatu, and New Caledonia to Fiji (the home of several recent coups). Peace talks ensued and a ceasefire was agreed to on 2 August 2000. Formal peace talks between the MEF and the IFM took place in Townsville, Queensland two months later and on 15 October 2000 the Townsville Peace Agreement (TPA) was signed. It provided for the laying down and collection of arms and a special non-armed International Peace Monitoring Group (IPMG) from overseas to monitor the process. It also provided amnesty and rehabilitation for the militants and economic development projects for remote parts of Malaita and Guadalcanal.

While the TPA represented a major settlement of the conflict between the IFM and the MEF, problems remained. One Guadalcanal militant, Harold Keke, leader of the Guadalcanal Liberation Front (GLF) on the eastern Weather Coast of Guadalcanal, refused to participate in the Townsville talks or sign the TPA and continued his fight against the Solomons government. In turn, the government organized a Joint Operation of police and former militants of both sides to go to the Weather Coast to fight Keke. These groups were quite undisciplined and Keke became paranoid about disloyalty in his own ranks. Ordinary people on the Weather Coast were caught in the middle and many were killed or tortured. In April 2002 Keke and GLF members killed six members of the Melanesian Brotherhood, an order of the Anglican Church of Melanesia, who were seeking a fellow member whom Keke had killed earlier that year; in August 2002 Keke killed the local member of parliament, Father Augustine Geve, a Roman Catholic priest. Nor had things entirely settled on north Guadalcanal and Malaita, with occasional killings continuing as militants returned home still eager to fight. The unarmed IPMG stood by powerless as acts of violence took place. In Malaita, where I lived, it was more violent after the TPA than before, as ex-militants returned home and terrorized villages. Violence also continued in the Western Solomons between the Black Sharks and locals.

Finally, in June 2003, the (new) prime minister of Solomon Islands, Allan Kemakeza, requested external military intervention to end the conflict. Until then, Australia had been strongly opposed to such intervention (Prime Minister Ulufa'alu had requested it when the conflict first began in 1999 but was refused) but post-9/11 security fears about the "arc of instability" prevailed and the intervention was agreed to. Australia, after a formal request from the Solomon Islands parliament, organized the Regional Assistance Mission to Solomon Islands (RAMSI). The missions was comprised of military and police units of Commonwealth countries in the Pacific region, including Australia, New Zealand, Papua New Guinea, Fiji, Samoa, and Tonga. Its troops arrived to a warm welcome on 24 July 2003. The troops quickly ended the conflict on the Weather Coast, arresting Keke and his cohorts; RAMSI line officers were placed in the provinces and the situation in Malaita and the west quickly settled. RAMSI, unlike the local police force, was armed and had power to intervene. While initially envisioned as a small and short intervention, RAMSI grew into a major military, police, and civil-service operation. Only now has it shrunk to almost nothing, though many fear the recurrence of ethnic conflict should it completely disappear.

    I hope this long historical introduction helps explain why Solomon Islands came to have a truth and reconciliation commission. About two hundred persons died in the conflict and many hundreds were injured, tortured, sexually assaulted, traumatized, run out from their homes (in most cases permanently), and deprived of their properties. Initially, Guadalcanal militants terrorized Malaita settlers; then the two militant groups fought one another, with the MEF having the advantage, drawing on the armaments of the state, including a patrol boat; each group killed and tortured members of the other group. But both militant groups terrorized their own people, too, whom they thought were disloyal; the IFM also employed child soldiers. The MEF in its occupation of Honiara stole from innocent civilians and intimidated members of the government. After the TPA, the Solomon Islands government participated in state terrorism through the human rights abuses committed as part of the Joint Operation. And Harold Keke and the GLF killed many Guadalcanal civilians. One striking conclusion of the TRC report was that the majority of human rights abuses were intra-ethnic rather than inter-ethnic. Only in the first stages of the conflict was it inter-ethnic. Thus the frequent description in the international media of the conflict as a "civil war" is not entirely accurate. The Roman Catholic archbishop of Honiara, Adrian Smith, described the conflict to me as one between two groups of displaced people: Malaitans on Guadalcanal and Weather Coast Guadalcanal people on north Guadalcanal. To say that the provinces were at war with one another is a gross overstatement. I lived fairly quietly in Malaita during the height of the conflict.

The Churches and the Genesis of the Truth and Reconciliation Commission

Solomon Islands is largely Christian and the "ethnic tension" caught many unawares, myself included. Christian evangelization began in the mid-nineteenth century, first with Anglicans, Roman Catholics, and Methodists; then later, South Sea Evangelicals (akin to Baptists), Seventh-day Adventists (SDAs), and many smaller groups; recently there has also been a proliferation of small new churches, many of them breakaways from the mainline churches. There are now small groups of Muslims. The Roman Catholic Church is predominant in rural Guadalcanal though there are also small groups of Anglican and South Sea Evangelical Church (SSEC) members. The western Weather Coast of Guadalcanal also includes what might be called a neo-custom movement, the Moro Movement, a group of former Roman Catholics who advocate a return to traditional Guadalcanal religion, custom, and lifestyle, including the rejection of Western religion, dress and technology. (Some of them appear in the film *The Thin Red Line*.) Many early IFM members came out of Moro and Roman Catholic backgrounds and IFM fighters frequently wore traditional Guadalcanal dress of a *kabilato* (bark loincloth) and relied on traditional magic to fight. MEF militants came out of largely Protestant backgrounds, especially members of the SSEC (the largest church in Malaita), SDAs, and Jehovah Witnesses, though there were some Anglicans, especially among the leaders. MEF members, however, also called upon Malaita custom magic in their fighting. On the western Weather Coast, Harold Keke, though initially Roman Catholic, identified himself as a member of the SSEC and his followers ascribed messianic qualities to him. But generally, the IFM-MEF conflict took on a certain Catholic versus Protestant quality, and the MEF limited the access of Roman Catholic leaders in Honiara to rural Guadalcanal.

However, once the character and scope of the conflict began to be understood, church leaders attempted to intervene to secure a peaceful resolution. The Peace Committee of the ecumenical Solomon Islands Christian Association (SICA), which included members of the Roman Catholic, Anglican, United (Methodist), and SSEC churches (with the SDAs as observers), proposed and promoted ceasefires and peace talks. Individual denominations tried to bring their members from the warring ethnic groups together for discussion. The Anglican religious communities (the Melanesian Brotherhood, the Sisters of Melanesia, the Society of St. Francis, and the Community of the Sisters of the Church), whose Honiara and mother houses were divided by the front line, were crucial in securing transportation across the checkpoints and providing counselling to both militant groups.[5] The General Synod of the Anglican Church of Melanesia passed resolutions and urged both the militant groups and the government to work for peace. The Anglican archbishop of Melanesia, Sir Ellison Pogo, participated in the Townsville peace talks as a representative of SICA.

As Church of Melanesia (Anglican) Bishop of Malaita, based in Auki, the capital of Malaita Province, I found myself in the middle of the conflict. I first worked in Solomon Islands as a Canadian missionary lecturer in theology at the Anglican theological college on Guadalcanal, the Bishop Patteson Theological Centre, from 1975 to 1981, before returning to Canada for graduate studies. I worked as Asia-Pacific mission coordinator of the Anglican Church of Canada from 1985 to 1996, during which time I visited the Solomons many times. In 1996 I was elected bishop of Malaita and returned to the Solomons, expecting a relatively quiet tenure touring the five hundred or so Anglican villages in the diocese. The rise of the conflict was a surprise but my experience of similar conflicts and human rights abuses in Sri Lanka, Burma, the Philippines, Korea, and elsewhere was invaluable.

When, after the 2000 coup, the Australian government advised all expatriates to leave Solomon Islands, there was no question but that I would stay. Indeed, the conflict did not excessively spill back over into Malaita until after the TPA, though there were incidents of kidnapping, murder, torture, and theft. While encouraging the diocese to stay out of the conflict and to work as peacemakers, I also spoke out in the media about human rights abuses, especially the cases of torture and murder I heard about. The Malaita churches also organized an ecumenical humanitarian assistance program for the twenty thousand Malaitans forced to return, some with nothing, when the conflict first began, with the support of New Zealand government aid. I was generally treated with respect by the MEF, though there were occasional threats: for example, they arrested one of my staff (I secured his release) and my truck was once commandeered. I believe the voice of all the churches at all levels across the country—bishops, clergy, laity, religious communities, women's groups, ecumenical organizations, synodical bodies, private interventions, etc.—prevented the conflict from becoming the genocidal situation it might have been.

Despite the TPA and the arrival of RAMSI, many scars from the conflict remained, not least kidnapped family members presumed to be dead but whose bodies were not locatable; those suffering from trauma, including the effects of sexual assault and torture; and ex-militants in need of rehabilitation and ultimately forgiveness. Shortly after the signing of the TPA, the SICA peace committee, influenced by the ongoing South African TRC chaired by Archbishop Desmond Tutu, proposed a Solomon Islands TRC to address some of these issues. After eight years of advocacy by the churches, the Solomon Islands national parliament passed the Truth and Reconciliation Act in 2008. It formed a TRC of five commissioners: three local (from Malaita, Guadalcanal, and the west) and two international (from Fiji and Peru), along with research staff. The international commissioners were chosen for their international human rights expertise rather than any knowledge of the Solomons. Local commissioners visited East Timor and South Africa in preparation for their work, and the TRC was launched with a visit from Archbishop Desmond Tutu. It worked from 2009 to 2011 through public and closed hearings and private interviews and presented its five-volume final report to Prime Minister Gordon Darcy Lilo at the end of February 2012.[6] The report then vanished from sight.

While I supported the formation of the TRC, as diocesan bishop and a senior bishop in the Church of Melanesia, I was very concerned with reconciliation at the local and national levels. Using church resources, we organized events locally in Malaita and eventually the Church of Melanesia brought together those separated by the conflict from Guadalcanal, Honiara, and Malaita in a conference in Honiara from 28 April to 1 May 2008. However, I did prepare a written submission to the TRC detailing some human rights abuses I was aware of and I was asked to attend a closed TRC hearing, which I did. I also provided the TRC's principal researcher with all my digital files of correspondence, notes, reports, and public statements related to the conflict, including press releases about torture and other human rights abuses. I can see that this material was used in the final report.

A couple of months before the final report was to be completed, the chair of the TRC, Father Sam Ata, an Anglican priest and a friend of many years, offered me a contract to do the final edit of the report: none of the commissioners or researchers spoke English as a first language. To this end, I spent January and February 2012 editing the report, sending back completed chapters one after another as I travelled in North America. As editor, I was impressed with the quality of the report and my editorial changes were largely confined to stylistic and grammatical issues. I finished the editing only a few days before it was submitted to the prime minister. About forty copies were printed under high security by the Provincial Press in Honiara and they were presented to the prime minister and cabinet. These copies apparently also vanished.

The decision by the prime minister to suppress the TRC's final report rather than tabling it in parliament, as required by the TRC Act, was very disappointing, especially to commissioners and staff of the TRC, the victims of the conflict, the churches, women's groups, and scholars of Solomon Islands history, politics, and society. In private, the TRC chair repeatedly urged the prime minister to release the report. By then, however, many of the militants had become politicians and some were now even members of the cabinet; indeed, one was deputy prime minister. The prime minister claimed the release of the report would reopen old wounds and even bring back violence. In truth, the TRC report was politically embarrassing as well as a potential source of much litigation and government compensation.

Finally, I should note that I retained a digital copy of the final report, though I had assumed it would be released immediately upon its presentation to the prime minister. It is a large document, 1,380 pages across five volumes. However, as 2012 turned into 2013, the prime minister announced it would be another nine months before the report would be released to the public (in other words, never). In consultation with some Solomon Islands friends, including some ex-militants, I therefore decided to release a digital copy of the report to anyone who wanted it. I felt it was better to make the report publically available to all rather than quietly secreting it to Western academics who were also asking for copies. By now it was clear that neither the TRC chair nor the other commissioners would release a copy and since

I was now living in Canada I had little to lose. I simply did not want to lose the valuable work that was done in the report. My release of the report was met with outrage and threats by the prime minister. The decision was generally well received by the public, although some other political leaders felt I had shown disrespect to the country and was engaging in self-promotion. The chair of the TRC did not agree with my decision, though he did not receive the punishment he feared. Other commissioners were supportive. The report is now freely available online.[7] Despite the prime minister's threats, I visited the Solomons in October 2013 without incident. I am told that eventually the prime minister did finally quietly table the report in parliament without a motion near the end of the 2014 parliamentary session; he promptly lost his seat in parliament in the national election that followed. The new prime minister, as noted above, is Manasseh Sogavare; he testified before the TRC and is much more comfortable with it. The TRC exonerated him of the common gossip that he was present at the Rove Armoury raid disguised with a balaclava.

Some Personal Reflections on the Solomon Islands TRC: Strengths and Weaknesses

I believe the greatest contribution of the Solomon Islands TRC is the very detailed documentation presented in the final report, especially the first three volumes, which cover the history of the conflict, the human rights abuses perpetrated in its course, and its sectoral impact, and present recommendations. These volumes are essential reading for anyone seeking to understand the conflict and empathize with its victims. These volumes also provide a road map to future justice and reconciliation, including efforts aimed at addressing the needs of those whose lives were damaged or destroyed by the conflict. Unfortunately, only until very recently successive Solomon Islands governments have simply ignored the document. I have noted a couple reasons for this above, namely political embarrassment and government liability. However, there are other, more complex reasons, too.

One of the peculiarities of the Solomon Islands TRC process is the relatively long gap (for a TRC dealing with a contemporary rather than a historical conflict) between the formal resolution of the conflict (the signing of the TPA in 2000) and the inauguration of the TRC (with the passing of the TRC Act in 2008). Much happened in these eight years. The amnesty provision of the TPA provided only for death and injury between militants in direct conflict with one another, not for the killing of civilians or the commission of human rights abuses such as torture or sexual violence. RAMSI intervention included a major strengthening of the judiciary sector and ex-militants from all sides were charged with criminal offenses, from murder down, convicted and sent to prison. Others were arrested and remanded for many months until it was decided if there would be a criminal case. Likewise, church and traditional cultural practices of reconciliation, adhering to both church and local customs, took place across the country; led by church and parachurch organizations, such as Sycamore Tree Ministries (dedicated to reconciling convicted criminals and the victims of their crimes). Several former militants experienced religious conversion. After these civil, custom, and religious experiences of justice and reconciliation, ex-militants re-entered their communities, and some entered politics and were elected to parliament. Solomon Islands has always had a strong tradition of ex-prisoners re-entering their communities with good family and community support, and this was the case for those who were convicted of crimes connected with the "ethnic tensions."

Therefore, for many ex-militants the TRC arrived rather late, after they had already served prison terms and even been reconciled with their victims. At least for Malaitans, once compensation has been paid for a wrong, the matter cannot be re-opened. For some ex-militants, the aura of double jeopardy hung over the proceedings and as a result they simply refused to testify. The TRC provided confidentiality and limited amnesty (TRC testimony could not be used in a court of law) but information gained in TRC interviews could result in new or reopened criminal files.[8] The TRC's amnesty provisions were seriously undercut when the police arrested a fugitive ex-militant after he testified at the TRC; someone had tipped off the police that he would be testifying.

Because the government changed soon after the passing of the TRC Act, the TRC operated with limited government funding; nor were foreign funders particularly generous or quick to offer money. Thus the TRC often did not operate at full capacity, which in turn meant it could not achieve its full potential. Researchers who went out to remote areas of Guadalcanal were able to acquire much credible testimony, and this remains invaluable. But the public hearings were rare and, at times, felt almost staged.

By now the MEF and IFM were a united force (they reconciled in Rove Prison, among other places) against the government, from whom they wanted compensation for their work in saving the nation from each other. Many people simply did not hear of the TRC's work and they did not feel it touched their lives in any way. In the cash-poor Solomons, the salaries and perks offered to TRC commissioners and staff caused jealousy among those who lost houses and other possessions in the conflict and who have never been compensated.

Likewise, the abrupt halt met by the TRC after the handing over of the final report to the prime minister—the TRC was dissolved, never to be constituted again—left some of its good work up in the air (for example, the exhumation of graves of victims and repatriation of bodies). In theory, the TRC's work was handed over to the government's Ministry of National Unity, Peace and Reconciliation (MNUPR), but without formal access to the TRC report (until very recently), there has been little continuity.

In early 2016 the Sogavare government convened a consultation on the TRC recommendations facilitated by Carol Laore, a former local TRC commissioner. The prime minister's office then hired her on contract to collate the TRC recommendations with an aim towards their implementation by the various government ministries. However, the key ministry in matters of reconciliation, the MNUPR, has remained disinterested in the TRC recommendations; it has instead pursued a policy of developing local customary leadership as a path to reconciliation.[9] The ongoing presence of ex-militant groups asking for financial compensation from the government (agreed to for the Malaita ex-militants at the end of 2015 and the Guadalcanal ex-militants at the end of 2016) has also distracted from efforts to compensate the conflict's true victims. Laore's TRC-implementation contract was not renewed, although there has been some very recent indication that the recommendations will soon be distributed to the relevant government ministries.[10] However, the TRC report has not yet been debated in parliament.

Also frustrating is the fact that because of the government's suppression of the report, followed by the legal limbo brought on by my informal digital release in April 2013, media in Solomon Islands has largely ignored it, probably fearing legal censure were they to reprint or quote it. It is also a very large document that needs condensation. While the report is freely available online, Internet service in the country is notoriously slow, unreliable, and expensive; to print a copy would be exorbitantly expensive; indeed, even downloading it is expensive. So the report is still not as freely accessible to the general population of Solomon Islands as one would like. Even parliament's secretive tabling of the report in late 2014 was designed to ensure it did not become public. There is no indication that the online publication of the report has caused any civil disorder. Those who read it are often deeply moved by it and readers have written me to tell me they read it with tears streaming down their cheeks.

Thus, I would argue that the final report remains the enduring monument of the Solomon Islands TRC. The first volume gives a nuanced and substantial account of the conflict and its root causes. The second volume details killings, abductions/detentions, torture/ill treatment, sexual violence, property violations, and forced displacement in all theatres of the conflict. The list of two hundred killed includes the victims' names and personal details. The third volume details the impact of the conflict on women and children, the economic, health, and education sectors, details the exhumation program, and presents final recommendations. The fourth volume includes most of the transcripts of the public hearings, already available on the TRC's website (now defunct). The fifth volume contains an institutional history of the TRC, biographical details of the commissioners and senior staff, texts of the Townsville and Marau Peace Agreements and the TRC Act, as well as extensive compensation claims lists. Together, these documents are an invaluable record of the conflict. However, it is also extremely painful reading and successive Solomon Islands governments have practiced avoidance, preferring instead to continue rewarding many of the perpetrators and ignoring the victims. However, I have hope that as the details included in the final report become more widely known, this situation will change. Editing the document immersed me in a pain that I still feel. Indeed, the chair of the TRC, Father Sam Ata, died in October 2014, partly from the stress of the work he pursued and the government's refusal to publish or implement the report. The report is also his monument and that of many other faithful TRC workers.

Notes

1. Some have questioned the appropriateness of the continued use of the term *ethnic* to describe the conflict as there were certainly other causes besides ethnicity. However, that is the term the final report of the Truth and Reconciliation Commission uses so I have retained it. For analysis of the conflict and truth commission, see Matthew G. Allen, *Greed and Grievance: Ex-Militants' Perspectives on the Conflict in Solomon Islands 1998–2003* (Honolulu: University of Hawai'i Press, 2013); Charles Brown Beu and Roselyn Nokise, *Mission in the Midst of Conflict: Stories from the Solomon Islands* (Suva, FJ: Pacific Theological College, 2009); Richard Anthony Carter, *In Search of the Lost: The Death and Life of Seven Peacemakers of the Melanesian Brotherhood* (Norwich, UK: Canterbury Press, 2006); Sinclair Dinnen, ed., *A Kind of Mending: Restorative Justice in the Pacific Islands* (Canberra, AU: Pandanus Books, 2003); Jon Fraenkel, *The Manipulation of Custom: From Uprising to Intervention in the Solomon Islands* (Canberra, AU: Pandanus Books, 2004); Holly L. Guthrey, *Victim Healing and Truth Commissions: Transforming Pain through Voice in the Solomon Islands and Timor-Leste* (Cham, CH: Springer, 2015); H. Guthrey and K. Brounéus, "Peering into the 'Black Box' of TRC success: Exploring Local Perceptions of Reconciliation in the Solomon Islands TRC," in *Transitional Justice in the Solomon Islands*, ed. R. Jeffrey (New York: Palgrave, 2017); Debra McDougall, *Engaging with Strangers: Love and Violence in the Rural Solomon Islands* (New York: Berghahn, 2016); Clive Moore, *The Happy Isles in Crisis: The Historical Causes for a Failing State in Solomon Islands, 1998–2004* (Canberra, AU: Asia Pacific Press, 2004); Clive Moore, "The Misappropriation of Malaita Labour: Historical Origins of the Recent Solomons Islands Crisis," *Journal of Pacific History* 42, no. 2 (2007): 211–32; Louise Vella, "Translating Transitional Justice: The Solomon Islands Truth and Reconciliation Commission," SSGM Discussion Paper 2014/2, Australian National University, https://openresearch-repository.anu.edu.au/bitstream/1885/11757/1/Vella%20Translating%20transitional%20justice%202013.pdf (accessed 17 July 2017).

2. Ulufa'alu, though from Malaita, was thought to be sympathetic with the IFM because of his Guadalcanal landholdings and in particular his Malaitan ethno-religious background (Langa Langa and Roman Catholic).

3. Sogavare is the current (as of 2017) prime minister though there have been several intervening prime ministers since 2000. While Sogavare denies it, there have been persistent accusations that he was in some way connected with, or at the very least tipped off about, the 2000 coup. The continuing financial payments (2015 and 2016) to ex-militants rather than their victims have further encouraged this perception.

4. Bougainville had in previous years had its own militant movement, the Bougainville Revolutionary Army, which fought against the PNG government and a large Australian-owned open-pit copper mine there; their presence in Honiara during those years of conflict possibly contributed to the rise of the GRA/IFM.

5. I have documented the work of these groups in an article, "The Role of Religious Communities in Peacemaking" *Anglican Religious Life Journal* 1 (2004): 8–18.

6   The text of the Truth and Reconciliation Act and the institutional history of the TRC are included in volume 5 of the TRC report, available online at: http://pacificpolicy.org/files/2013/04/Solomon-Islands-TRC-Final-Report-Vol-5A.pdf (accessed 17 July 2017).

7   For volume 1, see http://pacificpolicy.org/files/2013/04/Solomon-Islands-TRC-Final-Report-Vol1.pdf. The same site also has the subsequent volumes.

8   By the time the Solomons Truth and Reconciliation Act was passed in 2008, the weaknesses of the full amnesty provision of the South African TRC process had become apparent. Thus, only limited amnesty was provided.

9   Carol Laore, interview with author, Honiara, SB, 9 June 2016.

10 Government speakers at the RAMSI symposium, "Understanding RAMSI's Legacy and Lessons", Honiara, SB, 28 June 2017, spoke positively of the TRC report and indicated that the recommendations would be acted upon.

19

Women and Reconciliation in Solomon Islands

BETTY LINA GIGISI

My name is Betty Lina Gigisi, and I'm from Bubutoha village, Malango ward, in Central Guadalcanal Province. There were seven children in my family. My mother and father were all from the same province and were subsistence farmers. Today I am a mother of four children.

My own background working with communities is diverse, but I have maintained a focus on peace and reconciliation, gender equality, and women in leadership and decision making.

Solomon Islands suffered a civil war from 1998 to 2003, fought mostly between militants from Guadalcanal and Malaita who had settled in Honiara and around Guadalcanal Island. Guadalcanal militants wanted their *kastom* (customary) land back and were worried about many Malaitans living there, some of whom were squatters and some of whom had land leases.

The Solomon Islands Truth and Reconciliation Commission (SITRC) was mandated by an act of parliament in 2008. The commissioners were chosen by a national committee that was chaired by the chief justice and representatives from the government, opposition parties, and other stakeholders. From a list of names proposed by many sectors, five commissioners were chosen, three national and two non-national. They were SITRC chair Father Sam Ata (who died in 2014), Sofia Macher (the deputy chair, a non-national from Peru), Ratu Joni Madraiwiwi (a non-national from Fiji), Caroline Laore, and George Kejoa: three men and two women. The SITRC was launched with a public event opened by the South African TRC commissioner, Archbishop Desmond Tutu.

After the war, in 2007, a reconciliation ceremony was organized by the Ministry of National Unity, Peace and Reconciliation at Peochakuri village, South Guadalcanal. I was also at the ceremony, not as an official, but as a citizen of that particular constituency and as a gender advocate. Women were not participating in the event, nor were they recognized in the official program. They had no opportunity to express their emotional feelings to their government, as the prime minister was the guest of honour. Women's participation was confined to delivering traditional garlands to the official guests, and, as they were dressed in their traditional costumes, they did so while half naked. My question at the time was: is that the only strength that women have?

I am proud of my culture, but I would like to have a woman representative among the official guests, dressed according to custom. At the ceremony women approached me to see if I could negotiate for a change in the program so that they could have the time and voice to deliver their thoughts. I have a strong belief in the rights of women to have a voice in decision making, especially since most of Solomon Islands follows a matrilineal system of land allocation. Solomon Islands has only three women in parliamentary positions.

I prepared a media statement that highlighted my disappointment in the lack of women's participation in the peace ceremony. The statement came out in the media (via the Solomon Islands Broadcasting Corporation) on 1 January 2008.

The government of the day then offered me a position at the Ministry of National Unity, Peace and Reconciliation. I started there in February 2008 as a senior peace and reconciliation officer. My job was to make sure that women were participating in the peace process. I was involved in assisting the provincial liaison peace and reconciliation officer in organizing reconciliations at both the macro and micro levels.

In 2010 I was employed with the Solomon Islands Truth and Reconciliation Commission as the assistant exhumation officer. The purpose of the TRC was to "address people's traumatic experiences during the five-year ethnic conflict on Guadalcanal (1999–2004)." Its goal was to promote national unity and reconciliation.

My specific role in the commission entailed responsibility for the reunification of remains. The exhumation of remains is a process that brings up very painful feelings for all involved. Training for exhumation officers, forensic police officers, and the SITRC commissioners involved understanding the complex and sensitive nature of the exhumation process.

The process involved inviting relatives to a meeting to prepare them to understand and accept the process of exhumation. It was also intended to let them know that the Truth and Reconciliation Commission respected cultural procedures and that the SITRC was enacted in parliament in 2008 with a specific time frame of completion. The SITRC engaged two qualified counsellors to enact the healing process, as relatives receive counselling as part of their healing process.

One of my roles was to map graves in the southern part of Guadalcanal Province, where most of the people were killed and buried. But before and after this grave mapping a cultural procedure must be introduced to calm people's emotions. Some are mass graves with more than one person in them.

In a village a mother came to express herself emotionally: she wanted her husband's body returned in full; she got married to him in full, she said, not just to his head alone.

The commission worked with multiple stakeholders, including international experts, forensic police, non-governmental organizations, the Solomon Islands Christian Association (SICA), relatives of victims, and perpetrators. It investigated the cause, details, and effects of the ethnic tensions. It conducted public and closed hearings, gathered statements from individuals who were victims and perpetrators. It also organized research throughout the whole country. It determined that all parties had contributed to the breakdown of law and order, and committed human rights violations (namely killing, abduction, illegal detention, torture, sexual violation, property violations, and other human rights abuses). The SITRC concluded with some very good recommendations in its report, which was submitted to the government.

The SITRC report was tabled by the prime minister on the last day of the parliamentary session, after which parliament was adjourned. But he lost power in the 2010 elections, and the commission's report has never been debated in parliament. No reasons were ever given for this failure, but some of the commission's recommendations were partly addressed by the government. For example, progress is being made in constitutional and law reform, land reform, community policy, the early retirement of police officers who were involved in the conflict, and capacity building. There is much more to do, however, both on reconciliation and on the rights of Melanesian women.

SECTION VI
Bringing it Home

20

Reflecting on Reconciliation

MAGGIE HELWIG

To situate myself at the start—I am a settler in Turtle Island/Canada (henceforth referred to as "Canada" simply for convenience), of mixed English, Irish, and German ancestry, living on the traditional territories of the Mississaugas of the New Credit, the Haudenosaunee Confederacy, and the Huron/Wendat Nation. I was involved in the East Timor solidarity movement from the late 1980s until, more or less, Timor-Leste's emergence as an independent nation. I have been an Anglican priest since 2012, and previous to that an Anglican layperson, and as such was necessarily aware of the work of Canada's Truth and Reconciliation Commission on the residential school system, in which the Anglican Church played a large role. And, not incidentally, I am a novelist; one of my novels deals with the International Criminal Tribunal for the former Yugoslavia and another is set, in part, in Timor-Leste.[1] All of which is to say, I am someone with a broad general knowledge of many things, and a specialist knowledge of none, and that is the sort of chapter you are about to read, as I reflect on some of the aspects of the Canadian Truth and Reconciliation Commission (TRC), and possible links to issues of truth and reconciliation in East Timor, West Papua, and Indonesia.

Usually, truth and reconciliation commissions are set up as part of the transition from one form of government to another—this was the case, in varying ways, in South Africa, in El Salvador, in Haiti, in Guatemala, in Sierra Leone, among other places. It was the case in East Timor after it won its independence. It was the case in Solomon Islands, which as Betty Lina Gigisi and Terry Brown discuss in their chapters, was emerging from an internal conflict. If there is to be a commission for West Papua, it is likely to also come at a transitional moment. But in Canada, the settler-dominated regime which carried out the genocidal policies (and it is important that the commission stated, as a finding of fact, that the Canadian government and churches had committed cultural genocide) has remained in power. No significant political changes took place to cause the creation of the TRC—it was, rather, formed in response to several massive class action suits brought by residential school survivors, the only case so far in which a government has been compelled through legal action to create a truth commission.

This presented problems for the commission, but also some significant advantages. Most notably, once the TRC was set up and operating, it was far less beholden to power than most truth commissions. The TRC, in other words, was independent, not a government body. In general, a new regime, for good or ill, has particular interests that it wishes to see met by its truth commission, and the links between the regime and the commission, however much it may be formally independent, tend to be close enough to ensure that to a large degree this happens. As Patricia Hayner writes in her comparative analysis of truth commissions, they engage in "official truth-seeking."[2] The Canadian commission's lack of direct links to the government meant that it had no clear mechanism for the implementation of its recommendations, but it also meant that it could speak and act with unusual freedom.

The Canadian TRC began its work in 2008, following a settlement of legal battles over the toxic legacy left by the Indian residential schools that operated, many of them under church management but always as part of a federal government policy, from the passage of the Indian Act in 1876 until the last school closed in 1996. Some 150,000 Aboriginal children were compelled to attend residential schools apart from their families, where they were forced to work and forbidden to speak their own languages. The TRC held national hearings driven by survivor testimony and carried out extensive research in government and church archives before delivering its final report in 2015, featuring 94 "calls to action." Among other facts, it found that 4,000 children died in residential schools, and that the federal government had pursued a policy of "cultural genocide."[3]

It was, interestingly, the only truth commission so far which has had to deal with massive, systemic violations committed, as part of an institutional mandate, by mainstream Christian churches. This is important in large part because our vision of what truth commissions do and how they operate is still strongly influenced by South Africa, where the process was largely, and brilliantly, shaped by the Anglican archbishop Desmond Tutu, a figure of great moral authority and credibility who consciously drew on the Catholic sacrament of reconciliation to create the South African process. It is not a coincidence that most truth commission since then have been established in majority-Christian cultures—indeed, that the theological and liturgical imagination which Bishop Tutu brought to South Africa has become almost a defining feature of truth commissions in general. But in the Canadian case, the Anglican, United, Presbyterian, and Roman Catholic churches were among the greatest systemic offenders in the residential school system, and the "confessional" shape of the usual truth commission proceedings was thereby rendered quite problematic.

The Canadian situation also meant that the handful of surviving perpetrators, and the systems that had been created, were still very near at hand—unlike, for instance, the Timorese commission, which had to deal with the fact that most perpetrators were now living in another country—Indonesia—not necessarily either inclined or obliged to co-operate. On the other hand, because the Canadian commission's mandate extended back considerably more than a century, most perpetrators—whether individual offenders or architects of the genocidal policies—were no longer alive. Partly because of this, the commission made the unusual decision that it would not name names of perpetrators, nor would it seek testimony from them (though a very small number did speak). There was also, according to Frank Iacobucci,[4] who acted as the government's representative in the negotiations, a desire to avoid a prosecutorial framework: the commission therefore specifically rejected the South African model on a number of points, including the withholding of powers of subpoena, because, as Iacobucci said, "we didn't want it to become a lawyers' forum." (He also admitted that this led to a situation in which the TRC had to resort to judicial intervention after all to obtain archival records from the uncooperative federal government.)

The decision not to name names was greeted with some concern. It closed down space for the possibility of contrition, or for receiving the story of what was done wrongly; and it might have left little opportunity to sketch out the shape of reconciled community. The commission's stated policy of not naming names was historically and legally reasonable, since most accused perpetrators were no longer living, and therefore unable to speak in their own defence. But both Minow and Hayner,[5] in their comprehensive studies of truth commissions, concluded that naming names, in some form and with due caution, was important despite the many problems involved. Without names, the historical record is incomplete, and there is a danger that crimes committed by no one in particular cannot be properly remembered.

In the end, however, the decision not to name names may have, even if accidentally, contributed to what turned out to be the commission's greatest strength. The TRC's hearings were markedly less forensic and more discursive than most truth commissions; and by moving the focus away from the acts of individuals onto systems, they were able to dig very deeply into structures of racism and inequality. Their final report is, in some ways, only incidentally about residential schools—in fact, it is a sweeping indictment of the ongoing colonial situation in the country we call Canada. The commission, it is clear from its own materials, originally saw its role as twofold: helping the survivors heal from the trauma by giving them an opportunity to tell their stories, and compiling a comprehensive historical record. But ultimately, and after considerable struggle, the TRC did a great deal more than that. In the preface to their final report, the commissioners wrote:

> Getting to the truth was hard, but getting to reconciliation will be harder. It requires that the paternalistic and racist foundations of the residential school system be rejected as the basis for an ongoing relationship. Reconciliation requires that a new vision, based on a commitment to mutual respect, be developed. It also requires an understanding that the most harmful impacts of residential schools have been the loss of pride and self-respect of Aboriginal people, and the lack of respect that non-Aboriginal people have been raised to have for their Aboriginal neighbours. Reconciliation is not an Aboriginal problem; it is a Canadian one. Virtually all aspects of

> Canadian society may need to be reconsidered. ... Reconciliation will take some time.[6]

This is probably the first truth and reconciliation commission so far in history to end up calling for a complete reconsideration of all aspects of the society in which it is situated, and its ninety-four calls to action really do present a comprehensive picture of potentially massive social change.[7] Whether this extraordinary aim can be even partly fulfilled is another matter, but the report is, in itself, a small triumph.

The Canadian commission's turn to systems rather than individuals also meant that it was able to include some of the broader, more complex issues which sometimes escape the mandate of truth commissions. Todd Biderman and Jenny Munro, in their chapter, speak of the intimate relationship between the people of West Papua and the forest, and wonder if it could be possible for a commission to tell the truth about West Papua without including that relationship. Canada's First Nations, Inuit, and Metis people, it is clear, made sure that the commissioners heard very distinctly about their relationship with the land, and the impossibility of any reconciliation that did not include reconciliation with the non-human world. In this they built on the legacy of the 1996 Royal Commission on Aboriginal Peoples report.[8] As the TRC commissioners wrote in their final report:

> Reconciliation between Aboriginal and non-Aboriginal Canadians, from an Aboriginal perspective, also requires reconciliation with the natural world. If human beings resolve problems between themselves but continue to destroy the natural world, then reconciliation remains incomplete. This is a perspective that we as Commissioners have repeatedly heard: that reconciliation will never occur unless we are also reconciled with the earth. Mi'kmaq and other Indigenous laws stress that humans must journey through life in conversation and negotiation with all creation. Reciprocity and mutual respect help sustain our survival.[9]

Some of the unusual features of the Canadian TRC might be worth consideration by those looking at setting up truth commissions in other situations. It may not be an appropriate response in every case, and its merits must be weighed against the risk of never identifying real perpetrators and the possibility of leaving victims feeling less than fully heard—it is most appropriate in situations where larger systems and ideologies are being enacted by a large number of small-scale players. But arguably, this could be considered to be the case with the 1965 events in Indonesia, and a more discursive, less forensic, commission, perhaps accompanied by a range of local reconciliation activities, might be more achievable and reasonably effective.

The Canadian model might also serve countries that find the "confessional" model foreign or inappropriate, particularly if there are cultural story-telling and ceremonial traditions that can be employed as part of a commission's work; and it might help in trying to speak of issues like the relationship with non-human creation.

If we assume, in broad strokes, that the usual aims of a truth commission are generally to create a detailed and accurate historical record, to provide victims with some healing through the receiving of their stories, and to create some kind of political change, I think we can say that the Canadian TRC and East Timor's CAVR have both been quite successful in the first aim, as have most other truth commissions in the recent past. The *Chega!* document is and will continue to be extremely important in preserving in great human detail Timor-Leste's history during the occupation. The TRC's final report, likewise, stands as the definitive account of the often disputed history of the residential schools, and at least a partial history of other ravages of colonialism; it clearly names what took place as cultural genocide; and the combination of the very extensive online documentation that makes up the commission's full report, and the National Centre for Truth and Reconciliation in Winnipeg, create an impressive resource for a revised and more truthful account of this country's history.[10]

Of course, creating a historical record also involves, necessarily, creating a narrative, or in some cases a counter-narrative. It could be argued that the CAVR created a kind of consensus narrative of oppression and resistance, which the people of Timor-Leste in general can own as theirs, and which provides them with a resource for moving forward, while the TRC has created a counter-narrative, posed against a dominant Canadian narrative, which is still, for the most part, history as constructed by the colonizing power. And, in fact, among the TRC's calls to action, one of those most often identified as a priority is that of incorporating the survivors' narrative, the narrative of oppression and resistance, into the standard curricula for elementary and secondary schools, making it something like a consensus understanding. We are still a long way from turning this into reality. Yet in a small but very striking incident, the memorial plaque at the grave of the former head of the Department of Indian Affairs (1913–32), Duncan Campbell Scott, has been revised to include his role in the creation of the residential school system, and the words "cultural genocide" are explicitly used; if this truth-telling is sustained and expanded, we may yet see the dominant narrative begin to shift. Whether—as the TRC calls to action demand—there is a systematic effort to change the history curricula will be a key measure of success or failure. Church-driven responses, such as the campaign by ecumenical coalition KAIROS to make residential schools a mandatory aspect of all Canadian secondary school curricula, indicate movement in this direction.[11]

The second aim, providing healing for victims, is the hardest to measure. There has been a general hopeful assumption that telling one's personal story and having it respectfully received is, in some way, inherently healing. This is probably a largely Western assumption, and there's little evidence either for or against its general usefulness in situations of mass human rights violations. Holly Guthrey interviewed a small number of people who spoke to the commissions in East Timor and in Solomon Islands, almost all of whom seem to have reported that their experience was kind of good and kind of bad[12]—a finding that doesn't take us much further forward. The same indeterminacy and ambiguity appears to have marked the experiences of witnesses at the South African TRC.[13] Despite the weight that has sometimes been placed on truth commissions as a vehicle for individual healing, it may be that they simply cannot be evaluated on these grounds in isolation from the larger political picture and absent connected issues like reparations and political change.

And whether or not the TRC can be part of a movement towards real political change may be the final measure of its usefulness. As noted at the outset, there has not actually been any significant shift of political power in Canada. Most First Nations and Inuit people still live in conditions of appalling deprivation and face very significant discrimination at all levels; some communities have not had drinkable water for a generation.[14] Many live on lands poisoned by industrial development. The Aboriginal population is hugely over-represented in the prison system, suicide rates are extremely high, and the average life expectancy of First Nations and, especially, Inuit people is much shorter than average (most dramatically, an Inuit man can expect to live an average of sixty-four years, compared to seventy-nine years for a male settler).[15] Nearly two thousand Aboriginal women have been murdered or "disappeared" in recent years. The TRC calls to action included, as call 92, the demand that businesses and corporations "commit to meaningful consultation, building respectful relationships, and obtaining the free, prior, and informed consent of Indigenous peoples before proceeding with economic development projects." And yet, only a few months later, a Federal Court of Appeal threw out a case brought by the Chippewas of the Thames against the Enbridge Line 9 oil pipeline reversal project on their territory, a case based not even on an alleged violation of "free, prior and informed consent," but on an alleged failure to meet the arguably much lower bar of "duty to consult." In a statement issued after the decision, Chief Leslee White-Eye noted that, "this decision needs to be acknowledged as a step back in achieving reconciliation between the Crown and First Nations. Establishing processes which effectively remove the Crown from consultation with First Nations increases the potential for conflict, reduces the opportunity for respectful relations and entrenches the denial of Indigenous law."[16]

All of this suggests that—to borrow a term from Indonesia and Timor-Leste—the "socialization" of the Canadian TRC findings has so far been ineffective, at least at the political level. So far, the institutions that appear to have listened most carefully are the United and Anglican churches, both of whom are committed to engage as allies in political advocacy; the Anglican Church is also in the process of creating new internal structures that will give Aboriginal Anglicans greater self-determination and a stronger voice—for instance, through the appointment in 2006 of a national Indigenous bishop, the Right Reverend Mark MacDonald, whose responsibilities are not geographically defined, and the creation in 2014 of the Indigenous Spiritual Ministry of Mishamikoweesh, an Indigenous diocese encompassing over twenty-five First Nations communities and led by Bishop Lydia Mamakwa. However, these churches are now relatively marginal bodies in the broader society; their capacity to amplify the message of the TRC is real but limited.

The 2015 change of government in Canada will almost certainly mean some change for the better at the federal level; the new cabinet includes

Jody Wilson-Raybould, an Aboriginal woman, as minister of justice and attorney-general, and Carolyn Bennett, a settler woman who has engaged for some time with the issue of missing and murdered Aboriginal women, as minister for Indigenous affairs. Both of these appointments suggest some openness to constitutional change. Whether the extremely pressing issue of the exploitation of Aboriginal territories by heavy industry, especially the oil and gas industry, will be addressed is less clear. Educational reform will, due to the nature of Canada's educational system, have to be carried out at a provincial level, although messages from the federal government could certainly carry weight.

Canada also has work to do on its responsibilities in Timor-Leste, Tanah Papua, and Indonesia as well, work which might be furthered by a greater level of direct dialogue between the First Nations, Inuit, and Metis peoples in Canada, and people in Timor-Leste, Tanah Papua, and Indonesia, whether this occurs at the level of political leadership on both sides, or among grassroots activists. Promoting and supporting such dialogue could represent a valuable task for allies (the Pacific People's Partnership is already doing some of this work). The TRC's calls are ultimately about the undoing of colonialism, a task that must be carried out internationally as well as within Canada. The historic and ongoing violations of Indigenous rights, both in Canada and abroad, grow from the same root, and can only be fully addressed together.

Notes

1. Maggie Helwig, *Between Mountains* (Toronto: Knopf, 2004) and *Where She Was Standing* (Toronto: ECW Press, 2001).

2. Priscilla Hayner, *Unspeakable Truths: Facing the Challenge of Truth Commissions* (New York: Routledge, 2001), 8.

3. *Honouring the Truth, Reconciling for the Future. Summary of the Final Report of the Final Report of the Truth and Reconciliation Commission of Canada* (TRC online publication, 2015), http://www.myrobust.com/websites/trcinstitution/File/Reports/Executive_Summary_English_Web.pdf (accessed 11 June 2016).

4. Author's notes from Larkin-Stuart Lecture, Trinity College, University of Toronto, 3 November 2015.

5. Martha Minow, *Between Vengeance and Forgiveness* (Boston: Beacon Press, 1998), 86; Hayner, *Unspeakable Truths*, 132.

6. *Honouring the Truth, Reconciling for the Future*, vi.

7   The TRC calls to action can be found at http://www.trc.ca/websites/trcinstitution/File/2015/Findings/Calls_to_Action_English2.pdf.

8   Royal Commission on Aboriginal Peoples, *Report of the Royal Commission on Aboriginal Peoples* (Ottawa: Indian and Northern Affairs Canada, 1996), http://www.collectionscanada.gc.ca/webarchives/20071115053257/http://www.ainc-inac.gc.ca/ch/rcap/sg/sgmm_e.html (accessed 11 June 2016).

9   Murray Sinclair, Marie Wilson, Chief Wilton Littlechild, *What We Have Learned: Principles of Truth and Reconciliation* (Truth and Reconciliation Commission Canada, 2015), 123.

10 The National Centre for Truth and Reconciliation's online archive can be accessed at http://nctr.ca/map.php.

11 Resources for the KAIROS "winds of change" campaign are at http://www.kairoscanada.org/what-we-do/indigenous-rights/windsofchange-overview.

12 Holly L. Guthrey, *Victim Healing and Truth Commissions: Transforming Pain through Voice in the Solomon Islands and Timor-Leste* (Cham, CH: Springer, 2015).

13 Brandon Hamber, Dineo Nageng, and Gabriel O'Malley, "Telling It Like It Is: Understanding the Truth and Reconciliation Commission from the Perspective of Survivors," *Psychology in Society* 26 (2000): 18–42.

14 Current information on "boil water adviseries" in First Nations communities can be found at http://www.hc-sc.gc.ca/fniah-spnia/promotion/public-publique/water-dwa-eau-aqep-eng.php; as of 31 August 2017, ninety-eight communities were under short- or long-term "boil water advisories," excluding communities in British Columbia. According to this site, the Neskatanga First Nation has been under a "boil water advisery" continuously since 1995, and the Shoal Lake 40 Nation since 1997.

15 http://www.statcan.gc.ca/pub/89-645-x/2010001/c-g/c-g013-eng.htm (accessed 11 June 2016).

16 http://www.chiefs-of-ontario.org/node/1278 (accessed 11 June 2016).

21

Conclusion: Seeking Truth about Truth-seeking

DAVID WEBSTER

A tool developed for post-conflict zones in the global South, truth commissions have now come north—to Canada, where they have attempted to deal with the impact of colonial policies on Indigenous peoples, and to parts of Europe, where they have addressed the legacies of communism. Truth knows no borders. Increasingly, neither do truth commissions.

Truth commissions are at times thought to offer healing and reconciliation, allowing societies to "put the past behind them." The cases examined in *Flowers in the Wall* suggest that a valuable contribution of truth commissions is to unsettle dominant narratives, to tell new stories by drawing on new voices that disrupt and make transformation possible. Truth commissions emerge as vehicles for the mobilization of civil society, not just transient bodies reporting to governments and then closing their doors.

This book has sought, through a close look at aspects of the tricky truth and reconciliation experiences of Timor-Leste, Indonesia, and Melanesia, to contribute to global debates on truth commissions and transitional justice more broadly. Too often, as noted in chapter 2, truth commissions follow "strict forms and narratives" and base themselves on a global template in which Western knowledge is read as universal. Increasingly, analysts of truth commissions stress the importance of the local, of Indigenous traditions, of different ways of plotting stories. We use examples from the islands of Southeast Asia and the Southwest Pacific to add to the multiple locally driven studies that seek to "provincialize Europe" rather than seeing European-derived models and ways of constructing narratives as universal.[1]

The Timor-Leste section of *Flowers in the Wall* notes that the Commission for Reception, Truth and Reconciliation (CAVR) placed a high value on traditional ways of resolving conflict in Timorese communities. In chapter 4, Pat Walsh stresses the importance placed on community reconciliation processes, which rolled out "the big mat" and used local forms to seek a rapprochement between low-level offenders and their neighbours.[2] Though they are not of course identical from place to place, customary practices in the Indonesian archipelago tend to be lumped under the phrase *adat* (tradition). Lia Kent and Rizki Affiat explain in chapter 13 how the Timorese CAVR experience informed the creation of the new truth commission in Aceh. The effort to include a very different form of Indigenous Melanesian *kastom* (custom) in Solomon Islands is touched on by Terry Brown in chapter 18 and Betty Lina Gigisi in chapter 19. It is not impossible to combine the global truth commission template with Indigenous forms, something that both Timor-Leste's CAVR and the Solomon Islands Truth and Reconciliation Commission (SITRC) tried to do, and something that is among the goals of Aceh's new Truth and Reconciliation Commission (KKR). But it is a challenge.

On the other hand, omitting local factors seems to doom reconciliation processes to failure. In chapter 14, Arianto Sangadji calls top-down, government-led reconciliation processes in Poso district a failure. An illustration of the same problem comes in chapter 15, where Todd Biderman and Jenny Munro describe the shortcomings of Indonesian state reconciliation efforts in Indigenous Papuan communities. Where Sangadji calls for more attention to class than religious differences, Biderman and Munro note the omission of Indigenous perspectives, especially with regard to land tenure and environmental awareness. They conclude that an effective truth and reconciliation commission in Tanah Papua (the Land of Papua) must integrate these perspectives if it is to succeed. This is a point made very clearly in Canada's Truth and Reconciliation Commission, of course, as Maggie Helwig explores in chapter 20. In Canada's TRC report, Canadian Indigenous elder Stephen Augustin has suggested that the other dimensions of human experience, our relationship to the earth and all human beings, are also relevant in working towards reconciliation. Elder Reg Crowshoe similarly noted that reconciliation between Indigenous and non-Indigenous Canadians, from an Aboriginal perspective, requires reconciliation with the natural world.[3] It is worth adding that conflict in both Poso, Indonesia (chapter 14) and Guadalcanal, Solomon Islands (chapter 18), were in many ways conflicts over land alienation. Economic "development" can also be ecological destruction, as Ed McWilliams notes when writing in chapter 17 about the giant Freeport mine in Tanah Papua.

Truth commissions are not accustomed to examining economic factors. They turn on issues of individual civil and political rights first and foremost, with collective social and cultural rights noted at times and economic rights often omitted. When economics drives conflict, as it often does, this is a major gap in the work of post-conflict transitional justice. The central areas of Indonesia first experienced the economic changes brought about by integration into global trade and capitalism during Dutch colonial rule. But outlying regions of Indonesia, and areas later invaded by the Indonesian state, like Timor-Leste, were more peripheral to colonial capitalism. The blow of rapid economic change and growing economic inequality often came later. Aceh, Tanah Papua, and Poso each felt the blows of industrial resource extraction (mining, oil and gas) later on, at the hands of multinational companies and an Indonesian state that was, as Baskara Wardaya points out in chapter 10, hungry for foreign investment. This, too, fuelled conflict. The swift rivers that run with gold in Tanah Papua, described by Julian Smythe in chapter 16, were also desired by Western profit-seekers. These included Freeport and other mining companies who entered Tanah Papua with sometimes devastating effects—an entire mountain, sacred to the Amungme people, was transformed into an open-pit mine that now extends far below the ground. Should truth processes therefore include those companies and consider their impact, their role in fuelling conflict, and their responsibility for reconciliation?

Pat Walsh notes in chapter 4 the efforts to include economic rights in the Timorese CAVR's catalogue of human rights violations under Indonesian rule. In chapter 8, Fernanda Borges makes a similar point about the need for Timor-Leste to integrate "second-generation" economic, social, and cultural rights into its strong embrace of "first-generation" civil and political rights. This is something the CAVR attempted to do. The sections on economic rights may not be the strongest part of the CAVR report, but the commission's efforts to include economic rights are nonetheless pioneering. The SITRC makes a similar point in citing the uneven distribution of development assistance (centred on the capital, Honiara) and the effects of the 1990s financial crisis as contributing factors to "the tensions" in Solomon Islands. Truth commissions in other countries might usefully follow this direction of integrating economic rights in their larger analysis of human rights.

There is a negative lesson regarding economic factors from Timor-Leste's experience, too. In chapter 6, Laurentina Barreto Soares analyzes the post-independence development plan and is critical of its lack of attention to what came before. There was no effort even to review the development plan put through in the year 2000, let alone consider the scars of two and a half decades of occupation and attendant human rights violations and post-occupation trauma. Timorese development, it seems, was to be done without memory. It was as if the past was forgotten.

This sort of "official forgetting" looms as a serious problem for those who hope to see truth and reconciliation commission reports become blueprints for action rather than static documents left unpublished or quietly shelved in libraries. Rather than pushing against impunity for major human rights violators, the Timorese leadership has preferred good relations with Indonesia and consequently downplayed calls for justice. This means releasing indicted perpetrators and even repeating the excuses once used by the Indonesian government for non-action, as Geoffrey Robinson writes in chapter 3. But when a government denies the past in whole or in part, it does not heal wounds. It leaves them open.

Still, Timor-Leste has done far more on this aspect of memory than many others. In Solomon Islands, a five-volume truth commission report was as impressive in its way as the CAVR's own five volumes, now printed in handsome editions in Indonesian, Portuguese, and English (though not yet in the country's own language, Tetun). The SITRC report was not just shelved—it was never published in the first place. For its part, the Indonesian government has often promised truth commissions, but has not yet delivered on any of these promises. A truth commission into the mass killings of 1965 was promised in 2004, but went by the wayside in 2006. Though the pledge was revived in 2015, to date it has not been acted upon. The Indonesian government also promised a truth commission for Tanah Papua as part of the 2001 Special Autonomy Law, but the promise has not yet been kept. The 2006 Aceh peace deal also included a clause mandating a truth commission, but the Indonesian government failed to implement the commitment. This is not an impressive record: truth is dangled as a promise, but never delivered. The official forgetting of the New Order years continues, hampering a full post-dictatorship reform process.

This promise unkept in Aceh, however, has led to the interesting creation of a truth commission (the KKR) operating with a provincial government mandate. This limits the commission, since the central Indonesian government is not required to co-operate. In this, Aceh faces the same problem as Timor-Leste: the main perpetrators being beyond its reach, the commission is highly constrained in its work. In the CAVR case, this may have had benefits in forcing a focus on historical narrative and on community-level reconciliation. Time will tell whether or not the same can be said for Aceh.

Reliance on a local rather than national government mandate, however, need not be a barrier to success. A precedent exists in Jeju, South Korea.[4] During and after the Korean War, the island of Jeju was host to a severe conflict in which leftist political forces were attacked and—as a subsequent truth commission reported—14,028 people were killed. After extensive campaigning for historical justice, Jeju created a provincial truth commission that reported in 1995. Contested memories of the Jeju events became entangled in South Korea's national democratic transition. Still, the existence of a provincial truth commission and the findings of its final report helped spur the creation of a national truth commission into historical human rights violations in Jeju, mandated by the South Korean parliament in 1999. Four years later, that commission's report led to an apology from the president and other measures. A broader South Korean truth commission, with a mandate covering the entire country rather than just Jeju, followed in 2005. Changes at the national government level prevented it from finishing its work. Still, a provincial truth commission had led to national movement on truth and reconciliation. It is at least possible that Aceh's provincial truth commission, the first within Indonesia's borders, will spur movement on truth processes elsewhere in the country.

Aceh's KKR is also innovative, as Kent and Affiat indicate, in its permanence. Scholars of truth and reconciliation have seen weaknesses in the "episodic" truth commission model, starting with a government mandate and ending with a final report.[5] Timor-Leste's robust follow-up institutions to the CAVR are perhaps some of the best examples to date of trying to avoid this trouble. The "burying" of the Solomon Islands TRC report, meanwhile, provides one of the best examples of the lack of follow-up. Aceh has picked up on the suggestion for a permanent commission that carries on its work with interim deadlines but no final closing date. This frees it of a measure of dependence on government renewals of the mandate (even if it remains dependent on the provincial legislature for funding). It also frees it of the pressure to finish the job. Truth and reconciliation become process, not merely event.

In the introduction to this volume, we proposed considering truth and reconciliation as a process in which the convening and work of a truth commission was merely the middle phase of a three-phase process. The Timorese experience illustrates how there have also been a pre–truth commission phase of mobilizing for accountability, victim healing, and truth-seeking, as well as a post–truth commission phase of "socialization" in which the report's findings are disseminated and a popular sense of ownership and commitment to action are developed. In chapter 9, Manuela Leong Pereira describes the work in the post–truth commission phase of ACbit, the Timorese affiliate of the International Center for Transitional Justice (ICTJ), which works closely with Asian Justice and Rights (AJAR), the Indonesian NGO most active in upholding the rights of victims of past conflicts.[6] These NGOs' work of "socializing" the CAVR report will be aided considerably by the new Centro Nacional *Chega! Da Memória à Esperança* (*Chega!* National Centre: Though Memory to Hope) established in 2017. Timor-Leste's work in continuity of truth and reconciliation processes, it seems, has been picked up and expanded upon in Aceh in ways that, if the KKR meets its promise, could transcend the idea of phases. It shifts understandings of transitional justice towards processes rather than a "tool kit" approach, as Kent and Affiat write. It also has the potential to shift the narrative form of truth commission reports from finished documents to works in continual process. Aceh's experience will bear watching.

It is worth underlining that while truth commissions are mandated by and report to governments, the mobilizing phase beforehand and the socialization phase afterwards both rely on civil-society organizations. If there is no popular demand for truth and reconciliation, there is not likely to be a truth process. The SITRC would not have been formed without the work of NGOs led by the Solomon Islands Christian Association. The issue of truth in Tanah Papua would not exist without the calls for "straightening" history issuing from NGOs, church groups, and Indigenous networks. The KKR in Aceh exists only because NGO voices pushed for it and drew on Timorese and other advice from outside.

Similarly, the energy in advocating for official action on the CAVR report's recommendations came more from the NGO side than from inside the post-CAVR Technical Secretariat, which lost momentum due to lack of oversight and parliamentary inaction on the CAVR report. Without civil-society pressure, the CAVR report might have been shelved with much less action—and certainly non-government voices lobbying the Timorese government were vital to the Centro *Chega!* being approved. These same voices are working hard to socialize the CAVR's findings in Indonesia and internationally. Within Timor-Leste, the slogan "*Chega!* for Us" is not just the name of a group, but also an assertion that civil society, not government, "owns" the report. Without this socialization phase, implementation of truth commission reports seems much less likely. Certainly, despite the work of AJAR and other Indonesian NGOs in the face of official Indonesian resistance, there has been less work to socialize the CAVR report and the Timorese-Indonesian joint truth commission in Indonesia, leading to little follow-up action. Much the same is true in Solomon Islands, a situation that has left relatively little pressure on government to implement the SITRC's findings.

In all three countries examined, women are a distinct minority in government positions. Truth commission hearings have at times helped to open up more space for women's voices.[7] In the civil-society sector, women are far more visible, and are working in many cases to build border-crossing networks of shared experience. As Burma (Myanmar) entered a phase of democratic transition around its first free post-dictatorship elections in 2015, a group of women from that country travelled to Timor-Leste to learn from the work of Timorese women's victims groups. The trip was hosted by ACbit and funded by the Indonesian transitional justice group AJAR—another ICTJ affiliate. It is one example of the sort of transnational women's networks that have emerged in the spaces between more formal government-centred transitional justice work.[8]

Women emerge as "signs of disorder," Jacqueline Aquino Siapno writes in chapter 5. As Gigisi recounts in chapter 19, women have had to work to have their voices heard in truth and reconciliation processes. Yet in Tanah Papua, in Timor-Leste, in Solomon Islands and elsewhere, women are an important part of peacemaking processes.[9] The contributions in this book suggest that more disorder, more pressure, may help to make more successful commissions by including a more gendered awareness of reconciliation.

The case studies in *Flowers in the Wall* are mostly from majority-Christian societies, with civil-society groups often linked to religious institutions. This is truest in Solomon Islands, a country whose people are 98 per cent Christian. It is also true in heavily Catholic Timor-Leste, as Jess Agustin points out in chapter 7. Indeed, truth commissions often seem tied to the Christian faith and to Christian understandings of reconciliation.[10] The emergence of truth commissions in Muslim-majority countries is most evident in Morocco and, more recently, in Tunisia and Aceh. In each case, there are interesting divergences from the TRC model that emerged in South Africa and Latin America, such as a stress on reparation for harm done.[11]

What of the places in Indonesia that are still in *pre*–truth commission phases, that have been promised but denied truth and reconciliation processes, that are still home to civil-society organizations struggling for historical justice and accountability for human rights violations? We have already highlighted the need to take account of Indigenous rights and Indigenous perspectives, of relationships to the land, and of economic factors. These matter in local places under Indonesian rule, all the way from Sabang (in Aceh) to Merauke (in Tanah Papua), to once again evoke that Indonesian nationalist slogan. Then there are the "1965 events," the memory of a mass killing that remains unaddressed by government even while it is spoken about more and more in film, literature, and the conversations of non-governmental gatherings, as Wardaya describes in Chapter 10.[12] In Indonesia, it is now possible to publish individual stories of suffering like that of Gatot Lestario, which forms chapter 12 of this book. Now more than half a century old, the memories of 1965 will need to look more to historical justice than contemporary violations, as Bernd Schaefer writes in chapter 11. In Tanah Papua, too, "history needs healing and recognition," to borrow the words of the Papuan multi-faith "Land of Peace" initiative discussed in chapter 15. *Pelurusan sejarah*—setting straight the history, challenging the dominant state narrative that does violence to people's sense of who they are and what has happened in the past—is needed in order to permit healing and the resolution of conflict.

Historians have grappled with issues of memory and history, and the way memories of colonial rule have shaped post-colonial events.[13] Dialogue between different historical "master narratives" has been advanced as a tool to resolve conflict.[14] In many parts of Indonesia, clashing historical narratives, diametrically opposed versions of the past, are contributing factors to conflict. To resolve that conflict, it is necessary to attempt a dialogue between clashing narratives, for each side to at least acknowledge that the other side has a different history that shares its identity and its aspirations. Yet the Papuan call for historical dialogue, in the 2001 special autonomy package, became a commission empowered to "provide clarification of Papua's history in order to strengthen the people's unity in the State of the Republic of Indonesia."[15] Even that promise remains unkept. A 2005 protest in Papua could still demand the end to state violence committed against people "merely because they have a different understanding of history."[16] In the words of Muridan Widjojo:

> History should not be treated as a fixed position involving absolute truth and determining collective identity. Rather, history should be treated as a negotiable construction involving acceptance and compromise, and providing benefits for both parties rather than being the monopoly of just one side. Otherwise, history in Papua will perpetuate an endless cycle of violence.[17]

In the dialogue that achieved a peace deal in Aceh in 2005, both sides agreed to set aside their historical grievances and start fresh.[18] This helped achieve peace. But the continued struggles for truth-telling and accountability, mainly within civil society, continued for a decade. Not all was resolved: many people in Aceh still sought historical justice.

"Official forgetting," then, does not seem to end civil-society campaigning. The same may be true on the Indonesian national stage. While chapter 10 describes continued campaigning inside Indonesia, chapter 11 promotes the idea of a careful and document-driven historical commission. This recalls such earlier efforts to centre history and systems of oppression as Guatemala's Historical Clarification Commission. Indeed, the concept of historical clarification may be making a comeback. It is included in Papuan campaigning demands. It also lies at the centre of the truth commission into the history of slavery on the island of Mauritius, in the Indian Ocean. That country's Truth and Justice Commission had the longest historical sweep to investigate of any commission yet—370 years of slavery under Dutch, French, and finally British rule, with the goal of redressing poverty and other negative effects of slavery on the descendants of slaves and revealing, in the prime minister of the day's words, "the true history" of a dark colonial period.[19] More recently, the idea is moving north. It is the thread that ties together the Canadian TRC, which delved into the hidden history of "Indian residential schools" that separated children from their families and communities in an effort to assimilate them into settler society. Similarly, the concept of historical clarification animated Germany's "Commission of Inquiry for the Assessment of History and Consequences of the SED Dictatorship in [East] Germany." This truth commission aimed, at least in theory, to reveal the crimes of the East German communist government and thereby help heal a divided Germany.[20]

The latter examples imply a move towards looking at the effect of systems of oppression, from slavery to colonialism to an assimilationist model of residential schools that amounted, in the words of the Canadian TRC, to "cultural genocide."[21] Here there may be a global move, including from some of the cases examined in this book, away from the focus on individual rights. The South African TRC model remains powerful. The CAVR in Timor-Leste and the KKR in Aceh echo its name, as have commissions from Chile to Congo to Canada. Desmond Tutu wrote a foreword for the CAVR's report.[22] The Solomon Islands TRC very much drew on the South African model, from its name to Tutu's presence at its launch, creating what one author called "a performance of reconciliation in the theatre of post-conflict peacebuilding."[23] But from Papuan demands for a more connected understanding to Timorese efforts to include economic oppression in a truth commission report, the focus may be shifting a little towards groups and systemic violations of human rights.

At the same time, commissions are trying to remain victim-centred. For instance, the SITRC wanted to "restore the human dignity of victims and promote reconciliation by allowing victims to tell their stories about the violations and abuses suffered and providing for perpetrators to relate their experiences, creating a climate fostering constructive exchange between victim and perpetrator."[24] CAVR's "central principle," in the words of Isabel Guterres, one if its commissioners, was "to listen to and honour those who had suffered" and place "victims of violations at the centre of the national story of Timor-Leste."[25] The wording here is very much along the lines of global thinking about the value for victims of telling their stories, an assumption that is increasingly being challenged. But the commissions do appear, at least, to be trying to make something of the compiled stories. The CAVR effort to use victim voices to write the first history of Timor-Leste driven by Timor-Leste is one example. CAVR chief commissioner Aniceto Guterres Lopes analyzes the testimonies as a collective effort to "write the past for the sake of the future."[26]

The category of "victim" is fluid, as chapter 13 points out.[27] Yet in many cases groups that identify as victims form the core of campaigns for truth-seeking. Chapter 10 describes some of the groups of victims of the 1965 events and their supporters and their truth-seeking efforts to break down walls of silence. If Timor-Leste needed two truth commissions—the CAVR and the bilateral Timorese-Indonesian Commission on Truth and Friendship—it is perhaps because the first was victim-centred in its mandate and work, while the second was decidedly government-centred, designed in part to undermine civil-society campaigns against the impunity of perpetrators still at large in Indonesia. The CTF was designed to settle things. The CAVR and its post–truth commission socializers aimed instead to *un*-settle.

This "unsettling" may be among the key contributions that the Timorese experience of truth and reconciliation has to offer. Reconciliation can't simply ask those who have suffered to forgive their oppressors. The CTF had value in prompting an official Indonesian government acknowledgement of massive human rights violations during 1999, the final year of the country's occupation of Timor-Leste. But it also had "too much friendship, not enough truth," as Siapno writes above, and thus risked burying the very real ongoing legacy of those human rights violations. It tried in some ways to put reconciliation back in the shadows by placing the blame on anonymous institutions rather than the individuals with command responsibility, thereby frustrating the rights of victims and allowing impunity to continue. Problems with the CTF are compounded by its very limited distribution.

More broadly, there are dangers of a new official forgetting about crimes against humanity in East Timor. Official denials and official forgetting allow "non-truth" to flourish in Indonesia.[28] Equally worrying, they undercut interesting steps such as the CAVR effort to move towards "reparative justice"—justice that repairs the damage of conflict and human rights violations, rather than concentrating on accountability for perpetrators (retributive justice) or healing the wounds to society (restorative justice, the realm of most truth commission work).[29] CAVR attempted reparative justice by providing recognition, symbolic memorialization, and, in some cases, compensation to survivors. The SITRC also proposed a comprehensive reparation plan, mostly non-monetary measures such as apologies and educational assistance to conflict survivors and displaced people.

None of these measures are purely academic. They affect survivors, and they also affect the future of nations. In chapter 8 Borges argues that respect for human rights has become central to Timorese national identity. This is one legacy of the long fight for independence. Another is what Siapno calls, in chapter 5, clandestinity. Activists had to fight for freedom from the shadows, using secret names and secret identities, she writes. But how useful is this in independent Timor-Leste? Does it risk undermining the stability of democracy? Does it, perhaps, even threaten to undermine Timor-Leste's identity as a rights-respecting country?

Clandestine activism, in Siapno's account, often required leaving no written record, no trace that could be discovered. Truth-seeking requires opening up the archives and acknowledging the stories of survivors, letting them grow like flowers through the crumbling walls of official narratives.

So, stories and archives. Personal stories rely on memory and may be, as Zwierzchowski notes in her review of the field, an ineffective path to objective truth. But this is perhaps the point. Stories are messier than a single agreed-upon narrative, but they may get us closer to truths. They are told in the hopes of gaining a result—repentance from the perpetrator, reparations from the state, some other redress, or simply recognition. Stories are not always redemptive, as Kent and Affiat write. They do not always heal.[30] Yet they may allow new and more complex national narratives to emerge in place of the stories of "rainbow nations," heroic armed struggle against foreign rule, or redemption through suffering, to cite narratives on offer in South Africa and Timor-Leste. The new national narratives are important in overturning former colonial narratives that erased local understandings, but they too can become dominant master narratives that erase as much as they "nation build."

As for archival sources, these tend to be international. All the more so when local archives and other repositories of memory are themselves victims of violence. Guatemala's truth commission was able to draw on US archives. On his last visit to Argentina, President Barack Obama agreed to open up some US archival sources on Argentina's US-backed "dirty war" in the 1970s and '80s.[31] But more often than not, relevant archives are closed, making it hard to find the truth about past events. Among the exceptions, Timor-Leste again leads the way. Its truth commission was able to access some very revealing official records from Australia and the United States. This was due to tireless and vocal campaigning by Australian solidarity groups hoping to open the secrets of Australian government support for Indonesia's rule. In the United States, it was possible through the work of a remarkable non-governmental organization, the National Security Archive.[32] International civil-society groups backed up local civil-society campaigns. An effective Indonesian truth commission would need similar work to throw open archives, as Bernd Schaefer explains in chapter 11.

International linkages must mean more than the Indonesian-Timorese CTF, though that commission did provide a useful precedent for border-crossing truth commissions not linked to one government alone. In chapter 3 Geoffrey Robinson notes the selective compassion of the international community, which pressed hard for judicial mechanisms of retributive justice in Yugoslavia but discouraged anything similar in Timor-Leste or Indonesia. Holding Indonesian generals accountable had a much higher political cost than arresting militia leaders and politicians in the former Yugoslavia. More importantly, it would have exposed Western government complicity and active involvement in genocidal events in Indonesia and Timor-Leste.

The CAVR's final report included recommendations to the international community, including a call for reparations to be paid by the governments that backed, bankrolled, and armed the Indonesian army, thereby enabling mass atrocities in Timor-Leste. Western governments named in the report chose to ignore its record of their role, and the recommendations addressed to them. CAVR's recommendations to the international community therefore remain buried. The Timorese government, running a small country with a small population and reliant on good relations with its neighbours and with the great powers, is unlikely to take the lead in challenging this silence. Nevertheless, there are lessons from CAVR and from truth-seeking campaigns in the region. Truth processes must cross borders if they are to reveal the whole story and provide effective reconciliation. And again, that reconciliation must require action from the powerful, not just forgiveness from victims. Truth-seeking should lead to action, not to closure.

Notes

1 The phrase comes from Dipesh Chakrabarty, *Provincializing Europe: Postcolonial Thought and Historical Difference* (Princeton, NJ: Princeton University Press, 2007). See also Linda Tuhiwai Smith, *Decolonizing Methodologies* (London: Zed Books, 2012) and Joyce Green, ed., *Indivisible: Indigenous Human Rights* (Halifax, NS: Fernwood, 2014).

2 Dionísio Babo-Soares, "*Nahe Biti*: The Philosophy and Process of Grassroots Reconciliation (and Justice) in East Timor," *Asia Pacific Journal of Anthropology* 5, no. 1 (2004):15–33. For a more critical view of the problems in the district around Maubara, see Douglas Kammen, *Three Centuries of Conflict in East Timor* (Singapore: National University of Singapore Press, 2015).

3 *Honouring the Truth, Reconciling for the Future. Summary of the Final Report of the Truth and Reconciliation Commission of Canada* (Winnipeg, MB: TRC Canada, 2015), 17.

4 Hunjoon Kim, "Seeking Truth After 50 years: The National Committee for Investigation of the Truth about the Jeju 4.3 Events," *International Journal of Transitional Justice* 3, no. 3 (2009): 406–23.

5 Ray Nickson and John Braithwaite, "Deeper, Broader, Longer Transitional Justice," *European Journal of Criminology* 11, no. 4 (2014): 445–63.

6 On the ICTJ, see "About Us," https://www.ictj.org/about (accessed 21 May 2017).

7 Commission for Reception, Truth and Reconciliation, *Timor-Leste: Women and the Conflict* (Dili, TL: CAVR, 2005).

8 ACbit, "Burmese Women Activists Exchange Visit to Timor-Leste," ACbit report, 29 October 2015, http://chegabaita.org/en/2015/10/29/burmese-women-activists-exchange-visit-to-timor-leste/ (accessed 21 May 2017). On transnational women's networks more generally, see Pascale Dufour, Dominique Masson, and Dominique Caouette, eds., *Solidarities Beyond Borders: Transnationalizing Women's Movements* (Vancouver: University of British Columbia Press, 2010).

9 Lia Kent, "After the Truth Commission: Gender and Citizenship in Timor-Leste," *Human Rights Review* 17, no. 1 (2016): 51–70; Martha M. Wospakrik with Christy Reed, " 'The Woman Who Loves': Women as Guardians of Peace and Weavers of Life in Biak, Papua," in *Creating the Third Force: Indigenous Processes of Peacemaking*, ed. Hamdesa Tuso and Maureen P. Flaherty (Lanham, MD: Lexington, 2016); Jan Haaken et al.,

Speaking Out: Women, War and the Global Economy (Portland, OR: Ooligan Press, 2005).

10   There are forty truth commissions described in the most complete book, Priscilla B. Hayner, *Unspeakable Truths: Facing the Challenge of Truth Commissions* (New York: Routledge, 2010). Of these, thirty were in Christian-majority countries, five in countries with no single majority religion but with strong Christian influences (Ghana, Mauritius, Nigeria, Sierra Leone, and Togo), and five in countries with a non-Christian majority (Chad, Morocco, Nepal, South Korea, and Sri Lanka).

11   Susan Slyomovics, "Morocco's Justice and Reconciliation Commission," *Middle East Research and Information Project*, 4 April 2005, http://www.merip.org/mero/mero040405 (accessed 21 May 2017); Hayner, *Unspeakable Truths*, 42–44; Rim El Gantri, "Tunisia in Transition: One Year After the Creation of the Truth and Dignity Commission," International Center for Transitional Justice, September 2015, https://www.ictj.org/sites/default/files/ICTJ-Briefing-Tunisia-TJLaw-2015.pdf (accessed 21 May 2017).

12   See also John Roosa, "The State of Knowledge about an Open Secret: Indonesia's Mass Disappearances of 1965–66," *The Journal of Asia Studies* 75, no. 2 (2016): 281–97.

13   John Torpey, ed., *Politics and the Past* (Lanham, MD: Rowman & Littlefield, 2003).

14   Paul Scham, Benjamin Pogrund, and As'ad Ghanem, "Introduction to Shared Narratives: An Israeli-Palestinian Dialogue," *Israel Studies* 18, no. 2 (2013): 1–10.

15   Sekretariat Keadilan dan Perdamaian, Keuskupan Jayapura, *Catatan Perkembangan Terkini di Papua: Otonomi Khusus, proses dan hasil akhirnya [Social-Political Note on Recent Developments in Papua: The Special Autonomy Process and Final Results]* (Jayapura, ID: 2001).

16   Dewan Adat Papua protest demands, 12 August 2005.

17   Muridan S. Widjojo, "Negotiating the Past and Looking to the Future," *Inside Indonesia* no. 98 (October–December 2009), http://www.insideindonesia.org/negotiating-the-past-and-looking-to-the-future (accessed 21 May 2017).

18   See Timo Kivimäki, "Initiating a Peace Process in Papua: Actors, Issues, Process, and the Role of the International Community," *East-West Center Policy Studies* 25 (2006): ix–88.

19   Hayner, *Unspeakable Truths*.

20   United States Institute of Peace, "Truth Commission: Germany 92," http://www.usip.org/sites/default/files/file/resources/collections/commissions/Germany92-Charter.pdf (accessed 23 May 2017).

21   David MacDonald, "Five Reasons the TRC Chose 'Cultural Genocide,'" *Globe and Mail* (Toronto), 6 July 2015, http://www.theglobeandmail.com/opinion/five-reasons-the-trc-chose-cultural-genocide/article25311423/ (accessed 23 May 2017).

22   *Chega! A Plain Guide* (Jakarta: Gramedia, 2013).

23   Louise Vella, "Translating Transitional Justice: The Solomon Islands Truth and Reconciliation Commission," SSGM Discussion Paper 2014/2, Australian National

24   University, http://ssgm.bellschool.anu.edu.au/experts-publications/publications/1257/translating-transitional-justice-solomon-islands-truth-and (accessed 21 May 2017).

24   *Confronting the Truth for a Better Solomon Islands: Final Report of the Solomon Islands Truth and Reconciliation Commission* (Honiara, SB: Solomon Islands Truth and Reconciliation Commission, 2012), 1: 9–10. The report is online at http://pacificpolicy.org/files/2013/04/Solomon-Islands-TRC-Final-Report-Vol1.pdf.

25   *Rona Ami-nia Lia: Hear Our Voices* (Dili, TL: CAVR, 2005), 6.

26   Aniceto Guterres Lopes, preface to *Chega!*, 1: 2.

27   TRC Canada instead used the language of "survivors" and even "cross-generational survivors" to describe the families of survivors who had suffered at one remove. It set up a "survivor's committee" to oversee the commission and protect their centrality in its work.

28   John Braithwaite et al., *Anomie and Violence: Non-truth and Reconciliation in Indonesian Peacebuilding* (Canberra: Australian National University E-Press, 2010).

29   Joanna R. Quinn, ed., *Reconciliation(s): Transitional Justice in Postconflict Societies* (Montreal: McGill-Queen's University Press, 2009).

30   Lia Kent, *The Dynamics of Transitional Justice in East Timor* (New York: Routledge, 2012); Holly L. Guthrey, *Victim Healing and Truth Commissions: Transforming Pain through Voice in the Solomon Islands and Timor-Leste* (Cham, CH: Springer, 2015).

31   Greg Grandin, "Chronicles of a Guatemalan Genocide Foretold: Violence, Trauma, and the Limits of Historical Inquiry," *Nepantla* 1, no. 2 (2000): 391–412; Commission for Historical Clarification, *Guatemala: Memory of silence* (Guatemala City: CEH, 1999); Peter Kornbluh and Carlos Osorio, eds., " 'Declassified Diplomacy': Argentina," National Security Archive Electronic Briefing Book No. 556, 2016, http://nsarchive.gwu.edu/NSAEBB/NSAEBB556-Obama-administration-declassifies-documents-on-Argentina-military-human-rights-abuses/ (accessed 23 May 2017).

32   Brad Simpson, "The Indonesia/East Timor Documentation Project," National Security Archive, 28 January 2008, http://nsarchive.gwu.edu/indonesia/ (accessed 23 May 2017), and "Documenting Mass Violence: History, Truth, and Accountability," paper presented at "Legacies of Violence in Indonesia and East Timor," University of California–Los Angeles, 15 April 2011.

Bibliography

Adam, Asvi Warman. *Seabad Kontroversi Sejarah*. Yogyakarta, ID: Ombak, 2007.

———. "September Affair in History Courses." Paper presented at "The 1965–1966 Indonesian Killings Revisited," Singapore, 17–19 June 2009.

Afrida, Nani. "Army to join efforts to accelerate food sufficiency." *Jakarta Post*, 9 January 2015. http://www.thejakartapost.com/news/2015/01/09/army-join-efforts-accelerate-food-sufficiency.html.

Allen, Matthew G. *Greed and Grievance: Ex-Militants' Perspectives on the Conflict in Solomon Islands 1998–2003*. Honolulu: University of Hawai'i Press, 2013.

Amnesty International. "Indonesia: End Mass Arbitrary Arrests of Peaceful Protesters in Papua." 11 June 2015. https://www.amnesty.org/en/documents/asa21/1851/2015/en/.

———. "Indonesia: Investigate Military Attacks on Villagers in Wamena, Papua." 9 June 2012. http://www.amnesty.org.au/news/comments/28886/.

———. *Indonesia: New Military Operations, Old Patterns of Human Rights Abuses in Aceh*. London: Amnesty International, 2004.

Amstutz, Mark R. *The Healing of Nations: The Promise and Limits of Political Forgiveness*. Lanham, MD: Rowman & Littlefield, 2005.

Anderson, Benedict R. "Impunity and Reenactment: Reflections on the 1965 Massacre in Indonesia and its Legacy." *Asia-Pacific Journal: Japan Focus*, 15 April 2013. http://japanfocus.org/-Benedict-Anderson/3929/article.html.

———. "Indonesian Nationalism Today and in the Future." *Indonesia* 67 (1999): 1–11.

Anderson, Benedict, Ruth T. McVey, and Frederick P. Bunnell. *The Preliminary Analysis of the October 1, 1965 Coup in Indonesia*. Ithaca, NY: Cornell University Modern Indonesia Project, 1971.

Aragon, Lorraine V. "Communal Violence in Poso, Central Sulawesi: Where People Eat Fish and Fish Eat People." *Indonesia*, 72 (2001): 45–79.

———. "Elite Competition in Central Sulawesi." In *Renegotiating Boundaries: Local Politics in post-Suharto Indonesia*, edited by Henk Schulte Nordholt and Gerry van Klinken, 39–89. Leiden, NL: KITLV, 2007.

Aspinall, Edward. "Aceh: Democratization and the Politics of Co-option." In *Diminishing Conflicts in Asia and the Pacific: Why Some Subside and Others Don't*, edited by Edward Aspinall, Robin Jeffery, and Anthony J. Regan, 51–68. New York: Routledge, 2013.

———. "Combatants to Contractors: The Political Economy of Peace in Aceh, Indonesia," *Indonesia* 87 (2009): 1–34.

———. "The New Nationalism in Indonesia." *Asia & the Pacific Policy Studies*, 3 no. 1 (2016): 69–79.

———. *Peace without Justice? The Helsinki Peace Process in Aceh*. Geneva: Centre for Humanitarian Dialogue, 2008.

Aspinall, Edward and Fajran Zain. "Transitional Justice Delayed in Aceh, Indonesia." In *Transitional Justice in the Asia-Pacific*, edited by Renee Jeffery and Hun Joon Kim, 87–124. New York: Cambridge University Press, 2014.

Avonius, Leena. "Reconciliation and Human Rights in Post-conflict Aceh." In *Reconciling Indonesia: Grassroots Agency for Peace*, edited by Birgit Brauchler, 121–37. New York: Routledge, 2009.

Babo-Soares, Dionísio. "*Nahe Biti*: The Philosophy and Process of Grassroots Reconciliation (and Justice) in East Timor." *Asia Pacific Journal of Anthropology* 5, no. 1 (2004): 15–33.

Baja, Helder. "Timor Embraces China." *Macao Magazine*, 17 July 2012. http://macaomagazine.net/china/timor-embraces-china.

Bakiner, Onur. *Truth Commissions: Memory, Power and Legitimacy*. Philadelphia: University of Pennsylvania Press, 2016.

Barbara, Julien. "Rethinking Neo-Liberal State-building: Building Post-Conflict Development States." *Development in Practice* 18, no. 3 (2008): 307–18.

Barr, John. "A Veil of Silence is Killing Papua." *West Papua Media*, 22 December 2010. https://westpapuamedia.info/2010/12/.

Barreto Soares, Augusto, Hazem Galal, and Toshi Nakamura. "Capacity Development at the World's Newest Nation: Timor-Leste, Challenges and Lessons Learned from the Programme Approach." April 2005. http://www.sti.ch/fileadmin/user_upload/Pdfs/swap/swap413.pdf.

Barreto Soares, Laurentina. "Foreign Aid for State-Building: A Comparative Study between Australia and Chinese Aid Programs in Timor-Leste." MA Thesis, Ohio University, 2011.

Beeck, Christine. *Repaving the Road to Peace: Analysis of the Implementation of DD&R (Disarmament, Demobilization and Reintegration) in Aceh Province, Indonesia*. Bonn, DE: Bonn International Center for Conversion, Brief 35, 2007.

Belo, Carlos Filipe Ximenes. *The Road to Freedom: A Collection of Speeches, Pastoral Letters, and Articles from 1997–2001*. Sydney: Caritas Australia, 2001.

Beu, Charles Brown and Roselyn Nokise. *Mission in the Midst of Conflict: Stories from the Solomon Islands*. Suva, FJ: Pacific Theological College, 2009.

Boesenecker, Aaron P. and Leslie Vinjamuri. "Lost in Translation? Civil Society, Faith-Based Organisations and Negotiation of International Norms." *The International Journal of Transitional Justice* 5 (2011): 345–65.

Boraine, Alex. "South Africa's Truth and Reconciliation Commission from a Global Perspective." In *Peace versus Justice? The Dilemma of Transitional Justice in Africa*, edited by Chandra Lekha Sriram and Suren Pillay, 137–52. Scottsville, SA: University of KwaZulu-Natal Press, 2009.

Botman, H. Russell. "Truth and Reconciliation: The South Africa Case." In *Religion and Peacebuilding*, edited by Harold Coward and Gordon S. Smith, 243–60. Albany: State University of New York Press, 2004.

Braithwaite, John, Valerie Braithwaite, Michael Cookson, and Leah Dunn. *Anomie and Violence: Non-truth and Reconciliation in Indonesian Peacebuilding*. Canberra: Australian National University E-Press, 2010.

Brown, Terry M. "The Role of Religious Communities in Peacemaking." *Anglican Religious Life Journal*, no. 1 (2004): 8–18.

Brown, Wendy. "In the 'Folds of our own Discourse': The Pleasures and Freedoms of Silence." *The University of Chicago Law School Roundtable* 3, no. 1 (1996). http://chicagounbound.uchicago.edu/roundtable/vol13/iss1/8.

Budiardjo, Carmel and Liem Soei Liong. *West Papua: The Obliteration of a People*. London: Tapol, 1988.

Butt, Leslie. " 'Lipstick Girls' and 'Fallen Women': AIDS and Conspiratorial Thinking in Papua, Indonesia." *Cultural Anthropology* 20, no. 3 (2005): 412–42.

Carter, Richard Anthony. *In Search of the Lost: The Death and Life of Seven Peacemakers of the Melanesian Brotherhood*. Norwich, UK: Canterbury Press, 2006.

Centre for Religious and Cross-Cultural Studies. "Tolikara, Idul Fitri 2015: Tentang Konflik Agama, Mayoritas-Minoritas dan Perjuangan Tanah Damai." http://crcs.ugm.ac.id/news/3511/tolikara-idul-fitri-2015-tentang-konflik-agama-mayoritas-minoritas-dan-perjuangan-tanah-damai.html.

Chakrabarty, Dipesh. *Provincializing Europe: Postcolonial Thought and Historical Difference*. Princeton, NJ: Princeton University Press, 2007.

Chandler, David. *Empire in Denial: The Politics of State-Building*. London: Pluto Press, 2007.

———. "The Uncritical Critique of Liberal Peace." *Review of International Studies* 36, Special Issue S1 (2010): 137–55.

Chauvel, Richard. "Policy Failure and Political Impasse: Papua and Jakarta a Decade after the 'Papuan Spring.' " In *Comprehending West Papua*, edited by Peter King, Jim Elmslie, and Camellia Webb-Gannon, 105–15. Sydney, AU: Centre of Peace and Conflict Studies, University of Sydney, 2011.

———. *Intended to Fail: The Trials before the Ad Hoc Human Rights Court in Jakarta*. New York: International Center for Transitional Justice, 2003.

China, Information Office of the State Council of the People's Republic of. "China's Foreign Aid." Beijing: Information Office of the State Council, 2014. Cohen, David. *Indifference and Accountability: The United Nations and the Politics of International Justice in East Timor*. Honolulu, HI: East-West Center Special Reports Number 9, 2006.

China , State Council of the People's Republic of. "China's Foreign Aid (2011)." 21 April 2011. http://english.gov.cn/archive/white_paper/2014/09/09/content_281474986284620.htm.

———. "China's Foreign Aid (2014)." 10 July 2014. http://english.gov.cn/archive/white_paper/2014/08/23/content_281474982986592.htm.

Commission for Historical Clarification. *Guatemala: Memory of silence*. Guatemala City: CEH, 1999.

Commission for Reception, Truth and Reconciliation. *Chega! The Final Report of the Timor-Leste Commission for Reception, Truth and Reconciliation*. Jakarta: Gramedia, 2015.

———. *Chega! A Plain Guide*. Jakarta: Gramedia, 2013.

———. *Timor-Leste: Women and the Conflict*. Dili, TL: CAVR, 2005.

Craig, David and Douglas Porter. *Development beyond Neoliberalism? Governance, Poverty Reduction, and Political Economy*. New York: Routledge, 2006.

Cribb, Robert. *The Indonesian Killings of 1965–1966: Studies from Java and Bali*. Clayton, AU: Monash University Centre of Southeast Asian Studies, 1990.

———. Robert Cribb "Unresolved Problems in the Indonesian Killings of 1965–1966," *Asian Survey* 42, no. 4 (July/August 2002): 550–63.

Daly, Erin. "Truth Skepticism: An Inquiry into the Value of Truth in Times of Transition." *International Journal of Transitional Justice* 2, no. 1 (2008): 23–41.

Daly, Erin and Jeremy Sarkin. *Reconciliation in Divided Societies: Finding Common Ground*. Philadelphia: University of Pennsylvania Press, 2007.

Departamen Pendidikan dan Kebudayaan. *Sejarah Nasional, jilid 3 untuk SMA [National History for Upper-Level High Schools]*. Jakarta: Departamen Pendidikan dan Kebudayaan, 1981.

Dinnen, Sinclair, ed. *A Kind of Mending: Restorative Justice in the Pacific Islands*. Canberra, AU: Pandanus Books, 2003.

Dorling, Philip. "Timor Rejected Chinese Spy Offer." *Sydney Morning Herald*, 10 May 2011. http://www.smh.com.au/world/timor-rejected-chinese-spy-offer-20110509-1efv1.html.

Drysdale, Jennifer. *Sustainable Development or Resource Cursed? An Exploration of Timor-Leste's Institutional Choices*. PhD diss., Australian National University, 2007.

Dufour, Pascale, Dominique Masson, and Dominique Caouette, eds. *Solidarities beyond Borders: Transnationalizing Women's Movements*. Vancouver: University of British Columbia Press, 2010.

Dunn, James. *East Timor: A Rough Passage to Independence*. Double Bay, AU: Longueville, 2004.

Education Policy and Data Center. *Timor-Leste: National Education Profile Update 2014*. http://www.epdc.org/sites/default/files/documents/EPDC%20NEP_Timor%20Leste.pdf.

Eisenman, Joshua, Eric Heginbotham, and Derek Mitchell. *China and the Developing World: Beijing's Strategy for the Twenty-first Century*. New York: Routledge, 2015.

El Gantri, Rim. "Tunisia in Transition: One Year After the Creation of the Truth and Dignity Commission." International Center for Transitional Justice, September 2015. https://www.ictj.org/sites/default/files/ICTJ-Briefing-Tunisia-TJLaw-2015.pdf.

Embassy of the People's Republic of China in Timor-Leste. "China and Timor-Leste Bilateral Relations," 1 January 2010. http://tl.chineseembassy.org/eng/sbjx/.

Enloe, Cynthia. *Nimo's War, Emma's War: Making Feminist Sense of the Iraq War*. Princeton, NJ: Princeton University Press, 2010.

Everett, Silas. "U.S. Secretary of State Clinton's Timor-Leste Visit Highlights Growth." *The Asia Foundation*, 12 September 2012. http://asiafoundation.org/in-asia/2012/09/12/u-s-secretary-of-state-clintons-timor-leste-visit-highlights-growth/.

Faith Based Network on West Papua. "Papua Land of Peace." http://www.faithbasednetworkonwestpapua.org/papua_land_of_peace.

Fanon, Franz. *The Wretched of the Earth*. New York: Grove Press, 1963.

Federer, Juan. *The UN in East Timor: Building Timor-Leste, a Fragile State*. Darwin, AU: Charles Darwin University, 2005.

Feinstein, Andrew. *The Shadow World: Inside the Global Arms Trade*. New York: Picador, 2012.

Fernandes, Clinton. *The Independence of East Timor: Multidimensional Perspectives—Occupation, Resistance and International Political Activism*. Eastbourne, UK: Sussex Academic Press, 2011.

Fic, Victor M. *Anatomy of the Jakarta Coup, October 1, 1965: The Collusion with China Which Destroyed the Army Command, President Sukarno and the Communist Party of Indonesia.* New Delhi: Abhinav Publications, 2004.

Flint, Colin. "Terrorism and Counterterrorism: Geographic Research Questions and Agendas." *Professional Geographer* 55, no. 2 (2003): 162–69.

Fraenkel, Jon. *The Manipulation of Custom: From Uprising to Intervention in the Solomon Islands.* Canberra, AU: Pandanus Books, 2004.

Galtung, Johan. "After Violence, Reconstruction, Reconciliation, and Resolution: Coping with Visible and Invisible Effects of War and Violence." In *Reconciliation, Justice, and Coexistence: Theory and Practice*, edited by Mohammed Abu-Nimer, 3–24. Lanham, MD: Lexington Books, 2001.

Gatra. "Inilah Sejumlah Strategi Pemulihan Insiden Tolikara." *GATRAnews* (Jakarta), 3 August 2015. http://www.gatra.com/fokus-berita-1/158698-inilah-sejumlah-strategi-pemulihan-insiden-tolikara.

Gibson, James L. "Does Truth Lead to Reconciliation? Testing the Casual Assumptions of the South African Truth and Reconciliation Process." *American Journal of Political Science* 48, no. 2 (April 2004): 201–17.

Gietzelt, Dale. "The Indonesianization of West Papua." *Oceania* 59, no. 3 (1989): 201–21.

Grandin, Greg. "Chronicles of a Guatemalan Genocide Foretold: Violence, Trauma, and the Limits of Historical Inquiry." *Nepantla* 1, no. 2 (2000): 391–412.

———. "The Instruction of Great Catastrophe: Truth Commissions, National History, and State Formation in Argentina, Chile, and Guatemala." *The American Historical Review* 110, no. 1 (2005): 46–67.

Grayman, Jesse Hession. "Official and Unrecognized Narratives of Recovery in Post-conflict Aceh, Indonesia." *Critical Asian Studies* 48, no. 4 (2016): 528–55.

Gready, Paul. *The Era of Transitional Justice: The Aftermath of the Truth and Reconciliation Commission in South Africa and Beyond.* New York: Routledge, 2011.

Green, Joyce, ed. *Indivisible: Indigenous Human Rights.* Halifax, NS: Fernwood, 2014.

Guthrey, Holly L. *Victim Healing and Truth Commissions: Transforming Pain through Voice in the Solomon Islands and Timor-Leste.* Cham, CH: Springer, 2015.

Guthrey, Holly L. and Brounéus, K. "Peering into the 'Black Box' of TRC Success: Exploring Local Perceptions of Reconciliation in the Solomon Islands TRC." In *Transitional Justice in the Solomon Islands*, edited by Renée Jeffrey. New York: Palgrave, forthcoming.

Haaken, Jan, Ariel Ladum, Seiza de Tarr, Kayt Zundel, and Caleb Heymann. *Speaking Out: Women, War and the Global Economy*. Portland OR: Ooligan Press, 2005.

Hamber, Brandon. "Does the Truth Heal? A Psychological Perspective on the Political Strategies for Dealing with the Legacy of Political Violence." In *Burying the Past: Making Peace and Doing Justice after Civil Conflict,* edited by Neil Bigger, 131–48. Washington: Georgetown University Press, 2003.

Hamber, Brandon and Richard Wilson. "Symbolic Closure through Memory, Reparation and Revenge in Post-Conflict Societies." *Journal of Human Rights* 1, no. 1 (2002): 35–53.

Hayner, Priscilla B. *Unspeakable Truths: Facing the Challenge of Truth Commissions*. New York: Routledge, 2010.

Hernawan, Budi. *Papua Land of Peace: Addressing Conflict Building Peace in West Papua*. Jayapura, ID: Office for Justice and Peace, Catholic Diocese of Jayapura, 2005.

Hesegem, T., P. Wetipo, A. Logo, A. Itlay, Y. Yogobi, P. Aspalek. "Laporan hasil investigasi Wamena 6 Juni 2012: Penyerangan oleh Pasukan Batalion Yunif 756 Wimane Sili/WMS Wamena Kabupaten Jayawijaya." 2012.

Hill, Hal. *The Indonesian Economy*. Cambridge: Cambridge University Press, 2000.

Horta, Jose Ramos. *Funu: The Unfinished Saga of East Timor*. Boston: Red Sea Press, 1987.

Horta, Loro. "Timor-Leste: The Dragon's Newest Friend." *IRASEC Discussion Paper* 4, no. 18 (May 2009): 1–18.

Human Rights Watch. "Something to Hide? Indonesia's Restrictions on Media Freedom and Rights Monitoring in Papua." 10 November 2015. https://www.hrw.org/report/2015/11/10/something-hide/indonesias-restrictions-media-freedom-and-rights-monitoring-papua.

Ihsanuddin, Ican. "Umat Islam dan Umat Kristen Tolikara Sepakat Saling Memaafkan." *Kompas* (Jakarta) 11 August 2015. http://nasional.kompas.com/read/2015/08/11/1537387/Umat.Islam.dan.Umat.Kristen.Tolikara.Sepakat.Saling.Memaafkan.

Indonesia–Timor-Leste Commission on Truth and Friendship. *Per Memoriam Ad Spem: Final Report of the Commission on Truth and Friendship*. Denpasar, ID: CTF, 2008.

Ingold, Tim. *The Perception of the Environment: Essays in Livelihoods, Dwelling and Skill*. New York: Routledge, 2000.

International Center for Transitional Justice. "Challenging the Conventional: Can Truth Commissions Strengthen Peace Processes?" Multimedia website, March 2016. https://www.ictj.org/challenging-conventional-truth-commissions-peace/index.html.

International Coalition for Papua. *Human Rights in Papua 2013*. Wuppertal, DE: International Coalition for Papua, 2013.

———. *Human Rights in West Papua 2015*. Wuppertal, DE: International Coalition for Papua, 2015.

International Crisis Group. "Aceh: Post-Conflict Complications." Crisis Group Asia Report 139, 4 October 2007.

———. *How Indonesian Extremists Regroup*. Jakarta: International Crisis Group, 2012.

———. *Indonesia: Jemaah Islamiyah's Current Status*. Jakarta: International Crisis Group, 2007.

———. *Jemaah Islamiyah in South East Asia: Damaged but Still Dangerous.* Jakarta: International Crisis Group, 2003.

———. *Jihadism in Indonesia: Poso on the Edge*. Jakarta/Brussels: International Crisis Group, 2007.

———. "Stability at What Cost?" *Asia Report*, no. 246 (2013). http://www.crisisgroup.org/en/regions/asia/south-east-asia/timor-leste/246-timor-leste-stability-at-what-cost.aspx.

———. "Timor-Leste: Reconciliation and Return from Indonesia." *Asia Briefing* 122 (2011): 1–19.

Jeffery, Renee. "Amnesty and Accountability: The Price of Peace in Aceh, Indonesia." *International Journal of Transitional Justice* 6, no. 1 (2012): 60–82.

Jones, Lee. "(Post-)Colonial State-Building and State Failure in East Timor: Bringing Social Conflict Back In." *Conflict, Security & Development* 10, no. 4 (2010): 545–75.

KAIROS Canada. *Strength for Climbing: Steps on the Journey of Reconciliation*. Toronto: KAIROS Canada and Mennonite Church Canada, 2015.

Kammen, Douglas. *Three Centuries of Conflict in East Timor*. New Brunswick, NJ: Rutgers University Press, 2015.

Kammen, Douglas and Kate McGregor, eds. *The Contours of Mass Violence in Indonesia, 1965–68*. Singapore: National University of Singapore Press, 2012.

Karnavian, M. Tito. *Indonesian Top Secret: Membongkar Konflik Poso*. Jakarta: Gramedia Pustaka Utama, 2008.

Kartono, Alfian. "Belasan Kios dan Rumah Warga Hangus Dibakar Massa Tak Dikenal." *Kompas* (Jakarta) 17 July 2015. http://regional.kompas.com/read/2015/07/17/09461561/Belasan.Kios.dan.Rumah.Warga.Hangus.Dibakar.Massa.Tak.Dikenal.

Keagop, P. "Warga Honelama Kehilangan Rumah." 10 July 2012. http://www.suaraperempuanpapua.net/index.php/rubrikasi/hukum/item/665-warga-honelama-kehilangan-rumah.

Keefer, Edward C., ed. *Foreign Relations of the United States, 1964–1968, Volume XXVI, Indonesia; Malaysia-Singapore; Philippines*. Washington: United States Government Printing Office, 2000.

Kent, Lia. "After the Truth Commission: Gender and Citizenship in Timor-Leste." *Human Rights Review* 17, no. 1 (2016): 51–70.

———. *The Dynamics of Transitional Justice: International Models and Local Realities in East Timor*. New York: Routeldge, 2012.

———. *Unfulfilled Expectations: Community Views of the CAVR's Community Reconciliation Process in East Timor*. Dili, TL: Judicial Systems Monitoring Programme, 2004.

Kent, Lia, Naomi Kinsella, and Nuno Rodrigues Tchailoro. *Chega! Ten Years On: A Neglected National Resource*. Canberra, AU: State, Society and Governance in Melanesia Report, July 2016.

Kim, Hunjoon. "Seeking Truth After 50 years: The National Committee for Investigation of the Truth about the Jeju 4.3 Events." *International Journal of Transitional Justice* 3, no. 3 (2009): 406–23.

Kirksey, S. Eben. *Freedom in Entangled Worlds*. Durham, NC: Duke University Press, 2012.

Kivimäki, Timo. "Initiating a Peace Process in Papua: Actors, Issues, Process, and the Role of the International Community." *East-West Center Policy Studies* 25 (2006).

Klaehn, Jeffery. "Canadian Complicity in the East Timor Near-Genocide: A Case Study in the Sociology of Human Rights." *Portuguese Studies Review* 11, no. 1 (2003): 49–65.

Kohen, Arnold. *From the Place of the Dead: The Epic Struggles of Bishop Belo of East Timor*. New York: St. Martin's Press, 1999.

Kolimon, Mery, Liliya Wetangterah, and Karen Campbell-Nelson. *Forbidden Memories: Women's Experiences of 1965 in Eastern Indonesia*. Melbourne, AU: Monash University Publishing, 2015.

Komnas-HAM. "Statement by Komnas-HAM (National Commission for Human Rights) on the Results of its Investigations into Grave Violations of Human Rights during the Events of 1965–1966." TAPOL translation. 23 August 2012. http://www.tapol.org/sites/default/files/sites/default/files/pdfs/Komnas%20HAM%201965%20TAPOL%20translation.pdf.

Kornbluh, Peter and Carlos Osorio, eds., " 'Declassified Diplomacy': Argentina." National Security Archive Electronic Briefing Book No. 556, 2016. http://nsarchive.gwu.edu/NSAEBB/NSAEBB556-Obama-administration-declassifies-documents-on-Argentina-military-human-rights-abuses/.

KPP-HAM. *Laporan Penyelidikan Pelanggaran Hak Asasi Manusia di Timor-Leste*. Jakarta: KPP-HAM 2000.

Krishna, Sankaran. "The Moral Economy of Political Assassinations." Paper presented at "Political Violence in South and Southeast Asia," Colombo, LK, April 2007 and Kuala Lumpur, MY, August 2007.

Kumar, Deepa. "Political Islam: A Marxist analysis". *International Socialist Review* 76 (2001).

Lanteigne, Marc. *Chinese Foreign Policy: An Introduction*. London: Routledge Press, 2009.

La'o Hamutuk. *The La'o Hamutuk Bulletin* 11, no. 1–2 (2011). http://www.laohamutuk.org/Bulletin/2010/Feb/bulletinv11n1-2.html#donor.

———. "Letter to the National Procurement Commission of Timor-Leste: Tender ICB/017/MOE-2013 and Chinese Nuclear Industry Construction Company No. 22." 8 October 2013. http://www.laohamutuk.org/Oil/Power/2013/LHCNA-CNI22-8Oct2013.pdf.

Large, Daniel. "China & the Contradictions of 'Non-Interference' in Sudan." *Review of African Political Economy* 35, no. 115 (2008): 93–106. http://www.tandfonline.com/doi/abs/10.1080/03056240802011568?queryID=%24%7BresultBean.queryID%7D#preview.

Leach, Michael. "The Politics of History in Timor-Leste." In *A New Era? Timor-Leste After the UN*, edited by Sue Ingram, Lia Kent, and Andrew McWilliam, 41–58. Acton: Australian National University Press, 2015.

Lee-Koo, Katrina. "Gender at the Crossroad of Conflict: Tsunami and Peace in Post-2005 Aceh." *Feminist Review* 101 (2012): 59–77.

Leith, Denise. *The Politics of Power: Freeport in Suharto's Indonesia*. Honolulu: University of Hawai'i Press, 2003.

Lembaga Studi dan Advokasi Masyarakat (Elsam). *Pulangkan Mereka! Meringkai Ingatan Penghilangan Paksa di Indonesia*. Jakarta: Elsam, 2012.

Levi, Cunding. "Tolikara Pulih Ini Program Pemda untuk Rekonsiliasi." *Tempo*, 3 August 2015. https://m.tempo.co/read/news/2015/08/03/078688688/tolikara-pulih-ini-program-pemda-untuk-rekonsiliasi.

Li, Tania Murray. "Local Histories, Global Markets: Cocoa and Class in Upland Sulawesi." *Development and Change* 33, no. 3 (2002): 415–37.

Liotohe, Wimanjaya K. *Prima Dosa: Wimanjaya dan rakyat Indonesia menggugat imperium Suharto*. Pasar Minggu, ID: Yayasan Eka Fakta Kata, 1993.

Loen, Alexander. "Solidaritas PNS Papua Dukung Gubernor Kembalikan Otsus." *Tabloid Jubi* (Jayapura), 7 March 2016. http://tabloidjubi.com/2016/03/07/solidaritas-asn-papua-dukung-gubernur-kembalikan-otsus.

Lowry, Bob. "After the 2006 Crisis: Australian Interests in Timor-Leste." *Strategic Insights* 38 (2007): 1–16. https://www.aspi.org.au/publications/strategic-insights-38-after-the-2006-crisis-australian-interests-in-timor-leste/SI38_Timor_Leste.pdf.

MacDonald, David. "Five Reasons the TRC Chose 'Cultural Genocide.'" *Globe and Mail* (Toronto) 6 July 2015.

Magalhaes, Fidelis. "Past, Present and Future: Why the Past Matters." In *A New Era? Timor-Leste After the UN*, edited by Sue Ingram, Lia Kent, and Andrew McWilliam, 31–58. Acton: Australian National University Press, 2015.

Maier, Charles S. *The Unmasterable Past: History, Holocaust, and German National Identity*. Cambridge, MA: Harvard University Press, 2009.

Maite, J. Iturre and Carmen Amado Mendes. "Regional Implications of China's Quest for Energy in Latin America." *East Asia* 7, no. 1 (2010): 127–37.

Mambor, Victor. "Kronologis Insiden Tolikara Versi Masyarakat Karubaga." *Tabloid Jubi* (Jayapura) 24 July 2015. http://tabloidjubi.com/2015/07/24/ini-kronologis-insiden-tolikara-versi-masyarakat-karubaga/.

Marquette, Heather and Zoe Scott. "Marrying State-Building and Aid Policy: Civil Partnership or Irreconcilable Differences?" Paper presented at the SGIR 7th Pan-European International Relations Conference, Stockholm, SE, 9–10 September 2010.

Marquette, Heather and Danielle Beswick. "State Building, Security and Development: State Building as a New Development Paradigm?" *Third World Quarterly* 32, no. 10 (2011): 1703–14.

Marx, Karl. *The Eighteenth Brumaire of Louis Bonaparte*. 1852. https://www.marxists.org/archive/marx/works/1852/18th-brumaire/ch01.htm.

McDougall, Debra. *Engaging with Strangers: Love and Violence in the Rural Solomon Islands*. New York: Berghahn, 2016.

McKechnie, Alastair. *Managing Natural Resource Revenues: The Timor-Leste Petroleum Fund*. London: Overseas Development Institute, 2013.

McKenna, K. *Corporate Social Responsibility and Natural Resource Conflict*. New York: Routledge, 2015.

McRae, Dave. *A Few Poorly Organized Men: Interreligious Violence in Poso, Indonesia*. Leiden, NL: Brill, 2013.

Menegazzi, Silvia. "China Reinterprets the Liberal Peace." *Instituto Affari Internazionali Working Papers* 12, no. 30 (December 2012). https://www.ciaonet.org/attachments/22064/uploads.

Mensah, Chaldeans. "China's Foray into Africa: Ideational Underpinnings and Geo-Economic Interests." *African Journal of Political Science and International Relations* 4, no. 3 (2010): 96–108.

Merwe, Hugo van der. "Reconciliation and Justice in South Africa: Lessons from the TRC's Community Interventions." In *Reconciliation, Justice, and Coexistence: Theory and Practice*, edited by Mohammed Abu-Nimer, 187–208. Lanham, MD: Lexington Books, 2001.

———. "The Role of the Church in Promoting Reconciliation in Post-TRC South Africa." In *Religion & Reconciliation in South Africa: Voices of Religious Leaders*, edited by Audrey R. Chapman and Bernard Spong, 269–81. Philadelphia: Templeton Foundation Press, 2003.

Merwe, Hugo van der and Audrey R. Chapman. "Did the TRC Deliver?" In *Truth and Reconciliation in South Africa: Did the TRC Deliver?*, edited by Audrey R. Chapman and Hugo van der Merwe, 241–79. Philadelphia: University of Pennsylvania Press, 2008.

Ministry of Foreign Affairs of the People's Republic of China. "China's Initiation of the Five Principles of Peaceful Co-Existence." 2014. http://www.fmprc.gov.cn/mfa_eng/ziliao_665539/3602_665543/3604_665547/t18053.shtml.

Molnar, Andrea Katalin. *Timor-Leste: Politics, History, and Culture*. New York: Routledge, 2010.

Moon, Claire. *Narrating Political Reconciliation: South Africa's Truth and Reconciliation Commission*. Plymouth, UK: Lexington Books, 2008.

Moore, Clive. *The Happy Isles in Crisis: The Historical Causes for a Failing State in Solomon Islands, 1998–2004*. Canberra, AU: Asia Pacific Press, 2004.

———. "The Misappropriation of Malaita Labour: Historical Origins of the Recent Solomons Islands Crisis." *Journal of Pacific History* 42, no. 2 (2007): 211–32.

Mote, Octovianus. "West Papua's National Awakening." *Tok Blong Pasifik* 55, no. 2 (October 2001): 3–5.

Movanita, Ambaranie Nadia Kemala. "Komnas HAM Temukan Dugaan Pelanggaran HAM dalam Peristiwa Tolikara." *Kompas* (Jakarta) 8 August 2015. http://nasional.kompas.com/read/2015/08/10/11452461/Komnas.HAM.Temukan.Dugaan.Pelanggaran.HAM.dalam.Peristiwa.Tolikara?utm_source=RD&utm_medium=inart&utm_campaign=khiprd.

Munro, Jenny " 'HIV is our Problem Together': Developing an Indigenous-led Response to HIV in Tanah Papua." *In Brief* 5 (2015). Canberra: State, Society and Governance in Melanesia Program, Australian National University.

———. "Jokowi in Papua: Powerless or Duplicitous?" *In Brief* 29 (2015). Canberra: State, Society and Governance in Melanesia Program, Australian National University.

———. " 'Now we Know Shame': *Malu* and Stigma among Highlanders in the Papuan Diaspora." In *From "Stone-Age" to "Real-Time": Exploring Papuan Temporalities, Mobilities and Religiosities*, edited by Martin Slama and Jenny Munro, 169–94. Canberra: Australian National University Press, 2015.

———. "The Violence of Inflated Possibilities: Education, Transformation and Diminishment in Wamena, Papua." *Indonesia* 95 (2013): 25–46.

Munro, J., and L. Butt. "Compelling Evidence: Research Methods, Politics and HIV/AIDS in Papua, Indonesia." *The Asia Pacific Journal of Anthropology* 13, no. 4 (2012): 334–51.

Munro, J. and L. McIntyre. "(Not) Getting Political: Indigenous Women and Preventing Mother-to-Child Transmission of HIV in West Papua." *Culture, Health and Sexuality* 18, no. 2 (2016): 156–70.

Nesiah, Vasuki. "Truth vs. Justice? Commissions and Courts." In *Human Rights & Conflicts: Exploring the Links between Rights, Law, and Peacebuilding*, edited by Julie A. Mertus and Jeffrey W. Helsing, 375–98. Washington, DC: United States Institute of Peace Press, 2006.

Neves, Guteriano. "Timor: Where Has All the Aid Gone?" *Foreign Policy in Focus*, 20 June 2011. http://fpif.org/timor_where_has_all_the_aid_gone/.

Nickson, Ray and John Braithwaite. "Deeper, Broader, Longer Transitional Justice." *European Journal of Criminology* 11, no. 4 (2014): 445–63.

Nolan, C., S. Jones, and Solahudin. "The Political Impact of Carving up Papua." In *Regional Dynamics in a Decentralized Indonesia*, edited by Hal Hill, 409–32. Singapore: Institute of Southeast Asian Studies, 2014.

Norwegian Agency for Development Cooperation. *Review of Development Cooperation in Timor-Leste: Final Report*. Oslo: Norwegian Agency for Development Cooperation, 2007.

Office of the United Nations High Commissioner for Human Rights. *Report of the United Nations Independent Special Commission of Inquiry for Timor-Leste*. Geneva, 2 October 2006. http://www.ohchr.org/Documents/Countries/COITimorLeste.pdf.

Ottendorfer, Eva. "Contesting International Norms of Transitional Justice: The Case of Timor-Leste." *International Journal of Conflict and Violence* 7, no. 1 (2013): 23–35.

Oxfam Australia. "Childhood Malnutrition in Timor-Leste." 2015. https://www.oxfam.org.au/what-we-do/health/food-and-nutrition/childhood-malnutrition-in-timor-leste/.

Paat, Yustinus. "Pemda Bentuk Tim Pemulihan Insiden Tolikara." *BeritaSatu* (Jakarta), 24 July 2015. http://www.beritasatu.com/nasional/293380-pemda-bentuk-tim-pemulihan-insiden-tolikara.html.

Pang, Zhongying. "China's Non-Interference Question." *Global Responsibility to Protect* 1 (2009): 237–52.

"Papuans at U.N. Score Indonesia." *New York Times*, 20 October 1968.

Patey, Luke A. "Against the Asian Tide: The Sudan Divestment Campaign." *Journal of Modern African Studies* 47, no. 4 (2009): 551–73.

Poesponegoro, Marwati Djoened and Nugroho Notosusanto. *Sejarah Nasional Indonesia, VI: Zaman Jepang dan Zaman Republik Indonesia*. Jakarta: Balai Pustaka, 2008.

Quinn, Joanna R. *The Politics of Acknowledgement: Truth Commissions in Uganda and Haiti*. Vancouver: University of British Columbia Press, 2011.

Quinn, Joanna R., ed. *Reconciliation(s): Transitional Justice in Postconflict Societies*. Montreal: McGill-Queen's University Press, 2009.

Ramli, Hamid. "Bakar Batu Sudahi Pertikaian Wamena." *Kompasiana* (Jakarta) 14 June 2012. http://www.kompasiana.com/haramli/bakar-batu-sudahi-pertikaian-wamena_55111145a333110237ba94b9.

Rees, Edward. "Time for the UN to Withdraw from East Timor?" *Atlantic Monthly*, 21 December 2010.

Reid, Anthony. "War, Peace and the Burden of History in Aceh." *Asian Ethnicity* 5, no. 3 (2010): 301–14.

Richmond, Oliver and Ioannis Tellidis. "The BRICS and International Peacebuilding and Statebuilding." *Norwegian Peacebuilding Resource Centre*, 1 February 2013. http://www.peacebuilding.no/Themes/Emerging-powers/Publications/The-BRICS-and-international-peacebuilding-and-statebuilding.

Richmond, Oliver and Jason Franks. "The Emperors' New Clothes? Liberal Peace in East Timor." Paper presented at the Centre for Peace and Conflict Studies, University of St. Andrews, UK, 30 March 2007. http://www.academia.edu/1144446/The_emperors_new_clothes_Liberal_peace_in_East_Timor.

Robins, Simon. "Whose Voices? Understanding Victims' Needs in Transition." *Journal of Human Rights Practice* 1, no. 2 (2009): 320–31.

Robinson, Geoffrey. *The Dark Side of Paradise: Political Violence in Bali*. Ithaca, NY: Cornell University Press, 1995.

———. *East Timor 1999: Crimes against Humanity. A Report Commissioned by the United Nations Office of the High Commissioner for Human Rights*. Jakarta: HAK Association and Institute for Policy Research and Advocacy, 2006.

———. *If You Leave Us Here, We Will Die: How Genocide was Stopped in East Timor*. Princeton, NJ: Princeton University Press, 2010.

Roosa, John. "How Does a Truth Commission Find Out What the Truth Is? The Case of East Timor's CAVR." *Pacific Affairs* 80, no. 4 (2008): 569–80.

———. *Pretext for Mass Murder: The September 30th Movement and Suharto's Coup d'Etat in Indonesia*. Madison: University of Wisconsin Press, 2006.

———. "From the Dark Side" [Review of *Shades of Grey: A Political Memoir of Modern Indonesia, 1965–1998*], by Jusuf Wanandi. *Inside Indonesia*, 5 May 2013. http://www.insideindonesia.org/review-from-the-dark-side.

———. "The State of Knowledge about an Open Secret: Indonesia's Mass Disappearances of 1965–66." *Journal of Asia Studies* 75, no. 2 (2016): 281–97.

Ross, Michael L. "Blood Barrels: Why Oil Wealth Fuels Conflict." *Foreign Affairs* 87, no. 3 (May/June 2008): 2–8.

Rotberg, Robert I. "Apology, Truth Commissions, and Intrastate Conflict." In *Taking Wrongs Seriously: Apologies and Reconciliation*, edited by Elazar Barkan and Alexander Karn, 33–49. Stanford, CA: Stanford University Press, 2006.

Rothfield, Philipa. "Resistance and Reconciliation: Antimonies of Post-Traumatic Justice." In *Trauma, History, Philosophy*, edited by Matthew Sharpe, Murray Noonan, and Jason Freddi, 164–85. Newcastle, UK: Cambridge Scholars Publishing, 2007.

Rutherford, Danilyn. *Laughing at Leviathan: Sovereignty and Audience in West Papua*. Chicago: University of Chicago Press, 2012.

Sampaio, Antonio. "Chineses Querem Comprar Todo o Projeto de Oecussi." *Platforma Macau*, 2015. http://www.plataformamacau.com/lusofonia/timor-leste/chineses-querem-comprar-todo-o-projeto-de-oecussi/.

Sangaji, Arianto. "The Security Forces and Regional Violence in Poso." In *Renegotiating Boundaries: Local Politics in Post-Suharto Indonesia*, edited by Henk Schulte Nordholt and Gerry van Klinken, 255–80. Leiden, NL: KITLV, 2007.

Schaefer, Bernd and Baskara T. Wardaya, eds., *1965: Indonesia and the World / Indonesia dan Dunia*. Jakarta: Gramedia, 2013.

Schaffer, Kay. "Testimony, Nation Building and the Ethics of Witnessing: After the Truth and Reconciliation Commission in South Africa." In *Pathways to Reconciliation: Between Theory and Practice*, edited by Philipa Rothfield, Cleo Fleming, and Paul A. Komesaroff, 89–102. Burlington, VT: Ashgate, 2008.

Scham, Pul, Benjamin Pogrund, and As'ad Ghanem. "Introduction to Shared Narratives: An Israeli-Palestinian Dialogue." *Israel Studies* 18, no. 2 (2013): 1–10.

Scharfe, Sharon. *Complicity: Human Rights and Canadian Foreign Policy, the Case of East Timor*. Montreal: Black Rose Books, 1996.

Schrauwers, Albert. *Colonial "Reformation" in the Highlands of Central Sulawesi, Indonesia, 1892–1995*. Toronto: University of Toronto Press, 2000.

——. " 'Let's Party': State Intervention, Discursive Traditionalism and the Labour Process of Highland Rice Cultivators in Central Sulawesi, Indonesia." *Journal of Peasant Studies* 25, no. 3 (1998): 112–30.

Seddelmeyer, Laura M. *All the Way with LBJ: Australian Grand Strategy and the Vietnam War*. Athens, OH: Ohio University Press, 2009.

Sekretariat Keadilan dan Perdamaian, Keuskupan Jayapura. *Catatan Perkembangan Terkini di Papua: Otonomi Khusus, proses dan hasil akhirnya [Social-Political Note on Recent Developments in Papua: The Special Autonomy Process and Final Results]*. Jayapura, ID: 2001.

Sekretariat Negara Republik Indonesia. *Gerakan 30 September: Pemberontakan Partai Komunis Indonesia, Latar Belakung, Aksi dan Penumpasannya*. Jakarta: Sekretariat Negara Republik Indonesia, 1999.

Shaw, Rosalind. "Memory Frictions: Localizing the Truth and Reconciliation Commission in Sierra Leone." *International Journal of Transitional Justice* 1, no. 2 (2007): 183–207.

Siapno, Jacqueline A. "Brave Women Warriors, Unfinished Revolutions: Political Subjectivities of Women Ex-Falintil and Falintil-FDTL Combatants in East Timor." In *Women Warriors in Southeast Asia*, edited by Vina Lanzona and Tobias Rettig. New York: Routledge, forthcoming.

———. "The Politics of Reconstruction, Gender, and Re-Integration in Post-Tsunami Aceh." In *Tsunami in a Time of War: Aid, Activism and Reconstruction in Sri Lanka and Aceh, Indonesia*, edited by Malathi de Alwis and Eva-Lotta E. Hedman, 163–90. Columbo, LK: International Center for Ethnic Studies, 2009.

Simpson, Bradley R. "Documenting Mass Violence: History, Truth, and Accountability." Paper presented at "Legacies of Violence in Indonesia and East Timor," University of California–Los Angeles, 15 April 2011.

———. *Economists with Guns: Authoritarian Development and U.S.–Indonesian Relations, 1960–1968*. Stanford, CA: Stanford University Press, 2008.

———. "The Indonesia/East Timor Documentation Project." National Security Archive, 28 January 2008. http://nsarchive.gwu.edu/indonesia/.

Simpson, Graeme. " 'Tell No Lies, Claim No Easy Victories': A Brief Evaluation of South Africa's Truth and Reconciliation Commission." In *Commissioning the Past: Understanding South Africa's Truth and Reconciliation Commission*, edited by Deborah Posel and Graeme Simpson, 220–51. Johannesburg, SA: Witwatersand University Press, 2002.

Sitanggang, Poriaman. *Rona Ami-nia Lia: Hear Our Voices*. Dili, TL: CAVR, 2005.

Slama, M. and J. Munro. "From 'Stone-Age' to 'Real-Time': Exploring Papuan Temporalities, Mobilities and Religiosities: An Introduction." In *From "Stone-Age" to "Real-Time": Exploring Papuan Temporalities, Mobilities and Religiosities*, edited by Martin Slama and Jenny Munro, 1–38. Canberra: Australian National University Press, 2015.

Slovo, Gillian. "Truth and Reconciliation in South Africa." *Maisonneuve*, 1 June 2003. http://maisonneuve.org/article/2003/06/1/crime-and-no-punishment/.

Slyomovics, Susan. "Morocco's Justice and Reconciliation Commission." *Middle East Research and Information Project*, 4 April 2005. http://www.merip.org/mero/mero040405.

Smith, Aloys [Rodoplhe de Koninck]. "Timor Oriental devant la conscience de l'humanité." *Le Devoir* (Montreal), 20 December 1991.

Smith, Linda Tuhiwai. *Decolonizing Methodologies*. London: Zed Books, 2012.

Smythe, Patrick A. *"The Heaviest Blow": The Catholic Church and the East Timor Issue*. Münster, DE: LIT Verlag, 2004.

Solomon Islands Truth and Reconciliation Commission. *Confronting the Truth for a Better Solomon Islands: Final Report of the Solomon Islands Truth and Reconciliation Commission*. Honiara, SB: Solomon Islands Truth and Reconciliation Commission, 2012.

Sri Adhiati, Adriana. "Songs of Worries, Songs of Strength." *Down to Earth Special Edition Newsletter* 89–90 (November 2011): 23–5. www.downtoearth-indonesia.org/story/dte-newsletter-89-90-full-edition-download.

Subotic, Jelena. "The Transformation of International Transitional Justice Advocacy." *International Journal of Transitional Justice* 6, no. 1 (2012): 106–15.

Timor-Leste, Government of. "Address by His Excellency the Prime Minister and Minister of Defence and Security Kay Rala Xanana Gusmao at the Inauguration of the Building of the Defence and F-FDTL Headquarters." Press release, 3 April 2012. http://timor-leste.gov.tl/wp-content/uploads/2012/04/Inauguration-of-the-MD-and-F-FDTL-Headquarters-3.4.12.pdf.

Timor-Leste, Government of. "Guinea-Bissau 'Thanks for the Support and Help of Timor-Leste.' " Press release, 8 April 2014. http://timor-leste.gov.tl/?p=9942&lang=en.

Timor-Leste, Government of. "Mission of Support to the Electoral Process in Guinea-Bissau Completes its First Phase." Press release, 21 February 2014. http://timor-leste.gov.tl/?p=9743&lang=en. *Timor Post* (Dili). "Xina apoiu miliaun 13 ba dezenvolvimentu Timor-Leste." 15 September 2015.

Torpey, John, ed. *Politics and the Past*. Lanham, MD: Rowman & Littlefield, 2003.

Truth and Reconciliation Commission of Canada. *Honouring the Truth, Reconciling for the Future. Summary of the Final Report of the Truth and Reconciliation Commission of Canada*. Winnipeg, MB: TRC Canada, 2015.

United Nations. *Report of the International Commission of Inquiry on East Timor*. New York: United Nations, January 2000.

———. *Situation of Human Rights in East Timor*. New York: United Nations, December, 1999.

United Nations Development Programme. *Human Development Report 1996*. New York: Oxford University Press, 1996.

United Nations Population Fund. "Timor-Leste, Democratic Republic of." 8 February 2010. http://countryoffice.unfpa.org/timor-leste/2009/11/02/1482/timor-leste_democratic_republic_of/.

United Nations Secretary-General. "UN Secretary-General Briefing to the Security Council on Visit to Southeast Asia." Speech, New York, 29 February 2000.

United Nations Security Council. "Summary of the Report to the Secretary-General of the Commission of Experts to Review the Prosecution of Serious Violations of Human Rights in Timor-Leste (then East Timor) in 1999." New York: May 2006.

Van Klinken, Gerry. *Communal Violence and Democratization in Indonesia: Small Town Wars.* London: Routledge Contemporary Southeast Asia Series, 2009.

Vella, Louise. "Translating Transitional Justice: The Solomon Islands Truth and Reconciliation Commission." SSGM Discussion Paper 2014/2, Australian National University. http://ssgm.bellschool.anu.edu.au/experts-publications/publications/1257/translating-transitional-justice-solomon-islands-truth-and.

———. " 'What Will You Do with Our Stories?' Truth and Reconciliation in the Solomon Islands." *International Journal of Conflict and Violence* 8 no. 1 (2014): 91–103.

Wanandi, Jusuf. *Shades of Grey: A Political Memoir of Modern Indonesia, 1965–1998.* Jakarta: Equinox, 2012.

Webster, David. "Canadian Catholics and the East Timor Struggle, 1975–99." *Historical Studies* 75 (2009): 63–82

———. "History, Nation and Narrative in East Timor's Truth Commission Report." *Pacific Affairs* 80, no. 4 (2008): 581–91.

———. "Self-fulfilling Prophecies and Human Rights in Canada's Foreign Policy: The Case of East Timor." *International Journal* 65, no. 3 (2010): 739–50.

Weldemichael, Awet Tewelde. *Third World Colonialism and Strategies of Liberation: Eritrea and East Timor Compared.* Cambridge: Cambridge University Press, 2013.

West Papua Advocacy Team. "West Papua Report November 2007." http://www.etan.org/issues/wpapua/0711wpap.htm#forests.

West Papua Observer. "Like Thorn in Flesh is Free Papua Movement to Indonesian Colonial Government." *West Papua Observer* 3, no. 2 (December 1977–January 1978).

Westad, Odd Arne, Chen Jian, Stein Tonnesson, Nguyen Vu Tungand, and James G. Hershberg, eds. "77 Conversations between Chinese and Foreign Leaders on the Wars in Indochina, 1964–1977." Cold War International History Project Working Paper No. 22, Woodrow Wilson International Center for Scholars, Washington, DC, May 1998. https://www.wilsoncenter.org/sites/default/files/ACFB39.pdf.

Widjojo, Muridan S. "Negotiating the Past and Looking to the Future." *Inside Indonesia* 98 (October–December 2009). http://www.insideindonesia.org/negotiating-the-past-and-looking-to-the-future .

———, ed. *Papua Road Map: Negotiating the Past, Improving the Present and Securing the Future*. Jakarta: Lembaga Ilmu Pengetahuan Indonesia, 2008.

Wilde, Ralph. "Colonialism Redux? Territorial Administration by International Organizations, Colonial Echoes and the Legitimacy of the 'International.' " In *State-Building: Theory and Practice*, edited by Aidan Hehir and Neil Robinson, 29–49. New York: Routledge, 2007.

Wilson, Richard. *The Politics of Truth and Reconciliation in South Africa: Legitimizing the Post-Apartheid State*. New York: Cambridge University Press, 2001.

Wospakrik, Martha M. with Christy Reed. " 'The Woman Who Loves': Women as Guardians of Peace and Weavers of Life in Biak, Papua." In *Creating the Third Force: Indigenous Processes of Peacemaking*, edited by Hamdesa Tuso and Maureen P. Flaherty, 411–32. Lanham, MD: Lexington, 2016.

Zhou, Taomo. "Ambivalent Alliance: Chinese Policy towards Indonesia, 1960–1965." Cold War International History Project Working Paper No. 67, Woodrow Wilson International Center for Scholars, Washington, DC, August 2013. https://www.wilsoncenter.org/sites/default/files/CWIHP_Working_Paper_67_Chinese_Policy_towards_Indonesia_1960-1965.pdf.

Zifcak, Spencer. "Restorative Justice in Timor-Leste: the Truth and Reconciliation Commission." *Development Bulletin* 68 (2005): 51–54.

Zurbuchen, Mary S., ed. *Beginning to Remember: The Past in the Indonesian Present*. Singapore: Singapore University Press, 2005.

Index

A

Aboriginal. *See* Indigenous
ACbit (*Chega!* for Us association), 15, 44, 121–23, 314, 315
accountability. *See* impunity and accountability
Aceh, 7, 12, 17, 163, 164, 165, 167–84, 202, 203, 269, 311, 313, 314, 316, 317
    Helsinki Memorandum of Understanding, 7, 17, 165, 172, 173, 175, 177, 183n24, 313, 317
    Law for Governing of Aceh (LoGA), 168, 176, 183n24
    Peace Reintegration Agency (BRA), 172, 176
    Qanun (provincial legislation), 168, 169, 174
    tsunami, 2004 Indian Ocean earthquake and, 165, 176
    See also Bener Mariah, Aceh, Indonesia; Free Aceh Movement (GAM); Gayo people; militias: pro-Indonesia in Aceh; truth commission: Aceh (KKR)
Adat. See Indigenous traditions
African National Congress 29, 32
aid. *See* development
AIDS. *See* HIV/AIDS
Aidit, D.N. 148
AJAR. *See* Asia Justice and Rights
Ajikwa River, 266
Alkatiri, Mari, 50, 51, 53, 95
Alomang, Yosepha, 4, 247

Ambarita, Banjir, 253
Ambon. *See* Maluku
amnesties, 28, 29, 53, 55, 67, 70, 168, 175, 288
Amnesty International, 55, 263
Amungme people, 247, 265, 311
Anglican Church, 19, 31, 281, 283, 284, 285, 286, 299, 301, 306
    See also Ata, Father Sam; MacDonald, Bishop Mark; Mamakwa, Bishop Lydia; Tutu, Bishop Desmond
Annan, Kofi, 61n20
Ap, Arnold, 233, 234, 237–40, 243, 244, 245–47
APEC. *See* Asia Pacific Economic Cooperation
apologies, 27, 64, 139, 140, 174, 223, 313, 320
Arafura Sea, 266
Araújo, Fernando La Sama, 82, 88, 89, 90n8
Araújo, Rui Maria de, 73, 74, 95
archives, 70, 73, 129, 148, 149, 151, 152, 153, 300, 301, 320, 321
Argentina, 321
ASEAN. *See* Association of Southeast Asian Nations
Asia Justice and Rights (AJAR), 71, 73, 74, 121, 314, 315
Asia Pacific Economic Cooperation (APEC), 64
Asian Development Bank, 94

345

Association of Southeast Asian Nations (ASEAN), 97
Astra Agro Lestari, 189
Ata, Father Sam, 286, 290, 293
Augustine, Stephen, 310
Australia, 46, 47, 56, 64, 85, 94, 97, 101, 103, 113, 148, 276, 280, 282, 284, 321

B

Bakar batu (Papuan Indigenous feast), 218–20
Bali, 110, 132, 133, 140, 237
Barreto Soares, Abé, 1, 4
Belo, Bishop Carlos Ximenes, 110, 112, 113, 114
Benedict XVI, Pope, 114
Bener Mariah, Aceh, Indonesia, 167, 177, 178
Bennett, Carolyn, 307
Bere, Maternus, 45, 55, 59
Biak people, 235, 241, 242, 243
Black Brothers (musical group), 247
Bougainville, 281, 291n4
BRA. *See* Aceh: Peace Reintegration Agency
Brazil, 101, 102
Bridie, David, 245, 253
Briere, Elaine, 110
Buddhism, 214
Burma, 284, 315
Busby, Scott, 262
Bush, George W., 57, 267, 268
business networks and corporations, 3–4, 19, 87, 88, 133, 134, 137, 213, 227, 264, 269, 270, 306, 311

C

Cambodia, 6, 13, 110
Canada, 63, 64, 65, 113, 287, 299–307
    Department of Indian Affairs, 305, 307
    Indian Act, 300
    Indonesia, policy towards, 307
    Timor-Leste, policy towards, 64, 74, 94, 109, 307
    Residential schools system, 9, 20, 65, 299, 300, 301, 302, 304, 305, 318

    truth and reconciliation, global involvement, 307
    See also Bennett, Carolyn; Canada-Asia Working Group; Canadian Catholic Organization for Development and Peace; Canadian International Development Agency; Harper, Stephen; Iacobucci, Frank; KAIROS; National Centre for Truth and Reconciliation (Canada); Scott, Duncan Campbell; Shortliffe, Glen; Sinclair, Murray; truth commission: Canada (TRC); Wilson-Raybould, Jody
Canada-Asia Working Group, 63
Canadian Catholic Organization for Development and Peace, 10, 15, 109, 110, 112, 114
Canadian International Development Agency, 65
Caritas Australia, 113
Carouso, James, 262
cassette tapes, 239–40
Catholic Church, 15, 43, 47, 109–15, 214, 215, 281, 282, 283, 284, 301, 316
    See also Belo, Bishop Carlos Ximenes; Benedict XVI, Pope; Canadian Catholic Organization for Development and Peace; Caritas Australia; Catholic Youth Association (Papua); Costa Lopes, Martinho da; Domingo, Father; Erminia, Sister; Francis, Pope; Geve, Father Augustine; Indonesian Bishops Conference (KWI); Madeira, Father Hilario; Nascimiento, Bishop Basilio do; Silva, Bishop Ricardo da; Quevedo, Cardinal Orlando; Roche, Father Jim; Smith, Bishop Adrian; Vatican II reforms
Catholic Youth Association (Papua), 216
CAVR. *See* truth commission: Timor-Leste
censorship, 88, 131, 237, 238

Central Highlands Legal Advocacy and Human Rights Network (Papuan NGO), 216
Centre for Strategic and International Studies, 74
Centro Nacional *Chega!* Timor-Leste, 14, 74, 314, 315
Chega! See truth commission: Timor-Leste
Chega! for Us. *See* ACbit
children, 89, 96, 120, 216, 243, 250, 253, 275, 282, 290, 293, 300
China, 16, 43, 98, 270
   foreign ministry, 148, 149
   Indonesia, involvement in, 129, 146, 149–51
   Timor-Leste, aid to 94, 101–4
Christianity, 15, 17, 31, 165, 185, 188, 214, 215, 217, 275, 276, 283, 316
   See also Anglican Church; Catholic Church; Dutch Reformed Church; Evangelical Church of Indonesia (GIDI); Indonesian Bishops Conference (KWI); KAIROS; Presbyterian Church; Seventh Day Adventists; Solomon Islands Christian Association; United Church (Canada); South Sea Evangelical Church; United Church (Solomon Islands)
Church of Melanesia. *See* Anglican Church
CIA. *See* United States: Central Intelligence Agency
civil society, 9, 10, 11, 12, 15, 18, 43, 44, 111, 112, 113, 123, 128, 138, 141, 163, 164, 165, 173, 179, 207, 210, 217, 227, 263, 270, 275, 276, 309, 314–15, 316, 319, 321
clandestinity, 43, 80–89, 320
   definition of, 80–1
class analysis, 186–89, 192–96
Clinton, Bill, 55, 57, 268
Clinton, Hillary, 103
CNRT. *See* National Council of Timorese Resistance (resistance coalition);

National Congress for Timorese Reconstruction (political party)
Cohen, Leonard, 4, 63
Cold War, 147, 148–51, 152, 187
Colombia, 73
colonialism and colonization, 7, 14, 15, 42, 43, 48, 79, 80, 82, 84, 85, 100, 164, 186, 201, 202, 234, 235, 236, 249, 252, 302, 304, 307, 311, 317, 318, 320
Comarca. *See* monuments and museums
   See also truth commission: Timor-Leste
Commission on Reception, Truth and Reconciliation (CAVR). *See* truth commission: Timor-Leste
Commission on Truth and Friendship. *See* truth commission: Timor-Leste and Indonesia bilateral
Community of Portuguese-Speaking Countries, 97
Conference of the New Emerging Forces (CONEFO), 150
Congresso Nacional de Reconstrução de Timor (CNRT), *See* National Congress for Timorese Reconstruction
Conselho Nacional de Resistência Timorense (CNRT), *See* National Council of Timorese Resistance
Convention on the Elimination of All Forms of Discrimination Against Women, 84, 120
corruption, 47, 53, 80, 85, 87, 88, 99, 114, 210, 269
corporations. *See* business networks and corporations.
Costa Lopes, Martinho da, 111
Costa Rica, 72
Crowshoe, Reg, 311
CTF. *See* truth commission: Timor-Leste and Indonesia bilateral
Cuba, 97

D

Darul Islam, 164
Democratic party (Timor-Leste), 103
   See also Araújo, Fernando
democratization, 87, 99, 102, 114, 163, 267, 268, 269, 313

development, 14, 16, 70, 71, 82, **93–108**, 120, 187, 203, 207, 208, 211, 212, 213, 226, 243, 264, 305, 311, 312
  See also Canadian International Development Agency; development models; g7+ forum; HIVOS (Dutch development agency); Pacific Development Forum; United Nations: Development Programme (UNDP); United Nations: Special Development Goals
Development and Peace. *See* Canadian Catholic Organization for Development and Peace
development models
  Chinese, 14, 101–4
  Western, 14, 100
dialogue, 8, 9, 19, 83, 87, 112, 141, 201, 202, 215, 275, 317
Dili, Timor-Leste, 4, 5, 15, 45, 49, 51, 65, 98, 101, 103, 110, 111, 268
Domingo, Father, 110
Dutch Reformed Church, 31, 236

E

economic rights. *See* human rights: economic, social, and cultural
East Nusa Tenggara. *See* Nusa Tenggara Timur
East Timor. *See* Timor-Leste
East Timor Alert Network, 63, 110
education, 74, 93, 96, 98, 113, 120, 207, 211, 267, 290, 307, 320
elders, 67, 242, 310–11
Eluay, Theys, 252
environment, 18, 203, 206, 225–26, 227, 245, 254, 265–66, 269, 303, 310, 311, 316
Erminia, Sister, 55
Eritrea, 89
"ethnic" conflicts, 7, 17, 166, 185, 186, 187, 196, 223, 276, 282, 283, 288, 291n1, 295
European Union, 94

Evangelical Church of Indonesia (GIDI), 221–22, 223
exhumation, 289, 290, 294, 295

F

Falintil. *See* Timor-Leste: army
Fals, Iwan, 237
Fiji, 276, 281, 282, 285, 294
Ford, Gerald, 46
forests, 193, 225, 264, 265, 302
France, 64, 101, 148, 318
Francis, Pope, 114, 178
Free Aceh Movement (GAM), 7, 163, 164, 165, 167, 168, 171, 172, 173, 175, 177
Free Papua Movement (OPM), 205, 208
Freeport (mining company), 247, 265–66, 269, 311
forgiveness, 25, 26, 32, 35, 179, 285, 319, 322
Fretilin (Timorese political party), 49, 50, 51, 66, 103
  See also Alkatiri, Mari

G

g7+ forum, 97
Gadjah Mada University, 140, 141
GAM. *See* Free Aceh Movement
Gandhi, Mohandas, 234
Games of the New Emerging Forces (GANEFO), 150
Gates, Robert, 59
Gayo people, 177–79
genocide, 6, 46, 53, 56, 60n3, 233, 254, 262, 267, 300, 305, 318, 321
Germany, 94, 148
Geve, Father Augustine, 281
GIDI. *See* Evangelical Church of Indonesia
Goethe Institute, 151
Guadalcanal, Solomon Islands, 275, 276, 279, 280, 281, 282, 283, 284, 285, 288, 289, 293, 295, 311
Guadalcanal Liberation Front, 281, 282
Guadalcanal Revolutionary Army. *See* Isatabu Freedom Movement
  See also Keke, Harold
Guinea-Bissau, 97

Gusmão, Kay Rala Xanana, 45, 50, 51, 52, 53, 54, 55, 61n11, 66, 82, 95
Guterres, Eurico, 57
Guterres, Isabel, 319
Guterres Lopes, Aniceto, 319

H

Habibie, B.J., 128, 137, 214
Haiti, 97
Haiti, Badrodin, 195
Harper, Stephen, 114
healing, 5, 15, 24, 27, 115, 129, 173, 215, 275, 295, 302, 304, 305, 309, 312, 314, 317, 318, 320
health, 93, 96–97, 98, 114, 120, 141, 207, 264, 267, 290
Hinduism, 214
historical narratives, 6, 8, 9, 10–11, 12, 13, 20, 23, 29, 30, 34, 35, 36, 68–69, 71, 74, 128, 134–35, 146, 147, 170, 171, 173, 179, 196, 202, 203, 204, 207–10, 212, 214, 237, 304–5, 309, 313, 316–18, 320–21
history, 122, 123, 139, 206, 215, 302, 317
  oral, 146
HIV/AIDS, 202, 207, 209, 216
HIVOS (Dutch development agency), 121
Honduras, 268
Honelama, Papua, Indonesia, 216–20, 223
Honiara, Solomon Islands, 276, 279, 280, 282, 283, 284, 285, 286, 312
Hughes, Jen, 2
human rights, 10, 11, 13, 29, 30, 33, 35, 44, 54, 60, 68, 69, 72, 84, 100, 102, 117–20, 140, 146, 172, 174, 202, 203, 206, 210, 212, 213, 215, 223, 224, 225, 226, 262, 263, 267, 268, 269, 275, 284, 285, 287, 288, 290, 295, 319, 320
  crimes against humanity, 53, 54, 55, 57, 58, 60, 70, 118
  culture of, 73
  economic, social, and cultural rights, 33, 70, 118, 119, 311–12, 318

massacres and mass violence, 2, 3, 7, 8, 12, 13, 16, 41, 42, 44, 45, 58, 60n3, 69, 127, 133, 134, 148, 152, 262, 263, 268, 321
torture, 4, 69, 132, 133, 168, 213, 265, 275, 282, 284, 285, 288, 290, 295
See also ACbit; Amnesty International; Asia Justice and Rights; Human Rights Watch; TAPOL (Indonesian human rights campaign); United Nations: High Commissioner for Human Rights
Human Rights Watch, 263

I

Iacobucci, Frank, 301
impunity and accountability, 13, 44, 46, 53, 57, 59, 60, 70, 71, 85, 168, 174, 206, 269, 312, 314, 316, 319, 320
Inco, 189, 193
India, 86, 101, 102, 150
Indigenous peoples, 9, 10, 20, 31, 177–79, 212, 216, 220, 222, 224, 227, 263, 279, 302, 303, 305–7, 310, 315
Indigenous rights, 4, 204, 316
Indigenous traditions, 3, 18, 165, 169, 170, 219, 223, 275, 283, 294, 309, 310. See also *Bakar batu* (Papuan Indigenous feast)
Indonesia, 6, 7, 11, 16, 41, 45, 47, 48, 49, 50, 53, 59, 64, 70, 71, 73, 85, 98, 105, **127–271**, 299, 301, 306, 309, 311, 312, 316, 317, 319, 321
  ad-hoc human rights court, 57
  army (TNI), 57, 59, 70, 94, 110, 127, 128, 129, 132, 136, 139, 145, 147, 148, 149, 150, 152, 153, 163, 164, 166, 167, 173, 174, 177, 178, 185, 190, 191, 192, 202, 206, 211, 212, 213, 216, 217, 218, 220, 222, 223, 229n17, 243, 261, 265, 269, 270, 321
  coup and mass violence (1965), 12, 13, 16, 73, **127–54**, 163, 167, 170, 186, 196, 304, 316
  decentralization, 163, 208, 212, 213

Index 349

economic crisis (1998), 187
education system, 74, 179
migration and transmigration within Indonesia, 177, 188, 193–94, 195, 208, 209, 210, 262, 267 (*See also* Javanese settlers outside Java)
Ministry of culture and human development, 141
Ministry of home affairs, 221
Military operations zones, 164, 210
National Human Rights Commission (Komnas-HAM), 139, 141, 146, 182n16, 222
National Police (PNI), 174, 190, 191, 192, 195, 206, 212, 213, 218, 222, 223, 265
Territorial integrity 163, 208
See also Aidit, D.N.; Centre for Strategic and International Studies; Darul Islam; Evangelical Church of Indonesia (GIDI); Habibie, B.J.; Indonesia East Timor Program; Indonesian Bishops Conference (KWI); Indonesian Communist Party (PKI); Indonesian National Institute of Sciences (LIPI); Jemaah Islamiyah; Kalimantan (Borneo); Kopassus; Laskar Jihad; Laskar Jundullah; Murtopo, Ali; militias: pro-Indonesia; militias: pro-Indonesia in Timor-Leste; militias: Sulawesi; Mujahidin Indonesia Timur; Nahdatul Ulama; Nusa Tenggara Timur; Pancasila; Palu; Poso; September 30 Movement; Suharto; Sukarno; Sukarnoputri, Megawati; Sulawesi; Surakarta (Solo); TAPOL (Indonesian human rights campaign); Thukul, Wiji; United States: Indonesia; United States-Indonesia Society (USINDO); Untung; Wahid, Abdurrahman; Wanandi, Jusuf; Wibowo, Sarwo Edhie; Wiranto; Yudhoyono, Susilo Bambang

Indonesia East Timor Program, 63
Indonesian Bishops Conference (KWI), 111, 112
Indonesian Communist Party (PKI), 7, 16, 127, 128, 129, 132, 134, 135, 136, 138, 140, 145, 146, 147, 148, 151, 152, 155, 196
Indonesian National Institute of Sciences (LIPI), 215
inequality, 33, 85, 88, 114, 166, 193, 302
International Center for Transitional Justice, 44, 122, 314
International Coalition for Papua, 263
International Court of Justice, 98
international criminal tribunals, 6, 13, 26, 42, 57, 299, 321
   Timor-Leste, proposed, 54, 55–56, 57, 59
International People's Tribunal, 140
internet, 19, 71, 84, 221, 253, 275, 287, 289, 290, 304
ISIS. *See* Islamic State of Iraq and Syria
Islam, 7, 17, 137, 164, 165, 178, 194, 195, 209, 214, 220, 221, 283, 316
   See also Darul Islam; Islamic State of Iraq and Syria (ISIS); Jemaah Islamiyah; Laskar Jihad; Laskar Jundullah; Nahdatul Ulama; Mujahidin Indonesia Timur
Islamic State of Iraq and Syria (ISIS), 185, 195
Isatabu Freedom Movement (Solomon Islands militia), 280, 281, 282, 283, 289
   See also Keke, Harold

J

Jakarta, 114, 128, 132, 148, 150, 151, 212, 267
Japan, 49, 94, 236, 276
Java, 132, 133, 141, 186, 237
Javanese settlers outside Java, 177, 178, 179, 193, 227.
Jayapura, Papua, Indonesia, 222
Jayawijaya Women's Voice Foundation, 216
Jemaah Islamiyah, 185, 190, 191, 194, 195

justice
    reparative, 320 (*See also* apologies; reparations)
    restorative, 5, 6, 26–27, 29, 32, 35, 53, 320 (*See also* truth and reconciliation commissions
    retributive, 5, 6, 25, 26–27, 35, 42, 320, 321 (*See also* international criminal tribunals)
    rule of law, 46, 47, 56, 60, 100, 102, 118

K

KAIROS (Canadian ecumenical justice coalition), 10, 305
Kalimantan (Borneo), 164, 187, 264
Kamoro people, 265
Kanaky/New Caledonia 276, 281
Kapissa, Sam, 244
Karma, Filep, 242, 244
Karubaga, Papua, Indonesia, 221–24
Kastom. See Indigenous traditions
Kejoa, Geoge, 294
Keke, Harold, 281, 282, 283
Kemakeza, Allan, 281
Kissinger, Henry, 46
Kohen, Arnold, 113
Komisi Kebenaran dan Rekonsiliasi. *See* truth commission: Aceh
Komnas-HAM. *See* Indonesia: National Human Rights Commission
Kondologit, Edo 233, 250, 253–54
Kopassus, 48, 59, 60, 132, 139, 192, 265
Koreri millennial event, 235–36, 241, 242
KKR. *See* truth commission: Aceh
Kuwait, 101
KWI. *See* Indonesian Bishops Conference

L

land. *See* environment
land alienation, 188, 276, 279, 293, 311
La'o Hamutuk (Timorese NGO), 94
Laore, Carol, 289, 294
Laskar Jihad, 194
Laskar Jundullah, 194
Latief, Abdul, 132
Lautem, Timor-Leste, 54
Lilo, Gordon Darcy, 285, 286–87, 295

LIPI. *See* Indonesian National Institute of Sciences
Lobato, Rogerio, 51
LoGA. *See* Aceh: Law for Governing of Aceh
Lulik. See Indigenous traditions

M

MacDonald, Bishop Mark, 306
Macher, Sofia, 293
Madeira, Father Hilario, 2
Madraiwiwi, Ratu Joni, 294
Malaita, Solomon Islands, 19, 275, 276, 279, 280, 281, 282, 283, 284, 285, 288, 289, 293
Malaitan Eagle Force, 280, 281, 282, 283, 285, 289
Malaysia, 150, 194, 262
Maluku, Indonesia (Moluccas), 163–64, 187
Mamakwa, Bishop Lydia, 306
Mao Zedong, 145, 149
Malino Accord, 190, 192, 194, 196
Mambor, Victor, 222
Manufandu, Angganeka, 234–36, 240, 241, 242, 243, 244, 247, 248, 250, 251
Marcos, Ferdinand, 111, 113
Marques, Joni, 54
Masoka, Aristoteles, 252
massacres. *See* human rights: massacres and mass violence
media. *See* press
Melanesia, 6, 8, 11, 13, 18, 19, 275, 276, 296, 309
Melanesian Spearhead Group, 215, 276
memory and memorialization, 9, 12, 73, 74, 84, 127, 129, 135, 167, 173, 179, 238, 275, 302, 312, 313, 316, 317, 320
    See also monuments and museums
militarized masculinities, 90n4, 91n9
militias
    pro-Indonesia in Aceh 178
    pro-Indonesia in Timor-Leste 2, 45, 48–49, 52, 54, 58, 67, 70
    Solomon Islands 275, 276, 280, 281, 282, 283, 286, 288, 289 (*See also* Guadalcanal Liberation Front;

Isatabu Freedom Movement; Malaitan Eagle Force)
Sulawesi, 185, 190, 191, 194–95, 196
Yugoslavia, 321
Millennium Development Goals. *See* United Nations: Special Development Goals
mining companies. *See* natural resources and extractive capitalism
Mofu, Eddy, 240
Montreal, 110
monuments and museums, 2
   Archives and Museum of the Timorese Resistance, *81*
   Comarca, Dili, Timor-Leste, 4, *5*, 64, 65, 66, 74
   Liquica, Timor-Leste, *3*
   Museum Bergerak, Indonesia, 141
   Suai, Timor-Leste, 2
Moro National Liberation Front, 83
Morocco, 316
mourning, 71, 84, 90n6, 251
Mpur people, 225–26
Mujahidin Indonesia Timur, 191, 192, 195
Murtopo, Ali, 74
music. *See* songs
Myanmar. *See* Burma

N

Nahdatul Ulama, 137, 139
Nascimiento, Bishop Basilio do, 110
National Centre for Truth and Reconciliation (Canada), 304
National Congress for Timorese Reconstruction (CNRT), 50, 61n5, 103
   See also Gusmão, Kay Rala Xanana
National Council of Timorese Resistance (CNRT), 54, 55, 60n5
National Security Archive, 321
natural resources and extractive capitalism, 4, 164, 166, 189, 202, 203, 207, 208, 209, 226, 264, 279, 307, 311
Netherlands, 140, 164, 201, 208, 247, 318
New Caledonia. *See* Kanaky
New Guinea. *See* Papua
New Zealand, 282, 285
nickel mining. *See* Inco

Non-Aligned Movement, 150
non-governmental organizations. *See* civil society
"non-truth," 204, 205, 206, 320
non-violence, 234, 248, 249
Norway, 96, 104, 264
Nusa Tenggara Timur, 141, 193

O

Obama, Barack, 267, 268, 321
Oecusse, Timor-Leste, 97, 104
official truths. *See* truths, official
oil, 47, 96, 97, 105, 264, 306, 307
OPM. *See* Free Papua Movement

P

Pacific Development Forum, 97
Pacific Islands Forum, 215, 276
Pacific Peoples' Partnership, 10, 307
palm oil, 189, 264, 279
Pancasila, 132, 134
Palu, Indonesia, 190–91
Papua, 7, 8, 11, 12, 13, 18, 19, 21n14, 86, 87, 163, **201–71**, 275, 276, 281, 303, 310, 311, 316, 317
   "act of free choice," 202, 209
   "development approach," 201, 211, 212–13
   independence aspirations, 7, 8, 201, 202, 203, 205, 208, 209, 210, 211, 213–15, 242, 270
   "security approach," 201, 213, 270
   separation of Papua and West Papua provinces, 18, 21–22n14, 201, 212
   special autonomy, 8, 201, 202–3, 211–12, 214, 250, 267, 312, 317
   See also Alomang, Yosepha; Ap, Arnold; Biak people; Catholic Youth Association (Papua); Central Highlands Legal Advocacy and Human Rights Network (Papuan NGO); Eluay, Theys; Free Papua Movement (OPM); Freeport (mining company); International Coalition for Papua; Kamoro people; Kapissa, Sam; Karubaga, Papua, Indonesia; Kondologit,

Edo; *Koreri* millennial event; Manufandu, Angganeka; Masoka, Aristoteles; Melanesia; Mofu, Eddy; Mpur people; Papua New Guinea; Papua Original (musical group); Papua Peace Network; Papuan National Congress; Tebey, Neles; Telek, George; Wenda, Benny; United Liberation Movement of West Papua; West Papua National Committee
Papua New Guinea, 276, 281, 282
Papua Original (musical group), 253
Papua Peace Network, 215
Papuan National Congress, 213
peace, culture of, 15, 24, 72, 115, 214–15
  See also non-violence
peacebuilding, 67, 72, 87, 99–104, 109–15
peacekeeping 42, 103, 105
perpetrators 13, 26, 27, 28, 29, 30, 34, 36, 41, 42, 44, 48, 57, 58, 61n20, 67, 68, 71, 119, 146, 151, 168, 170, 171, 178, 191, 193, 194, 217, 218, 227, 290, 295, 301, 302, 304, 312, 313, 318, 319, 320
Peru 285, 294
Philippines, 15, 83, 98, 111, 113, 194, 284
  See also Marcos, Ferdinand; Moro National Liberation Front; Quevedo, Cardinal Orlando
phases of truth-seeking, 11, 12, 129, 164, 165, 170, 203, 314, 316
PKI. *See* Indonesian Communist Party
PNI. *See* Indonesia: National Police
Pogo, Ellison, 284
Poso, Indonesia, 164, 165, 166, **185–98**, 203, 311
political prisoners, 4, 17, 89n1, 112, 136, 138, 155–60, 168, 251
Portugal, 49, 85, 94, 97, 98
poverty, 14, 89, 98, 114, 119, 120, 187, 192–96, 202, 211, 213, 233, 318
Presbyterian Church, 301
press, 47, 80, 87, 88, 249, 252–53, 262, 263
prisoners. *See* political prisoners
propaganda, 74, 84, 85, 132, 135, 146
psychology, 82, 87

PT PN XIV (Indonesian corporation), 189, 193, 194

Q

Qaeda, al, 185, 191, 194
Quevedo, Cardinal Orlando, 113

R

racism, 227, 233, 243, 302
radio, 129
Ramos Horta, José, 52, 53, 54, 95
RAMSI. *See* Regional Assistance Mission to Solomon Islands
reconciliation, 9, 14, 17, 18, **23–36**, 53, 54, 55, 59, 71, 84, 105, 111, 112, 138, 164, 172, 173, 180, 196, 204, 269, 285, 287, 293, 302, 309, 311, 316, 319, 322
  attitudes of Christian churches, 31, 301
  business and, 306, 311
  community reconciliation ceremonies, 67, 169–70, 310, 313
  education and, 10, 68, 71, 72, 73, 113, 122, 123, 171, 173, 179, 305
  Indigenous and non-Western models, 25, 33, 34, 66–67, 169, 170, 206, 207, 219, 224–26, 227–28, 288, 289, 304, 310, 311
  international aspects of, 42, 56–60, 64–66, 129, 153, 203, 206, 321–22
  state-sponsored forms, 130, 166, 185, 190, 207, 210–12, 216–24, 310, 319
  women and, 2, 10, 19, 69, 121, 184n40, 275, 276, 294–96
Regional Assistance Mission to Solomon Islands (RAMSI), 276, 282, 285, 288
Reinado, Alfredo, 51, 52
Reis, Filomena dos, 2
remembrance. *See* memory
reparations, 29, 65, 70, 73, 118–19, 170, 172, 174, 175–77, 180, 316, 320, 321
repertoires of violence, 48, 49
reserve army of labour, 186, 189, 193, 194
Riwu, Marinus, 193, 194
Roche, Father Jim, 2
Rodrigues, Roque, 51

Index   353

Roma (musicians), 237
Ruak, Taur Matan, 101
rule of law. *See* justice: rule of law
Russia, 101, 102
Rwanda, 6, 13

S

Salsinha, Gastão, 52
Samoa, 282
Santoso, 191, 192, 195
scholars, role of, 88–89, 90n4
Scott, Duncan Campbell, 305
September 30 Movement, 132, 136, 137
Seventh Day Adventists, 283, 284
sexual violence. *See* violence against women
Shortliffe, Glen, 64
Sierra Leone, 6
silence, 16, 19, 59, 79, 80, 82, 84, 85, 88, 127, 128, 129, 136, 139, 172, 266, 313, 319
Silva, Bishop Ricardo da, 110
Silva, Dominggus da, 193
Simanjuntak, Lina, 250
Sinatra, Frank, 252
Sinar Mas, 189
Sinclair, Murray, 10, 22n15
Singapore, 95, 100, 194
  National University of, 138
SITRC. *See* truth commission: Solomon Islands
Smith, Bishop Adrian, 282
social movements. *See* civil society
socialization, 9, 12, 20, 44, 71, 121–23, 138, 171, 180, 277, 306, 314, 315
Soepardjo, 132
Sogovare, Manasseh, 280, 287, 289, 291n3
Solomon Islands, 8, 11, 13, 72, 275–96, 311, 312, 315, 316
  independence, 8, 279
  Ministry of National Unity, Peace and Reconciliation, 289, 294
  parliament, 282, 285, 286, 288, 290, 294
  Royal Solomon Islands Police Force, 280, 281, 296
  Townsville Peace Agreement, 281, 282, 284, 285, 287, 288

  See also Guadalcanal; Guadalcanal Liberation Front; Isatabu Freedom Movement (Solomon Islands militia); Laore, Carol; Lilo, Gordon Darcy; Malaita; Malaitan Eagle Force; militias: Solomon Islands; Pogo, Ellison; Seventh Day Adventists; South Sea Evangelical Church; Regional Assistance Mission to Solomon Islands; Solomon Islands Christian Association; Sogovare, Manasseh; truth commission: Solomon Islands; Ulufa'alu, Bartholemew
Solomon Islands Christian Association, 275–76, 284, 295, 314
Solomon Islands Truth and Reconciliation Commission. *See* truth commission: Solomon Islands
songs, 18, 178, 183n39, 203, **233–54**
South Africa, 101, 102, 285
  See also truth commission: South Africa; Tutu, Bishop Desmond
South Korea, 100, 101, 284
  See also truth commission: South Korea
South Sea Evangelical Church, 283, 284
Soviet Union, 16, 146, 149, 153, 195
Sri Lanka, 284
stories, 12, 33, 180, 250, 304, 305, 309, 318, 320–21
Suai, Timor-Leste 2, 45, 98
suffering, 29, 117, 127, 153, 172, 249, 316, 320
Suharto, 7, 16, 46, 59, 64, 74, 111, 129, 132, 133, 134, 135, 136, 137, 138, 142, 145, 147, 149, 152, 153, 186, 212, 234, 265, 267, 269, 270
  fall of, 46, 128, 133, 187, 202
Sukarno, 7, 132, 133, 134, 135, 137, 145, 147, 149, 150, 151, 152, 153, 237
Sukarnoputri, Megawati, 128, 137, 250, 252
Sulawesi, 8, 17, 141, 164, 188, 195
  See also militias: Sulawesi; Poso
Sumatra, 132, 140, 264
Surakarta (Solo), Indonesia, 128, 138, 140

T

Taiwan, 73, 100, 103
Tanah Papua. *See* Papua
TAPOL (Indonesian human rights campaign), 17
Tebey, Neles, 222, 225
Telek, George, 253
Thailand, 101, 194
theatre of the oppressed, 250
Thukul, Wiji, 4, 131, 142, 142n1
Tibet, 103
Tibo, Fabianus, 193
Timika, Papua, Indonesia, 266
Timor-Leste, 6, 11, 13, 14, 15, **41–123**, 127, 163, 173, 202, 267, 268, 269, 285, 299, 306, 309, 310, 311, 312, 313, 315, 316, 318, 320, 321
    army (Falintil), 49, 50, 51, 83
    Chinese community, in 98–99
    election (2017), 95
    famine (1970s), 64, 69
    foreign advisers, in 85, 86, 88, 94
    independence referendum and ensuing violence, 41, 45, 47, 56, 95, 112
    Indonesian invasion (1975), 41, 64, 73
    judiciary, 58, 118
    Ministry of Education, 72
    Ministry of Finance, 84
    Ministry of Foreign Affairs, 72
    Ministry of Social Solidarity, 121, 122
    National Parliament, 44, 66, 71, 96, 99, 117, 118, 315
    petroleum fund, 96
    police, 49, 51, 52
    political crisis (2006), 48, 50–52, 56, 94, 95, 105, 115
    Prime Minister's office, 99, 122
    restoration of independence (2002), 6, 93, 95
    strategic development plan, 95–96
    veterans (ex-guerrillas), 48, 49, 51, 52, 68, 71, 81, 82, 87, 89
    women in, 96
    See also Alkatiri, Mari; Araújo, Fernando La Sama; Araújo, Rui Maria de; Barreto Soares, Abé; Belo, Bishop Carlos Ximenes; Bere, Maternus; clandestinity; Costa Lopes, Martinho da; Democratic party (Timor-Leste); East Timor Alert Network; Fretilin (Timorese political party); Gusmão, Kay Rala Xanana; Guterres, Eurico; Guterres, Isabel; Guterres Lopes, Aniceto; international criminal tribunals: Timor-Leste, proposed; La'o Hamutuk (Timorese NGO); Lobato, Rogerio; Marques, Joni; militias: pro-Indonesia in Timor-Leste; Nascimiento, Bishop Basilio do; National Congress for Timorese Reconstruction; Oecusse, Timor-Leste; Ramos Horta, José; Reinado, Alfredo; Reis, Filomena dos; repertoires of violence; Rodrigues, Roque; Ruak, Taur Matan; Silva, Bishop Ricardo da; Suai, Timor-Leste; truth commission: Timor-Leste; United Nations: administration in Timor-Leste; United Nations: commission of experts on Timor-Leste; United Nations: serious crimes process in Timor-Leste; United States: Timor-Leste involvement; UDT (Timorese political party); Viqueque, Timor-Leste
TNI. *See* Indonesia: army
Tonga, 282
torture. *See* human rights: torture
transparency, 86, 96, 172, 218
trauma, 43, 115, 119, 127, 282, 294
TRC Canada. *See* truth commission: Canada
TRC South Africa. *See* truth commission: South Africa
truth and reconciliation commissions, 4, 11, **23–36**, 172–74, **309–24**
    follow-up institutions, 4, 8, 11, 44, 72, 73, 74, 123, 275, 313
    permanence, 171–72, 180, 313

public hearings, 28–29, 32, 33, 67, 285, 288, 295, 300, 305
truth commission,
  Aceh (KKR), 7, 9, 164, 165, 168–84, 310, 313–14, 315
  Canada (TRC), 5, 9, 10, 20, 65, 165, **299–306**, 309, 310, 318
  El Salvador, 299
  Germany, 5, 318
  Guatemala, 299, 317, 321
  Haiti, 299
  historical, 151, 317, 318
  Indonesia, proposed, 128–29, 137, 139, 163, 312, 321.
    possible scope, 151–53.
  Latin America, 23, 66, 129, 299, 316
  Mauritius, 318
  Papua, proposed, 201, 203, 216, 226–28, 300, 312, 318
  Sierra Leone, 299
  Solomon Islands (SITRC), 9, 19, 165, 275, 276, 277, **285–90, 293–96**, 300, 305, 310, 312, 313, 314, 315, 318, 320
  South Africa (TRC), 5, 12, 24, **28–36**, 42, 66, 72, 165, 275, 276, 285, 294, 299, 301, 305, 316, 318
  South Korea, 313
  Timor-Leste (CAVR), 4, 9, 13, 14, 41, 42, 44, 55, 58, 59, **63–76**, 84, 105, 114–15, 117, 118, 121–23, 169, 170, 171, 173, 299–300, 301, 304, 305, 310, 311, 313, 319, 320, 321, 322 (*See also* Centro Nacional Chega! Timor-Leste)
  Timor-Leste and Indonesia bilateral (CTF), 6, 9, 13, 14, 54, 68–69, 70–71, 73, 127, 129, 315, 319, 321
truth-seeking, 9, 14, 16, 17, 26, 33, 67, 128, 138, 169, 170, 203, 215, 300, 314, 319, 320, 322
  Western understandings, 23, 35, 171, 224, 309–10
truths, official, 7, 9, 16, 84, 135, 300, 312, 313, 317
Tunisia, 316
Tutu, Bishop Desmond, 31, 72, 276, 285, 294, 301, 318

U

UDT (Timorese political party), 66
Ulufa'alu, Bartholomew, 280, 282, 291n2
UN. *See* United Nations
UNDP. *See* United Nations: Development Programme
United Church (Canada), 301, 306
United Church (Solomon Islands), 284
United Kingdom, 46, 64, 101, 148, 152, 276, 318
United Liberation Movement of West Papua, 206, 215
United Nations, 13, 14, 47, 58, 59, 64, 70, 86, 87, 88, 103, 121, 150
  administration in Timor-Leste, 41, 42, 43, 47, 52, 56–57, 58, 66, 93, 94, 95
  commission of experts on Timor-Leste, 58–59
  Development Programme (UNDP), 93, 213
  High Commissioner for Human Rights, 59
  serious crimes process in Timor-Leste, 58, 65, 181n6
  Special Development Goals, 97, 119
  UN Women, 120 (*See also* Convention on the Elimination of All Forms of Discrimination Against Women)
United States 14, 16, 18, 57, 85, 97, 101, 103, 152, 279
  Central Intelligence Agency (CIA), 148
  Congress, 262, 263, 268
  Department of State, 204, 261, 262
  Indonesia involvement
    coup (1965), 129, 145–46, 148–51
    military ties with, 57, 59, 60, 261, 262, 265, 267–69, 270 (*See also* United States-Indonesia Society [USINDO])

Invasion of Iraq, 195
Papua involvement, 201, 203, 239, 252, 261–71
Timor-Leste involvement, 46, 56, 64, 94, 103, 321
See also Busby, Scott; Bush, George W.; Clinton, Bill; Clinton, Hillary; Ford, Gerald; Gates, Robert; Kissinger, Henry; Obama, Barack.
United States-Indonesia Society (USINDO), 263, 264
University of California, Los Angeles, 138
Untung, 132
US. *See* United States
usable past, 12
USINDO. *See* United States-Indonesia Society
Uzbekistan, 268

V

Vancouver, 64, 110
Vanuatu, 276, 281
Vatican II reforms, 112
victims, 28, 34, 35, 42, 63, 66–67, 68, 70, 71, 105, 118, 121, 128, 129, 133, 170, 173, 174, 175–77, 178, 187, 193, 196, 227, 275, 290, 304, 305, 314, 315, 318–19, 322
Vietnam, 98, 262, 268
Viqueque, Timor-Leste, 56
violence against women/sexual violence, 45, 69, 85, 120, 176–77, 179, 243, 275, 282, 285, 288, 290, 295
See also Convention on the Elimination of All Forms of Discrimination Against Women

W

Wahid, Abdurrahman, 128, 137, 139
Wamena. *See* Honelama, Papua, Indonesia
Wanandi, Jusuf, 74
Wanimbo, Edi, 221
"War on terror," 8, 57, 59, 166, 191
Wenda, Benny, 245
West Papua. *See* Papua
West Papua National Committee, 205
White-Eye, Chief Leslee, 306
Wibowo, Sarwo Edhie, 132, 139
Widodo, Joko (Jokowi), 128, 140, 212, 213, 215, 222, 263, 269
Wiranto, 110
Wilson-Raybould, Jody, 307
women, 84, 89, 114, 176–77, 227, 275, 276, 290, 293, 294, 296, 306, 307, 315
political participation of, 96, 114
See also Convention on the Elimination of All Forms of Discrimination Against Women; Jayawijaya Women's Voice Foundation; reconciliation: women and; Timor-Leste: women in; Violence against women/sexual violence; United Nations: UN Women
World Bank, 86, 94, 187

Y

Yogyakarta, 140, 141
YouTube, 240, 241
Yudhoyono, Susilo Bambang, 70, 128, 139
Yugoslavia, 6, 13, 150, 321
See also militias: Yugoslavia
Yusuf, Irwandi, 175

Contributors

RIZKI AMALIA AFFIAT is a Researcher at the International Centre for Aceh and Indian Ocean Studies.

JESS AGUSTIN is a Programs Officer with the Canadian Catholic Organization for Development and Peace.

LAURENTINA "MICA" BARRETO SOARES is a PhD candidate at Swinburne University of Technology, Melbourne.

TODD BIDERMAN has worked extensively with Indigenous communities in remote areas of Indonesia and West Papua since 2001.

FERNANDA BORGES is a former Minister of Finance and Member of Parliament in Timor-Leste.

TERRY M. BROWN served as Anglican Church of Melanesia bishop of Malaita in Solomon Islands from 1996 to 2008.

BETTY LINA GIGISI was a Chief Exhumation Officer with the Solomon Islands Truth and Reconciliation Commission.

MAGGIE HELWIG is an author and Rector of St. Stephen-in-the-Fields Anglican Church, Toronto.

LIA KENT is a Fellow in the School of Regulation and Global Governance at the Australian National University.

GATOT LESTARIO was accused of being an activist in the East Java branch of the Indonesian Communist Party. He was executed by firing squad in 1985.

Maria Manuela Leong Pereira works with the Assosiasaun Chega! Ba Ita, the Timorese affiliate of the International Center for Transitional Justice.

Edmund McWilliams is a member of the West Papua Advocacy team, consultant with the East Timor and Indonesian Action Network, and retired Political Counselor at the U.S. Embassy, Jakarta.

Jenny Munro is a Lecturer in Anthropology at the University of Queensland, Australia.

Geoffrey Robinson is a Professor of History at the University of California Los Angeles.

Arianto Sangadji is a PhD candidate at York University and former coordinator of the non-governmental organization Yayasan Tanah Merdeka in Sulawesi, Indonesia.

Bernd Schaefer is Senior Scholar with the Woodrow Wilson International Center's Cold War International History Project and a Professional Lecturer at George Washington University.

Jacqueline Aquino Siapno is the co-founder of Universidade de Paz (UNPAZ) and Centro Para a Mulher e Estudos do Genero.

Julian Smythe is a pseudonym for a researcher who has spent more than 10 years learning about and living in Indonesia.

Pat Walsh is an Australian human rights advocate and author with a long background in Indonesian and Timorese affairs.

Baskara Wardaya is a Professor of History at Sanata Dharma University, Yogyakarta, Indonesia.

David Webster is Associate Professor of History at Bishop's University.

Sarah Zwierzchowski has worked as a research assistant, teaching assistant, and translator in the field of history since 2013.

www.ingramcontent.com/pod-product-compliance
Lightning Source LLC
Chambersburg PA
CBHW061253230426

43665CB00027B/2927